A PATHWAY INTO THE PSALTER

A PATHWAY INTO THE PSALTER

The Psalms: Their History, Teachings and Use

WILLIAM BINNIE

SOLID GROUND CHRISTIAN BOOKS
BIRMINGHAM, ALABAMA USA

Solid Ground Christian Books
2090 Columbiana Rd, Suite 2000
Birmingham, AL 35216
205-443-0311
sgcb@charter.net
http://solid-ground-books.com

A PATHWAY INTO THE PSALTER
The Psalms: Their History, Teachings and Use

William Binnie (1823-1886)

The Psalms: Their History etc. was first published in 1870
Revised edition first published in 1886 by Hodder & Stoughton, London

Solid Ground Classic Reprints

First printing of new edition December 2005

Cover work by Borgo Design, Tuscaloosa, AL
Contact them at nelbrown@comcast.net

*Special thanks to Ric Ergenbright for permission to use
the image on the cover. Visit him at ricergenbright.org*

SPECIAL THANKS: We are grateful to Andy Wortman and
Dr. Ben Shaw of Greenville Presbyterian Theological Seminary
for their help and encouragement with this project. We are also
grateful to Reformed Presbyterian Theological Seminary,
in Pittsburgh, PA for permitting us to use their copy of Binnie.

ISBN: 1-59925-034-9

New Introduction

William Binnie is a good example of the sort of man with which the history of the church is full. He labored faithfully in the place of God's appointment, wrote some, and has been largely forgotten in after years, illustrating the forgetfulness of the race that Solomon pointed to in Eccles 1:11. A search of his name on the internet, that source of all knowledge, produces little in the way of information about him. He is mentioned in passing in an article about his father Thomas, and there are links to some reprints of extracts from some of his work that have been done by modern conservative Presbyterians.

The *Dictionary of Scottish Church History and Theology* has a brief article on Binnie from which we find that he was born in 1823 and died in 1886. He studied in Berlin under Neander and Hengstenberg. He apparently pastored in the Stirling Reformed Presbyterian Church from 1849 until 1862, when he was appointed Professor of Systematic Theology at the Divinity Hall. He moved to the Free Church in 1876 and was appointed as the first Professor of Church History at Aberdeen, where he taught until his death. The article lists four books published by Binnie. The first was his work on the Psalms (1870). This was followed by *The Proposed Reconstruction of Old Testament History* (1880); *The Church* (1882); and *Sermons*, published posthumously in 1887. The article does not note, however, that he published a second edition of his work on the Psalms in the year of his death. It is that work for which this essay provides a brief introduction.

There has never been a shortage of books devoted to the study of the Psalms. Church history is replete with commentaries, devotional guides, and specialized studies on the Psalms, and the present day is no exception. It seems a legitimate question, then, to ask why this particular work should be reprinted. The short answer is that it is a very good work, deserving space on the pastor's shelf. However, the short answer is not really an adequate answer, so a more thorough answer is needed.

I first came across the book (the first edition) more than a decade ago when I was researching material on the Psalms for the students in my Hebrew exegesis classes. As I studied the book, it occurred to me that here was a lost treasure. The work does a number of things that were not done by earlier works on the Psalms. In addition, it does a number of things that might be found in a current work on the Psalms, but does them differently. The result is that the book really has no comparison with other works on the Psalms.

First, rather than being a commentary, it falls more into the realm of what might today be called a theology of the Psalms. Such a work, whether devoted to the Psalms or to some other Biblical book, was almost unheard of in the nineteenth century. Such works have become much more common in the 20th and 21st centuries, but they have been heavily influenced by both critical scholarship and by what might be called the secular use of the Psalms. Binnie's work avoids both of these difficulties.

The work itself is divided into three books. The first focuses on the history and structure of the Psalms. In this part, Binnie traces the development of the Psalms *as a book* from the time of Moses down to the post-exilic period. He takes seriously the information given in the titles of the Psalms and the relevant notices in the historical books of the Old Testament. This is something that most modern treatments of the Psalms do not do. He concludes the first book with a treatment of the structure of the individual psalms, describing the characteristics of Hebrew poetry, and including extended treatments of both parallelism and the acrostic psalms. The issues of the characteristics of Hebrew poetry and parallelism are still debated today, and Binnie's well-considered comments can make a fruitful contribution even to the modern discussion. His treatment of the acrostic psalms is almost unparalleled, either in the preceding or subsequent literature.

The second book focuses on the theology of the psalms, that is, on what they teach. The first part treats of Christ in the psalms. This is a most important discussion, if for no other reason than that modern treatments usually consider the messianic psalms to be primarily devoted to the kings of Israel, referring only in a secondary fashion to Christ. Binnie's division of the messianic character of psalms into several types helps clarify the issues for the modern reader, and shows conclusively that the modern dismissal of distinctly messianic psalms reflects an inadequate reading of them.

Book two, part two, deals with personal religion in the psalms, while part three deals with social religion in the psalms. This careful distinction is especially helpful to those who would read the psalms primarily, if not exclusively, as guides to individual piety. The last section of book two, added in the second edition of the work, shows the relationship between the psalms and the earlier portions of the Old Testament, particularly the Pentateuch. This is again a helpful corrective to modern treatments that tend to see the relationship of the psalms to the Pentateuch as minimal, if not non-existent.

The third book is a history of the use of the psalms in the church, from its beginnings in the Old Testament through the history of the church. Again, this helps remind the reader that the Book of Psalms is a book for the church. In an age when the use of the Psalms in Christian worship has almost vanished, this provides an encouraging call to the church to regain the rich heritage that God has given her, and that most of the church through her history has benefited from.

This brief introduction can only hope to encourage the reader, particularly the student or pastor who will make use of the psalms in his pastoral labors, to discover anew the riches found in the Book of Psalms, and to feed his people from the resources found there.

Dr. Benjamin Shaw
Greenville Presbyterian Theological Seminary

PREFACE TO THE NEW EDITION.

THIS work has now been out of print for several years, and an apology for the delay in bringing out a new edition is due to the many kind friends who have been inquiring after it. I was very sensible that the book needed revision, and I did not find it easy to secure the necessary leisure. Latterly, another consideration weighed with me. I thought it might be expedient to delay completing the revision until the publication of the Revised Version of the Old Testament should have enabled me to take advantage of the Revisers' labours. The examination which I have been able to make of the Psalms, in their new dress, has left on my mind so favourable an impression that, in the present edition, I have, as a rule, made the necessary quotations from the Revised Version, and have dropped the translations which I had myself ventured to give in the former edition. A large proportion of the emendations which I had deemed necessary find a place in the Revised Version, which is, besides, much more perfect in other respects, than my attempts at translating could pretend to be.

But while quotations are usually made from the Revised Version, there are a few exceptions. One of these is in the instance of the Alphabetical Psalms. Without calling in question the wisdom of the Revisers in declining to reproduce these Psalms in the form of English acrostics, it still seemed to me that, in such a work as the present, it would be a pity not to make at least an attempt to exhibit to the eye of the English reader a form of literary structure so remarkable. For a similar reason, I have not been content to adopt merely the Revisers' "arrangement in *lines,* so as to exhibit

the parallelism which is characteristic of Hebrew poetry," *
but have, moreover, grouped the lines so as to exhibit the
strophic arrangement which is likewise found in Hebrew poetry,
especially in the Psalms. The Revisers have tacitly done this
in a few instances, such as the Second Psalm ; but there are
many others in which the strophic arrangement is quite as
unmistakable, and I have treated them accordingly. I may
refer for examples to Psalms xxxvii., xlix., lxxx., and lxxxii., as
they are quoted at pages 90, 148, 263, and 335 of this volume.

During the sixteen years which have passed since the former
edition appeared, all questions relating to the Old Testament
have been deeply affected by the new reading of the history of
Israel which has been worked out and strenuously advocated
by the "advanced" section of the critical school. According to
this reading, the account which the Pentateuch gives of the promulgation of the Levitical law, the appointment of the Aaronic
priesthood, the erection of the Tabernacle, the organisation and
marshalling of the Tribes, is not true history. What the
Pentateuch relates as the *terminus a quo* of the Israelitish
history was in reality the *terminus ad quem.* The Levitical
system, unfolded in the Pentateuch along with much else which
purports, like it, to have been delivered to Israel by the ministry
of Moses at Sinai, is now held to have been put together, for
the first time, during the Captivity or shortly afterwards, and to
have been largely composed of rites and ordinances which had
grown up spontaneously under the kings. As for the *Torah*—
the great compilation styled in the Old Testament " the Book
of the Law of Moses "—its true date, we are told, is to be sought
in the age of Ezra the scribe. It is not denied that the sacred
writers, to whom we owe the historical books from Joshua to
Chronicles, took the same view of the Old Testament history as
that which has hitherto found general acceptance, and that many
passages in those books distinctly imply it. It is admitted, for
example, that the old view is everywhere implied in the account
given in the Chronicles of David's rearrangement of the Tabernacle
service. But then it is maintained that the compilers of the

---

* Preface to Revised Version of Old Testament.

historical books misunderstood the old records in their possession, and that anyhow the true history of Israel is that which
has now at length been worked out by the advanced critics.

It is plain that if we are to accept this Reconstruction of the
Old Testament History, we must readjust our conceptions of
everything else relating to the Old Testament; and, among
other things, the history of the Psalter must be rewritten. For,
not to mention other considerations, the Law and the Psalter
are related to each other as the voice and its echo. In the Law,
God reveals His mind and will to Israel; in the Psalms, Israel
gives utterance to the thoughts and feelings which that revelation
has awakened in its soul.* This being so, you cannot throw
forward the date of the Law without being obliged to throw
forward the date of the Psalms also. There is a notable example
of this in the Fifty-first Psalm. The title ascribes it to David,
on occasion of his great fall, and the contents are so strikingly
accordant with this account of the authorship that it has been
approved all along by the general verdict of Jewish and Christian readers, and even Bleek† (who is universally recognised as
a worthy representative of modern criticism) declares that it is
"without doubt" correct. There is only one reason for calling
it in question. The writer of the Fifty-first Psalm was a man
who lived under the Levitical system. The allusions to the
Levitical rites are such as to make this perfectly plain. Accordingly, the advocates of the new reading of the History
attribute the Psalm to some unknown poet belonging to the age
of the Captivity, or to some age even less remote.

The anxiety of the advanced critics to apply to as many as
possible of the Psalms the same treatment which has been
found necessary in the instance of the Fifty-first is not dis-
creditable to their sagacity. They perceive that the allusions,
of one kind or another, to the Torah are much more numerous
and more generally distributed than the ordinary reader has
any conception of. They are haunted with a well-founded

---

* Compare *The Pentateuch, its Origin and Structure,* by E. C. Bissell, D.D.,
especially chapter x., "The Law and the Psalms." I regret that Dr. Bissell's
work did not reach me till the present volume was in the press.

† *Einleitung,* Wellhausen's Ed., p. 512.

apprehension that perhaps there is not a single Psalm of any considerable length in which such allusions may not be detected. This is well exemplified in the Eighteenth Psalm. One who has not had occasion to scrutinise it closely might have supposed that this Psalm, at least, would be suffered to pass as a genuine product of David's pen. It is ascribed to him in the title, and the contents agree with this account of its origin. It is the song of a warrior, of a royal warrior, of a poet who has the true lyric touch, and there is in it a vein of powerful originality. To crown all, the author of the memoirs relating to David, in the great historical record which is the source of almost all our knowledge of his life, not only mentions that David wrote such a song, but engrosses it in his narrative at the proper place. But there is one phrase in the Psalm which, in the judgment of the new critics, outweighs all these proofs of Davidic author- ship. It lurks in verse 22 :—

> All His judgments were before me,
> And I put not away His statutes from me.

His judgments and His statutes, or, to reverse the order of the words, *His statutes and judgments;* it is a Pentateuchal phrase. It occurs six times in Leviticus, and some sixteen times or more in Deuteronomy. Clearly, this psalmist is a man who knows the Law, a man in whose ear the characteristic phrases of the Law are familiar as household words. In Professor Reuss's judgment, this is fatal to the Davidic authorship. "The mention of the laws and commandments of God in verse 22 agrees better (he thinks) with a less ancient date." *

When so well-authenticated a product of David's muse is thus taken from him and thrown indefinitely forward, one is not surprised to find that the new critics are more and more inclined to doubt whether there exists a single Psalm belonging to the age of David. "The doubt (says Wellhausen †) is not whether there are any post-exilian, but whether there are any pre-exilian Psalms." Dr. Cheyne, with all his favour for

---

* *Psautier*, p. 107.
† In his edition of Bleek's *Einleitung*, p. 507.

the new reading of the Old Testament History, naturally enough recoils from such a sweeping conclusion. With reference to the question "whether any of the Psalms can be Davidic," he well observes that "a reasonable respect for tradition would incline us to reply affirmatively;" yet he is so far carried away by the stream as to find it, "at any rate, a great relief to realise that only a very small number of Psalms can reasonably be ascribed to David."* I do not doubt that, to those who believe in the post-exilian origin of the Law, it really is a relief to think that poems, in which allusions to the Law are so apt to turn up in unexpected places, are being comfortably transferred by the critics to some later age. Anyhow, Dr. Cheyne himself goes so far in this direction that he ascribes the First Psalm to some "Pharisee of the better sort," who lived nobody knows when or where, but certainly after the time of Ezra; and he sees in the latter part of the Nineteenth Psalm (a Psalm hitherto referred, without doubt, to David's pen, on the concurrent evidence of the title and the contents) an example of a way of regarding the Word of the Lord which grew up among the Jews as the fruit of the teachings and exhortations of the prophet Malachi!

The acceptance of conclusions differing so widely from those hitherto prevalent among the learned, whether Jewish or Christian, proves this at least, that if the Pentateuchal writings and institutions are relegated to the age of Ezra, the Psalms must not only follow suit, but must be thrust forward to a time very considerably more recent. Writings and institutions must have been in existence for several generations, men must have grown up under them and been moulded by them from their childhood, and this must have been going on through successive generations, before hymns so thoroughly imbued with their spirit and so full of all sorts of allusions to them, as the Psalms admittedly are, could have been written. This is true not only of such Psalms as the Hundred-and-nineteenth, but of the Fifteenth, the Nineteenth, the Twenty-

---

* *Psalms*, pp. xi., xii.

fourth, the Fifty-first, and others too many to name. I do not know whether this has yet been fully realised by the neophytes of the new school; but the venerable father of it, Professor Reuss, of Strassburg, has certainly done so. In his recently published work on the History of the Sacred Scriptures of the Old Testament, he has, with iron consistency, assigned to the Psalter the last place in the chronological series of the Old Testament writings; and this place is—where does the reader suppose ? *In the age of the Maccabees!* The bulk of the Psalms belong not to the age of David, not to the age of Isaiah, not to the age of Ezekiel and Daniel, not even to the age of Ezra and Nehemiah, but to a time long posterior,— a time which is later even than the conquests of Alexander the Great and only about a century and a half earlier than the birth of Christ! This conclusion is probably inevitable, on the supposition of the post-exilian origin of the Levitical institutions and the Pentateuch; but, in that case, the supposition itself becomes liable to a glaring *reductio ad absurdum.* Referring the reader to the fuller discussions in Book I. (see especially at pages 54, 112, and 118-120), it will be enough to mention here that the Alexandrian translation of the Psalms was executed certainly not later than the age of the Maccabees, and the superscriptions to the psalms, as they appear in that Version, present features which have convinced the critics (Professor Reuss, strange to say, among the rest) that the Hebrew original was already so ancient that the meaning of them had fallen hopelessly into oblivion!

At one time I thought it might be necessary to preface this new Edition with an attempt to vindicate the credibility of the received history of the Psalms. But I soon perceived that such a vindication would, of necessity, involve the discussion of the whole question of the Credibility of the Old Testament History generally. The only serious assault on the received history of the Psalms with which we have to reckon at present proceeds on the assumed incredibility of the Old Testament History in its main line, and particularly on the incredibility of the parts of it delivered in the Pentateuch and Joshua, and in the Chronicles. A discussion so extensive would, of course, be impossible in this place.* And it is by no means of very urgent necessity. If the critics imagine that they have extensively undermined the faith of intelligent and serious Bible readers in the credibility of the Old Testament History, they are certainly mistaken. With regard to the new reading of the History of the Psalms in particular, I cannot imagine that well-informed and thoughtful Christians are likely to be shaken in mind by a hypothesis which requires them to believe that an age like that of the Maccabees, which knew and sorrowfully confessed † that it no longer enjoyed the ministry of prophets, was nevertheless the golden age of inspired Psalmody,—a hypothesis which, at any rate, asks them to believe that great Psalms, such as the Fiftieth and the Seventy-third, the Fifty-first, the Hundred-and-third, and the Hundred-and-thirty-ninth, in which the Church, both Jewish and Christian, has hitherto felt the hand of known and distinguished men, like David and Asaph, were written by men utterly unknown to history and tradition and so shadowy that the authors of the hypothesis have not ventured to give to one of them a name.

I ought perhaps to explain that, besides additions of smaller extent which have been introduced here and there, especially in the earlier chapters, the present Edition contains an entire chapter which is new. I refer to the last chapter of Book II., entitled *The Law of the Lord,* in which an endeavour is made to open up the Teaching of the Psalms regarding Holy Scripture, or the written Word, as the previous chapters had opened up the Christology of the Psalms and their Teachings regarding Personal and Social Religion. The remark made before with respect to those earlier chapters is still more applicable to the one now added. In preparing it, I have not derived much assistance from previous writers. The subject is of such uncommon interest and importance that I suppose it must have been previously discussed; but, if so,

---

* The reader who desires to possess, in short compass, a learned and able review of the whole controversy, may be confidently referred to the volume entitled *Moses and the Prophets*, by W. H. Green, D.D., Professor in Princeton, N.J., 1883.

† 1 Maccab. iv. 46 ; ix. 27 ; xiv. 41.

I have not been able to lay my hands on any of the treatises in which this has been done, and have been obliged to forego the advantage which the perusal of them would doubtless have conferred. In another respect, the present Edition has been more fortunate. From several kind friends I have received suggestions and criticisms of various kinds, which have been very helpful, and for which I trust they will accept my warm thanks.

In sending forth this volume on its new voyage, I would humbly commend it anew to the blessing of the Lord, and pray Him to make use of it still for confirming the faith of His people and for leading many into the green pastures and beside the still waters which are disclosed to view in the Psalms.

ABERDEEN, 15*th March*, 1886.

PREFACE TO THE FIRST EDITION.

IT will be seen at a glance that this volume is not a Commentary on particular Psalms, but an Introduction to the study of the Psalter generally. It is meant to be the kind of book which Tyndale the Martyr would have entitled, *a Pathway into the Psalter.* I have long thought that there was room for such a book. The objects it is intended to serve are not fulfilled by commentaries on the Psalms in detail. For, in the first place, the Psalter being a whole literature in itself, the study of it, even for those practical purposes on account of which it is resorted to by all Christian readers, is greatly facilitated by some prior acquaintance with the writers whose pens were employed upon it, the circumstances which induced them to write, and the literary qualities of their style. Moreover, it is useful to know something of the history of the Psalter since it was first launched into the public view, especially the use that has been made of it by the successive generations of God's people. Beyond any other book that can be named, it has moulded the sentiments of individuals, and influenced the life and movements of whole communities. Some acquaintance, therefore, with the place the Psalms have occupied in the Church during so many centuries will add exceedingly to the interest with which they are studied.

These considerations will explain the historical character of two of the books into which the following work is divided; the *First* being mainly occupied with the history of the Growth of the Psalter; the *Third* containing some notices regarding the

Use which has been made of the Psalms in the Church, and the Estimation in which they have been held.

The *Second* Book is of a different character, being intended to open up the views of divine Truth and of the divine Life which pervade the Psalms. Referring the reader to the introductory remarks at the beginning of the first chapter of this Book, I may be allowed to say here that the subject with which it deals is one which has appeared to me peculiarly important. The fact that the Psalter, like the Lord's Prayer, is an authentic and divinely approved utterance of the heart of God's people, and that, in a degree far exceeding even the Lord's Prayer, it is the utterance of their *whole* heart—that one fact, I say (were there nothing else), would suffice to show how important it must be to get a distinct and comprehensive view of the features of the piety here expressed. It is only of late that much has been done in working this vein. The first attempt to open it up, as far as I am aware, was the one made twenty-four years ago (in 1845) by the late Dr. Hengstenberg of Berlin—a theologian to whose academic prelections and published works I would take this opportunity of expressing my deep obligations. In the Appendix to his Commentary, he introduced some chapters on the *Theology of the Psalms*, which, although short, and dealing only with two or three topics, are very valuable, and have moved succeeding writers to do something in the same direction. Of separate treatises on the subject, I know only two : the one being a little volume by Kurtz, "A Contribution to the Theology of the Psalms ; " * the other a considerable volume, "The Theology of the Psalms," by Dr. Kœnig, Professor of Theology in the Roman Catholic University of Freiburg.† But the former deals with hardly anything

---

* *Zur Theologie der Psalmen,* Dorpat, 1865, pp. 173.

† *Die Theologie der Psalmen.* Von Dr. J. Kœnig.   Freiburg im Breisgau, 1857, pp. 521.

save the Messianic Psalms, and with them in a way that I cannot regard as satisfactory. The latter, although written by a Roman Catholic, follows close in the track of Dr. Hengstenberg. Its author manifests sympathy with the divine word very pleasing to meet with in the Romish Communion ; but he is fettered by the Tridentine Theology, and lacks the freshness of insight into Scripture which can alone vivify these investigations. These works, therefore, have not been of much service to me. Besides—and the remark is largely applicable also to the great commentaries to be presently mentioned—they are purely academic treatises ; whereas the present volume addresses itself to a wider circle. This has so materially affected, not only the style of treatment, but the choice of topics itself, that, in the doctrinal part of the work, I have been obliged to depend mainly on my own investigations.

The works to which I have been principally indebted for assistance in the course of my studies in the Psalms are the three great commentaries that have been published during the last quarter of a century by Professors Hengstenberg, Hupfeld, and Delitzsch. Of the value of these it would be difficult to speak too strongly. Dr. Hengstenberg's work,[*] notwithstanding its defects in point of literary taste and an occasional eccentricity of opinion, marks an epoch in the reverent and erudite study of the Psalms. The example set by the Berlin Professor has been ably followed by the other two critics. The former, Dr. Hupfeld of Halle, whose massive commentary [†] is the ripe fruit of the labours of some thirty years, may be regarded as representing the more rationalistic side, while Dr. Delitzsch of Erlangen [‡] (now of Leipsic), who, for acquaintance with Hebrew literature and

---

[*] *Commentar ueber die Psalmen,* 4 vols. Berlin. 1842-1847.

[†] *Die Psalmen,* 4 vols. Gotha, 1855-1862 ; 2nd Edition, edited by Riehm, 1867-1869.

[‡] *Commentar ueber den Psalter,* 2 vols. Leipzig, 1859, 1860 ; 3rd Edition, 1874.

deep spiritual insight into Scripture, is second to no living divine, represents the orthodox and believing side, of modern German theology. The present work had taken shape before the appearance of Mr. [now Dean] Perowne's valuable Commentary but it also has been found very serviceable. Perhaps Calvin's great work on the Psalms ought to have been mentioned first, for the Genevan reformer retains his place as the prince of commentators, and I have constantly consulted him.

The volume now laid before the reader has been the pleasant companion of my leisure hours for a good many years. It is sent forth, at length, with the prayer that the God of all grace may be pleased to make use of it, to His own glory, in confirming the faith, advancing the knowledge, and helping the joy of all into whose hands it may come.

STIRLING, *December* 1869.

ERRATUM.

At p. 97, l. 22, for *joining* read *writing.*

NOTICES OF FIRST EDITION.

"We have derived very great satisfaction from the examination of this work. It is a valuable contribution to our theological literature, and all the more so that it sets an example of a new method of treating the most important books of Scripture, which is likely to draw after it many imitations. . . . Dr. Binnie, while making use of German methods and materials, has done so in a way at once so independent, so judicious, and so edifying, that no sensible reader can fail to acknowledge that what is new to him in the book is also true, and that a British divine may, after all, intromit with German sources without incurring the odium of Germanising."—*Edinburgh Daily Review.*

"Dr. Binnie has done for the Psalms what Conybeare and Howson have done for the Life and Epistles of Paul. . . . He has invested the subject with an interest and charm which belong to himself alone."—*United Presbyterian Magazine.*

"Ministers of the gospel will come to reckon it an indispensable equipment ere they venture to expound the Psalms to their people ; for we know not where else (certainly not in the English language, and, as far as we know, in no other language) they can find such a repertory of almost all that should be known by them in the way of introduction to the study of the Psalter."—*British Messenger.*

"On every page the book bears marks of much thought, of extensive reading, and of accurate scholarship. The style is easy, quiet, and graceful, yet forcible enough when there is occasion. . . . These three chapters alone (on the Messianic Psalms) would have formed a valuable contribution to theological literature." —*Aberdeen Free Press.*

"In his chapters on the Theology of the Psalms he (Dr. Binnie) maintains the most commonly received views respecting the Messiah, a Future Life, the Imprecations, etc.; but he handles these subjects with learning and moderation."—*Dean Perowne on the Psalms : Preface to Second Edition.*

"It deserves to be known far and wide throughout the Church. . . . The transparency of Dr. Binnie's style allows a clear light to fall upon everything he holds up to view, and even the most unlearned will follow him with satisfaction and appreciation."—*Rev. J. F. McCurdy, Princeton, N.J., in " Bibliotheca Sacra."*

"Not an Exposition, but can readily be used as such. . . . Dr. Binnie reviews with great skill and intense devotion the various sacred poems contained in the book of Psalms, and gives the general run and character of each one. His work is unlike any other, and supplies a great desideratum."—*Mr. Spurgeon in his " Catalogue of Commentaries,"* 1876, where it is ranked among " the books most heartily recommended."

"A work which merits attention among us also. Written in a warm and elevated style, and grounded on comprehensive exegetical studies, particularly of the German commentators, it constitutes an animated and graphic introduction to the contents of the Psalter, in a form of such interest and attractiveness for the educated laity as is hardly to be found in any German book."—*Neue evangelische Kirchenzeitung.*

CONTENTS.

BOOK I.

HISTORY AND POETICAL STRUCTURE OF THE PSALMS.

BOOK II.

THE THEOLOGY OF THE PSALMS.

CHRIST IN THE PSALMS.

PERSONAL RELIGION IN THE PSALMS.

SOCIAL RELIGION IN THE PSALMS.

HOLY SCRIPTURE IN THE PSALMS.

BOOK III.

NOTICES REGARDING THE USE OF THE PSALMS IN THE CHURCH.

BOOK I.

THE HISTORY AND POETICAL STRUCTURE OF THE PSALMS.

CHAPTER I.

INTRODUCTION.

THE Psalter is distinguished from the other books of Holy Scripture by peculiar features that are broad and obvious. It is not one continuous composition, but a collection of one hundred and fifty poems of various length. It does not come from one pen, but is the product of very many. No one generation can claim the honour of having given it birth, for the history of the poems of which it is made up runs parallel to that of the whole Hebrew Scriptures, beginning with Moses and ending with the contemporaries of Ezra and Malachi. Moreover, it refuses to be assigned as the peculiar possession of either the Old Testament or the New. In language and date and literary character, it belongs to the older dispensation ; but, in a degree peculiar to itself, it has passed over into the possession of the Christian Church. It has "become the sacred book of the world, in a sense belonging to no other part of the Biblical records." "Not only was it used more than any other part of the Old Testament by the writers of the New, but it is, in a special sense, the peculiar inheritance of the Christian Church through all its different branches ;" and, "if we descend from Churches to individuals, there is no one book which has played so large a part in the history of so many human souls." *

Such being the singular nature and history of the Psalter, it becomes an interesting subject of inquiry, What are the features which distinguish from the rest of the sacred writings the compositions here collected ? In other words, What is a Psalm ?

The question is one that cannot be better answered, than by

* Stanley, *Lect. on Jewish Church*, ii. 146, 147.

passing in review the several designations, or descriptive titles, employed in the superscriptions with which so many of the psalms are furnished. Whatever opinion may be entertained regarding the origin and authority of the superscriptions, no one can doubt that the designations employed in them bring out, distinctly, the nature and scope of the psalms. Five of them especially claim notice here.

1. The psalms are sometimes entitled PRAYERS. The term *Tephilloth* (singular *Tephillah*), which is thus rendered by our translators, occurs five times in the superscriptions.* It occurs also in the note appended to the Seventy-second Psalm : "The prayers of David the son of Jesse are ended." This note will claim careful consideration when we come to speak of the Psalter as a whole. Meanwhile I simply remark, that it relates not so much to the particular psalm to which it is annexed, as to the book or division of the Psalter which ends with that psalm—the second of the five books of which the whole is made up. It implies therefore that every Psalm of David may be correctly described as a Prayer of David. There are other designations in much more frequent use, but this of *Tephillah* or Prayer deserves to be mentioned first, because it not only seems to be older † than any other, but is certainly more comprehensive than any, and brings out the first characteristic of the psalms which it is important to keep in view. A Psalm, whatever else it may be, is a Prayer ; it is an utterance of the soul before God. It is not a soliloquy ; much less is it the utterance of the soul's emotions for the gratification of a human auditory ; it conducts us into the presence-chamber of the great King, and teaches us how to pour out our hearts before His throne. A psalm is the Church's response to those two primary articles of the faith, that *God is*, and that *He is a Rewarder of them that seek after Him*. The psalms accordingly are pervaded everywhere with the consciousness of God. The most of us are so much accustomed to the use of them, so much accustomed also to the use of other

---

* Psalms xvii., lxxxvi., xc., cii., cxlii., also Hab. iii. 1, where the hymn which fills the whole chapter is entitled, " A Prayer of Habakkuk the prophet."

† Not only does it occur, as above noted, in the title subscribed to the oldest Collection of psalms, viz., Books I. and II. ; it is found, moreover, in the superscription of the oldest psalm—the " prayer of Moses the man of God " (Ps. xc.). Comp. Delitzsch on title of Ps. xvii.

sacred lyrics written under their influence and imbued with
their spirit, that we seldom give due heed to this quality; but
it has never failed to strike with astonishment serious persons
who have read much in the hymns and poems of pagan nations.
In these the gods are no doubt celebrated, their names come
up often enough, but there is no reality about the beings thus
addressed; they are impersonal, unsubstantial, airy nothings.
It is the high prerogative of the psalms, that they not only
name the name of God, but bear us into His presence. They
bring us face to face with our Maker and Judge, a personal
God, who has an ear to hear and a hand to help, and of whom
the weakest saint on earth may say, " I am poor and needy,
yet the Lord thinketh upon me."

2. The designation most frequently employed in the superscriptions is the one which almost all the modern versions
render PSALM. It stands at the head of no fewer than fifty-
seven of the Psalms; so that we cannot wonder that it has
come to be the current designation of the whole book. When
the Jews of Alexandria, in the third century before Christ,
translated the Old Testament into the language which
Alexander's conquests had made the common speech of the
world, they chose the Greek word *psalmos,* which properly
denotes *a strain of music,* to represent the *Mizmor* of the superscriptions; and their example has been generally followed by
succeeding translators. Curiously enough, this Hebrew term
Mizmor, although of such frequent use in the superscriptions,
is never found anywhere else,—a circumstance which has led
some to conjecture that it was coined by David to describe his
sacred poems. Its etymology is doubtful. Not to mention
older Hebraists, Lowth thinks it properly denotes *a poem cut
up into short sentences and pruned from all superfluity of words,*
and with this agrees Hengstenberg's definition of it as *a poem
artfully elaborated.* Delitzsch thinks it rather denotes *the musical
accompaniment,* which is the opinion of Oehler * also, who
observes that " among the religious songs it appears to denote
only such as were *musically* prepared for the purpose of
singing in public worship." Gesenius and Hupfeld have each
set forth more than one interpretation in successive works.

---

* Art. "PSALMS" in Fairbairn's Imperial Bible Dict.

But amid this diversity, all the best authorities are agreed that the general idea which the term expresses is that of *a song which is, or may be, wedded to an appropriate strain of music.*

This, then, is a second point to be noted in the psalms. They are prayers, and they are something more. There are elements essential to them which are not found in ordinary prayers. A prayer is not a work of art. On the contrary, the more artless a prayer is, the more perfectly does it answer its end. Prayer is the simple, unadorned outpouring of the heart before God. The true idea of it is seen in the petition presented by a child at its father's knee. This is the conception of prayer taught by our Lord Himself, "When ye pray, say, Our Father which art in heaven." The true idea of a psalm takes in more than this. Every psalm is a prayer, but every prayer is not a psalm. To the production of the psalms art was required,—the art of the poet and the art of the musician. It is evident from the memorials of the primitive times preserved in Genesis, that Music and Poetry, as they rank amongst the noblest of the arts, so they were amongst the first to be cultivated; and God has been pleased to sanctify them by assigning to them a place and a function in the ordinances of His worship. It is His will that we should worship Him not only with the spontaneous and unstudied effusions of our hearts, but also with the musical recitation of poems that have been composed with care and cultivated taste.

3. The word SONG is another designation that occurs with great frequency. It stands for the Hebrew term *Shir*, which is found in no fewer than thirty of the superscriptions. The fifteen " songs of degrees " may be referred to as the most remarkable of the class. Unlike the designation just explained, it is often found in the body of the psalms, as well as in their superscriptions. The general idea expressed by *psalm* and *song* is the same ; they denote a poem of the lyrical order,—a poem framed to be sung rather than read. And here it may be remarked, that these two titles not only distinguish the psalms from ordinary prayers, and from such prose compositions as we possess in the Bible histories and epistles, but also from such poetical compositions as are found in Job, in the Proverbs, and in the Prophets. The poetry in these, with the exception of a few passages here and there, is of the didactic order, and was

meant to be read or recited, not sung. The psalms, on the contrary, were all meant to be sung. It may be doubted whether sufficient heed has been given to the fact that the element of song enters so largely into Scriptural devotion. No one can have failed to observe that the expressing of any sort of sentiment with the assistance of poetry and music reacts powerfully upon the sentiment. The singing of a good song— a song of which the words and the music give felicitous expression to feelings with which the mind happens to be charged —who does not know how powerfully it moves the heart! It adds fresh delight to every sort of gladsome emotion, and assuages the tumult of sorrow. The book of Psalms bears witness that it is the will of God that we should call in this office of minstrelsy to the assistance of our religious emotions. If a great prophet was fain to call for a minstrel to play before him when he desired that the hand of the Lord might come upon him,* much more may we expect powerful assistance, in the cultivation of a right state of mind and feeling towards God, from the singing of the psalms to appropriate melodies.

Respecting the precise sense of the word *Shir* or *Song* in the superscriptions, there is some difference of opinion. According to Hengstenberg, it denotes a joyous lyric, and is therefore less comprehensive than the modern *song*. To this Dr. Oehler objects, and points to the circumstance that the title in question is found in the superscription of the Eighty-eighth Psalm, which is emphatically a cry out of the depths. He supposes the *Shir* to have differed from the other psalms only with respect to the musical execution. The *Shir* may have been delivered in the way that we should still describe as singing, whereas the other psalms may have been merely cantillated, that is to say, recited in a musical tone of voice. The two explanations are not altogether incompatible. The more elaborate style of music, although it might, on a rare occasion, be employed to deepen the effect of an elegiac poem, would more commonly be employed in connection with songs of thanksgiving and praise. With two exceptions, the psalms which bear the title in question are characteristically joyous. It

---

* 2 Kings iii. 15.

is repeatedly used * in addition to the more general title of
Mizmor or *psalm.* Thus the Sixty-fifth and the Ninety-second
Psalms are both entitled *" a Psalm or Song,"* and they are of a
peculiarly bright and sunny complexion.

4. The Hundred-and-forty-fifth Psalm is, in the superscription, entitled *David's Tehillah,* that is to say, " David's Psalm
of Praise." It is rather remarkable that this title, *Praise,* or
Psalm of Praise (it is one word in the Hebrew), should be
found only in a single superscription, for the word is of perpetual occurrence in the Psalter, and is more or less applicable
to every one of the Psalms. A vein of praise runs through all.
It was, no doubt, a sense of this which led the Jews to fix on
this title, rather than any of those before mentioned, as the
fittest to describe the whole book. What the Greek translators
and the modern versions after them call *The Psalter* or *Book of
Psalms* is denominated in the Hebrew Bible *Sepher Tehillim*
—the Book of Praises. It is a beautiful title, and gives prominence to an aspect of the Psalms as important as any other.
They are not only Prayers and Songs, but *Hymns* also ; that is
to say, they are songs which have for their chief scope the
glory and praise of God. Like the golden censers in which
the sons of Aaron burnt fragrant incense in the Holy Place,
they are the vessels in which our thanksgivings are to be
offered before the throne of God. There is a passage in one
of Augustine's popular discourses on the psalms (it occurs
in the introduction to the one he preached, A.D. 411, on
Ps. lxxii.) which strikingly brings out the combined force
of the three titles last mentioned : " Psalms are the praises of
God accompanied with song ; psalms are songs containing the
praise of God. If there be praise, but not of God, it is not
a psalm. If there be praise, and praise of God, if it is not
sung, it is not a psalm. To make a psalm there go these
three—praise, God's praise, and song." Let it be remembered,
then, that the Psalter is the Book of Praises. There are
several psalms which, like the five at the close of the book,
begin and end with *Hallelujah ;* and that inspiring word
is a kind of key-note to the whole book. The psalms are

---

* In thirteen places, viz., Psalms xxx., xlviii., lxv., lxvi., lxvii., lxviii., lxxv.,
lxxvi., lxxxiii., lxxxvii., lxxxviii., xcii., cviii., to which may be added xlv.

Praises. We do not sing them aright unless we come before the Lord with grateful adoration, as men who feel themselves impelled to bless His holy name.

5. There is yet another word, of frequent occurrence in the superscriptions, which claims a moment's notice. I refer to the term *Maschil*, which is prefixed to thirteen psalms. The English translators of 1611 did not venture to do more, in the *text*, than simply print the word in English characters; in the *margin*, however, they rendered it, as the Geneva version had done before them, "to give instruction." In the Revised Version it is left untranslated. The interpretation set down in the old margin, as it is the most ancient, so it is sustained by the great preponderance of authority.* It agrees remarkably with the contents of the Thirty-second Psalm, which affords the earliest instance of its use; for that psalm is pre-eminently didactic. Its scope is to instruct the convicted soul how to obtain peace with God and be compassed about with songs of deliverance. The title, although prefixed only to a few, is less or more applicable to all the psalms. It holds forth, as one of the purposes they were designed to serve, the edification of souls in the truth and ways of the Lord. It is true, as we may afterwards have occasion to show, that there is very little *revelation*, strictly so called, in this part of the divine word—little disclosure of new truth to the Church. The Psalter is rather the response of the Church to God's revelations elsewhere made, than itself the vehicle of new revelations. But it is a very instructive response. Many a time has it happened that the psalms learned by a child at his mother's knee have deposited in his heart the seeds of divine knowledge, and kept them alive till they sprang up, long after, in a harvest of salvation. The psalms, then, besides being songs and hymns, are designed "to give instruction."

---

* The LXX. and Vulgate are ambiguous, but Jerome in his version from the Hebrew renders it *eruditio ;* and in this he is followed by the modern translators generally. Of recent critics, Gesenius and Hengstenberg render it *a didactic song,* Hupfeld *a doctrine* or *instruction,* and Delitzsch *a pious meditation.* Ewald and Mr. Perowne take the meaning to be, *a skilfully composed song, ein feines Lied,* and refer to Ps. xlvii. 7, where the same term is rendered "*with understanding*" (margin, *in a skilful psalm*).

It may not be unnecessary to add, that in thus commenting upon the designations of the psalms that are found in the prefixed titles, I by no means wish to convey the idea that they are all equally descriptive of every psalm. The way they are severally employed in the superscriptions obviously implies the contrary. Still it seemed expedient to gather them together, inasmuch as they indicate the elements that principally enter into these Bible songs. Besides, although particular elements may predominate, one in one psalm, another in another, there is not a psalm but contains something of each. There is not a psalm of instruction but contains something of prayer and praise, and the psalms of praise are psalms of instruction also.

One other remark here. The psalm differs from some other kinds of sacred song in these two points, that it is, in every instance, the fruit of supernatural inspiration ; and that it is, in every instance, designed for permanent use in the public worship of God. The former point requires no demonstration in this place. The manner in which our blessed Lord and the apostles cite and comment upon this portion of the Hebrew Scriptures clearly implies its supernatural inspiration and divine authority.* The other point is also capable of abundant verification. We find in the Bible many other sacred songs ; for instance, the Song at the Red Sea, the Song of Moses, the Songs of Deborah and Hannah, the Song of Habakkuk, the Songs of Zacharias, and Mary, and Simeon. But it is obvious that these were, for the most part, meant to be sung only on the occasions which gave them birth,—at least there is no evidence that they were made a part of the stated services of the public worship. It was otherwise with the Psalms. No fewer than fifty-five of them are formally inscribed FOR THE CHIEF MUSICIAN, that is, for the Leader of the service of song. They were, therefore, from the first, in use in the sanctuary. It is universally admitted that the Psalter was the one hymn-book of the Jewish Church under the Second Temple. It is true, some learned men, like Hupfeld, while concurring in this admission, contend that many of the psalms must have been written originally without any view to the public use to which

---

* Comp. *Bengelii Gnomon* at Heb. x. 8.

they were afterwards put. They ground this opinion on the circumstance, that some of them,—the Fifty-first, for example,—are too personal to permit the thought that the writers ever could have designed them for other than private use. But this consideration, interesting and suggestive as it is, will not sustain the inference grounded upon it. The case of Cowper and his hymns is exactly in point. Not even the Fifty-first Psalm is more intensely personal than one or two of the hymns we owe to the bard of Olney; yet we know that the employment of the Olney Hymns in public worship took place within the poet's lifetime, and with his consent.

Passing from these prefatory explanations regarding the characteristic qualities of the psalms, we proceed to trace the History of Sacred Psalmody in the Hebrew Church. In doing so, we shall take note of the men of God who, during many generations, were raised up in Israel, endowed by the Holy Spirit with appropriate gifts, and moved by His supernatural energy to give voice to the feelings of the Church in divine songs. The psalmists are not all known to us, even by name, but enough is known to invest this part of the subject with undying interest. We shall take note of those movements of God's providence towards the chosen people, which gave occasion to very many of the psalms; and we shall endeavour to estimate, with such an approach to accuracy as may now be possible, the amount of the contributions which the successive periods of the history brought into the great treasury of holy song.

The first poem preserved in Scripture is Lamech's Song, in the fourth chapter of Genesis, addressed to his two wives, Adah and Zillah. Lamech was of the seed of Cain; and his song, however interesting as a relic of antediluvian art, has no further relation to our present subject, for it was not sung in worship of the living God. We do not possess a vestige of sacred song that is more ancient than the time of Moses. The poetry of the patriarchal blessings was didactic, not lyric. Probably it would be unwarrantable to conclude from these facts, that the antediluvian and patriarchal Church was never cheered with the melody of hymns. Whether it be true or not, that poetry and song were first cultivated by the race of

Cain, it is not likely that God suffered those arts to be appropriated exclusively to the solace of the world and the inflaming of earthly passions during the long centuries of the primeval dispensations. It may be confidently assumed, that the first hymn we meet with in the Bible,—the triumphal ode over Pharaoh and his host, which was sung by the tribes of Israel in responsive bands at the Red Sea,—could not have been sung by a people unaccustomed to sacred music. How many communities are there, even now, sufficiently trained in music to attempt the responsive chanting of so elaborate a song ?

The Song at the Red Sea sufficiently proves that Moses, besides his other manifold endowments, was a poet of the highest order. This faculty was not suffered to slumber. His dying legacy to the tribes he had conducted out of Egypt was a song. It is of great length, occupying nearly all the thirty-second chapter of Deuteronomy. The splendour of its imagery is only surpassed by that rare combination of tenderness and strength in virtue of which it still, after so many ages, stirs the blood of every reader. The man of God was enabled to foresee the temptations which were to befall the tribes in Canaan; and he knew that as they could not in those days possess copies of the law in their several dwellings, the hearing of it, once a year, at the autumnal festival would be but an ineffectual barrier against forgetfulness of the testimonies of the Lord. To fortify and perpetuate the influence of the law, he was moved by the Spirit to compose a song which the people might carry in their memories, and teach to their children and children's children—a song which, being sung in the towns and villages and tents of Israel, from Lebanon to the wilderness, and from Bashan to the sea, might be an ever-present memorial of the Lord, of His terrible majesty, His unslumbering righteousness, His mighty acts in the redemption of His people.

During the period of the Judges, we meet with two odes of great power—the Song of Deborah and the Song of Hannah (Judges v. ; 1 Sam. ii.). The latter, which has been aptly styled the *Magnificat* of the Old Testament Church, possesses a special interest for us at present, as having been composed by the mother of the prophet whom God commissioned to call forth and consecrate "the son of Jesse, the anointed of the God of Jacob, and the sweet psalmist of Israel" (2 Sam. xxiii. 1).

Respecting the Song of Deborah it may be mentioned, that it is almost universally accepted as a genuine monument of the period of the Judges, being recognised as such by the greater number even of those who refuse to acknowledge the authenticity of the books of Moses ; and that critics of every name are agreed in esteeming it one of the most perfect examples of lyrical poetry extant in any language.

Besides the religious interest that must always attach itself to the sacred lyrics which have come down from the times of Moses and the Judges, they possess great literary and historical interest in connection with the subject of Psalmody. They demonstrate that the Israelitish people in those primitive times, however rude their manner of life may have been, were not barbarians, as some have hastily imagined. A poetical literature which included such songs as Deborah's and Hannah's,— songs which, considered simply as works of art, have never been surpassed in their kind,—could neither have been produced nor appreciated in a barbarous community. Reasoning back, as we are entitled to do, from the literary style and the tone of sentiment exhibited in the songs, to the attainments in culture and piety of the people for whom they were composed, and who eagerly caught them from the lips of the authors, we can have no hesitation in affirming that "the Israelite of those remote times was one whose religious beliefs, and whose modes of feeling, and whose social habitudes, were such as to place him far in advance of any among his contemporaries, or even of the men of much later times."*

It is more important, for our present purpose, to remark, that in this early period of the Jewish history, the first stone of the fair edifice of the Psalter was laid. One of the psalms has come down to us from the age of Moses, and from the pen of the great lawgiver himself. The NINETIETH is entitled, *A Prayer of Moses the man of God*, and its contents are in remarkable harmony with this account of its authorship. Some modern critics, indeed, discredit the testimony of the superscription. Ewald, for example, would assign the psalm to the period of the later kings. But this is simply to save his theory regarding the book of Deuteronomy, which he supposes to have been written

---

* Isaac Taylor, *The Spirit of the Hebrew Poetry*, p. 139.

at that late period. He perceives that Deuteronomy and the
psalm are near of kin; and he admits that the latter is " so
full of vigorous originality that it might well have been attributed to Moses, if we only knew better the historical grounds
which led the editor of the Psalter to prefix his name to it." *
The truth is, that " there is hardly a monument of antiquity
which so brilliantly justifies the traditional account of its
origin. Both in its contents and in its linguistic peculiarities it
altogether agrees with Moses." †

It would not be correct to say that there is anything personal
to Moses in the psalm, or anything pertaining exclusively to the
generation by whom it was first sung. It contains nothing local
or temporary. It is the first instalment of the inspired hymnology of the catholic Church, and will never become obsolete till
the vicissitudes of time come to an end, and the songs of this
lower sanctuary are swallowed up in the songs of the heavenly
temple. Nevertheless, the interest with which one reads it is
greatly heightened by recollecting the circumstances of its
birth. It is the cry that arose from the congregation in the
wilderness when they beheld their ranks melting away, in
fulfilment of the oath of God that they should not enter into His
rest. It can hardly be necessary to repeat the familiar story,
how, after God had brought His people out of Egypt, and given
them the law at Sinai, and conducted them through the
howling deserts of Paran to the border of Canaan, and shown
them the pleasant southern hills of that land of ancient promise,
their hearts fainted within them, they disbelieved His word, and
refused to enter in; and how, for their unbelief, they were
commanded to face the desert once more, not now to travel
through it, but to spend in it their lives and leave their bones
in its thirsty solitudes. Among the tribes, there were many
besides Caleb and Joshua who were " Israelites indeed." Aaron,
for instance, was a saint of God, although he was involved in
the general penalty. There would be many, therefore, even of
the generation that had come out of Egypt by Moses, and many
more belonging to the generation which grew up in the wilder-

* *Die Psalmen*, p. 127.
† Delitzsch, *Der Psalter*, ii. 3. See more in Note at the end of the present
Chapter.

ness, whose hearts were contrite under God's mighty hand. To them the psalm was delivered, that in its plaintive measures they might utter their penitent grief in the ear of God. And it was carefully framed to be the expression of something better than a barren and hopeless sorrow. It opens grandly with the profession of a strong faith in the Eternal, as the dwelling-place of His people in all generations; and it closes with an importunate and hopeful prayer for the generation that was to come after and possess the promised inheritance.

1. Lord, Thou hast been our dwelling-place
   In all generations.
2. Before the mountains were brought forth,
   Or ever Thou hadst formed the earth and the world,
   Even from everlasting to everlasting, Thou art God.
3. Thou turnest man to destruction;
   And sayest, Return, ye children of men.*
4. For a thousand years in Thy sight
   Are but as yesterday when it is past,
   And as a watch in the night.
5. Thou carriest them away as with a flood; they are as a sleep:
   In the morning they are like grass which groweth up.
6. In the morning it flourisheth and groweth up:
   In the evening it is cut down and withereth.
7. For we are consumed in Thine anger,
   And in Thy wrath are we troubled.
8. Thou hast set our iniquities before Thee,
   Our secret sins in the light of Thy countenance.
9. For all our days are passed away in Thy wrath:
   We bring our years to an end as a tale that is told.
10. The days of our years are threescore years and ten,
    Or even by reason of strength fourscore years;
    Yet is their pride but labour and sorrow;
    For it is soon gone, and we fly away.
11. Who knoweth the power of Thine anger,
    And Thy wrath according to the fear that is due unto Thee?
12. So teach us to number our days,
    That we may get us an heart of wisdom.
13. Return, O LORD, how long?
    And let it repent Thee concerning Thy servants.
14. O satisfy us in the morning with Thy mercy;
    That we may rejoice and be glad all our days.
15. Make us glad according to the days wherein Thou hast afflicted us,
    And the years wherein we have seen evil.

* Gen. iii. 19.

16. Let Thy work appear unto Thy servants,
    And Thy glory upon their children.
17. And let the beauty of the LORD our God be upon us:
    And establish Thou the work of our hands upon us;
    . Yea, the work of our hands establish Thou it.

Three thousand years and more have passed away since the
congregation of Israel made the solitudes of the wilderness
vocal with the plaintive music of this Ninetieth psalm. There
is probably not another song now sung in any nation under
heaven that possesses such a hoary antiquity.* And yet there
is about it the freshness of a perpetual youth. In what nation
have God's people ceased to employ it? It forms part of the
English Order for the Burial of the Dead, and in all Christian
nations is, in one form or another, devoted to a similar use.
Moreover, as each New Year comes round, bringing its train of
saddening memories and summoning us to count our days, who
does not turn to the Prayer of Moses for the most adequate
expression of the thoughts and feelings awakened by the season?
In the Protestant churches of Hungary it is sung every New
Year's Day, and the same custom is widely prevalent in other
countries. It is a solemnising and stimulating thought, that
when we lift up our voices to the Eternal in this psalm, we put
ourselves into communion with the Church of all generations
and of all lands, and yield our hearts to the guidance of a
song given three-and-thirty centuries ago by the inspiration of
the Holy Spirit, which has been a fountain of pensive comfort to God's saints in all the hundred generations that have
lived and died since its notes first awoke the echoes of the
desert.

Dr. Hengstenberg of Berlin, a divine who has done as much
as any other man of this age for the elucidation of the psalms,
remarks in his Commentary,† that the concurrence of three
conditions was requisite in order to an efflorescence of divine

---

* Professor Max Müller assigns the same date, the sixteenth century B.C.,
to the oldest hymns of the Veda; but I suppose it is many centuries since the
Hindoo race sang these in their vernacular. They are therefore, at the best,
a kind of fossils, the long-disused memorials of a civilisation contemporary with
Moses.

† Vol. IV., ii. pp. 212, 213 (Berlin, 1846).

psalmody. There was required, in the first place, a wide-spread *Revival of Religion* in the Church. A psalm is not the voice of a solitary individual; it is the voice of the Church, and new songs can only proceed from the bosom of a quickened Church. It was necessary, in the second place, that there should be found in the Church persons, more or fewer, gifted with the *Poetical Faculty*,—men of genius and cultivated taste, who might express the thoughts and feelings of the quickened Church in poetry and song. Lastly, there was required the *Supernatural Inspiration* of the Holy Spirit, elevating and controlling the exercise of the poet's genius, so that he might speak as one who was moved by the Holy Ghost. It is evident that these three conditions found place at the time of the sojourn of the tribes in the wilderness. How genuine and deep was the revival of religion in that age appears from the terms of regretful affection with which it was commemorated long after, " I remember thee, the kindness of thy youth, the love of thine espousals ; when thou wentest after me in the wilderness, in a land that was not sown. Israel was holiness to the Lord, and the first-fruits of his increase " (Jer. ii. 2, 3). The poetical faculty and the super-natural inspiration were both found in Moses the man of God. And so the first of the Psalms was given to the Church in the wilderness.

NOTE TO CHAPTER I.

THE MOSAIC AUTHORSHIP OF PSALM XC.

" BY a very singular caprice of tradition, or rather of the Jewish *savans*, this psalm passes for the oldest of all the psalms, and is attributed to Moses, although there is in the text itself absolutely nothing of a kind fitted to suggest such a high antiquity." Such is the judgment of Professor Reuss,[*] and he expresses the mind of all the critics who go in for the Reconstruction of the Old Testament History. The unwary reader is apt to imagine that such a peremptory judgment must rest on grounds of corresponding strength. For this reason, and also because of the intrinsic interest of the point at issue, room must be made for a summary statement of the evidence available on both sides.

    1. The *testimony of the superscription* was doubtless that on the

---

[*] *Le Psautier*, 1875, p. 291. This is Volume V. of the author's Commentary on the Bible.

ground of which the Mosaic authorship was accepted in the first instance. It is a mistake, however, to suppose that this testimony furnishes the sole reason for attributing the psalm to the great lawgiver. The harmony between the contents of the psalm and the origin thus assigned to it is (as we shall see by-and-by) so perfect that the Mosaic authorship might well have been accepted on a more slender external testimony than that furnished by the superscription. What is more, the harmony referred to, although perfect, is so deep and unobtrusive as to suggest that the superscription cannot have been the result of a happy conjecture, but must have been founded on some documentary or other evidence now lost.

2. The arguments urged in disproof of the Mosaic authorship are quite remarkably weak. (1) From the opening words, which he renders, "Lord, Thou hast been unto us an asylum from age to age," Mr. Cheyne * deduces the inference, "Israel then is no longer a young nation;" as if Moses and the faithful of his time did not know, or had forgotten, that the Eternal had been the asylum and dwelling-place of Abraham and Isaac, of Jacob and Joseph, in their generations! (2) Reuss and Hupfeld strangely assert that there is nothing in the psalm answering specially to the circumstances of the exodus and the long sojourn in the wilderness—strangely, I say, for to very competent judges, like Herder and Ewald, and certainly to the majority of Christian readers who have considered the matter, it has seemed that the psalm, from beginning to end, breathes the air of the desert, and answers in every feature to the circumstances implied in the Mosaic authorship. (3) As for the difficulty some have felt on account of the place in which the psalm is found—not in the Pentateuch along with the other Mosaic songs, nor in the beginning of the Psalter, but in the heart of the book— it disappears on fuller acquaintance with the history of the Psalter. (See Chapter VI. of this book.)

3. The most important piece of evidence relative to the date of the psalm is furnished by the surprisingly close correspondence subsisting, at many points, between it and the book of Deuteronomy, as the following table will show :—

PSALM XC.	DEUTERONOMY.
Title—"The Prayer of *Moses the man of God.*"	xxxiii. 1. "The blessing wherewith *Moses the man of God* blessed the children of Israel."
Ver. 1. "*A dwelling-place* hast Thou been to us" (*ma'on*, a habitation, refuge, asylum).	xxxiii. 27. "The Eternal God is thy dwelling-place" (*ma'on*).
"*In all generations*" (lit. in generation and generation).	xxxii. 7. "Consider the years of many generations" (lit. of generations and generations).
Ver. 13. "Let it *repent Thee concerning Thy servants.*"	xxxii. 36. "Will *repent Himself concerning His servants*" (comp. Exod. xxxii. 12).
Ver. 15. "The days wherein Thou hast afflicted (lit. *humbled*) us."	viii. 2. "To *humble* (or afflict) thee."

* *Book of Psalms*, 1884, p. 246.

PSALM XC.	DEUTERONOMY.
Ver. 16. " *Thy work* " (*po'al*, it is a stately word, *Thy doing*).	xxxii. 4. "His work (*po'al*) is perfect." (The earliest occurrence of the word in Scripture.)
" Thy glory" (*hadar*, Thy beauty and majesty).	xxxiii. 17. "His glory (*hadar*) is like the firstling," etc.
Ver. 17. " *The work of our hands* " (*ma'aseh yadenu*).	ii. 7. "In all the *work of Thy hands.*" (So at chaps. xiv. 29, xvi. 15, xxiv. 19, xxviii. 12, xxx. 9, xxxi. 29.

But, in truth, the coincidences between Deuteronomy and the Psalm are closer and deeper than a table of this sort can exhibit. In both cases, the voice which we hear is that of a man who has attained a great age, whose life has been spent in public service, whose heart is filled with solicitude for the people whom he is soon to leave behind amidst the temptations of the present life. In both cases, moreover, we are conscious of a certain stern sublimity of thought and feeling— sublimity as of a grander Milton—which is not found elsewhere.

The circumstance that Ps. xc. and the book of Deuteronomy can be shown to have had a common author does not, of course, suffice to prove that Moses was he. If it could be made out that Deuteronomy was written in the age of Hezekiah, the identity of authorship would only prove that the psalm was also written in that age. I cannot turn aside to discuss the question of Deuteronomy here, and will therefore only remark that to the other formidable difficulties which the impugners of the Mosaic origin of Deuteronomy have to encounter—difficulties critical, historical, and moral—this has to be added, that the prophet who, on their hypothesis, concocted Deuteronomy must have been a man capable of writing also the Ninetieth Psalm.

4. The testimony of the superscription is strongly supported by the circumstance that, while the psalm contains no allusion to any passage of Scripture or to any historical event of later date than the death of Moses, there are in it allusions which remarkably accord with the Mosaic authorship. Not to repeat what has been already said about the coincidences between the psalm and Deuteronomy, which, if they had not demonstrated a common authorship, would have certainly proved that the author of the psalm was uncommonly familiar with Deuteronomy, I ask the readers to observe ver. 3, " Thou turnest frail man to dust; and sayest, Return, ye children of men," or, as it is rendered by Mr. Cheyne,

> " Thou turnest mortals back to dust,
> And sayest, Return, ye sons of the earth-born."

There is here an unmistakable allusion to Gen. iii. 19, " In the sweat of thy face shalt thou eat bread till thou return unto the ground; for out of it wast thou taken: for dust thou art, and unto dust shalt thou return." Not only is the psalmist acquainted with that primal curse, but his mind is very much occupied with the truth which it is the leading purpose of the whole context to unfold, namely that death is the wages of sin. It cannot be said that this truth crops up often in the Old Testament. Yet it must have been familiar to Moses; for it is everywhere implied in the ordinances of the ritual respecting death and the treatment of the bodies of the dead. Coincidences like these, so close and yet so recondite, strongly support the Mosaic authorship.

CHAPTER II.

DAVID THE PSALMIST OF ISRAEL.

MOSES, the earliest writer of Holy Scripture, was also the first of the psalmists; and it was long ere another stone was built on the foundation he laid. For nearly four hundred years, his prayer stood alone, of its kind. During the times of Joshua and the Judges, the harp of *prophecy* was not altogether mute; but those stormy centuries have bequeathed to us no psalm. Moses remained the only psalmist till David.

But if the efflorescence of sacred song was long delayed, it came, at length, with a sudden and magnificent outburst, insomuch that ere David was gathered to his fathers, the Church was in possession of nearly two-thirds of the lyrical treasures laid up in the Psalter. The half of the psalms, or thereby, are believed to have been written by David himself; and there were other pens besides his employed in the same work during the later years of his life. This is offered for the present only as an approximate estimate. There is still a good deal of obscurity, and consequent difference of opinion, on several points necessary to be determined before the precise number of the psalms contributed by David can be ascertained; and the subject is so full of interest, that we must revert to it hereafter. Meanwhile the approximate estimate is sufficient to show that the reign of David was, beyond all controversy, the Augustan age of sacred psalmody. It is plain, therefore, that however deep the interest attaching to the history of the one psalm of Moses, and however deep and various the interest attaching to the history of the fifty or sixty that were written between the time of Solomon and the cessation of prophecy, the age which we are principally concerned to study, with a view to the history of the psalms, is the age of King David.

The Spirit and Providence of God had been making preparation for the great outburst of holy song long before David was born at Bethlehem. The Lord never works by unpremeditated and extemporised strokes of power, least of all in the production of those fruits of His wisdom and love which are the enduring possession of His Church. Long before April clothes the trees in their gay and hopeful livery of blossoms, there are hidden motions under the bark, and the buds are being silently prepared to unfold when their full time is come. So was it with the psalms of David. Their history, if it is to be worthy of the name, must not commence with the day when the first of them flowed from David's pen, but must take note of the steps of God's providence and grace in raising up so great a psalmist in Israel.

Foremost among the influences which prepared the way for the golden age of psalmody, we must make mention of the religious revival with which the Lord blessed Israel towards the close of the period of the Judges. It is unnecessary to relate here the life of Samuel, whom God honoured to be the principal instrument in that revival: how he was raised up in a godly house belonging to the tribe of Levi; how his mother, in particular, was eminent not only for piety but for spiritual gifts, being, like Deborah, a prophetess, and the writer of one of the few sacred lyrics which broke the silence of the long period between Moses and David; how, after years of childless wedded life, she asked a son from the Lord, and received Samuel as God's answer to her prayer; how from his mother's womb the Lord separated the child to be His servant; how, as he grew up, "the Lord was with him, and did let none of his words fall to the ground; and all Israel from Dan even to Beersheba knew that Samuel was established to be a prophet of the Lord" (1 Sam. iii. 19, 20); how, with a disinterested zeal, which no man could impeach, he from the first devoted his life to the nation and Church of Israel, judging all the tribes, and labouring, as none of the Judges who preceded him had done, to instruct the people in the law of Moses and so to imbue them with the knowledge and fear of the living God. It is more necessary, in relation to the present subject, to observe that Samuel, no doubt by divine direction, took steps to multiply and prolong the benefits of his personal service by means of a remarkable Institution, the first mention of which in the sacred history occurs in connection with his name. I refer to the famous Schools of the Prophets. It is possible some institution of the kind may have existed from the age of Moses ; more probably Samuel was the founder. It is certain, at least, that it was in Samuel's hands that the prophetical schools became institutions of far-reaching influence, and rose to the honourable place within the Hebrew commonwealth which they seem henceforth to have occupied till the Captivity. If the question is asked, What precisely were these prophetical schools ? for what end were they set up and maintained ? this at least is to be said, that they were a kind of College or Theological Hall (if so modern a phrase may be allowed), into which Samuel received such young men as seemed to be qualified by gifts and piety to act as prophets in Israel, and regarding whom it might be presumed that the Lord was calling them by His Spirit into that office. The principal study, we may be sure, would be the Book of the Law, which was now, after the lapse of four hundred years, a somewhat ancient document ; and we know for certain that, in addition to that supremely important study, the arts of Music and Poetry were cultivated. It may well be believed that, from his childhood, Hannah's son would be no stranger to arts in which she was herself so eminent.

The earliest notice of the company of the Prophets is that which relates how Saul met them coming down from the hill of God, on the day that Samuel anointed him king ; and it describes them as coming down from the High Place with a psaltery and a timbrel and a pipe and a harp before them, and prophesying as they went (1 Sam. x. 5), all which sufficiently attests the assiduity with which the company had been trained in sacred music and song. It is worthy of remark, that the prophesying of these " sons of the prophets " is so described, as to suggest that the singing or chanting which greeted the newly-anointed king on his homeward journey was, on this occasion, prompted and sustained by a supernatural motion of the Holy Spirit. They spoke and sang as men who were swayed by a divine and irresistible energy ; for the same motion of the Spirit came on Saul, and he prophesied also. It seems to have been a motion of the Spirit closely resembling that which came down on the disciples to signalise the Mission of the Comforter on the day of Pentecost. It differed from that great New Testament miracle chiefly in this respect, that the sons of the prophets were moved to utter their hearts in *song*, whereas the disciples at Pentecost

uttered theirs in *divers tongues*. This miraculous quality of
the prophesying of Samuel's disciples is important to be noted ;
for it was a kind of seal affixed by God Himself on the newly-
founded Institution—a sign from heaven by which the Lord gave
testimony to the school and declared that His blessing rested
upon it. We might say of Samuel, what the Epistle to the
Hebrews says of the apostles, that God bare witness to him
" with gifts of the Holy Ghost " (Heb. ii. 4).

It has not yet been ascertained what eminence of Southern
Palestine was the Ramah of Samuel's residence and of the Prophetical School. Dean Stanley * enumerates as many as eight
localities, on behalf of which claims have been urged. Of these,
four have respectively received the suffrages of such high
authorities as Dr. Robinson, Van de Velde, Gesenius, and Mr.
Finn, the English consul at Jerusalem ; and it is remarkable that
the four eminences fixed upon by these careful scholars and
investigators are all situated within a few miles of Bethlehem.
One of them, the site favoured by Gesenius and adopted by the
English surveyors, is in its immediate neighbourhood, lying
about three quarters of a mile to the east of the town.† We
may be very sure that such an institution as Samuel's college
would have a powerful attraction for the godly among its
Bethlehemite neighbours ; and that such a youth as David, the
son of such a man as Jesse, would be no stranger among the
sons of the prophets. This supposition is confirmed by the
fact, that David had attained to such skill in sacred minstrelsy,
ere his boyhood was well past, that his fame had reached the
court of Saul, and he was spoken of to the king as the fittest
person to play before him when the evil spirit from God
darkened his mind. A further confirmation is found in the
circumstance, that some years later, when he fled from Saul's
envious javelin, he betook himself to the *Naioth*, or Cottages, at
Ramah, where the sons of the prophets dwelt in company with
the venerable man of God whom Providence had appointed over
them as their father (1 Sam. xix. 18). It is unlikely that David,
on the occasion of that first danger, would have thought of Ramah
if he had been a stranger either to the place or its inmates.

---

* *Sinai and Palestine*, pp. 222, 233.

† See the Palestine Exploration Fund map of Western Palestine, and compare
Gesenius's *Thesaurus*, s.v.

Whatever may be thought of the conjecture that David resorted in his youth to the school of the prophets, it is certain that he was anything but a novice in the peculiar exercises of the place when persecution constrained him to seek safety within its walls. He was descended from a family of great distinction in Israel. He was of the tribe of Judah, on which God had, from the first, set a note of pre-eminence above the rest ; and Nahshon, who was Prince of the tribe in the wilderness, was his ancestor. After examining the several notices of the family that occur in the Scriptures from first to last, one is struck with the fact that its distinction in the nation was anything but factitious—anything but the sort of distinction that mere Heraldry can bestow. God raised the family to its predicted and predestined distinction, by bestowing upon it a rich dower of diversified intellectual ability. The roll of the eminent men whom it furnished to Church and commonwealth is a long and brilliant one ; and many facts concur to show that the general mental power which characterised the family for centuries and was transmitted like an heirloom from father to son never shone out with more lustre than in Jesse and his immediate descendants. Thus it is remarkable that David's most distinguished generals, Joab, Abishai, Amasa, were found in the circle of his near kinsmen, as were also several counsellors who attained distinction during his reign.*

In David himself the general hereditary ability was associated with the poetical faculty in its highest form. No competent critic has ever affected to deny that the son of Jesse was a poet born, and a poet of the first rank. And the family into which he was born—was it not an admirable nursery for the man who was to be, not the song-writer of his country merely, but the Psalmist of God's Israel? I have just referred to the *force of mind* which perpetually showed itself in the line of our Lord's ancestry. Let the reader turn to the genealogy in the first chapter of Matthew, or to the other version of the same genealogy in the third of Luke, and he will find that, all along the line from Adam and Abraham to Mary and Joseph, *true godliness* also

---

* Jonathan, described in 1 Chron. xxvii. 32 as " a counsellor, a man of understanding, and a scribe," was either his uncle or his brother's son ; and Jonadab, the " very subtile " adviser of unhappy Amnon, was the son of Shimeah, and therefore the king's nephew.

can be traced, with only an occasional intermission. If I do not greatly err, a perception of the mercy which God had thus shown to the house of her fathers contributed to swell the flood of tender thankfulness which filled the heart of the " blessed among women ;" for in her song, among the other instances of the Lord's kindness which called for notice in connection with the circumstances of the Incarnation, she tells how " His mercy is unto generations and generations on them that fear Him."*   It is certain that, during the stormy times of the Judges, the family at Bethlehem was eminent among those which remained faithful to the Lord.   The delightful picture of domestic piety that imparts such a charm to the Book of Ruth is a memorial of the manners prevalent among David's im- mediate ancestors, and of the benign and heavenly influences that blessed his infancy and boyhood.   I do not suppose that the Twenty-third Psalm was written in the Psalmist's child- hood ; but it is at least a reminiscence of it, and brings vividly before us the scenes and the feelings which his memory recalled when it reverted to the golden morning of his life.   We have good reason to believe that the regenerating hallowing grace of God's free Spirit accompanied—if indeed it did not anticipate —the teaching and godly nurture he received from his parents. There is not the faintest trace of his having passed through such a crisis as we see in the lives of Moses and Paul.   I am much inclined to think that his was a case of infant regenera- tion ; certainly it was a case of early piety.   Touching proof of this is found in the SEVENTY-FIRST Psalm.   The psalm, I am aware, is anonymous, and is by many recent critics referred to some later writer ; but I am satisfied that Venema and Heng- stenberg have adduced sufficient reasons for retaining the opinion of Calvin and the older expositors, that it is from David's pen, and is the complaint of his old age.   It shows us the soul of the aged saint darkened by the remembrance of his great transgression, and by the sorrows with which that sin filled all his later years.   But he finds comfort in reverting to the happy days of his childhood, and especially to the irre- vocable trust which he was then enabled to repose in God. The thoughts and feelings expressed remind one of those which invest with such a solemn, tender interest the second epistle to

* Luke i. 50.

Timothy,—the repository of the great apostle's dying thoughts. Like Paul, David takes a retrospect of the Lord's dealings with him from the beginning, and utters himself in words which are an anticipation of those in which the apostle declared his hope in Christ, " I am not ashamed; for I know Him whom I have believed, and I am persuaded that He is able to guard that which I have committed to Him against that day " (2 Tim. i. 12). Only, there is this notable difference between the two, that while Paul gathered confirmation of his faith from the experience of a thirty years' walk with his Lord, David's experience stretched over a tract of more than twice so many years; for it began with his childhood. Let us hear the confession of his faith :—

1. In Thee, O LORD, do I put my trust :
   Let me never be ashamed.
2. Deliver me in Thy righteousness, and rescue me :
   Bow down Thine ear to me, and save me.
3. Be Thou to me a rock of habitation, whereunto I may continually resort :
   Thou hast given commandment to save me ;
   For Thou art my rock and my fortress.
4. Rescue me, O my God, out of the hand of the wicked,
   Out of the hand of the unrighteous and cruel man.
5. For Thou art my hope, O Lord GOD ;
   Thou art my trust from my youth.

   .   .   .   .

9. Cast me not off in the time of old age ;
   Forsake me not when my strength faileth.

   .   .   .   .

17. O God, Thou hast taught me from my youth ;
    And hitherto have I declared Thy wondrous works.
18. Yea, even when I am old and gray-headed, O God, forsake me not ;
    Until I have declared Thy strength unto the next generation,
    Thy might to every one that is to come.
19. Thy righteousness also, O God, is very high ;
    Thou who hast done great things,
    O God, who is like unto Thee ?
20. Thou, which hast showed us many and sore troubles,
    Shalt quicken us again,
    And shalt bring us up again from the depths of the earth.

    .   .   .   .

23. My lips shall greatly rejoice when I sing praises unto Thee ;
    And my soul, which Thou hast redeemed.

It is evident, then, that in David there was a remarkable concurrence of circumstances favourable to the production of sacred
psalmody. He was raised up at a time when the Lord had
visited His people and vouchsafed a copious effusion of the
Holy Spirit ; so that there were in Israel a numerous people,
God's "hidden ones," in whose name a psalmist might sing.
He knew the Lord from his childhood. The poetical faculty
with which his nature was so richly endowed he had been in a
position to cultivate, having had access to instruction in the
law of the Lord and in the arts of music and poetry. For, as
Augustine, who was himself an adept in music, remarks in his
City of God, "David was a man erudite in song, a man who
loved musical harmony, not for the sensible delight merely, but
of set purpose and from a principle of faith."* It remains to
be added that David afterwards enjoyed the supernatural
motions of the Holy Spirit. He was a PROPHET. He is so
designated in Peter's Pentecostal sermon (Acts ii. 30). From
the day that Samuel sent for him to the field and anointed him
in his father's house at Bethlehem, the Spirit of the Lord
came upon him, and this not only to endow him with counsel
and might with a view to the kingdom, but also, and in the
first instance, to enable him to set forth the praises of God in
song. The courtier who first mentioned his name to Saul
did not speak of him as a mere harper or minstrel, but as a
man of valour and prudence, of whom it could be said, "The
Lord is with him." When it is remembered that Saul's dis-
temper was not a mere case of natural melancholy, but was
the effect of "an evil spirit from God upon him," it will readily
be believed that the relief ministered to him by David was
something more than the soothing effect of sweet music,—that
it was the effect rather of David's wise and kindly use of *a
spiritual gift*, a gift of sacred song with which he was endowed
by the good Spirit of God, who had departed from Saul and
rested on him. It was the motion of this Holy Spirit, acting
upon, and by means of, rare natural endowments and cultivated
skill, which thenceforward impelled and enabled David to
indite psalms. Hence the combination of titles by which he
describes his place and function, in his "last words" (2 Sam.
xxiii. 1): "the man who was raised up on high, the

* Lib. xvii., c. 14.

anointed of the God of Jacob, and the sweet psalmist of Israel." The combination implies, and was doubtless intended to suggest, that David was raised up on high and anointed by the God of Jacob, in order that he might be the sweet psalmist of the Church. He was a prophet, not a whit behind the very chiefest of the prophets ; and it is the constant testimony of the Apostles, and of the Lord Jesus Himself, that it was " in the Spirit," that is, as one who was moved by the Holy Ghost, that he indited his hymns and songs.

The most of the qualifications hitherto enumerated, and especially the one last named, were essential to the office of a psalmist, and were found in others besides David. But the son of Jesse possessed some, besides, that were peculiar to himself. It has been remarked, and I think with truth, that he is the only psalmist whose *personal history* comes up very prominently in the Psalter. References to the more remarkable passages in David's life occur in places without number. There are psalms not a few which it is impossible for any one to read without being reminded that they are his. This is to be accounted for by adverting to David's singular position in Israel. He was not only the king, but the man after God's own heart; he was "an Israelite indeed," the genuine representative of the Hebrew nation and Church, insomuch that when he expressed his personal experience and diversified feelings in song, he produced psalms that were felt by the whole people to be exactly suited to express their feelings also before God. His psalms were from the first "the Psalms of Israel."* This, we may remark in passing, is one of the points in respect to which David was a type of our Blessed Lord. For we know that Christ, although He was in the form of God, condescended to be made like unto the brethren whom He came to redeem ; submitted Himself to a condition in which He knew that He should, though without sin, be in all points tempted even as we are ; condescended to be so perfectly made like unto His brethren, that in addressing the Father He could employ, and did employ, the very words of David and of the Church in the Book of Psalms. It is impossible to do full

* "(David) the Anointed of the God of Jacob, and pleasant in the Psalms of Israel" (2 Sam. xxiii. 1, Heb. and margin of Revised Version).

justice to David and his psalms without bearing in mind his singular position as the man who was thus raised up on high. He was not a private individual. He was " the Anointed One of the God of Jacob," the head or chief of the people of the Lord ; and so was both entitled to speak in their name and moved by the Holy Spirit to do so.

To qualify David to be " the Psalmist of Israel " in this high and honourable sense, to qualify him to write hymns in which there should be a living, warm, true expression of the very thoughts and inmost feelings of God's Israel, his experience required to be, beyond example, intense and diversified. A poet cannot give vivid expression to feelings to which he is himself an entire stranger. Among uninspired hymns those only succeed in rooting themselves in the minds and hearts of God's people which (like Luther's *Eine feste Burg* and the best of Cowper's hymns) embalm the actual feelings of a believing soul in some season of high emotion. The *Pilgrim's Progress* (which is a poem too) owes as much of its fascination to the wonderfully varied experience of its author as to his matchless genius ; for the characters and scenes in the allegory are the reflection or idealised reproduction of characters Bunyan had known, and scenes he had passed through, in his time. With respect to this qualification, the fact that they enjoyed the inspiration of the Spirit did not alter the case of the sacred writers, at least of the psalmists. It belongs to the very idea of a psalm that it is the expression of the genuine feelings of the writer. God may, in a few exceptional instances, have employed the tongue of an ungodly man in the utterance of a prophecy or the revelation of a doctrine ; but it may be affirmed with much confidence that He never employed, in the composition of a psalm, any man whose heart was dead to the sentiments expressed. There was a Balaam among the prophets, a Judas among the apostles ; but there was no Balaam or Judas among the psalmists. There was required, therefore, in the man who was to be, by way of eminence, " the Psalmist of Israel," a saint of manifold experience.

And such a man was David. Into his single life were crowded the vicissitudes of many lives. His boyhood made him acquainted with the deep-flowing, tranquil joys of a godly and well-ordered home (a better home than his manhood or old age ever knew); it made him acquainted also with the hardships and the pleasures of country life among the pastoral expanses of Southern Palestine. After he was anointed by Samuel, Providence called him to ply the minstrel's art before Saul, and initiated him into the life of a court. Having returned home, he received a second and more brilliant introduction to the court in consequence of the victory over Goliath. Thereafter, for a succession of years, his life was spent amidst continual perils and trials. Persecuted by Saul, he had bitter experience of the worst vices of the ungodly in Israel; he was thrown for a time into the company of outlaws, and was obliged, more than once, to reside for a season among the idolatrous heathen, being driven forth, as he complained, from the heritage of the Lord. Nor did his trials cease when Saul's death on the field of Gilboa opened his way to the throne. Israel in his reign was a figure of the Church militant; he ruled, but it was in the midst of his enemies. First he had the Philistines to make head against and drive back to their maritime plain. Then he had to confront a succession of formidable coalitions among the principal nations to the east and north—the Ammonites, the Moabites, the Syrians—so that years were spent in wars which taxed his utmost energies and the resources of the kingdom. At length victory crowned his arms on every side, so that his sway extended from the Euphrates to the river of Egypt. This might have brought him peace, but he forfeited the blessing by presumptuous sin. The evening of his life, which had held out the promise of a serene, unclouded sky, was vexed with storms more terrible than all that went before. The transgression of an unguarded day planted in his house a root of bitterness which troubled all his years. Incest and murder showed their frightful visage in the palace. One son after another rose in rebellious against him, which were only quenched in their blood. His heart—a heart that beat with an intensity of natural affection never surpassed—was broken with anguish, and his gray hairs were brought down with sorrow to the grave.

I do not think it needful to spend many words in vindicating David's character from the reproaches with which some have been pleased to load it. The fact is significant (I believe it to

be a fact), that the quarters whence these reproaches come are
not those in which the highest ideal of moral excellence prevails.
It is not the men of unbending rectitude, of tender conscience,
of holy life, who find it most difficult to understand how David
should have been an eminent saint for all his sins, and who can
perceive nothing but whining hypocrisy in his confessions. The
psalms which he wrote on occasion of his great fall have gone
home to the hearts of the best and holiest men that ever walked
the earth. No sermon of Augustine's betrays more tender
emotion, more deep and thrilling sympathy with his subject,
than the one he preached to the people of Carthage on the
Fifty-first Psalm. A great modern preacher gives similarly
touching expression to his sense of the indubitable truth and
sincerity of the king's penitence. " In commenting on some of
these psalms," writes Mr. Spurgeon, "I have been overwhelmed
with awe, and said with Jacob, 'How dreadful is this place! It
is none other than the house of God.' Especially was this the
case with the Fifty-first. I postponed expounding it week after
week, feeling, more and more, my inability for the work.
Often I sat down to it, and rose up again without having penned
a line. The Psalm is very human; its sobs and cries are of one
born of woman; but it is freighted with an inspiration all
divine, as if the great Father were putting words into His
child's mouth. Such a psalm may be wept over, absorbed into
the soul, and exhaled again in devotion, but commented on—
ah! Where is he who, having attempted it, can do other than
blush at his defeat?" * Nothing can well be plainer, than that
psalms which for ages have thus found their way to men's
hearts must have come from the heart.

One who would appreciate the character of the Psalmist
must remember that he was a man of prodigious energy. What
he did, he did with his might. Moreover, he was a king, an
oriental king, to whom law and universal custom permitted
polygamy, and who was thus put in the way of being tempted
by the foul sin which was the death of his domestic peace.
Nor ought it to be forgotten that the sacred history has
narrated David's fall with a judicial severity full of the terror
of the Lord. The chapter which records his offence sets down

---

* Spurgeon's *Treasury of David*, Preface to Vol. II., 1870.

every hateful feature in it with an unextenuating, inexorable circumstantiality, unparalleled in all biography, and, to a thoughtful reader, suggestive of the indictment that might be preferred against a criminal at the bar of the Most High. These considerations are not adduced to cloak David's transgression. Its enormity is undeniable, and is denied by none. He sank to a depth of guilt into which few of God's children have ever been suffered to fall. Yet this very fact contributed to fit him to be the Psalmist of God's Israel. It was not in spite of his fall, but because of it, that God made choice of him to be the spokesman of the Church in penitential song. The Church is not a company of angels, but of ransomed men ; of men who were sinners, who are often sinning still. David well knew that the record of his fall and his forgiveness would furnish to sin stricken souls in after-times a strength of encouragement which nothing else could yield. In crying for mercy, this was the plea he urged, " Restore unto me the joy of Thy salvation ;—then will I teach transgressors Thy ways ; and sinners shall be converted unto Thee " (Ps. li. 12, 13). Being forgiven, he felt, like the converted persecutor of the Church, that his God had furnished in him " a pattern to them which should hereafter believe in Him to life everlasting." How wonderfully has this anticipation been realised ! It is a merciful provision that, however profound may be the depths into which a man may be cast by his sins, he finds that the Psalmist has been there before him, and has furnished him with words in which " out of the depths " he may cry to the Lord. There is not a poor publican in all God's temple who, as he smites on his breast and cries, " God be merciful to me a sinner," does not find, on turning to the Book of Psalms, that the mercy of God has there provided for him songs that express every feeling of his convicted soul— songs, too, originally written by as great a sinner as himself, in the agony of his repentance. Till the judgment day it will never be known how many souls, who would otherwise have cast themselves down in despair, have been encouraged by David's example, and assisted by his psalms, to embrace the promise and to hope in the mercy of God.*

---

* " The force of David's character was vast, and the scope of his life was immense. His harp was full-stringed, and every angel, of joy and of sorrow, swept over the chords as he passed ; but the melody always breathed of heaven.

We have not exhausted the catalogue of David's qualifications to be the Psalmist of Israel. We have said nothing of his remarkable love for the tabernacle and the solemn worship there offered. Yet this was one of the strongly marked features of his character. It impressed all who knew him, and, when he was gathered to his fathers, the generation that came after continued to speak with affection of " David and all his affliction," all his anxious labour for the House of God—how he lamented for the ark all the years it lay neglected at Kirjath-jearim— how he coveted its presence in his own city, as the fairest jewel in his diadem—how he pitched for it a Tabernacle, and desired to build for it a Temple (Ps. cxxxii.). If David ever had a ruling passion, it was his zeal, his consuming zeal, for the House of God. He could say with rare truth, " The zeal of Thine house hath eaten me up" (Ps. lxix. 9). How strongly is this expressed in the Twenty-seventh Psalm :—

4. One thing have I asked of the LORD, that will I seek after ;
   That I may dwell in the house of the LORD all the days of my life,
   To behold the beauty of the LORD, and to inquire in His temple.
5. For in the day of trouble He shall keep me secretly in His pavilion :
   In the covert of His tabernacle shall He hide me ;
   He shall lift me up upon a rock.

In David's position, and with his love for the tabernacle service, an uninspired poet might have so framed his hymns that, however suitable to the typical dispensation, they would

---

And such oceans of affection lay within his breast, as could not always slumber in their calmness. For the hearts of a hundred men strove and struggled together within the narrow continent of his single heart ; and will the scornful men have no sympathy for one so conditioned, but scorn him, because he ruled not with constant quietness the unruly host of diverse natures which dwelt within his single soul ?

" Such oceans of feeling did God infuse into his soul, and such utterance of poetry He placed between his lips, and such skilful music He seated in his right hand, in order that he might conceive forms of feeling for all saints, and create an everlasting psalmody, and hand down an organ for expressing the melody of the renewed soul. The Lord did not intend that His Church should be without a rule for uttering its gladness and its glory, its lamentation and its grief ; and to bring such a rule and institute into being, He raised up His servant David, as formerly He raised up His servant Moses, to give to the Church an institute of Law. And to that end He led him the round of all human conditions, that he might catch the spirit proper to every one, and utter it according to truth. He allowed him not to curtail his being, by treading the round of one function, but by every variety of functions He cultivated his whole being, and filled his soul with wisdom

have become obsolete when the temple was given to the flames, and the cumbrous ritual, in which the fathers of the Old Testament worshipped God, was finally supplanted by a system of simple and spiritual ordinances. But David " spake as he was moved by the Holy Ghost ; " and, accordingly, in his character of Psalmist, we may say of him, with Augustine, that "although he lived under the Old Testament, he was not a man of the Old Testament." * He seized on the spiritual elements and import of the tabernacle service, and wove these alone into the fabric of his songs ; so that when " the things that might be shaken " were removed, his Psalms were found to belong to " the things which could not be shaken," and remained fixed in the worship of the catholic Church.

The most important, in some respects, of all David's qualifications, remains yet to be noticed. " He was a prophet, and knew that God had sworn with an oath to him, that of the fruit of his loins he would set One upon his throne " (Acts ii. 30). Through Nathan he learned that the Promised Seed, the Hope of Israel, was to be born of his family and to be the Heir of his throne. He was thus taught to regard himself as a man who had been raised up to foreshadow his Lord, and his kingdom as one that was not only to foreshadow, but to pass into the kingdom of that divine Son. Thus he was put in a position to write, not only psalms that were strictly prophetical of Christ, but other psalms besides, which, although in some sense applicable to himself and his people, looked beyond him and them to the person and kingdom of the Son.

---

and feeling. He found him objects for every affection, that the affection might not slumber and die. His trials were but the tuning of the instrument with which the Spirit might express the various melodies which He designed to utter by him for the consolation and edification of spiritual men. And though we neither excuse his acts of wickedness, nor impute them to the temptation of God, Who cannot be tempted of evil, neither tempteth any man, we will also add that by his loss the Church hath gained ; and that, out of the evil of his ways, much good hath been made to arise ; and that, if he had not passed through every valley of humiliation, and stumbled upon the dark mountains, we should not have had a language for the souls of the penitent, or an expression for the dark troubles which compass the soul that feareth to be deserted by its God."—Edward Irving : *Introduction to Horne on the Psalms* (Collected Writings, Vol. i. pp. 418-420).

* *Expositio Epistolæ ad Galatas,* sect. 43.

CHAPTER III.

DAVID'S PSALMS.

ONE who is in search of the facts and testimonies which must be taken into account in forming an estimate of the number of David's psalms naturally turns, in the first place, to the *superscriptions*. Of these no fewer than seventy-three exhibit the name of the royal psalmist. Thus the number of the psalms that are expressly ascribed to him wants only two of amounting to half the entire collection. Proceeding on this datum alone, we should be entitled to infer that his single contribution is, as nearly as may be, equal to those of all the other psalmists put together—so well is he entitled to be denominated, by way of eminence, The sweet Psalmist of Israel.

I am aware, of course, that the trustworthiness of this source of information has been challenged. The "advanced" school of critics, holding as they do, that much the greater number of the psalms were written after the Captivity and that it is doubtful whether David was a psalmist at all, have no patience with the superscriptions, and brush them aside as so much rubbish. Others (and this class probably includes the majority of recent critics), while acknowledging that the authors of the superscriptions, whoever they were, must have been in possession of genuine traditions regarding the authorship of a good many psalms, so that their testimony is entitled to respectful consideration, nevertheless are of opinion that the superscriptions neither proceeded from the psalmists themselves nor from any other authoritative source, and that they can not unfrequently be convicted of error. According to this view (which, I repeat, is probably the one most in favour at present among sober-minded critics) the titles resemble, in respect to trustworthiness and authority, the little notes appended to the Pauline Epistles in the *textus receptus*. These, as every one knows, form no part of the original text, are full of errors, and have been left out of the Revised Version.

This question of the superscriptions involves several points of considerable importance, and I must revert to it in a note at the end of the chapter. One consideration may be mentioned at present as furnishing a presumption in their favour. The case of the notes affixed to the Pauline Epistles, which has been cited as parallel, shows this at least, that in ordinary hands, and indeed in any hands except perhaps those of men who happen to be uncommonly expert in the modern art of criticism, the attempt to assign author and date to fugitive compositions, after the lapse of many years, is precarious in the extreme, or rather is sure to result in conjectures which can be easily convicted of error. Do we find, then, that, like the notes referred to, the superscriptions are always worthless and often demonstrably erroneous ? Certainly not. On the contrary, the indications of authorship and date and occasion due to them are, in many instances, found to harmonise quite remarkably with recondite features in the psalms themselves, which have been brought to light in the progress of critical research. One example of this has already fallen under our notice, in the Ninetieth Psalm. Other examples are seen in the "psalms of the Sons of Korah," the "psalms of Asaph," and the so-called "songs of degrees." It is as certain as anything of the sort can well be, that the several collections of psalms thus bound together by a common title constitute groups which have much in common and really are of a piece. What is even more to the purpose, the correspondences by which the learned have been able to make out that the psalms composing these several collections are near of kin to each other are for the most part so covert as to show that the titles were not suggested by them. Facts like these sufficiently prove that the scepticism with which it is the fashion at present to regard the titles is unreasonable, and that their testimony possesses great weight.

This conclusion is farther strengthened by the circumstance that attempts made, soon after the completion of the Old Testament Canon, to deal with the psalms as the early critics dealt with the apostolic epistles in the notes they appended, were quite as unsuccessful. The superscriptions, as they stand in the Septuagint, contain statements regarding the authorship and occasion of certain psalms, without warrant from the original Hebrew, and which doubtless are the product simply of the conjectural criticism of the Alexandrian Jews, to whom we owe that priceless version of the Old Testament. Thus Ps. xxvii. is entitled, "a psalm of David before he was anointed;" Ps. xcvii., "a psalm of David when his country was restored;" Ps. cxxxix., "(a psalm) of David, a psalm of Zacharias in the Dispersion." In Ps. cxxxvii. the title in the Septuagint not only names David as the writer, but associates with him the prophet Jeremiah in the authorship, although it is certain that neither of these holy men could have had a hand in writing a psalm which celebrates the sorrows of the exiles " by the rivers of Babylon." The version which contains these conjectural titles is believed to have been executed about two centuries after the age of Malachi; yet the conjectures are not only quite unreliable, but, in a large proportion of instances (as in the four just cited), demonstrably, and by universal admission, erroneous. If the superscriptions in the Hebrew had rested on no better basis than conjecture, they must have, in like manner, bristled with gross and palpable errors; which certainly they do not. Questions may still be, not unfairly, raised regarding some of the instances in which the name of David occurs in the titles. Thus it has been observed that in four of these, near the end of the Psalter (namely Psalms cxxii., cxxiv., cxxxi., cxxxiii.), the name of David is not found in the Septuagint. The four psalms from which David's name is thus omitted in the Greek include the two which perhaps suit least the age of David; and it is not impossible that this is a case in which the Septuagint has preserved the truer reading. But any deduction which may have to be made for such reasons as these will, after all, affect only a very limited number of psalms, and we shall not be far from the mark if, on the ground of the superscriptions, we ascribe to David seventy or thereby of the psalms.

Do these constitute David's entire contribution? or are we to set down to his account some of the rest, although not exhibiting his name? The whole of these he certainly did *not* write. That other pens besides his were employed on the psalms is not only universally acknowledged by modern critics, but has been known all along. It is hardly fair in some recent writers * to cite the opinion of Augustine and Chrysostom, who imagined that all the psalms were David's, as if that had been the general opinion of the primitive times. " We know," wrote Jerome, " that they are in error who suppose that all the psalms were written by David, and not by those whose names are inscribed upon them." † Besides, we have already had occasion to observe, that the title prefixed to the Book in our Bibles, which seems to ascribe the whole to one psalmist, is not the most ancient. The title in the Hebrew Bible is not " the Psalms of David," but *Sepher Tehillim*, " the Book of Praises ; " and the title found in the most ancient manuscripts of the Septuagint is *The Psalter*, or *The Psalms*. It would have been strange if the primitive students of the Scriptures had failed to discover the truth in this matter ; for the superscriptions are quite as express in ascribing some psalms to Asaph and the sons of Korah, as they are in ascribing so many to David. Moreover, of those which are not furnished with superscriptions—" the orphan psalms," as the Jewish writers style them—not a few can be demonstrated to be of later date than David's reign. There are several which bear on the face of them indubitable evidence of having been first sung, either by the exiles who hanged their harps on the willows by the rivers of Babylon and wept as they remembered Zion, or by the remnant who returned with songs to the hills of Judah, and drank again of the soft-flowing waters of Siloa.

All this, however, still leaves undecided the authorship of a considerable number of psalms, especially towards the latter part of the collection—psalms which, although not bearing David's name in their titles, exhibit nothing, either in their titles or contents, that is plainly inconsistent with his having been the writer. What shall we say regarding these ? Shall we set them all down to David's account? or shall we refuse

---

* Stanley, *Jewish Church*, ii. 145.

† *Epist. ad Cyprianum Presbyter* (Opp. ed Migne i. 1166). Comp. *Præf. in librum psalmorum, ad Sophronium:* " Psalmos omnes eorum testamur auctorum, qui ponuntur in titulis, David scilicet, Asaph, et Idithun, filiorum Core, Eman Esrahitæ, Moisi. et Salomonis, et reliquorum " (Migne ix. 1123). Also *Comment. in Mat.* xiii. 35 (Migne vii. 92).

to attribute to him any save the seventy-three that bear his name? It must be admitted that any answer that can be given as yet to these questions can only claim to be regarded as a more or less probable conjecture. Critics of great note have taken up a position on either extreme. Dr. Lightfoot,* for example, the famous Cambridge Hebraist, maintained that we are to presume that any given psalm is David's unless the contrary can be proved; that all are his whose titles or contents do not distinctly point to some other pen. So far as my observation goes, this is the view that pervades the writings of our older British divines, and indeed also of most of the recent divines, who have not made the subject a special study. The grand objection to it is the obvious one, that it seems to leave nothing for the Davidic superscriptions to do. If the Ninety-ninth Psalm, for example, although anonymous, is to be ascribed to David, as a matter of course, simply because there is nothing in it but might well enough have been written by him, it is difficult to see what use there was in prefixing his name to the Hundred-and-first. There is such obvious force in this objection, that one is not surprised to find that the tendency of late years has been to refuse to recognise David's pen except in the psalms which bear his name. That this is a good general rule to go by, I do not doubt; nevertheless, room must be left for a few exceptions. For example, the Second Psalm, like the First, bears no title, and is on this account referred to some later writer, not only by Hupfeld and Ewald, but by Delitzsch and Perowne. But the contents are so hard to reconcile with any reign except David's that the ancient opinion which assigns the authorship to him seems likely to keep its ground; and the absence of his name may be accounted for by the position occupied by the psalm, as constituting along with the First a kind of Introduction to the whole book. A possible call for other exceptions is suggested by the fact that the Greek version, while dropping (as we have seen) David's name from some of the titles where it is found in the Hebrew, inserts it in more than twice as many others in which the Hebrew does not exhibit it.† However, any addition which may have to be made to the number of Davidic psalms for these and such-like reasons

---

* *Comment. on Acts*, at chapter iv. 25 (Works, i. 761).

† Psalms xxxiii., lxvii., xci., xciv., xcv., xcvi., xcvii., xcviii., xcix., civ.

must be small, and will leave unaffected the conclusion to which we have been led that nearly one half of the psalms proceeded from the pen of David.

In view of the contempt so freely expressed for the superscriptions, it is right to observe that the conclusion deduced from them regarding the comparative amount of David's contribution to the Psalter is well sustained by other testimony. We possess other odes from his pen which prove that the son of Jesse was a poet of the first rank. Need I name the Lament for Saul and Jonathan, the Dirge over Abner, or the " Last Words of David " ? * In one signal instance, the testimony of a title is expressly endorsed by the sacred history.† In 2 Chron. xxix. 30, it is related that when Hezekiah reformed the psalmody of the Temple-service, the Levites were commanded " to sing praise unto the Lord with the words of David and of Asaph the seer," which shows that David was traditionally known as having been a distinguished writer of psalms. Finally, the description given of David in 2 Sam. xxiii. 1 as, by way of eminence, " the sweet psalmist of Israel "—*egregius psaltes Israel* ‡—implies not only that he wrote a great number of the psalms, but that he occupied a unique place in relation to this honourable kind of service. It was he who wrote those odes which served as models to all succeeding psalmists, so that the popular voice has not failed to hit the substantial truth of the matter in entitling the whole collection The Psalms of David.

More interesting than the computation of the number of David's psalms is the attempt to allocate them to their respective periods in his chequered life. It must be admitted that this cannot be done with anything like completeness or perfect accuracy. The psalms have not been arranged in chronological order; and although the titles, viewed in connection with the contents, sometimes indicate the date, they quite as often leave us in the dark.

This impossibility of fixing the chronology of so many of the sacred lyrics, let us remark in passing, is by no means to be deplored. It is fitted rather to awaken a sentiment of gratitude, recalling as it does one of the most precious characteristics of

---

* 2 Sam. i. 19–27 ; iii. 33, 34 ; xxiii. 1–7.

† Comp. title of Ps. xviii. with 2 Sam. xxii.

‡ So the descriptive appellation is rendered by Jerome in the Latin Vulgate.

some that are very memorable. Take the Nineteenth Psalm, or the Twenty-third, the Thirty-seventh, the Hundred-and-third, the Hundred-and-thirty-ninth, the Hundred-and-forty-fifth, —these are all from David's pen, but who will venture to affix a date to one of them? They present an entire absence of such allusions to David's personal history, or to other contemporary events, as would have fixed them down to some particular period in his life. If the superscriptions had not informed us that they came from David's pen, the psalms themselves would have afforded no hint of their origin, except, indeed, that their inimitable power, freshness, thoughtfulness, and beauty, might have warranted the conjecture that they could have proceeded from no other harp than David's. They are the most catholic songs that were ever sung since the making of the world, the most entirely free from those local and temporary elements which might have bound them to the age and country of their birth. One consequence is, that while the lyrics of Gentile antiquity have, in every instance, failed to strike root in any nation of modern Europe, these psalms of David are domesticated everywhere—"familiar in the ear as household words." The metrical version of the Twenty-third Psalm in use in Scotland is a translation and nothing more; it is really David's psalm in English verse; yet it has taken as kindly to the soil as any of the native songs, and is lodged in the memory of every child. I mention this singular quality of David's finest lyrics at the present stage of our inquiry, that the reader may not think it an oversight if he should find that some of these have had no place assigned them in our chronological arrangement.

These explanations being premised, it will serve a useful purpose to point out the historical position of the most noteworthy of those psalms of David whose date can be determined with tolerable certainty.

It may be affirmed without hesitation that the Psalter contains no psalm written by David before he was anointed at Bethlehem; indeed, it is very doubtful whether there is any psalm prior in date to the victory over Goliath. The sorrows of David's life began with the envy and jealousy consequent on the defeat of the Philistian champion; and his sanctified genius did not give forth its perfect fragrance till it was bruised in God's chastening hand. It was the storm of affliction that awoke the full harmonies of David's harp. We know for certain that a very considerable number of the psalms were written in the course of the ten years, or thereby, that Saul's persecution lasted—not fewer than ten, perhaps as many as sixteen. The character of these is remarkable. They often take the form of complaint. " How long wilt Thou forget me ? Shall it be for ever ? Why standest Thou afar off, O Lord ? Why hidest Thou Thyself in times of trouble ?" This is not surprising. It may well be believed that David found it difficult to hold fast his faith in God, when he saw himself a fugitive and an outlaw on account of the jealousies awakened by honours which he had never grasped at, which the providence of God had thrust on him unsought. It is to be remembered, moreover, that David was conscious not only of sincerity towards God, but of the most perfect rectitude, both of intention and conduct, towards Saul and the royal house. Accordingly we find that the psalms belonging to this period are not of the penitential order. On the contrary, they abound in protestations of rectitude, and appeals to God to bear witness of that rectitude. Indications, indeed, are not wanting, even here, that the psalmist was sensible of his unworthiness before God, that he knew very well that he was not clean in God's sight. The leaven of the Pharisees is nowhere found in the Psalter. But in the passages now under consideration, the thing principally insisted upon is the fact, that in relation to the men who sought his life, the psalmist was blameless and could therefore, without misgiving, appeal from their unrighteous judgment to the judgment of the Most High, and could even venture humbly to remonstrate with Him for so unaccountably exposing His servant to the fury of their malice. This is well exemplified in the Seventh Psalm :—

    1. O Lord my God, in Thee do I put my trust:
        Save me from all them that pursue me, and deliver me.
    2. Lest he tear my soul like a lion,
        Rending it in pieces, while there is none to deliver.
    3. O Lord my God, if I have done this ;
        If there be iniquity in my hands ;
    4. If I have rewarded evil unto him that was at peace with me;
        (Yea, I have delivered him that without cause was mine
          adversary :)
    5. Let the enemy pursue my soul, and overtake it ;
        Yea, let him tread my life down to the earth,
        And lay my glory in the dust.

6. Arise, O Lord, in Thine anger,
   Lift up Thyself against the rage of mine adversaries,
   And awake for me; Thou hast commanded judgment.
7. And let the congregation of the peoples compass Thee about:
   And over them return Thou on high.
8. The Lord ministereth judgment to the peoples:
   Judge me, O Lord, according to my righteousness, and to
   mine integrity that is in me.

The Fifty-seventh Psalm may be referred to as exemplifying
a somewhat different aspect of the Psalmist's exercise of soul
during these years of peril and unrest.   We hear in it also a
cry for mercy and an appeal to the just judgment of God, but
the thing that principally strikes a thoughtful reader is the
unwavering confidence expressed in the Divine faithfulness.
David's faith, soaring above the clouds and tempest, bathes
itself in the light of God's countenance :—

1. Be merciful unto me, O God, be merciful unto me ;
   For my soul taketh refuge in Thee :
   Yea, in the shadow of Thy wings will I take refuge,
   Until these calamities be overpast.
2. I will cry unto God Most High ;
   Unto God that performeth all things for me.
3. He shall send from heaven and save me ;
   When he that would swallow me up reproacheth ;
   God shall send forth His mercy and His truth.

   .   .   .   .

7. My heart is fixed, O God, my heart is fixed :
   I will sing, yea, I will sing praises.
8. Awake up, my glory; awake, psaltery and harp :
   I myself will awake right early.
9. I will give thanks unto Thee, O Lord, among the peoples :
   I will sing praises unto Thee among the nations.
10. For Thy mercy is great unto the heavens,
    And Thy truth unto the skies.
11. Be Thou exalted, O God, above the heavens ;
    Let Thy glory be above all the earth.

" I will give thanks unto Thee among the peoples : I will sing
praises unto Thee among the nations."   These are remarkable
words.   They show that David, from his early days, was filled
with the presentiment that he was inditing songs in which not
Israel only, but the Gentiles far and near, would one day praise
the God of Abraham.   How remarkably has the anticipation

been fulfilled! David now "sings praises to God among the nations," in this very psalm which so many nations have already learnt to use.

It is not likely that David's muse went to sleep when the death of Saul at Gilboa opened his way to the throne, or that it produced nothing but such comparatively secular songs as the Lament for Saul and Jonathan.* It is rather remarkable, however, that there is not a single psalm of which one can affirm with confidence that it was written during the seven years and a half that David reigned at Hebron over the tribe of Judah. If Hebron was the birthplace of psalms, they must have belonged to the class formerly described as containing no trace of the circumstances of their origin, a class that, including such psalms as the Hundred-and-third and Twenty-third, are in some respects the most honourable and precious of all. It is a pleasing thought that some of these golden songs may have been first heard in the ancient frontier city, where the ashes of the patriarchs await in hope the resurrection of the just. An exception to this general remark about the Hebron psalms may perhaps be found in the HUNDRED-AND-THIRTY-FIRST, the brief song which, teaching us to " become as little children," and breathing the very spirit of little children, has always been such a favourite in the nursery. If it was not written during this period of the royal prophet's life, it certainly expresses the feelings which were then predominant in his heart :—

1. LORD, my heart is not haughty, nor mine eyes lofty;
   Neither do I exercise myself in great matters,
   Or in things too wonderful for me.
2. Surely I have stilled and quieted my soul ;
   Like a weaned child with his mother,
   My soul is with me like a weaned child.
3. O Israel, hope in the LORD
   From this time forth and for evermore.

This very pleasant ode, I may remark, is in the title ascribed to David, and furnishes one of the instances in which the testimony of the titles is summarily rejected by many recent critics. Having, first of all, made up their minds that there are no psalms of David so far on in the Psalter, they either, like Dr.

---

* 2 Sam. i. 17.

Hupfeld, set aside the testimony of the title, as "unworthy of refutation," or at best they take it to mean no more than that this is a psalm written "after David's manner." This latter explanation is adopted by Dr. Delitzsch, who, however, admits that the sentiments of the psalm agree perfectly with all we know of David. The truth is, that the grounds on which the testimony of the inscription has, in this instance, been set aside, are fitted to confirm the impression that the scepticism with which these have come to be regarded cannot be justified. Dr. Delitzsch is undoubtedly in the right when he says that "David was a pattern of the sentiment expressed in this psalm," and that "resignation to God's guidance, submission to His dispensations, contentment with whatsoever He was pleased to mete out, were among the essential features of his noble character." By some of his many critics, the royal prophet has been accused of ambition; and it is by no means unlikely that his youth showed some blossomings of that proud flower, the "last infirmity of noble minds." The sharpness with which his brothers accused him of pride, when they saw his valour roused by the disdainful challenge of the Philistine, would seem to indicate that the family at Bethlehem had observed in him abilities and aspirations which looked beyond the tending of Jesse's flocks. But if ambitious thoughts found entrance into his mind, they were not cherished, or permitted to betray him into the measures characteristic of ambitious men. In all the brilliant company of gifted men who have risen from a low rank to sit amongst the mighty, the Princes, Statesmen, Warriors of the world, it would be hard to point out a single individual who could have sung the Hundred-and-thirty-first Psalm with such perfect truth and fitness as the son of Jesse. His exaltation was of God's doing rather than his own. Samuel's call found him among the sheep; it was the king's commandment that introduced him to the court; it was what men call a mere chance that brought him to the battle-field where Goliath fell by his sling; and if, after that victory, he obtained the hand of Michal and so reached the steps of the throne, it was the king who pressed on him the alliance. When Saul was in his power, he refused to deal the blow that would have ended his wanderings and put the crown on his brow. Even after Saul and Jonathan were taken out of the way by the sword of the

Philistines, he quietly suffered Ishbosheth to set up his throne at Mahanaim, and was content to wait long years, till, without word or deed from him, the Lord moved all the tribes to offer him their allegiance.

When the whole house of Israel chose David for their king, and the throne was established at Jerusalem, the new capital, he lost no time in bringing up the ark from Kirjath-jearim, and restoring the tabernacle service with more than its ancient splendour. And these great events were accompanied with a gush of sacred melody. They constituted the most memorable epoch in the history of the Hebrew Church, between the Exodus and the Incarnation. Accordingly, the songs belonging to this period are of a peculiarly lofty and joyful character. How does the psalmist exult in the reunion of the whole House of Israel, in the HUNDRED-AND-THIRTY-THIRD PSALM, a song which has, times without number, enabled God's people to give fit utterance to the grateful feelings of their hearts when " the Lord has built up Jerusalem, and gathered together the dispersed of Israel."

1. Behold, how good and how pleasant it is
    For brethren to dwell together in unity!
2. It is like the precious oil upon the head,
    That ran down upon the beard,
    Even Aaron's beard;
    That came down upon the skirt of his garments;
3. Like the dew of Hermon,
    That cometh down upon the mountains of Zion:
    For there the LORD commanded the blessing,
    Even life for evermore.

The Prophet-King, when he found himself established in his palace at Jerusalem, crowned with the uncontested sovereignty over all Israel, did not forget that the increase of power and honour was attended with an increase also of responsibility and of danger. Accordingly, in at least one psalm, the HUNDRED-AND-FIRST, we find him offering up to God vows appropriate to his new circumstances, and prayers for that continual presence of the Lord which would enable him to perform the duties of his new station.

2. I will behave myself wisely in a perfect way:
    Oh when wilt Thou come unto me?
    I will walk within my house with a perfect heart.

5. Whoso privily slandereth his neighbour, him will I destroy:
   Him that hath an high look and a proud heart will I not
   suffer.
6. Mine eyes shall be upon the faithful of the land, that they may
   dwell with me:
   He that walketh in a perfect way, he shall minister unto me.
7. He that worketh deceit shall not dwell within my house:
   He that speaketh falsehood shall not be established before
   mine eyes.
8. Morning by morning will I destroy all the wicked of the land;
   To cut off all the workers of iniquity from the city of the
   LORD.

This is the psalm which the old expositors used to designate
"The Mirror for Magistrates;" and an excellent mirror it is.
If magistrates could only be persuaded to dress themselves by
it every time they go forth to perform the functions of their
Godlike office, their administration would do much to hasten
forward the time when every nation shall be Christ's possession, and every capital a city of the Lord.   When Sir George
Villiers became the favourite and prime minister of King James,
Lord Bacon, in a beautiful Letter of Advice, counselled him to
take this psalm for his rule in the promotion of courtiers.   "In
these the choice had need be of honest and faithful servants, as
well as of comely outsides who can bow the knee and kiss the
hand.   King David (Ps. ci. 6, 7) propounded a rule to himself for the choice of his courtiers.   He was a wise and a good
king: and a wise and a good king shall do well to follow such
a good example; and if he find any to be faulty, which perhaps
cannot suddenly be discovered, let him take on him this resolution as King David did, *There shall no deceitful person dwell in
my house.*"   It would have been well, both for the Philosopher
and the Favourite, if they had been careful to walk by this rule.
   The Twentieth and Twenty-first Psalms belong to the same
class as the one just mentioned, and may be very probably
referred to the same time; also the Thirtieth, which, as we
learn from the title, expresses the exercises of David's heart
when he took up his residence in the house he had built
for himself in Jerusalem.   To these I am inclined to add
the Hundred-and-forty-fourth, which concludes with such a
pleasant picture of national felicity—the felicity of the people
whose God is the Lord.

It was observed before, that David's ruling passion was zeal for the house and worship of God. He could take no pleasure in his palace so long as the ark lay neglected at Kirjath-jearim. I believe, therefore, that if he had been asked what were the brightest days in his life, he would have named among the first the day that saw the representatives of the twelve tribes bearing the Ark of God in solemn procession from Obed-edom's house, and depositing it in the new tabernacle erected in Jerusalem,—the day when the Lord of hosts, with the ark of His strength, came within the gates of Sion, and Sion became the City of the Great King. No one can read the Twenty-fourth Psalm without perceiving that it must have been composed for the purpose of being sung at this great solemnity. The Fifteenth Psalm also appears to have been written on the same occasion.

No sooner was the Ark established in the city, than David resolved to rear on the rocky summit of Moriah a temple whose magnificence might worthily express his reverent love of the Lord, his zeal for the Lord's worship and glory. " It came to pass, when the king dwelt in his house, and the Lord had given him rest from all his enemies round about, that the king said unto Nathan the prophet, See now, I dwell in an house of cedar, but the Ark of God dwelleth within curtains " (2 Sam. vii. 1, 2). We may well imagine that the king was disappointed when he learned from Nathan the next day, that the approbation which the prophet had expressed was recalled, and that the project on which his heart was set must be abandoned. He had shed much blood, and must therefore relinquish the hope of building the sanctuary, in which the typical glory of the Old Testament Church was to be manifested in its utmost splendour. The honour he so much coveted was to be reserved for another generation. But if this was a disappointment, it was more than counterbalanced by the oracle which followed. Nathan was commissioned to let the king know that it was well that his heart had been so occupied with projects for the honour of God's name. The Lord whom he had thought to honour had prepared honour for him, and for his house after him. When his days should be fulfilled, and he should sleep with his fathers, his throne was not to perish, as Saul's had done. He was to be the founder of a stable dynasty, a dynasty that should continue as long as the sun. "Thine house and thy kingdom shall be made sure for ever before thee; thy throne shall be established for ever." These were astonishing disclosures, and David did not fail to perceive and appreciate their drift. He connected them with former promises made to the fathers. He saw that the promise of redemption by the Seed of the woman which first kindled hope in Adam's heart, the promise whose accomplishment Abraham was afterwards taught to expect in connection with his seed, and which was at a later time linked to the tribe of Judah, was now linked to his own house and lineage. He perceived that his Lord, the Star of Jacob, the Anointed One, the Christ of God, was to be his Son, the Heir of his throne, and that He would extend its dominion over all the nations and establish it in perpetuity.

The king was deeply moved. The prayer in which he poured out his heart before God on the occasion expresses just those feelings which were to be looked for in such a man, on hearing disclosures so far-reaching and so glorious. He is not jubilant, as when he welcomed the ark into Sion. It is not exactly gladness that possesses his mind. Rather it is awe, adoring reverence, an overwhelming and almost oppressive sense of his unworthiness, his nothingness, in the presence of God. "Who am I, O Lord God? And now, O Lord God, the word that Thou hast spoken concerning Thy servant, and concerning his house, confirm Thou it for ever, and do as Thou hast spoken. For Thou, O Lord of hosts, hast revealed to Thy servant, saying, I will build Thee an house: therefore hath Thy servant found in his heart to pray this prayer unto Thee." It would seem that David's feelings were too much oppressed to find vent in song. No psalm can be traced to the day of this oracle, although it was the Psalmist's brightest day. It marks, nevertheless, an epoch in the history of the psalms. From this time forward there are new strings audible in David's harp. Henceforth there is continual articulate mention of Christ, the divine King and Hope of Israel. The reader will recall the Twenty-second Psalm, where the prophet celebrates Messiah's Cross and Crown, "the sufferings of Christ and the glories that should follow them." He will recall also the Hundred-and-tenth, the psalm which furnished our Lord with the dilemma that silenced the Pharisees, and which holds forth

David's Son as David's Lord, a Priest on His throne like Melchizedek. Even had those psalms not borne David's name, we
might confidently have attributed them to his pen. And
internal evidence, as well as the place it occupies in the Psalter,
warrants us to add to them the Second also, which tells how
Christ establishes His throne in the midst of His enemies.
These are the most prominent examples of a class—the Messianic Psalms of David—to which it may be impossible to affix
exact dates, but in which we undoubtedly hear the echo of
Nathan's oracle.

The delivery of this great predictive oracle marks the highest
noon of David's felicity. Thenceforward its sun declined. It
was not long afterwards that the king fell into the sin which
darkened all his sky. After what was said before regarding
that great transgression and the manner in which it was over-
ruled by God for the enrichment of the treasury of penitential
song, nothing need be added, except that it is to this period
that we owe the Thirty-second and the Hundred-and-forty-
third Psalms as well as the Fifty-first—three which (along with
the Hundred-and-thirtieth, from a later pen) Luther loved to
describe as the Pauline Psalms.

Another fruitful occasion of psalms in the same middle period
of David's reign was found in those great foreign wars with
the nations to the east and north, in the course of which the
fate of the throne, and even of the nation, seemed more than
once to tremble in the balance. The superscription of the
Sixtieth Psalm connects it with one of these wars ; and one
of the most beautiful of the Songs of Degrees, the Hundred-
and-twenty-fourth Psalm, seems to have been composed at
the restoration of peace. This happy event called for a
solemn national thanksgiving, and there is ground for the
conjecture that it was on the occasion of some such solemnity
that the king delivered into the hands of the Levites and congregation the Sixty-eighth Psalm. This is the earliest in date
of the great historical odes, and is in every respect remarkable
even among David's writings. It is a magnificent triumphal
anthem, sparkling with gems from the earlier scriptures, and is
by many critics esteemed the loftiest effusion of David's muse.

The rebellion of Absalom was in David's pilgrimage a valley
of the shadow of death. But if the sorrows it brought him

were dark and chilling, God gave him " songs in the night," insomuch that the Psalter owes to this period some of its most precious treasures. To it we owe, among others, the Third and the Fourth Psalms, the Morning and Evening Hymns of the Church. From the midst of it proceeded also those expressions of unquenchable thirst for God which have made the Sixty-third Psalm so dear to the hearts of God's people that its echo rings through all Christian literature and devotion.

1. O God, Thou art my God, early will I seek Thee;
   My soul thirsteth for Thee, my flesh longeth for Thee,
   In a dry and weary land, where no water is.
2. So have I looked upon Thee in the sanctuary,
   To see Thy power and Thy glory.
3. For Thy loving-kindness is better than life;
   My lips shall praise Thee.

The able and unscrupulous men who participated in Absalom's revolt were moved to do so, in part, by hostility to the cause of religion, of which David was the main representative and bulwark. Accordingly, it is in the psalms belonging to this period—the Fifty-fifth, for example, and the Sixty-ninth—that we meet with those denunciations of God's judgments on the enemies of the king of which a handle has so often been made to depreciate the morality of the Old Testament Scriptures. Without anticipating what is to be afterwards urged by way of vindicating them from the imputation of vengefulness and cruelty, I will only say this, that sober and devout readers will think twice before they brand, as full of hatred and cursing, Bible songs which were written by a man whose unrevenging, placable spirit was as remarkable as his genius, and which the Lord Jesus sanctified by making them His own.

The Eighteenth Psalm was written by David in celebration of the Lord's goodness in delivering him from all his enemies; and the Seventy-first, from which citations have been already given, was the plaintive song he uttered on his harp in his old age, when his sun was setting amidst clouds. The immediate occasion of the Sixteenth and Seventeenth Psalms is unknown. They are both from David's pen, and may be named here, in the last place, on account of the expression they give to the faith with which the royal saint contemplated the approach of the king of terrors.

xvi. 9. Therefore my heart is glad and my glory rejoiceth :
My flesh also shall dwell confidently.
10. For Thou wilt not leave my soul to Sheol :
Neither wilt Thou suffer Thine holy one to see corruption.
11. Thou wilt show me the path of life :
In Thy presence is fulness of joy ;
In Thy right hand there are pleasures for evermore.

xvii. 15. As for me, I shall behold Thy face in righteousness :
I shall be satisfied, when I awake, with Thy likeness.

NOTE TO CHAPTER III.

THE SUPERSCRIPTIONS OF THE PSALMS.

A FULL discussion of this subject would lead into details appropriate only in a Critical Commentary. But it may be possible to present in a short note the points of principal importance.

The superscriptions are designed to serve a variety of purposes.

1. They sometimes indicate THE WRITERS of the respective psalms. The psalmists thus named in them are Moses, David and Asaph, Solomon, the sons of Korah, and the Ezrahites. It is remarkable that while, in the case of other psalmists, the custom is to set down the name without any farther intimation of the occasion on which the psalm was written, the mention of *David's* name is in many instances accompanied with a historical notice indicating the particular occasion in his life to which the psalm relates. Thus Psalms vii., lix , lvi., xxxiv., lii., lvii., cxlii., liv. are assigned to the period of persecution under Saul's reign; Psalms iii. and lxiii. to the time of Absalom's rebellion ; Ps. xxx. to the solemnity of the dedication of David's house ; Ps. li. to the time of his great transgression ; Ps. lx. to the year of the Syrian war.

2. Sometimes they indicate THE CHARACTER of the Psalms. One is entitled, " A (psalm of) Praise ; " others " A Song," or " A Psalm and Song ; " very many " A Psalm ; " a considerable number " A *Maschil*," or Instruction. *Michtam* and *Shiggaion* are understood to be words of the same order ; but their meaning has not been quite ascertained.

3. Sometimes they convey DIRECTIONS REGARDING THE MUSIC. Thus " *on Nehiloth* " (Ps. v.) denotes the accompaniment of " flutes " or other " wind instruments ; " " *on Neginoth* " (Psalms iv., vi., liv., lv., lxvii., lxxvi. ; also Ps. lxi.), the accompaniment of " stringed instruments." Other terms indicate the tone : thus " *on Alamoth* " (Ps. xlvi.), " in the manner of the virgins," denotes the treble ; " *on Sheminith* " (Psalms vi. and xii.), which is rendered literally in the Geneva version " on the eight (tune)," denotes the bass. The exceedingly obscure sentences which occur in a considerable number of superscriptions, and are left

untranslated in our version, such as *Aijeleth hash-shahar*, literally, " the hind of the morning" (Ps. xxii), are most probably the opening words of certain Hebrew songs, the melodies of which were to be used in singing the Psalms to which they are prefixed.

Although it is a little out of place, I may here notice the word *Selah*, inasmuch as it also would seem to be of musical import. It is found only in the Psalter and the Prayer of Habakkuk: in the latter it occurs thrice, in the former seventy-one times, usually in Psalms inscribed "for the Chief Musician." The meaning is quite uncertain; tho most likely conjecture being that it is an instruction with regard to the instrumental accompaniment.

4. Several superscriptions relate to the sort of use for which the Psalms were designed. Thus fifty-five are inscribed " for the Chief Musician," and in three of these the name of Jeduthun is added, who was one of the three leaders of the song in David's time. Fifteen are entitled " Songs of Degrees" or " of Ascents," being appropriated to the use of the people in their annual goings up to Jerusalem to the feasts. The Ninety-second Psalm is entitled " A Psalm or Song for the Sabbath-day," and is thus marked as the one which was constantly sung in the temple on that day.

So much for the Contents of the superscriptions; their Origin and Authority must next be noticed. The older interpreters received them without misgiving, as having been prefixed either by the psalmists themselves or, at the latest, by the person who finally edited the Old Testament Canon, and as, in either case, reliable and authoritative. Latterly, and especially since the middle of last century, their authority has been much contested, the rationalist critics in particular treating them with contempt. Even Mr. Cheyne * is so far infected with this sceptical feeling about them as to aver that " in most cases a little common sense will dissolve them into thin air." Enough has been said above to show that the facts of the case will not accommodate themselves to this low estimate of the titles; and other arguments in favour of their value are not wanting.

For one thing, they are undoubtedly very ancient. The authors of the Septuagint found them in the Hebrew text from which they made their translation. Unfortunately the date at which the *Psalter* was translated cannot be made out with the same certainty with which we can assign the date of the translation of the *Law*. The latter is known to have been executed in the beginning of the third century before Christ; the former, although by a different hand, and presumably of later date, cannot reasonably be thrust down more than a century later. In the Prologue to the Wisdom of Sirach, mention is made of the Law and the Prophets and the rest (of the books) in such a way as, in the opinion of Bleek,† implies that the Hagiographa, or the principal books in the collection so named, were in circulation in Greek by the

---

* *Book of Psalms*, Introd. p. xi.
† *Einleitung in das A. Test.*, 3rd Ed. p. 576.

year 130 B.C. And indeed, apart from any external testimony, we may well believe that the same causes which led to the translation of the Pentateuch into Greek about the year 270 B.C. would ere long lead to the translation of the Psalms also. Next to the Law, the Psalter would be in constant demand among the Greek-speaking Jews. The use of the Septuagint in the New Testament is such as to show that it had been long in circulation among the Jews in all the countries of their dispersion, and this remark applies to the Psalter as much as to any other part. This datum also points to the earlier half of the second century before Christ as the latest period to which the Greek translation of the Psalms can be assigned. As the superscriptions are found in the LXX. along with their respective psalms, they must have formed part of the Hebrew original from which the translation was made.

When we examine the renderings which the LXX. give of the super-scriptions we are carried back yet another step, and a long one. When the student, puzzled with the enigmatic terms which meet his eye in the titles as they appear in the English Bible, betakes himself to his Septuagint for farther light, he finds that the Alexandrian Jews were quite as much in the dark as the English translators. Even in their time, the superscriptions were so ancient that the true sense of a great part of them was irrecoverably lost, and the attempts to render them into Greek have all the appearance of guess-work. In regard to the *musical notes*, for example, which constitute so considerable a part of the titles, Professor Reuss hardly exaggerates when he remarks :— "The Alexandrian translators, notwithstanding that they were them-selves Jews, find themselves already in the utmost perplexity in view of these notes, and in the greater number of instances their attempts at interpretation either tell us nothing or are fitted to lead us farther astray." *

What a curiosity, by the way, is this remark of the Strassburg divine ! According to Dr. Reuss the age of the Maccabees was the Augustan age of Hebrew psalmody. The psalms belong, not to David's century, but to the middle of the second century before Christ ! Yet here, in presence of the phenomena presented by the LXX., he so far forgets his theory as to record the opinion that the Alexandrian translators, writing (be it remembered) not later than the middle of the second century— probably a generation or two earlier—not only find the superscriptions in existence, but find them already so old that they are unable to make out what they mean ! The truth is that when men commit themselves to a paradox like this of the Maccabean origin of the psalms, they lay for themselves a trap into which not even such learning and ability as Professor Reuss's will save them from falling.

But to return from this digression. Reuss may have exaggerated the

---

* *Le Psautier :* Introd. p. 38. "Déjà les traducteurs alexandrins, qui pourtant étaient juifs eux-mêmes, se sont trouvés dans le plus grand embarras en face de ces notes, et dans la plupart des cas leurs essais d'interprétation ou bien ne nous apprennent rien ou sont plutôt de nature à nous égarer davantage."

perplexity of the LXX. in presence of the superscriptions; but perplexed they certainly are, and Professor Delitzsch mentions that the oldest traditions of the Synagogue betray the same perplexity. All this points to a date for the superscriptions prior to the making up of the Canon in the age of Ezra. The circumstance that the superscriptions abound most in the earliest psalms points to the same conclusion. They are found almost exclusively in the psalms which were written either by David and his contemporaries, or by members of the Levitical choirs founded by him. Not one post-exilian psalmist is so much as named in them.

It is alleged, indeed, that in many cases the contents of the psalms contradict the account of the authorship and date given in the superscriptions. Without entering into details which belong to the Commentator, I can only say that I have not found this conclusively established in a single instance; whereas there is often such harmony between the superscriptions and the contents as cannot well be accounted for except on the supposition that the former embody an early and authentict radition. I do not refer merely to such instances as the Fifty-first Psalm, where the contents are irresistibly suggestive of David and his great offence; for in these it might be argued that the titles are the fruit of easy conjecture. I refer chiefly to instances of a harmony so covert as to have only very recently attracted notice. The fact, brought out for the first time by Delitzsch, that the "Asaph psalms" constitute a group the members of which are distinguished by certain well-defined features common to them all, is a case in point. The same may be affirmed of the eleven (or twelve) psalms ascribed to "the sons of Korah," viz., Psalms xlii.–xlix., lxxxiv., lxxxv., lxxxvii., lxxxviii. These, it will be observed, do not all occur in one place; yet the unity of authorship asserted in the titles is well sustained by the tone and substance of the contents. For proof I may refer to Delitzsch's note on Ps. xlii. and to Dean Plumptre's essay on "the Psalms of the Sons of Korah" in his *Biblical Studies in the Old Testament.* One may doubt whether the latter critic has succeeded in his attempt to refer all the Korahite psalms to the age of Hezekiah; but at least he has established this, that these psalms are so far of a piece as to make it hard to believe that their common title is a mere freak of conjecture. "If," writes Dean Plumptre, "the final editing of the book of Psalms was, as is probable in itself, and as the Jewish tradition reports, the work of a priest or Levite, we are, I believe, as free from the chance of error as the case admits of in ascribing the superscriptions of these psalms to an authentic tradition" (p. 152).

Besides, there are instances in which the contents of a title are of such a kind as to agree best with the supposition that it is contemporaneous, or nearly so, with the psalmist. The Seventh Psalm, for example, is entitled, "Shiggaion of David, which he sang unto the LORD, concerning the words of Cush, a Benjamite." On this Professor Riehm, who is by no means partial to the authority of the titles, remarks that "the mention here made of a person and event otherwise totally unknown to us shows that the superscriptions originated in an age when men were in possession of other sources of information regarding the history of David than those now extant in the Old Testament.''

On the whole, then, it may be confidently affirmed that, whether the superscriptions were written by the psalmists themselves or were prefixed by the persons who first began to make collections of psalms, their testimony regarding the origin of the respective psalms comes to us from a time so ancient as to invest it with great weight. Taking a general survey of the facts bearing on the case, we seem shut up to the belief that the men who finally made up the Old Testament Canon found the titles already prefixed to the psalms. At any rate, the very lowest view which can reasonably be taken is that which sees in them an embodiment of the current tradition of the Hebrew Church about the time when the Canon was completed, and which, if not always bowing to them as a final and conclusive authority, regards them as establishing, at least, a strong presumption that the psalms come to us from the writers and the occasions specified in them.

CHAPTER IV.

DAVID'S ORDINANCES FOR THE SERVICE OF SONG.

ALTHOUGH the psalms we owe to David are so numerous, it would be doing injustice to his memory if we did not look beyond them in estimating the whole amount of the contribution he was honoured to make to the hymnology of the Church. His services were not of one kind only, but manifold, insomuch that it would not be going too far were we to affirm that, if the son of Jesse had not written a single psalm, he would still have deserved to be held in everlasting remembrance as one of the principal instruments by whom God taught the Church to sing His praise. It has been already remarked that he was a Prophet, not a whit behind the very chiefest of the prophets. In this character he was commissioned by the Lord to introduce into Israel ordinances or institutions which exercised an immense influence on psalmody in many ways, especially in forming the minds of the succession of psalmists who took part in the composition of new songs, both in his own time and in the generations that followed, down to the cessation of prophecy and the close of the canon.

David's ordinances were twofold. In the first place, being called by the providence of God and moved by His Spirit to rearrange the whole Levitical ministrations, he introduced into the House of the Lord a Service of Song, and set apart a numerous company, selected from the three principal families of the sacred tribe, to minister continually in this new office. In the second place, he formed in Jerusalem a School of Psalmody in connection with the sanctuary. The elucidation of these very interesting Ordinances of David is the more necessary inasmuch as the facts relating to them have received comparatively little attention, and will be new to many readers.

It is remarkable that the Law of Moses made no provision for a stated SERVICE OF SONG in the tabernacle. It is not to be imagined, indeed, that till David's reign the Church was utterly unfurnished with such a service; that the saints who lived under Moses and the Judges had no divine songs to cheer their pilgrimage. On the contrary, as it has been already remarked, the Song of Moses lived in the memories of the people, and was sung everywhere in their dwellings. They possessed, moreover, the Song of the Red Sea, the Ninetieth Psalm, and latterly, the songs of Deborah and Hannah. And there were other lyrics partaking more or less of the same sacred character. To judge from the lines quoted in Num. xxi. from the Book of the Wars of the Lord, this Book would seem to have been a Collection of national songs commemorative of certain stirring passages in the early history of Israel. If the Song of the Bow is a fair sample of the contents of the Book of Jashar, it also must have been a lyrical collection.* It is very evident that there was no lack of song in the School of the Prophets at Ramah. Respecting the *uses* to which the divine songs were put by the body of the people, it is impossible to speak particularly. The information we possess is scanty. However, it does not seem likely that their use was confined to the family circle and the School of Ramah. I am much inclined to think that when the New Moons and the Sabbaths came round, they would be sung likewise in more public religious assemblies, resembling those we are familiar with in the synagogues of a later age.† However, it is certain that there was no psalmody in the original Tabernacle Service. With the single exception of the Aaronic benediction, prescribed in the sixth chapter of Numbers, the ordinances which the Law of Moses appointed for the Tabernacle were purely ceremonial, the shadow of good things to come. It was not the least of the honours put on the man after God's own heart, that he was commissioned to enrich the Levitical ministrations with such a spiritual heavenly Ordinance as the Service of Song. This, taken in connection with the erection of the Temple (which may be said also to have been David's work, since Solomon found the plan and the materials lying ready to his hand), constituted the only considerable alteration in the

---

* See, in the Revised Version, Num. xxi. 14–18, 27–30, and 2 Sam. i. 18–27.

† Comp. Delitzsch, I. 563.

service of the sanctuary during the continuance of the Old Testament dispensation. " God by David perfected the Jewish worship, and added to it several new institutions. The law was given by Moses, but yet all the institutions of the Jewish worship were not given by Moses ; some were added by divine direction. So this greatest of all personal types of Christ did not only perfect *Joshua's* work, in giving Israel the possession of the promised land, but he also finished *Moses'* work in perfecting the instituted worship of Israel, . . . Thus David as well as Moses was made like to Christ, the Son of David, in this respect, that by him God gave a new ecclesiastical establishment and new ordinances of worship."*

This great reformation in the worship of the Hebrew Church was not accomplished all at once, like the introduction of the Levitical system. It was brought in by a succession of measures, distributed over many years. Detailed information respecting these can be gathered from a series of contemporary documents which have been carefully engrossed in the first book of The Chronicles. As they possess much interest, and shed not a little light on the subject at present in hand, a brief notice of them here will not be out of place.

There is reason to believe that the prophet Samuel, among his other measures for the reformation of religion in Israel, had it in his heart to introduce some new arrangement of the Levitical ministrations, in room of that which Moses had set up and which altered circumstances had now rendered obsolete. And it would seem that, before his death, he communicated his thoughts on the subject to David—the man who, as God's anointed king and prophet, would one day be able to carry them out. Hence the remarkable collocation of the names of " David and Samuel the seer " in 1 Chron. ix. 22. They were the joint authors of the new distribution of service amongst the families of the sacred tribe. However, nothing was done in the matter till David's throne was established in Jerusalem, and he was able to give effect to his long-cherished desire to bring forth the ark of the Lord from the obscurity in which it lay at Kirjath-jearim, and establish it in his own city. To this epoch we can trace the first of his Ordinances for the Service of Song. We

* Edwards's *History of Redemption*, Period II. Part 5.

have already seen that David's harp awoke to ecstasy at this time, and that among other psalms which date from it, there is one that was evidently composed for the purpose of being sung at the solemn removal of the ark. I do not know that there is sufficient ground for affirming, with many critics, that the psalm in question—the Twenty-fourth—was sung in responsive choirs by the congregation. But whatever opinion may be formed on that point, there can be no doubt that the psalm is one which demanded no little musical skill on the part of those who sang it, as they marched on that High Day, bearing the ark of the Lord of hosts within the ancient gates of the city of Melchizedek.

1. The earth is the LORD'S, and the fulness thereof;
   The world, and they that dwell therein.
2. For He hath founded it upon the seas,
   And established it upon the floods.

3. Who shall ascend into the hill of the LORD?
   And who shall stand in His holy place ?
4. He that hath clean hands and a pure heart;
   Who hath not lifted up his soul unto vanity,
   And hath not sworn deceitfully.
5. He shall receive a blessing from the LORD,
   And righteousness from the God of his salvation.
6. This is the generation of them that seek after Him,
   That seek Thy face, O God of Jacob.

7. Lift up your heads, O ye gates ;
   And be ye lift up, ye everlasting doors :
   And the King of glory shall come in.
8. Who is the King of glory ?
   The LORD strong and mighty,
   The LORD mighty in battle.

9. Lift up your heads, O ye gates ;
   Yea, lift them up, ye everlasting doors :
   And the King of glory shall come in.
10. Who is this King of glory ?
    The LORD of hosts,
    He is the King of glory.

No one who studies this psalm with attention will doubt that David, when he composed it to be sung in a solemn national assembly, knew he could reckon on the services of a numerous body of thoroughly trained musicians. Where were these found ? The answer to that question is furnished by the chapter in The Chronicles which narrates at great length the arrangements made for the solemnity. Among other things, we are told that "David *spake to the chief of the Levites to appoint their brethren* the singers, with instruments of music, psalteries and harps and cymbals, sounding aloud and lifting up the voice with joy;" and that, being thus admonished, the Levites appointed Heman, Asaph, and Ethan, with fourteen others "of the second degree." And it is added that "Chenaniah, the chief of the Levites, was over the song; he instructed about the song, because he was skilful." * From all this it is evident that, although under the law of Moses there was nothing in the ministrations assigned to the Levites that obliged them to pay special attention to music and song, some leading men in the tribe had been led to do so, and had attained great proficiency. It is instructive, in this connection, to remark that the prophet Samuel was himself a Levite, that he was the son of a prophetess skilled in minstrelsy, and that Heman, one of the three Levitical masters of song, was his grandson. This reminds us of the fact we took notice of before, that in Samuel's school at Ramah sacred music and song were among the most prominent studies in which the prophets were exercised. We may well suppose that Heman would not be the only member of the sacred tribe who profited by the studies of his grandfather's School, and that it was by those studies that the Levites were prepared for the honourable office which God had in store for them in His House. It is worthy of notice that, all along, there was great intimacy between David and certain families of the Levites. Among the valiant men who joined him at Ziklag were a band of the sons of Korah, † for the Levites of that age were quite as much at home in the camp as in the sanctuary; and we may well believe that the psalms which, like so many constellations, beautified and cheered the long night of his early sufferings, would often be sung by his men. When the ark was to be brought up, David put himself into communication with the Levites. He let them know that it was his heart's desire that there should be a solemn procession, and that the ark should be welcomed with psalmody into the place he had prepared for it. He put into

---

* I Chron. xv. 16–22.   † I Chron. xii. 6.

their hands the Twenty-fourth Psalm, and enjoined them to make arrangements among themselves for having it chanted to an appropriate tune, not without a grand instrumental accompaniment. " So the singers, Heman, Asaph, and Ethan, were appointed with cymbals of brass to sound aloud," in order that with these clear-toned instruments they might effectually sustain and guide the voices of the multitude of singers. Eight other Levites were appointed to accompany the song with psalteries, and six with harps. In all these arrangements the king took the deepest personal interest. He was himself an enthusiastic and accomplished musician. Long after, when the prophet Amos launched his invective against the *dilettanti* of degenerate Israel—men who spent their days in music for the mere carnal delight—he described them as " devising for themselves instruments of music, like David."* Among the instruments used at the bringing home of the ark, there would doubtless be, therefore, some of the king's own invention. Nothing which the musical science of the age could supply was wanting on the occasion. The sacred historian relates that, when the High Day arrived, the king threw off the conventionalities of royal state, arrayed himself in a linen robe and ephod, and danced and played before the Lord in the solemn procession.

The next step David took was to arrange for the continuance of this Levitical Service of Song, as a perpetual Ordinance before the Lord. The narrative of this comes immediately after that of the bringing up of the ark into the City of David. Among other things, we are informed that the king " appointed certain of the Levites to minister before the ark of the LORD, and to celebrate, and to thank and praise the LORD, the God of Israel;" and it is added, " So he left there, before the ark of the covenant of the LORD, Asaph and his brethren, to minister before the ark continually, as every day's work required."† It will be remembered that, when the ark was deposited in the new tent prepared for it in David's city, no attempt was made to remove the Tabernacle of the wanderings, or the great altar of burnt sacrifice, from the station they had long occupied on the high place at Gibeon. It was there, and not at Jerusalem, that the

---

* Amos vi. 5 ; comp. 1 Chron. xxiii. 5. † 1 Chron. xvi. 4, 37.

sons of Aaron offered the burnt-offerings for all Israel till the temple of Solomon was finished. David, therefore, was careful to provide for a service of song at both sanctuaries. While Asaph and his brethren were appointed to minister before the ark in Jerusalem, Heman and Jeduthun, with their brethren, were appointed to minister under Zadok the priest, at Gibeon, singing and playing on musical instruments when the morning and evening oblations were offered, " giving thanks to the LORD, because His mercy endureth for ever." *

What were the particular psalms appointed to be sung, day by day, by these Levitical choirs, we are not informed. It is known with tolerable certainty that proper psalms were appointed for every day of the week in the Second Temple ; and a cycle 'of psalms, beginning with the Hundred-and-thirteenth —the " Hallel," as it is called—was regularly sung at the passover and the other solemn feasts.† It may be presumed that some arrangement of the kind would be made by David from the first. ' But on this the sacred history is silent. There is a passage, indeed, in the chapter which relates David's appointment of the continual service of praise before the Lord, which might seem to intimate that the Hymn which fills the greater part of the chapter was, on that occasion, delivered by the royal psalmist into the hand of the Levites. This is evidently the light in which our old translators regarded the passage ; for they render it thus, " Then on that day David delivered first *this psalm* to thank the LORD, into the hand of Asaph and his brethren : Give thanks unto the LORD, call upon His name, make known His deeds among the people," ‡ etc. But, as thus rendered, the statement is erroneous. The hymn which the chronicler has set down, and which it is impossible to read without perceiving its singular appropriateness for the temple service, is a kind of lyrical mosaic. It is a composition made up of portions of Psalms cv., xcvi., and cvi. Now it is certain that these were not, and could not be, delivered by *David* into the hand of Asaph. One of them bears evident marks of having been written during the Babylonish captivity ; and it is next to certain that none of them is of an

* 1 Chron. xvi. 39–41 ; comp. chap. vi. 31, 32.
† Lightfoot · *Temple Service*, vii. 2, xii. 5. See below, Book III. c. 1.
‡ 1 Chron. xvi. 7, 8.

earlier date than the reign of Jehoshaphat or Hezekiah. It will be observed that the words *this psalm* are printed in italics, to intimate that they are wanting in the Hebrew, and were supplied by the translators to complete what they took to be the sense of the historian. The verse is more correctly rendered in the Revised Version thus, "Then on that day did David first ordain to give thanks unto the Lord, by the hand of Asaph and his brethren." This, it may be added, is the sense assigned by almost all the translators, ancient and modern, from the Seventy to Luther and De Wette.* Bishop Patrick's note brings out the meaning quite correctly: "*This David appointed or ordained in the first place at that time,* namely, that God should be praised by Asaph and his colleagues in the manner following. Which solemn service began on the day when he brought up the ark, and ever after was continued." What the historian meant to state was simply that this was the first occasion on which David gave charge to Asaph to minister before the Lord in the service of praise. Having made this statement, he inserts in his narrative, at this point, those portions of the Psalter which, in his time, had come into daily use in the temple service. There is, of course, a *prolepsis* in the insertion of the composition in connection with David's ordinances ; but it is just such a *prolepsis* as is of frequent occurrence in The Chronicles, and cannot justly be censured as involving either error or oversight.†

David having thus established the continual service of song in the hands of Asaph, Heman, and Jeduthun, with their brethren, nothing more was done in the matter till near the close of his life. Meanwhile, the Lord had, by Nathan, signified His approval of the king's project of erecting a temple in the room of the ambulatory Tabernacle. It was plain that the old distribution of duty among the members of the sacred tribe, according to which certain Levitical families were set apart to the business of carrying the sacred vessels and the several parts of the tabernacle, when the sanctuary removed from

---

* Thus the Geneva Bible :— "Then at that time David did appoint at the beginning to give thanks to the Lord by the hand of Asaph and his brethren." By some oversight, Mr. Cheyne speaks of "the psalm *ascribed to David* in I Chron. xvi. 7-36 " (*Book of Psalms:* Introd. p. xvi.).

† Hengstenberg, *Commentar* IV. i. 168.

place to place, was no longer appropriate and might with advantage be set aside. The royal prophet, accordingly, a short time before his death, made a new distribution of service: " For David said, The Lord, the God of Israel, hath given rest unto His people; and He dwelleth in Jerusalem for ever; and also the Levites shall no more have need to carry the Tabernacle and all the vessels of it for the service thereof."* The particulars of the redistribution are given in the twenty-third and twenty-fifth chapters of the first book of Chronicles. The only points we are concerned to take notice of at present being those relating to psalmody, it is sufficient to observe, that of the Levites, no fewer than four thousand were appointed for song, " to stand every morning to thank and praise the Lord, and likewise at even." These singers were divided into four-and-twenty courses, of which fourteen were presided over by the fourteen sons of Heman the Korahite, four by the four sons of Asaph, and six by the six sons of Ethan.

Before passing from the consideration of these ordinances of David for the Levitical service of song, I am anxious to put in a caveat against a possible misapprehension of their design. It would certainly be a mistake to imagine that the singing of the psalms by the Levitical choirs, with the accompaniment of instrumental music, was either the principal or the most honourable use for which they were designed by the Holy Spirit. No doubt the service was a very magnificent and imposing one; and we have already pointed out that there was in it a larger infusion of the spiritual element than was found in the original Levitical ordinances. Yet, after all, the psalmody of the Temple was a part of the ceremonial worship of the old covenant, inferior therefore in real honour, because inferior in spirituality and truth, to the service of praise that ascended to God day by day from the dwellings of the godly in the land. An attentive consideration of the Psalms of David leaves on one's mind the impression that, although perhaps none of them was absolutely unfit for use in the Levitical service, the greater number were much better adapted for the simpler worship offered in families, and in such religious assemblies as gathered round the prophets

---

* 1 Chron. xxiii. 25, 26.

on New Moons and Sabbaths, to hear the word of God.* It was to this kind of worship, rather than to the stately ceremonial of the Temple, that they most naturally lent themselves ; and for it they were principally designed from the first. The Psalter has sometimes been styled the Hymnal of the Temple, and I will not impugn the accuracy of the title ; but if the psalms were meant for the Temple, they were more obviously and emphatically meant, as they were more perfectly fitted, for the Family, the Synagogue, and the Catholic Church.

David, we have said, besides introducing a Levitical service of song, founded at Jerusalem a SCHOOL OF PSALMODY. This institution derives extraordinary importance from the fact that, with one or two doubtful exceptions, all the psalms which are expressly ascribed to other pens than those of Moses and David are ascribed to men who were educated in, or owed their impulse to, this school at Jerusalem. A statement of the facts that have been ascertained in relation to the institution will throw light, therefore, on all the subsequent history of Bible psalmody.

That David founded in Jerusalem a school of *sacred music* needs no proof. It was implied in the dedication of four thousand Levites, *with their children after them*, to the service of song. That something more than music, however, was to be taught in the school might have been surmised from the circumstance, that the presidents of the families of singers were something more than musicians. Let the reader turn to the twenty-fifth chapter of first Chronicles, and mark the terms there applied to Asaph, Jeduthun, and Heman. First, we are told that the function of all three was to "*prophesy* with harps, with psalteries, and with cymbals ;" then Asaph is described as one who "*prophesied* after the order of the king ;" Jeduthun as one "who *prophesied* in giving thanks and praising the Lord ;" and Heman is styled "*the king's seer* in the words of God." These terms are significant, and ought not to be passed lightly over. They show that the presidents of the Levitical families were not mere *artistes*, mere musical performers. They were men to whom God was wont to vouchsafe those supernatural motions of the Spirit which were witnessed in the Seventy Elders whom Moses ordained in the

* See 2 Kings iv. 23, and comp. Ezek. viii. 1.

wilderness, and which attested the gracious presence of God in Samuel's school at Ramah. In regard to some of them, we have warrant to go further. It may perhaps be doubted whether the Heman and Ethan-Jeduthun, whose names occur in the super-scriptions of the Eighty-eighth and Eighty-ninth Psalms, are to be identified with the famous singers who bore those names in David's reign; but it is certain that the Asaph of David's reign was a writer of psalms. It is certain also that, whether Heman was a psalmist or not, his brethren the sons of Korah, over whom he presided, enjoyed that honour. These Levites, therefore, were "men who spake from God, as they were moved by the Holy Ghost."* Having, like David himself, been trained in poetry and song, they, like him, enjoyed the super-natural inspiration of the Spirit, that they might be qualified to bring gifts into the treasury of divine praise. The school which had such men for presidents was something more than a musical academy.

I am much inclined to think that what David did in this matter was, in effect, the transplantation to Jerusalem, or the reproduction there, of the School of the prophets, which Samuel so long taught at Ramah and to which David had been so much indebted in his youth. Let such facts as the following be carefully weighed, and I believe they will be found to sustain this conjecture. First of all, let it be remembered that Samuel's School at Ramah had proved itself exceedingly useful in promoting the comprehensive scheme of reformation which it was the aim of Samuel to accomplish. The more the Israelitish history is investigated, the more clearly does it appear that, whether regard is had to the diffusion of the knowledge of the divine law and of the history of the chosen people, or to the revival of living religion, or to the cultivation of spiritual gifts, Samuel's School exerted a greater influence than any other institution in the country. This was so well known, that when Elijah and Elisha, some generations after-wards, were moved to attempt, in the kingdom of the Ten Tribes, a reformation similar to that which Samuel had accomplished in the undivided nation, they took a lesson from his example and set up Prophetical Schools at Gilgal, at Jericho,

* 2 Pet. i. 21.

and at Bethel. These homes of "the sons of the prophets," it will be observed, all lay within the Ten Tribes. After Samuel's death, we do not meet with a single notice of such an institution in the kingdom of Judah. How is this to be explained? Is it to be supposed that Judah was less favoured in this matter than her sister Samaria? that while the kingdom which had broken away from the throne of David and the House of the Lord had colleges in which her young men were taught in the Law and trained in the exercises of piety under holy prophets, the more faithful kingdom was restricted to the carnal ordinances of the Levitical system? Above all, can it be believed that a prince like David, who knew so well the value of Samuel's institution, would suffer it to go down without setting up some similar School to continue its work? These are questions which admit of only one reply. We cannot doubt that, when David chose Jerusalem for the capital of the kingdom and learned that the Lord had chosen it for His dwelling-place, the seat of the ark and the solemn worship, and when he gathered to it the heads of the sacred tribe, he not only founded a School of sacred music, but made it, in effect, a Prophetical School also,—an institution in which the sons of Levi might be trained in the knowledge of the Law, and in which, especially, the families of Heman, Asaph, and Jeduthun might receive such instruction in music and song as would fit them for giving voice to the feelings of the Church in new songs, if God by His Spirit should ever call them to that honourable duty. The Korahites were Samuel's kinsmen,—for he was a Levite of the family of Korah,—and Heman was the old prophet's descendant. It would have been strange indeed if David had allowed the grace, the spiritual gifts, the cultivated taste of these seers, to be exercised only in personal services, which would, for the most part, die with themselves. Our conjecture is, that David's School of Sacred Song was, in effect, the reproduction at Jerusalem of Samuel's Prophetical School, in closer connection than ever with the Levitical tribe. It agrees with this that Heman, the grandson of Samuel, is always represented as the chief of David's Levitical seers, having Asaph on his right hand, and Ethan-Jeduthun on his left.* The conjecture derives

* 1 Chron. vi. 39, 44.

confirmation from the fact that when Jehoshaphat, in the beginning of his reign, commiserating the ignorance and spiritual destitution of the people, sent chosen men in circuit through the whole kingdom, to teach in the cities of Judah the law of the Lord, it was in the tribe of Levi that the necessary learning was found ; * from which it may be reasonably inferred that there existed in Jerusalem some such Levitical School as we have supposed David to have founded.

The importance of the service which David thus rendered to the cause of Bible psalmody is best illustrated by referring to the extent and value of the contributions made to the Psalter by the Levites who presided over his institution, or were trained within its walls. Interesting facts bearing on this will come before us when we reach the times of the later kings, the Captivity, and the Return. For the present, it will suffice to call attention to the psalmists who were David's contemporaries. Without a single exception, they were Levites, and belonged to the families which were dedicated to the service of song.

A word or two must be said at this point on a question relating to certain of the superscriptions. Every reader knows, that while some of these, as they stand in our Authorised English Version, declare who were the *writers* of the respective psalms, running thus,—"a psalm *of* David," "a psalm *of* Asaph," "a prayer *of* Moses the man of God," others declare rather the persons for whose benefit they were designed, or the singers who were entrusted with the musical delivery of them in the sanctuary. Thus, one psalm is entitled "a psalm *for* Solomon;" and several are stated to be "*for* the sons of Korah." In the Hebrew it is the same preposition that is used in all these cases ; and a glance at the margin will show that our translators were by no means confident that they had done well to vary the rendering in English. In every instance in which they use *for* in the text, they have set down *of* in the margin. I think it would not be difficult to assign the reason which deterred them from adopting a uniform rendering. They were haunted with the feeling that David was the real author of the psalms which bear the names of Solomon and the sons of Korah in their titles; that the Forty-second and Forty-third, for example,

---

* 2 Chron. xvii. 7–9.

were written by him when he fled beyond the Jordan before the face of Absalom. A touch of the same feeling shows itself in some of our best modern critics. Dr. Hengstenberg is so strongly moved by it, that he has betaken himself to the very unlikely hypothesis, that although the sons of Korah were the writers of the two psalms referred to, they wrote in the king's name, and it was the feelings and exercises of his heart, rather than their own, that they uttered in song. Dr. Hupfeld, again, thinks these psalms are without doubt from David's pen, and summarily rejects the titles for naming the sons of Korah as the writers. I mention these opinions simply as an act of justice to our venerable translators; for they show this at least, that the rendering of the superscriptions was not varied through caprice or carelessness. However, there can be no doubt that the rendering they gave in the margin, and which has been adopted by our Revisers, is the better of the two. The design of the preposition is to indicate the authorship.*

One other preliminary remark. Among the psalms ascribed in the titles to Asaph and the sons of Korah are some which cannot have been written before the reign of Jehoshaphat. In the case of the Korahite psalms this need occasion no difficulty, for the sons of Korah continued to officiate as singers in the temple down to the fall of the monarchy. And the case of the Asaph-psalms may well be explained on the same principle. The posterity of the great Asaph, the contemporary and prophet-psalmist of King David, were singers till long after the Captivity; and it is a reasonable conjecture that the psalmists raised up from among them may have superscribed their psalms with their great ancestor's name.

These observations premised, let us take note of the psalmists who were David's contemporaries, and the contributions they were honoured to make to the Psalter. The circumstance that, without exception, they were Levitical singers, and that they did not begin to write till the ark was established on Zion, is exceedingly significant, as an indication of the predominant influence exercised by David in the domain of psalmody. They all shared in the remarkable relation to David denoted by the

---

* Comp. Isa. xxxviii. 9, and Hab. iii. 1, where the same preposition is employed in superscriptions, to declare the authorship of the "writing" or "prayer" that follows.

title given to Heman in particular, "the king's seer in the words of God" (1 Chron. xxv. 5).

We have had occasion* already to remark that twelve psalms are, in the titles, ascribed to the SONS OF KORAH.   The persons so designated were a Levitical family of the line of Kohath, and derived their name from their ancestor Korah—the same whose name is commemorated with infamy in the history of the wanderings.   Both by the original Mosaic ordinance and by the ordinance of "David and Samuel the seer," "the oversight of the gates of the house of the Lord" was committed to them†—a circumstance that sheds new interest on the sentiment expressed by them in the Eighty-fourth Psalm: "I had rather be a door-keeper in the house of my God, than to dwell in the tents of wickedness."   When it became known that the Lord had rejected Saul and anointed David to the kingdom by the hand of their kinsman Samuel, certain martial Korahites were among the first to cast in their lot with the youthful hope of Israel, as his helpers in war. ‡   In the person of Heman, the grandson of Samuel, the family furnished David with one of his three prophet-psalmists; and of the twenty-four courses of singers, fourteen were presided over by Heman's sons.   "All these were under the hands of their father for song in the house of the LORD, with cymbals, psalteries, and harps, for the service of the house of God." §   As Singers, the Korahites are mentioned as late as the reign of Jehoshaphat; ‖ as Porters, they are mentioned as serving in the second temple.¶   How many of the Korahite psalms were written by David's contemporaries is quite uncertain.   The Forty-fourth is generally believed to have been written in the crisis of David's Syrian and Edomite wars, when destruction seemed impending over the kingdom; although some of the best critics favour a much later date.   The Forty-second and Forty-third (which go together) were almost certainly written by the Korahites who accompanied David in his flight beyond the Jordan during Absalom's rebellion.

xlii. 1. As the hart panteth after the water-brooks,
         So panteth my soul after Thee, O God.

·   ·   ·   ·   ·   ·   ·

---

* In the note regarding the superscriptions, appended to the foregoing chapter.
† 1 Chron. ix. 23.   § 1 Chron. xxv. 6.   ¶ Neh. xi. 19.
‡ 1 Chron. xii. 1-6.   ‖ 2 Chron. xx. 19.

6. O my God, my soul is cast down within me :
   Therefore do I remember Thee from the land of Jordan,
   And the Hermons, from the hill Mizar.

11. Why art thou cast down, O my soul?
    And why art thou disquieted within me?
    Hope thou in God : for I shall yet praise Him,
    Who is the health of my countenance, and my God.

To the same occasion we may refer also the Eighty-fourth
Psalm. It everywhere breathes the same fervent thirst for
that communion with the living God which is enjoyed by the
faithful when they resort to the sanctuary.

1. How amiable are Thy tabernacles,
   O LORD of hosts :
2. My soul longeth, yea, even fainteth for the courts of the LORD;
   My heart and my flesh cry out unto the living God.

4. Blessed are they that dwell in Thy house :
   They will be still praising Thee.

If David is, without controversy, the prince of the psalmists,
ASAPH stands next to him in honour. The psalms in which the
Levites sang praise to the Lord in the days of Hezekiah are
called "the words of David and of *Asaph the seer*" (2 Chron.
xxix. 30). The emphatic manner in which the prophetic title
is here annexed to Asaph's name suggests that he was favoured
with a larger measure of the prophetic spirit than any of the
Levitical prophets who were his contemporaries. The facts
known respecting him are few. He was a Levite, of the family
of Gershon. He was one of the three presidents of the Levitical singers, standing at Heman's right hand, as Ethan-
Jeduthun did at his left. His four sons presided, under him,
over four companies. Their descendants continued to minister
in the service of song so long as the first temple stood, and are
mentioned in this connection in the histories of Jehoshaphat
and Hezekiah.* They mustered, to the number of one hundred and twenty-eight, among the exiles who returned to
Jerusalem with Zerubbabel, and are found ministering in the
second temple, before the cessation of prophecy. When Zerubbabel and Jeshua laid the foundation of the house, amidst the

---

* 2 Chron. xx. 14 ; xxix. 13.

tears and shoutings of the remnant who had returned, it was
the sons of Asaph who praised the Lord with cymbals, "after
the order of David king of Israel." And we are told that "they
sang one to another in praising and giving thanks unto the
Lord, saying, For He is good, for His mercy endureth for ever
toward Israel."*

There appear to have been several members of this family who
inherited at once their father's name and his gift of minstrelsy;
for of the twelve Asaph psalms, several are of a date long
subsequent to David's reign. It deserves to be noticed, however, as confirmatory of the testimony of the superscriptions in
prefixing the name to all the twelve, that they constitute a
class by themselves. They are the following: Psalm l. and
Psalms lxxiii. to lxxxiii. inclusive. Dr. Delitzsch, who was
the first to call attention to the peculiarities which characterise them, remarks, among other things, that "they are
distinguished from the Korahite psalms by their prophetical
and judicial character. Like the prophetical books, they frequently introduce God as the speaker. After the manner of
the prophets, they contain lengthened representations of God
as the Judge of all, as well as somewhat lengthened discourses
spoken by Him in that character (Psalms l., lxxv., lxxxii.).
Besides their predictive aspect, the Asaph-psalms present a
historical aspect also, frequently commemorating facts pertaining
to the ancient times; and one of them, the Seventy-eighth, is
altogether devoted to holding forth the ancient history of the
nation as a mirror for the present generation to look into.
The consecutive perusal of the twelve Asaph-psalms brings to
light this other curious peculiarity, that Joseph and the tribes
descended from him are mentioned more frequently in them
than in any other." The reader may easily verify this last
remark by turning to Psalms lxxvii. 15 ; lxxviii. 9, 67 ;
lxxx. 1, 2 ; lxxxi. 5.

Of the Asaph-psalms which there is some reason to suppose
were written by David's illustrious contemporary himself, three
may be named as worthy of special notice. The SEVENTY-
EIGHTII is one of the earliest, as it is the most remarkable, of
the great historical odes. It recapitulates the history of the

---

* Ezra iii. 10, 11 ; comp. Neh. xi. 22.

chosen people from the Exodus to the reign of David; and it comes behind no psalm of its class for depth of insight into the treasures of instruction which the Spirit of God has stored up in the sacred history for the edification of all generations.* The SEVENTY-THIRD Psalm is another of Asaph's; and it is one for which God's people will always honour his name. It is a kind of lyrical epitome of the argument expanded in the book of Job. It delineates the trial and triumph of grace in a believer, whose faith, after staggering at the sight of prosperous wickedness, recovers on observing the sudden destruction of the ungodly, and especially on recollecting (what he feels he ought never to have forgotten) that the chief end and felicity of man is, after all, to be found in God, not in worldly prosperity but in the participation of God's favour.

The FIFTIETH Psalm is from the same pen. It is remarkable for this, that although written at the time when the Levitical ritual was celebrated with its utmost splendour, and by a *Levite*, whose office called him to act a principal part in some of its most splendid services, it contains as energetic a protest as the apostle Paul himself ever uttered against the imagination that ceremonies are intrinsically well-pleasing to God. It preaches, from the midst of the ritual magnificence of the age of David and Solomon, the very doctrine which our blessed Lord unfolded to the astonished woman of Samaria at Jacob's well, that God is a Spirit and they that worship Him must worship Him in spirit and in truth. What could be plainer or bolder than these words?—

> 7. Hear, O My people, and I will speak;
>   O Israel, and I will testify unto thee:
>   I am God, even thy God.
> 8. I will not reprove thee for thy sacrifices;
>   And thy burnt-offerings are continually before Me.
> 9. I will take no bullock out of thy house,
>   Nor he-goats out of thy folds.
> 10. For every beast of the forest is Mine,
>   And the cattle upon a thousand hills.
> 11. I know all the fowls of the mountains:
>   And the wild beasts of the field are Mine.
> 12. If I were hungry, I would not tell thee:
>   For the world is Mine, and the fulness thereof.

---

* It will be noticed again in another connection (Book II. chap. 8).

13. Will I eat the flesh of bulls,
    Or drink the blood of goats?
14. OFFER UNTO GOD THE SACRIFICE OF THANKSGIVING;
    AND PAY THY VOWS UNTO THE MOST HIGH:
15. AND CALL UPON ME IN THE DAY OF TROUBLE;
    I WILL DELIVER THEE, AND THOU SHALT GLORIFY ME.

These last are golden sentences! The hecatombs that Solomon and the congregation offered at the dedication of the House were, doubtless, acceptable in God's sight; but they owed their acceptance to the joyful faith and thankfulness that animated the offerers,—to their humble reverence and unreserved devotion to the God of Israel. And there is not a poor troubled one on earth this day, there is not a soul crushed beneath a load of sorrow, in whom, if he will but importunately call on God, "making known to Him his requests with thanksgiving,"* God will not take a higher delight than He did in the costly and magnificent offering of the king.

---

* Phil. iv. 6

CHAPTER V.

PSALMODY UNDER SOLOMON AND THE LATER KINGS.

THE river of sacred song which gladdened the reign of David dwindled into a brook when the great psalmist died. Of the Hundred-and-fifty psalms, not more than four can be traced to the age of Solomon. This is certainly a much smaller number than might have been expected, considering the intellectual brilliance of the age, and especially considering that the wise king and his contemporaries had been nurtured amongst the songs of Zion. In explanation of this, it has been well observed by Dr. Delitzsch, that the age of Solomon was one rather of reflective study than of direct and deep feeling, that the yearning after higher things, which marked the preceding generation, had given place to the lust of present enjoyment, and that if, of the Thousand-and-five songs which the king wrote, all have perished save two or three, the reason is to be found in the fact that he spake of all things, from the cedar to the hyssop, directing his studies rather to the arcana of nature than to the mysteries of grace. An additional explanation may perhaps be found in another direction. We know that the function of the Psalms was not so much to set forth new revelations, as to aid the Church in appropriating and responding to the revelations already given. May it not be that the material of which psalms are woven,—the prior revelations of divine truth,—had been so far exhausted by David and his contemporaries, that a long time had to elapse,—the Church's stock of knowledge had to be enlarged by new revelations and new experiences,—before there could be a copious flow of new songs ? Certain it is, as we shall afterwards see, that the only period which was very fruitful of psalmody after the reign of David was preceded by that marvellous disclosure of God's purposes regarding the Church and the world which took place by the ministry of Isaiah and the other prophets who lived about the same time.

Two psalms bear SOLOMON's name in their titles. One of these is the HUNDRED-AND-TWENTY-SEVENTH, entitled, *A Song of Ascents; of Solomon.*

> 1. Except the LORD build the house,
>   They labour in vain that build it:
>   Except the LORD keep the city,
>   The watchman waketh but in vain.
> 2. It is vain for you that ye rise up early, and so late take
>   rest,
>   And eat the bread of toil:
>   For so He giveth unto His beloved sleep.
> 3. Lo, children are an heritage of the LORD:
>   And the fruit of the womb is His reward.
> 4. As arrows in the hand of a mighty man,
>   So are the children of youth.
> 5. Happy is the man that hath his quiver full of them:
>   They shall not be ashamed,
>   When they speak with their enemies in the gate.

Some recent critics throw doubt, here also, on the trustworthiness of the superscription. But there is certainly nothing in the psalm itself shutting us up to a later date; and we agree with Luther, Calvin, and the generality of the older commentators, in thinking that it is so exactly in the manner of the wise author of the Proverbs, that one need not hesitate to attribute it to his pen. It is the lyrical expression of thoughts which run through the sayings of that book. The first part of it, for instance, is a beautiful reproduction of Prov. x. 22: " The blessing of the Lord, it maketh rich, and He addeth no sorrow therewith ; " and the correspondence will be still closer if we translate the latter clause, as in the margin of the Revised Version, "And toil addeth nothing thereto." Familiar as the Proverb has become in the speech of every Christian nation, the Psalm is yet more familiar. From it the pious builders of a former generation borrowed the NISI DOMINUS FRUSTRA, which may be read on the lintels of houses in our older streets ; an admirable confession of faith to be made by any man who is called to be a builder in Church or Commonwealth ! It is the Lord's blessing that builds the House and keeps the Town ;

that fills the House with the stir of children, and peoples the Town with valiant sons, who, with unabashed brow, will speak with the enemies in the gate.

Solomon's other psalm is the SEVENTY-SECOND, and here also the traces of his pen are unequivocal. A mistaken interpretation of the note appended to it, " The prayers of David, the son of Jesse, are ended," led most of the older commentators to attribute the psalm to David, and to suppose that it was a prayer offered in his old age "for Solomon," as the peaceful prince who was to succeed him on the throne. The note in question is now on all hands understood to refer to the whole of the preceding portion of the Psalter; and there can be no doubt that the title can only be translated "of Solomon." Calvin (whose sagacity in this kind of criticism has never been excelled), although he thought himself obliged, by the note at the end of the psalm, to attribute the substance of it to David, felt Solomon's touch so sensibly, that he threw out the conjecture that the prayer was the father's, but that it was afterwards thrown into the lyrical form by the son. The Messianic interpretation of this psalm will call for notice in a subsequent chapter; for the present it will be enough to remark that, properly speaking, it is not " for Solomon " at all. If it refers to him and his peaceful reign, it does so only in so far as they were types of the person and kingdom of the Prince of Peace. The psalm, from beginning to end, is not only capable of being applied to Christ, but great part is incapable of being fairly applied to any other.

The FORTY-FIFTH is another Messianic psalm belonging to this period. It was not written by Solomon, but by "the sons of Korah,"—the same Levitical family who had made such precious contributions to the Psalter in the preceding reign. Its theme, —I venture to say, its primary and proper theme,—is the glory of the Lord Christ and the Church's marriage to Him ; and this is celebrated with gorgeous imagery, everywhere reminding us of the reign of King Solomon. The King's house is an ivory palace, fragrant with myrrh and aloes and cassia. The Queen is arrayed in gold of Ophir, and the daughter of Tyre brings in her hand the wealth of the nations for a wedding gift. The parallel between the Song of Solomon and the Psalm cannot escape any reader, and we may very confidently attribute them both to the brilliant age of the son of David.

The great event of Solomon's reign was the building of the Temple. It was a high day in Israel when, at the close of the great prayer which was offered at the consecration of the House, the fire came down from heaven upon the altar of burnt-offering, and the cloud of the divine glory filled the sanctuary. Did the harp of inspired song hang silent on the wall that day ? On the contrary, we can with much probability trace to this time one of the greater Messianic psalms. As the Twenty-fourth was composed by David to be sung at the bringing up of the ark to the Tabernacle on Mount Zion, so the HUNDRED-AND-THIRTY-SECOND appears to have been composed by Solomon, or by some Levitical psalmist in concert with him, to be sung when the ark was borne into its final resting-place within the golden chamber of the Temple. Solomon's prayer on the occasion, as it is reported in the Chronicles, concludes with petitions which constitute the burden of the psalm, "Now therefore arise, O LORD God, into Thy resting-place, Thou, and the ark of Thy strength : let Thy priests, O LORD God, be clothed with salvation, and let Thy saints rejoice in goodness. O LORD God, turn not away the face of Thine anointed : remember the mercies of David Thy servant."* I do not forget that some, like our old translators, judge the psalm to have been written by David for a " prayer at the removing of the ark," and suppose that it is he who here " commendeth unto God the religious care he had for the ark ;" nor do I forget that other critics connect the psalm with the consecration of the second temple. But neither supposition corresponds perfectly to the tenor of the psalm. God did not say of David's new Tabernacle, " This is My rest for ever ; here will I dwell :" and as for the second temple, we know indeed that its builders might well have prayed, like Solomon, " Arise, O LORD, into Thy rest," but they could not have added, " Thou and the ark of Thy strength ;" for the ark never entered that second House. Moreover, is it not most natural to suppose that it was Solomon and the Levites his contemporaries, the men who had been eye-witnesses of the late king's solicitude about the erection of a fit dwelling-place for the God of Jacob, who gave utterance to the affectionate reminiscence with which the psalm opens ?

---

* 2 Chron. vi. 41, 42.

1. LORD, remember for David
   All his affliction ;
2. How he sware unto the LORD,
   And vowed unto the Mighty One of Jacob :
3. Surely I will not come into the tabernacle of my house,
   Nor go up into my bed ;
4. I will not give sleep to mine eyes,
   Or slumber to mine eyelids ;
5. Until I find out a place for the LORD,
   A tabernacle for the Mighty One of Jacob.

The historian of Solomon's reign has preserved the names of some of the sages who graced his court, and who may have stood related to him in his studies in much the same way as Asaph and the other Levitical seers to David. The list occurs in the encomium on the wisdom of Solomon, which tells how "he was wiser than all men (that is to say, wiser than all the men of his own age and country); than Ethan the Ezrahite, and Heman, and Calcol, and Darda, the sons of Mahol ; and his fame was in all the nations round about" (1 Kings iv. 31). Questions not a few have been raised respecting the sages here enumerated—the wise satellites who revolved around the wisest king. Were they of the tribe of Judah, the king's own tribe, as the insertion of their names in 1 Chron. ii. 6 has been thought to imply ? Or were they not rather Levites, registered among the families of Judah, because their lot had fallen to them within the inheritance of that tribe ? These questions must remain unanswered here. I quote the list at present simply to call attention to the fact that two of the names that occur in it are found also in the superscriptions of the EIGHTY-EIGHTH and EIGHTY-NINTH Psalms. The former has the singular peculiarity of possessing two superscriptions, for it is entitled both "A song, a psalm *of the sons of Korah,*" and a " Maschil of *Heman the Ezrahite*" : the latter is entitled, "Maschil of *Ethan the Ezrahite.*" Is the coincidence of these names with those of Solomon's sages a mere accident ? or are the Heman and Ethan of the superscriptions to be identified with the Heman and Ethan of the history ? We are not in a condition to determine the point with certainty. The superscriptions are obscure ; and it must be admitted that neither the authorship nor the date of the psalms has yet been established with certainty. Without going into any of the discussions that have been raised, I can only say that I think Calvin hit the truth when he conjectured that the Eighty-ninth Psalm was written by some prophet of Solomon's time, who lived on into the disastrous reign of Rehoboam; and that it was written to give expression to the sorrow with which the godly in Judah had witnessed the disruption of the kingdom and the collapse of the short-lived glory of David's house. We know that it was not the sentiment of patriotism merely, but the deepest religious feelings of the people, that were wounded, when the Ten Tribes fell away from the house of David. The glories reserved for Israel in the latter days had been announced in connection with the promise to David that his seed and throne should be established for ever. The calamity that had befallen the monarchy seemed therefore to involve a breach of covenant with the Lord's anointed and with the Church. Hence the complaint in Psalm lxxxix. 38, 39 :—

> Thou hast been wroth with Thine anointed :
> Thou hast abhorred the covenant of Thy servant :
> Thou hast profaned his crown even to the ground.

The faith of the people was wounded quite as much as their patriotism, when the monarchy which had been the subject of so many great and far-reaching promises, and from which such great things had been hoped, was despoiled of its glory ere the reign of the third king had well begun. The days of its youth were shortened ; it was covered with shame. With regard to the Eighty-eighth Psalm, one must speak with more hesitation. Neither author nor date is at all certain. It is a tearful song, standing alone in the Psalter, in this respect, that no ray of light breaks the gloom of the suppliant. Were it not that he calls upon God, in the opening verse, as " the LORD, the God of his salvation," the whole might have seemed the cry of despair, rather than of struggling faith. Dr. Hengstenberg, and some other commentators of note, are of opinion that the two psalms go together. If so, it may be possible to identify the Heman the Ezrahite of the one superscription, and the Ethan the Ezrahite of the other, with the Heman and Ethan of Solomon's time. Some go further, and identify them with Heman and Ethan-Jeduthun, the Levitical seers and psalmists whom David appointed, along with Asaph their kinsman, to preside over the service of song. It is just possible they may be the same ; but in that case they must have lived to extreme old age. The forty years of Solomon's reign, in addition to some of the last years of David's, intervened between the establishment of the Levitical choirs and the disruption of the kingdom. However this may be, since the Eighty-ninth Psalm is a voice from the calamitous reign of Rehoboam, the circumstances of its origin must ever invest it with a certain melancholy interest, as being the last utterance of the Holy Spirit, in this kind, for a long time,—the last pulsation of the mighty tide of inspired psalmody which commenced to flow when David was anointed at Bethlehem.

Between the death of Solomon and the cessation of prophecy, there intervened about 525 years. This period is parted by the Captivity into two unequal divisions. The former, embracing nearly four centuries, extends from B.C. 975, the date of Rehoboam's accession and Jeroboam's revolt, to B.C. 588, when Jerusalem was burnt by the Chaldeans and Judah carried into captivity; the latter extends from the captivity of Judah to the time of Malachi's prophesying,—a period of rather more than a century and a half.* Fixing our attention, for the present, on the former period,—the four centuries during which the family of David reigned over the House of Judah, —what are the outstanding features that strike the eye? It was an eventful time. The years were crowded with incident, and that of a kind which the Spirit of inspiration judged worthy of being commemorated in Scripture, in a double narrative, for the instruction of succeeding times. There were times of apostasy and times of revival; reigns in which the people sat every man under his vine and his fig tree, and reigns in which the feet of hostile armies traversed the land. There are two names, however, which tower above the rest, as the names of kings who were a signal blessing to the nation and Church. JEHOSHAPHAT came first. He was the fourth in the succession from Solomon, and came to the throne sixty-one years after that king's death. HEZEKIAH inherited the crown about two hundred years later, when the monarchy was obviously declining to its fall. Both kings were God-fearing men;

---

* I have followed the chronology of Ussher, which is adopted by Prideaux, Winer, and Kurtz.

both walked in the ways of David their father, and were honoured to do eminent service to Church and commonwealth in their generations ; in behalf of both, God, in an astonishing way, put invading armies to flight, making bare His arm for the defence of His people ; best of all, the reigns of both were times in which special efforts were made for the religious instruction of the people, and in which there was a genuine revival of religion.

These chronological notices are not a digression from our subject. The reader will remember the connection formerly pointed out between times of revival and the production of new psalms. It is a remarkable fact, that the two reigns upon which the sacred history, especially in the Chronicles, expatiates with marked affection, as seasons of religious awakening in Judah,—the reigns of Jehoshaphat and Hezekiah,—and after them the period of the Captivity and return, were just the periods in which psalmody revived. So far as success has attended the effort to trace to their origin the forty or fifty songs of the later psalmists, they are found to belong mainly to the three periods of quickened religious life.

The psalms we owe to the reign of JEHOSHAPHAT are not many. Of only *two* are we quite certain ; there may be, perhaps, *four* or *five*. Some think the Forty-sixth and Forty-seventh,—both of them Korahite psalms,—belong to the period. Certainly we owe to it the Forty-eighth and the Eighty-third,—the former a Korahite psalm, the latter "a song and psalm of Asaph." The character of these odes reminds us that it was the pressure of a public danger that at this epoch awoke for a short time the harps of the Levitical seers. They make mention of an invasion which, as we learn from the historical books, for a time threatened to sweep away Jehoshaphat's throne, and even to annihilate the kingdom. The nations bordering on Judah to the east and south, Moab, Ammon, Edom, entered into a coalition against it, and secured the alliance of several more distant powers. They invaded the land from the south, and marched without check till they reached the wilderness of Tekoa, within ten miles of Jerusalem, whence, looking northwards, they could descry the battlements of the city and the glittering pinnacles of the temple. In this extremity of danger, Jehoshaphat and the people betook themselves to prayer. Having received, through one of the prophets, the promise of deliverance, king and people sallied forth in a solemn procession, in the van of which there marched a band of Levites, singing and praising the Lord. When they came in sight of the enemy, they found that God had sown mutual suspicions in the motley host, so that they had turned their swords against each other and were utterly discomfited. It deserves to be remarked in connection with our subject, that the prophet by whom God's comfortable message was delivered to the king was Jahaziel, the son of Zechariah, "a Levite of the sons of Asaph;" and that among the Levites who sang praise to the Lord, mention is made of a band "of the children of the Korahites." * It is an interesting and significant coincidence, that of the two psalms known to date from this epoch, one is marked in the superscription as an Asaph-psalm, and the other is assigned to the sons of Korah. The Asaph-psalm is the EIGHTY-THIRD, and is the prayer of the congregation when the danger was at its height. It speaks of a confederation of "the tents of Edom and the Ishmaelites; of Moab, and the Hagarenes; Gebal, and Ammon and Amalek;" and, among the more distant allies, mention is made of Tyre, and of Assyria itself. Their cry is, "Come, and let us cut them off from being a nation; that the name of Israel may be no more in remembrance." The cry of Judah, in response, is toward heaven: "O my God, make them like the whirling dust," or, as Milton translates the prayer,—

> "My God, oh make them as a wheel,
>   No quiet let them find;
> Giddy and restless let them reel,
>   Like stubble from the wind.
>
> As when an aged wood takes fire,
>   Which on a sudden strays,
> The greedy flame runs higher and higher,
>   Till all the mountains blaze;
>
> So with Thy whirlwind them pursue,
>   And with Thy tempest chase."

Such was the prayer. The answer which God gave, in the flame of discord that consumed the confederate host, is celebrated by the sons of Korah in the FORTY-EIGHTH Psalm.

---

* 2 Chron. xx. 14, 19.

1. Great is the LORD, and highly to be praised,
      In the city of our God, in His holy mountain.
2. Beautiful in elevation, the joy of the whole earth,
      Is Mount Zion, on the sides of the north,
      The City of the Great King.

3. God hath made Himself known in her palaces for a refuge.
4. For, lo, the kings assembled themselves,
      They passed by together.
5. They saw it; then were they amazed;
      They were dismayed, they hasted away.
6. Trembling took hold of them there;
      Pain, as of a woman in travail.

7. With the east wind
      Thou breakest the ships of Tarshish.
8. As we have heard, so have we seen,
      In the city of the LORD of hosts, in the city of our God.
      God will establish it for ever.

9. We have thought on Thy loving-kindness, O God,
      In the midst of Thy temple.
10. As is Thy name, O God,
      So is Thy praise unto the ends of the earth:
      Thy right hand is full of righteousness.
11. Let Mount Zion be glad,
      Let the daughters of Judah rejoice,
      Because of Thy judgments.

12. Walk about Zion, and go round about her:
      Tell the towers thereof.
13. Mark ye well her bulwarks,
      Consider her palaces;
      That ye may tell it to the generation following.

14. FOR THIS GOD IS OUR GOD FOR EVER AND EVER:
      HE WILL BE OUR GUIDE EVEN UNTO DEATH.

Some expositors have found a difficulty in the last verse, deeming such a profession of personal faith an inappropriate termination for a national song. Even Dr. Delitzsch, a wise and devout interpreter, shares in this notion; going, indeed, so far as to throw out the surmise, that some word must have been lost from the Hebrew text. To me it seems that the verse, as it stands, is admirably in harmony with the song, and is its crowning beauty. When the Lord does great things for Church or nation, He means that all the faithful, however humble their station, should take courage from it, should repose in Him fresh confidence, and cling to Him with a firmer hope, and say, "This God shall be our God for ever; He will guide us even unto death."

A century and a half elapsed between the death of Jehoshaphat and the accession of HEZEKIAH. This long tract of years was anything but devoid of interest. But it made no addition to the Psalter, or none that can now be identified with any certainty. Perhaps the Eighty-second—the short but striking psalm which has for its theme *the judgment of the gods by the God of gods*—may have come from this time. The Ninety-fourth may also be assigned to it with much probability. Both psalms bear the marks of having been written under one of those disastrous reigns in which the persons of the wicked found acceptance in high places and the foundations of the earth were out of course.

At length there came a glorious outburst of holy song. God having raised up, in Hezekiah, a king every way worthy to sit on David's throne, and granted a time of clear shining to cheer His people, the harp of psalmody awoke from its long sleep and poured forth strains so rich and various, that it seemed as if the golden time of David had come again.

The psalms of this epoch may be distributed into three classes, corresponding to the three characteristic features of the time.

1. The reign of Hezekiah was a time of REUNION IN THE CHURCH. It witnessed the resumption of the long-interrupted ecclesiastical communion between Judah and the Ten Tribes. It will be remembered that when Jeroboam cast off his allegiance to the house of David and founded the kingdom of Israel, he erected an idolatrous worship at Dan and Bethel and forbade the people to resort to the feasts of the Lord at Jerusalem. The defection was a grave one and sufficiently calamitous; but to imagine, as many do, that the Ten Tribes ceased thenceforward to belong to the commonwealth of Israel and the Church of the Living God, is certainly a mistake. The Lord did not cast off the house of Joseph. He withdrew from them neither the ministry of His Word nor the saving grace of the Spirit. Generation after generation, He gathered to Himself,

out of the Ten Tribes, a remnant according to the election of grace.   Even in the dark days of Ahab and Jezebel, when the Sidonian idolatry became the state religion, He testified that He had reserved to Himself seven thousand in Israel who had not bowed the knee to Baal; and the ruler of Ahab's own house was one of them.   Prophets, too, were raised up.   Elijah and Elisha ministered within the northern kingdom.   Obadiah concealed a hundred prophets at once in a time of persecution. It is certain, therefore, that God did not, during all those two hundred-and-fifty years, *unchurch* the Ten Tribes.   Nevertheless, during all that time, there was an entire *cessation of Church-fellowship* between the house of Judah and the house of Joseph. Never once did they resort together to the solemn feasts.   Individuals occasionally, as at the accession of Jeroboam and in the reign of Asa, left their homes in the North and cast in their lot with Judah, because of the house of the Lord;* but that was all.   At length a partial reunion gladdened the Church in the first year of Hezekiah.   The recent captivity of two tribes and a half had weakened the northern kingdom; and Hoshea, who was Hezekiah's contemporary and the last of its kings, was led by a sense of duty to break the evil custom which his predecessors had inherited from Jeroboam the son of Nebat, " who sinned, and made Israel to sin."   He suspended the law against going up to Jerusalem.   Hezekiah's posts were permitted to carry to every part of the kingdom the invitation to unite again with Judah in celebrating the Passover in the city which God had chosen out of all the tribes of Israel.†   The invitation, scorned by many, was gladly accepted by some; and a Passover was celebrated the like of which had not been seen in Israel, since the days of Solomon and the undivided kingdom.

So happy a reunion—happy in itself, twice happy as the pledge of the promised time when Ephraim should no more envy Judah, and Judah no more vex Ephraim, but they should be one stick in the Lord's hand‡—could not fail to call forth new songs.   There is, I think, sufficient ground to attribute to it the EIGHTY-FIRST Psalm.   It is, obviously and by universal consent, a Festal song.   The reference to the exodus from Egypt shows that, although framed to suit all the three Feasts,

---

* 2 Chron. xi. 13, 14; xv. 9.   † 2 Chron. xxx.
‡ Isa. xi. 13; Ezek. xxxvii. 17.

it had a special connection with the Passover; and the emphatic reminder that the feast had been ordained in *Joseph* for a testimony—especially when this is taken in connection with the terms of the reference to Joseph in the psalm next to be noticed—may be fairly interpreted as pointing to an occasion when Ephraim and Manasseh, the sons of Joseph, participated with Judah in the solemn rite. There is an undertone of sadness towards the end which reminds us that the desolation of the northern kingdom was at hand; but it opens as with a blast of trumpets :—

1. Sing aloud unto God our Strength ;
    Make a joyful noise unto the God of Jacob.
2. Take up the psalm and bring hither the timbrel,
    The pleasant harp with the psaltery.
3. Blow up the trumpet in the new moon ;
    At the full moon, on our solemn feast-day.
4. For it is a statute for Israel,
    An ordinance of the God of Jacob.
5. He appointed it in Joseph for a testimony,
    When He went out against the land of Egypt :
    Where I heard a language that I knew not.

There were circumstances in the condition of the Ten Tribes in the age of Hezekiah which were fitted, as indeed they were designed, to blow into a flame the ancient brotherly affection of Judah and Joseph. Fourteen years before his accession, the northern kingdom was bereft of the Transjordanic tribes by the first of the great Assyrian invasions. A second invasion under Shalmanezer, five years after Hezekiah's accession, brought Hoshea's reign to an end and completed the captivity of the kingdom. This was B.C. 721, eight years before Sennacherib's attempt against Judah. Bearing these dates in mind, they will be found to shed an interesting light on a song of complaint which is set down in the Psalter by the side of the Festal hymn we have just noticed. That that hymn was first sung at Hezekiah's passover, I have stated merely as a probable conjecture. That its sister psalm, the EIGHTIETH, belongs to that age, may be asserted as something more than a conjecture. It is a lament over the devastations that were now being wrought by the heathen among the tribes of the Lord, and the reference to the northern tribes is reiterated and express. It may interest the reader to see the whole psalm printed so as to exhibit the strophic arrangement :—

1. Give ear, O Shepherd of Israel,
   Thou that leadest Joseph like a flock ;
   Thou that sittest upon the Cherubim, shine forth.
2. Before Ephraim and Benjamin and Manasseh, stir up Thy might,
   And come to save us.
3. TURN US AGAIN, O GOD,
   AND CAUSE THY FACE TO SHINE, AND WE SHALL BE SAVED.

4. O LORD God of hosts,
   How long wilt Thou be angry against the prayer of Thy people ?
5. Thou hast fed them with the bread of tears,
   And given them tears to drink in large measure.
6. Thou makest us a strife unto our neighbours ;
   And our enemies laugh among themselves.
7. TURN US AGAIN, O GOD OF HOSTS ;
   AND CAUSE THY FACE TO SHINE, AND WE SHALL BE SAVED.

8. Thou broughtest a vine out of Egypt :
   Thou didst drive out the nations, and plantedst it.
9. Thou preparedst room before it ;
   And it took deep root, and filled the land.
10. The mountains were covered with the shadow of it,
    And the boughs thereof were like cedars of God.
11. She sent out her branches unto the sea,
    And her shoots unto the River.

12. Why hast Thou broken down her fences,
    So that all they which pass by the way do pluck her ?
13. The boar out of the wood doth ravage it,
    And the wild beasts of the field feed on it.
14. TURN AGAIN, WE BESEECH THEE, O GOD OF HOSTS.
    Look down from heaven, and behold, and visit this vine ;
15. And the stock which Thy right hand hath planted,
    And the branch that Thou madest strong for Thyself.
16. It is burnt with fire, it is cut down :
    They perish at the rebuke of Thy countenance.

17. Let Thy hand be upon the man of Thy right hand ;
    Upon the son of man whom Thou madest strong for Thyself.
18. So shall we not go back from Thee ;
    Quicken Thou us, and we will call upon Thy name.
19. TURN US AGAIN, O LORD GOD OF HOSTS :
    CAUSE THY FACE TO SHINE, AND WE SHALL BE SAVED.

It has long been felt that this psalm must have been written with reference to the gradual desolation of the Ten Tribes. This was pointed out by Calvin, and he has been followed by the best subsequent expositors. The reference to the Ten Tribes being evident, the psalm, according to Calvin, is a prayer of Judah for her afflicted sister. There was a time when, as the Lord complains by the prophet Amos,* the people of Judah, being " at ease in Zion," were " not grieved for the affliction of Joseph ; " there was a time when they would have taken pleasure in the captivity of the northern kingdom, looking upon it as the removal of their rival. But they have been brought to a better mind, and have learned to pray for their brethren. That this represents the general drift of the psalm is unquestionable. But it would require to be taken with some modification. Those who, like Dr. Hengstenberg, adhere to the letter of Calvin's view, are obliged to maintain that Benjamin, which is named along with Ephraim and Manasseh, belonged to Israel, not to Judah. If the psalm is a prayer for Ephraim, it is a prayer for Benjamin also. We get rid of all this difficulty if we look on the psalm as the joint prayer of all the tribes, *the prayer in which the house of Joseph and the house of Judah, so long estranged from one another, unite again in calling on the God of Abraham, and Isaac, and Jacob.* The psalm has Asaph's name in the superscription, and is inscribed " for the Chief Musician." It is therefore a Song of the Temple. What more likely than that it was first sung in the Temple in those early years of Hezekiah's reign when Benjamin found himself once more associated with Ephraim and Manasseh, his mother's sons, in the solemn worship of the Lord ; that it is the prayer in which the whole seed of Jacob, now happily restored to complete religious fellowship, united in spreading before the Lord the calamities of the nation, and prayed Him to restore them again and cause His face to shine ?

2. The reign of Hezekiah witnessed just such another INVASION and DELIVERANCE as had been seen in Jehoshaphat's time. The facts already noticed remind us that this was the age in which the Assyrian monarchy had attained the highest

---

* Amos vi. 6.

noon of its splendour. The Assyrian kings were rearing at
Nineveh those great palaces whose sculptured slabs have
lately lent a new attraction to the museums of Europe. Shalmanezer, who carried the Ten Tribes into captivity, had been
succeeded by Sennacherib, and the new monarch was resolved
to measure his strength with the King of Egypt. That he
might leave no hostile fortress to threaten his rear, he determined to capture Jerusalem and remove the people to share
the captivity of their brethren. The sacred writers have narrated in great detail the history of this attempt : the impious
letter of the Assyrian king ; the arrogant pride of Rabshakeh
his lieutenant ; Hezekiah's prayer as he spread the letter before
the Lord in the Temple ; the comfortable answer sent by
Isaiah ; the stroke of the angel of the Lord which laid low
180,000 men, the flower of Assyria, in one night ; the flight
of Sennacherib in shame to his own land. As in Jehoshaphat's
time, the danger and the deliverance are both celebrated in
psalms. It is certain that the SEVENTY-SIXTH Psalm celebrates the *deliverance;* and the SEVENTY-FIFTH bears traces
of having been written in the crisis of the *danger.* An unfortunate mistranslation in the second verse of the latter psalm
is apt to mislead the reader of the Authorised Version. The
verse, let it be observed, expresses God's purpose, not the
purpose of the psalmist. " When I shall find [or take] the set
time, I will judge uprightly :" * God may hide Himself long,
but when the fit time, the time of His own appointment, comes,
He will make bare His arm in the defence of the oppressed :—

7. But God is the Judge :
   He putteth down one, and lifteth up another.
8. For in the hand of the LORD there is a cup, and the wine
   foameth ;
   It is full of mixture, and He poureth out of the same :
   Surely the dregs thereof, all the wicked of the earth shall wring
   them out, and drink them.

The Seventy-sixth Psalm was evidently written in the first
flush of the grateful joy with which the marvellous discomfiture
of the Assyrians brightened every countenance in Jerusalem.

* So the Geneva Bible, " When I shall take a convenient time, I will judge
righteously."

It is rendered with exquisite skill and spirit in the English Bible (and, I may add, in the Scots Metrical Version also), and citation is unnecessary. Let the reader compare it with the narrative given in Isaiah and the historical books, and he will not marvel that the critics, divided as they are in opinion regarding the origin of so many other psalms, are almost unanimous in connecting this one with the mysterious discomfiture of Sennacherib's host.

To some it may seem that a psalm which originated in an event so marvellous, and which bears such strongly-marked traces of its origin, must be little adapted for the subsequent use of God's people, and therefore must be out of place in the Psalter of the Church catholic. But facts refute such a notion. Times without number the psalm has been sung, as furnishing the fittest expression of the thoughts and feelings of God's people in view of deliverances wrought for them. When the Covenanters at Drumclog closed their ranks to meet the onset of Claverhouse and his dragoons, they sang the opening verses, to the tune of Martyrs :—

> " In Judah's land God is well known,
>   his name's in Isr'el great :
> In Salem is His tabernacle,
>   in Zion is His seat.
>
> There arrows of the bow He brake,
>   the shield, the sword, the war.
> More glorious Thou than hills of prey,
>   more excellent art far.
>
> Those that were stout of heart are spoiled,
>   they slept their sleep outright ;
> And none of those their hands did find
>   that were the men of might."

A century earlier, in 1588, when the first rumour of the discomfiture of the Spanish Armada reached Edinburgh and the citizens assembled to render thanks to God, Robert Bruce, addressing them in the West Kirk, took this psalm for his text, and the two noble sermons * he preached on the occasion were, from beginning to end, little more than a running commentary on the psalm. And every hearer must have felt that the whole

---

* Bruce's *Sermons*, pp. 278-323.

was as appropriate to the circumstances as if the psalm had been written for the occasion.

3. The other feature of Hezekiah's reign which remains to be noticed, as affecting the complexion of the psalms of the period, belongs to it in common with the times which followed, and will be most fitly noticed in connection with the whole period of the captivity and the return.

CHAPTER VI.

THE PSALMS OF THE CAPTIVITY AND THE RETURN.

IN the reign of Hezekiah, the kingdom of Judah entered on a period of its history which may be described as the eve of the Babylonish Captivity. That terrible overthrow, it is true, was still a great way off. Nearly a century intervened between the death of Hezekiah and the first appearance of the Chaldean armies on the frontier, and twenty years more elapsed before the desolation of the kingdom was complete. But during all this period of four generations, the Captivity projected its dark shadow on the devoted nation. All who had eyes to see saw it coming on. Prophets had foretold it. Micah, who prophesied in the days of Jotham, Ahaz, and Hezekiah, had declared that Zion should be ploughed as a field, and Jerusalem should become heaps ; * and there is evidence that the prediction excited attention, and was remembered in the capital.† Nor was this the first intimation of the Lord's purpose. So early as the year that King Uzziah died, the approaching desolation of the land had been signified in vision to Isaiah, who was then entering on his protracted and memorable ministry.‡ Some years later, the prediction received an ominous confirmation from the successive Assyrian invasions, which resulted in the carrying away of the Ten Tribes. The tide of invasion, indeed, was turned back from Zion and the house of David, when the angel of the Lord smote the host of the Assyrians. But thoughtful persons, who pondered the word of prophecy and marked how the clouds continued to gather on the northern horizon, felt that the discomfiture of Sennacherib, marvellous as it was, meant only respite, not deliverance, to the kingdom of Judah; and their misgivings would be strengthened when

---

* Micah iii. 12.   † Jer. xxvi. 18.   ‡ Isa. vi. 11, 12.

they observed how Hezekiah " rendered not again according to the benefit done unto him ; for his heart was lifted up."* These facts are necessary to be remembered, if one would fully understand either the age of Hezekiah or the psalms to which it gave birth. It was not only a time of rekindled affection between the two houses of Israel, and of signal deliverance for Judah, but a time, moreover, in which the hearts of God's people were chilled by the shadow of a great calamity which they saw approaching.

This characteristic, also, of the period commencing with the reign of Hezekiah, has left its mark on the Psalter. It has done so in two kinds of psalms. There are some in which the Church pours out penitent sorrow before the Lord. The Eighty-first has been already commented upon—a Festal Psalm, in which the whole people of Israel seem to have praised the Lord during the four or five years that intervened between the resumption of communion between Ephraim and Judah and the captivity of the northern kingdom. It is impossible to read the latter part of the psalm without perceiving that the joy of those years was clouded by the anticipation of the calamities that were coming on the whole nation :—

> 8. Hear, O My people, and I will testify unto thee :
>   O Israel, if thou wouldst hearken unto Me !
> 9. There shall no strange god be in thee ;
>   Neither shalt thou worship any strange god.
>   .   .   .   .
> 11. But My people hearkened not to My voice ;
>   And Israel would none of Me.
> 12. So I let them go after the stubbornness of their heart,
>   That they might walk in their own counsels.

It is plain that the generation which first sang thus had ceased to hope that the predicted desolation of the country might be averted. The SEVENTY-SEVENTH,—another " Psalm of Asaph,"—may with all confidence be likewise referred to the Eve of the Captivity. From the way in which the psalmist gathers comfort by the recollection of the past, "the days of old, the years of ancient times," " the years of the right hand of the Most High," it is sufficiently plain that his sorrow was not a private grief, but flowed from his sympathy with the

---

* 2 Chron. xxxii. 25.

calamity of Zion. It is pleasant to note here also the continued working of the brotherly love lately renewed between Israel and Judah. Joseph participated along with the other tribes in the redemption from Egypt, and the psalmist calls that fact to mind, that he may comfort himself with the hope that the children of Joseph will be remembered when the Lord shall turn the captivity of His people. "Thou art the God that doest wonders : Thou hast made known Thy strength among the peoples. Thou hast with Thine arm redeemed Thy people, the sons of Jacob and Joseph."

The Eve of the Captivity was blessed with psalms of a more cheerful order—psalms which take rank amongst the brightest and the most joyous the Church ever sang. As the coming on of night brings into view the far-off starry worlds, so God made choice of the age when the temporal glories of David's house were sinking into darkness for disclosing to the faith of the godly the higher glories He had in store for that house and for His people. The century and a half which preceded the Captivity was a period wonderfully favoured in this respect, enjoying the ministry of such prophets as Isaiah and Jeremiah, Hosea, Joel, Amos, Micah. This was the age in which the joining of the Prophetical Books of the Old Testament was begun. Prior to this time, indeed, God raised up a succession of prophets in the Church, and since the days of Samuel, the succession had been uninterrupted. By men like Gad and Nathan in Judah, Elijah and Elisha in Israel, the Lord sent His word to the people, generation after generation. But the function of these earlier prophets was rather to stir up men's minds by way of remembrance than to invite them to expatiate upon the future. They were preachers of righteousness, inculcating the law of Moses, and bearing witness against the sins of their times. The additions which some of them were moved to make to the canon of Scripture took the historical rather than the predictive form. The reign of Hezekiah may be said to mark the commencement of a new order of things—the commencement of the ministry of the "writing prophets."* Henceforward one principal function of the holy men of God

---

* Edward's *Hist. of Redemption*, Period I., Part V., Sect. 19. Oehler, in Herzog's Encyclopedia, Art. "*Prophetenthum d. A. Test*," vol. xii. p. 224.

was to be the opening up of the future.   The decline of the temporal grandeur of the nation was fitted, as it was no doubt intended, to wean God's people from that transitory glory, and to prepare them for listening to the announcement of something more excellent.   It was at this epoch, accordingly, that the divine purposes regarding the Church and the world in the latter days, began to be fully opened up by the prophets, and especially by Isaiah.   Assuming that the predicted captivity would certainly come to pass, they spoke of a happy return to Zion ; and with their announcement of that return were mingled intimations regarding the advent of the Messiah, His sufferings and the glories that were to follow, the mission of the Comforter, the calling of the Gentiles, the establishment of the kingdom of God in all the earth.   Occasionally, as in the twelfth chapter of Isaiah, the predictions of the prophets blossom into song.   It would have been strange if, at such a time, the stock of psalmody in actual use had not been enriched with an increment of new psalms,—anthems in which the Church might express her faith in the disclosures God had made, and the gladness with which they filled her heart.

There are discoverable several psalms of the character anticipated.   The middle of the Psalter derives a peculiar brightness from a constellation of them, the decade, I mean, which closes with the Hundredth Psalm.   With perhaps one or two exceptions, all the ten belong to the prophetic order. They are Messianic in the sense of celebrating the *kingdom* of Christ, although not Messianic in the narrower sense of celebrating His *person*.   They soar far above the general level of the Old Testament economy, bearing the mind forward and upward to a state of things such as even the apostolic age never saw.   Dr. Delitzsch has, with much felicity, entitled them *apocalyptic psalms;* some of them I should prefer to call *the Songs of the Millennium*.   The Hundredth Psalm, for instance, how grandly does it anticipate the Millennial time, and summon all the nations to unite in the high praises of the Lord !

> All people that on earth do dwell,
>   sing to the Lord with cheerful voice :
> Him serve with mirth, His praise forth tell,
>   come ye before Him and rejoice.

> Know that the Lord is God indeed;
> without our aid He did us make:
> We are His flock, He doth us feed,
> and for His sheep He doth us take.*

The NINETY-THIRD, another star in this constellation, may be cited entire. The drift of it cannot be better expressed than in the two words with which it opens, JEHOVAH REIGNETH. It is a kind of proclamation, in which God's people are invited to declare before men and angels that the Lord is King, He and He only. It is the response of the Church to the preaching of the gospel, so rapturously hailed in Isaiah †—the preaching of the messenger "that bringeth good tidings, that publisheth peace; that bringeth good tidings of good, that publisheth salvation; that saith unto Zion, Thy God reigneth!"

1. The LORD reigneth; He is apparelled with majesty;
   The LORD is apparelled, He hath girded Himself with
       strength:
   The world also is stablished, that it cannot be moved.
2. Thy throne is established of old:
   Thou art from everlasting.
3. The floods have lifted up, O LORD,
   The floods have lifted up their voice;
   The floods lift up their waves.
4. Above the voices of many waters,
   The mighty breakers of the sea,
   The LORD on high is mighty.
5. Thy testimonies are very sure:
   Holiness becometh Thine house,
   O LORD, for evermore.

What has been said regarding this psalm applies to the NINETY-SEVENTH also. It is quoted in the Epistle to the Hebrews

---

* This noble version, *Old Hundred*, is, I believe, the most ancient metrical psalm now in common use in our language. It is certainly one of the very best, faithful to the original, and yet full of grace and strength. It was first printed in the Psalm-book published for the English exiles at Geneva in 1561; and is believed to have been written by William Kethe, a native of Scotland, who joined the exiles at Geneva in 1556. See the Third of the learned and valuable Dissertations by the Rev. Neil Livingstone, prefixed to his sumptuous reprint of *The Scottish Metrical Psalter* of 1635 (Glasgow, 1864). From an allusion in Shakespeare (*Merry Wives of Windsor* II. 1), the psalm in this version and the well-known melody named after it would appear to have been as great favourites in Queen Elizabeth's time as they are among ourselves.

† Isa. lii. 7.

as having just such a reference as we have explained to the second advent of Christ and the Church's future prosperity under His reign. "When He again bringeth in the First-born into the world, He saith, And let all the angels of God worship Him."* The quotation is from the seventh verse of the psalm ("worship Him, all ye gods"), according to the translation of the LXX. The meaning is that Christ being the First-born and Heir, "He shall be brought again into the world of men and installed into His inheritance; and then shall all the angels worship Him."†

How many of these Psalms of the Kingdom come down to us from the Eve of the Captivity cannot be determined with any certainty. Dr. Hengstenberg very confidently sets down the whole of the decade already mentioned as having been written during the reign of Hezekiah, but on insufficient grounds. Some of them may very well have been written after the return from Babylon. Nevertheless, the present seemed on several accounts the fittest place at which to take note of them as a class. In the first place, they stand related, in a close and vital manner, to the heart-stirring word of prophecy which, as we have seen, constitutes the peculiar glory of the hundred-and-fifty years preceding the Captivity. Let any one who doubts this compare the Ninety-sixth or Ninety-eighth Psalm with the prophecies of Isaiah. The connection cannot be mistaken. The one voice is a clear articulate echo of the other. Moreover, some of the psalms in question contain allusions which warrant us to attribute them either to the reign of Hezekiah or the period immediately after it. The EIGHTY-SEVENTH is an instance in point. It celebrates the Church's latter-day glory in modes of representation borrowed from the age which listened to the predictions of Isaiah and Micah. I name these two prophets because the psalm takes up, and makes answer to, a prediction which was delivered by them in common. "It shall come to pass in the latter days, that the mountain of the LORD's house shall be established in the top of the mountains, and shall be exalted above the hills; and all nations shall flow unto it. And many peoples shall go and

---

* Heb. i. 6.
† *Epistle to the Hebrews, with Introd. and Notes,* by A. B. Davidson, LL.D., p. 48.

say, Come ye, and let us go up to the mountain of the Lord, to
the house of the God of Jacob : . . . for out of Zion shall go forth
the law, and the word of the LORD from Jerusalem."* The
incorporation of the Gentiles with God's Israel, which the prophets here so boldly announce, is precisely the theme of the
psalm. And how wonderfully it is celebrated! Not content
with representing the great Gentile nations as coming up to
Zion, year by year, to seek the Lord and rejoice with the gladness of His nation, the psalmist, waxing bolder, announces the
advent of a time when the Lord will enrol them among the
native citizens of Jerusalem.

This remarkable ode presents considerable difficulty to the
translator,—differing, in this respect, from the ordinary style of
the later psalmists, which is easy and perspicuous. The structure and scope are so well brought out in Hupfeld's German
version that a useful purpose may be served by reproducing it
here in an English dress. I have a special reason, in the
present instance, for making use of this eminent critic's assistance. His bias is all to the rationalist side ; and it has
occurred to me that many readers may feel a certain satisfaction
in perceiving that the prophetical glory of the psalm is not due
to the evangelical feeling of our English translators, but is
inherent in the Hebrew and shines out in any faithful translation.

1. His foundation on the holy mountains Jehovah loveth,
   Even the gates of Zion before all dwellings of Jacob.
2. Glorious things are spoken [promised] concerning thee,
   O city of God. (Selah.)
3. I will name Rahab [Egypt] and Babel as confessors of Me :
   Behold Palashet and Tsor, with Cush :
   " *This man was born there.*"
4. And of Zion it shall be said, "One and all are born in her,
   And He will stablish her, even the Most High."
5. Jehovah shall count, at the enrolment of the peoples,
   " *This man was born there.*" (Selah.)
6. And they sing and skip for joy
   All who dwell in thee.

The reader will mark the names that occur in this catalogue
of the nations which are one day to be enrolled among the

---

* Isa. ii. 2, 3 ; Micah iv. 1, 2.

citizens, the born citizens, of Zion. Egypt and Babylon, Philistia and Tyre, with far-off Ethiopia ; these are precisely the nations which had proved formidable to Israel in the ages preceding the Babylonish captivity, precisely those which would have arrested the attention of a psalmist of the reign of Hezekiah or Josiah, who, taking his stand in imagination on a pinnacle of the temple, had thence surveyed the panorama of the world. We hold ourselves warranted, therefore, to assign the Eighty-seventh Psalm to the Eve of the Captivity ; and if this bright millennial star cheered the deepening gloom of that period, we may be sure that others of the class belong to it also.

The PSALMS OF THE CAPTIVITY, strictly so called, fall under three heads, according as they were written in the first anguish of the carrying away, or after the exiles had settled down in their new abodes in Mesopotamia, or when the time fixed for the return drew near.

To the first class belong the SEVENTY-FOURTH and SEVENTY-NINTH. In reading them we seem to hear the cry of the people rising to heaven as the Chaldeans scale the wall, and fire the city, and desecrate the sanctuary. They are both entitled Psalms of Asaph ; and the vividness with which they describe the desolations wrought by the Chaldeans, with sword and with fire, leaves the impression that they must have come from the pen of Levites who were eye-witnesses of the dismal scene. In the former of the two, the godly complain, " There is no more any prophet ; neither is there among us any that knoweth how long." This has led some commentators to think that, whatever may be the true date of the psalm, it cannot refer to the Chaldean invasion ; for it is certain that at that epoch the congregation enjoyed the ministry of distinguished prophets, and Jeremiah, who was one of them, foretold how long the Captivity was to last. The occurrence of the complaint is indeed, by some, deemed sufficient to show that the psalm belongs to the age of the Maccabees, and has reference to the sufferings inflicted on the Jews by Antiochus Epiphanes. This subject of Maccabean psalms will come up again ; meanwhile it is enough to say that the one before us cannot well have been written after the Captivity, inasmuch as the Second Temple was never consumed with fire till its final destruction by the Romans. The truth is, that complaints uttered in the first pressure of sore affliction are not to be interpreted too literally. The eye dimmed with sudden tears sees only the dark side of things, and is unable, for a while, to do justice to the rays of light which mitigate the darkness of its affliction. That the psalmist's words must be taken with some qualification is apparent from the fact, that the same complaint which he utters is found in the Lamentations of Jeremiah himself. He was certainly a prophet, and never ceased to see the visions of God; yet he exclaims, " The Lord hath cast off His altar : He hath purposed to destroy the wall of the daughter of Zion : yea, her prophets find no vision from the Lord " (Lam. ii. 7-9). Let us hear the Psalmist :—

1. O God, why hast Thou cast us off for ever?
   Why doth Thine anger smoke against the sheep of Thy pasture?
2. Remember Thy congregation, which Thou hast purchased of old,
   Which Thou hast redeemed to be the tribe of Thine inheritance,
   And Mount Zion, wherein Thou hast dwelt.

   .   .   .   .

4. Thine adversaries have roared in the midst of Thine assembly;
   They have set up their ensigns for signs.
5. They seemed as men that lifted up
   Axes upon a thicket of trees.
6. And now all the carved work thereof together
   They break down with hatchet and hammers.
7. They have set Thy sanctuary on fire ;
   They have profaned the dwelling-place of Thy name even to the ground.
8. They said in their heart, Let us make havoc of them altogether:
   They have burnt up all the synagogues of God in the land.
9. We see not our signs:
   There is no more any prophet:
   Neither is there among us any that knoweth how long.
10. How long, O God, shall the adversary reproach?
    Shall the enemy blaspheme Thy name for ever?

Such is the former half of the psalm. The latter half is of a more cheerful tenor. The Church remembers God's mighty works in nature and in grace, and her grief is assuaged. With recovered faith she betakes herself again to prayer : " Have respect unto the covenant ; for the dark places of the earth are full of the habitations of violence."

So much for the psalms that date from the great overthrow. The condition of the exiles in their new abode was attended with much less of hardship than the mention of captivity might suggest. It is a mistake to think of them as in a state of slavery, like their fathers in Egypt. They were transported beyond the Euphrates, not to be made slaves of, but that they might help to replenish the central parts of the Babylonish empire with an industrious population. They were subjected to no crushing disabilities; and in fact great numbers of them rose rapidly to wealth and political distinction. Hence they soon got rooted in the new soil;—so deeply rooted, that only a small remnant could ever after be persuaded to return to the place of their fathers' sepulchres. In a worldly point of view, the exiles were better off in Babylon than they could hope to be, for many a day, at Jerusalem. These facts will afford assistance in appreciating the true design of the HUNDRED-AND-THIRTY-SEVENTH Psalm, which is a voice out of the midst of the Captivity. The recent commentators seem, with one consent, to regard it as a *reminiscence* of the Captivity, on the part of the remnant who returned. For myself, while not insensible to the force of the considerations they adduce, I am disposed to hold by the opinion, that the psalm was actually written by some captive Levite, dwelling among his brethren by the Ulai and the Chebar:—

1. By the rivers of Babylon,
     There we sat down, yea, we wept,
     When we remembered Zion.
2. Upon the willows, in the midst thereof,
     We hanged up our harps.
3. For there they that led us captive required of us songs,
     And they that wasted us required of us mirth, saying,
     Sing us one of the songs of Zion.
4. How shall we sing the LORD'S song
     In a strange land?
5. If I forget thee, O Jerusalem,
     Let my right hand forget her cunning.
6. Let my tongue cleave to the roof of my mouth,
     If I remember thee not;
   If I prefer not Jerusalem
     Above my chief joy.
7. Remember, O LORD, against the children of Edom
     The day of Jerusalem;

Who said, Rase it, rase it,
Even to the foundation thereof.
8. O daughter of Babylon, that art to be destroyed ;
Happy shall he be that rewardeth thee
As thou hast served us.
9. Happy shall he be, that taketh and dasheth thy little ones
Against the rock.

The air of pensive melancholy which imparts such a charm to this ode may seem hardly consistent with what has been said regarding the advantageous condition of the exiles. But it is to be remembered that their very prosperity was pregnant with danger to their highest good, and therefore might well cause painful concern to a man like the psalmist—a man who set Jerusalem above his chief joy. The ordinances God had appointed for the Old Testament Church, and which were such a well-spring of blessing whilst the Levitical dispensation lasted, were unalterably bound to the land of promise ; they could only be celebrated in the city which the Lord had chosen to place His name there. So long as the Captivity lasted, they ceased. Hence the tears of tender regret with which the psalmist remembers Zion ; hence his determination to regard the place of his present abode as "a strange land," and to reserve for the Temple the Temple Songs. The design of the psalmist is to guard the people against allowing their affections to settle in the place of their sojourn. With this view he labours to strengthen within their hearts the affectionate remembrance of Jerusalem, the hope and desire to return in God's good time, and the assured expectation that the haters and oppressors of Zion shall be overthrown.

The HUNDRED-AND-SECOND Psalm brings before us the Captivity in its third phase. The Lord had, by Jeremiah, announced a return after seventy years. This was done in express terms. We are not surprised therefore to find that, as the years wore away, the fearers of God among the exiles began to look out for the fulfilment of the prediction. Daniel had come to understand "by the books the number of the years, whereof the word of the LORD came to Jeremiah the prophet, for the accomplishing of the desolations of Jerusalem, even seventy years." He knew more. He knew that when God promises blessings, He desires to be inquired of by His Israel with respect to them.   Accordingly, he "set his face unto the Lord God, to seek by prayer and supplications, with fasting;" and the burden of his prayer was that the Lord would at length turn the captivity of His people.   "O our God, cause Thy face to shine upon Thy sanctuary that is desolate, for the Lord's sake."*   I refer to these exercises of the man greatly beloved because I am persuaded that the chapter which relates them furnishes the best and most apposite commentary on the Hundred-and-second Psalm.   I do not suppose that the psalm is Daniel's; yet it certainly gives expression to the very thoughts and feelings which filled his soul as the time fixed for the return drew near.

> 13. Thou shalt arise and have mercy upon Zion:
>   For it is time to have pity upon her; yea, the set time is come.
> 14. For Thy servants take pleasure in her stones,
>   And have pity upon her dust.
> 15. So the nations shall fear the name of the LORD,
>   And all the kings of the earth Thy glory.
> 16. For the LORD hath built up Zion,
>   He hath appeared in His glory.
> 17. He hath regarded the prayer of the destitute,
>   And hath not despised their prayer.
> 18. This shall be written for the generation to come:
>   And a people which shall be created shall praise the LORD.

The change which passed upon the Jewish Church during the Captivity can scarcely be exaggerated.   It was great, and it has been permanent.   In one of the prophecies of Ezekiel announcing the return, there was coupled with that announcement the promise of a deep and abiding religious reformation. "I will take you from among the nations, and gather you out of all the countries, and will bring you into your own land. And I will sprinkle clean water upon you, and ye shall be clean: from all your filthiness and from all your idols will I cleanse you.   A new heart also will I give you."†   The promise did not fall to the ground.   The people received a new heart, and were cleansed from their idols.   Since the Babylonish captivity the Jews have never once bowed the knee to graven images; and this decisive and final abandonment of idolatry may be taken as the index of a genuine religious

---

* Dan. ix. 2, 3, 17.   † Ezek. xxxvi. 24-26.

awakening at the time of the return. Bearing in mind the connection we have traced all along between seasons of quickened life in the Church and the production of new psalms, we are prepared to find that the century which followed the return was more fruitful of inspired psalmody than any other period, with the single exception of the age of David.

The RETURN has itself left its mark on the Psalter. The Eighty-fifth Psalm may, with great probability, be ascribed to this time. "The sons of Korah" are named in the superscription (it is the last occurrence of their name), whence we may infer that it was written by one of those Levitical singers, of the family of Korah, who, when the edict of Cyrus brought liberty, gladly took down their harps from the willows, and returned to resume the Lord's song in Zion.* The HUNDRED-AND-TWENTY-SIXTH is still more evidently a song of the exiles who came back. In common with the Eighty-fifth, it reminds us of the intermingled weeping and shouting at the laying of the foundation of the temple.† Laughter and tears chase each other on the cheek of the daughter of Zion; she rejoices to find herself in her own land again, but a touch of sadness checks her joy as she marks her impaired strength and beauty :—

    1. When the LORD turned again the captivity of Zion,
        We were like unto them that dream.
    2. Then was our mouth filled with laughter,
        And our tongue with singing:
        Then said they among the nations,
        The LORD hath done great things for them.
    3. The LORD hath done great things for us,
        Whereof we are glad.
    4. Turn again our captivity, O LORD,
        As the streams in the South.
    5. They that sow in tears shall reap in joy.
    6. Though he goeth on his way weeping, bearing forth the seed;
        He shall come again with joy, bringing his sheaves with him.

The first care of the people, after their arrival in the holy city, was to rear again the altar of burnt-offering and resume the daily sacrifice. Their second care was to set forward the

* The Korahites are named among those who dwelt at Jerusalem after the return (1 Chron. ix. 19-31).

† Ezra iii. 12, 13.

rebuilding of the temple. Their hands were greatly strengthened in this work by the prophesying of Haggai and Zechariah ;
and the same Spirit who moved those prophets to speak to the
people moved psalmists to cheer them with new songs. Who
these psalmists were we do not know. We cannot name one
of them. We cannot even determine with certainty the tribes
from which they sprang. In the absence of any hint to the
contrary, we can only conjecture that, like the greater number
of the psalmists after David, they belonged to the Levitical
families whose inheritance was the service of song in the
temple. We know from the history that, when the Levitical
singers were carried to Babylon, they neither abandoned the
honourable office transmitted to them from their fathers nor
suffered their right hand to forget its cunning. And they
mustered strong in the remnant who returned.* The sons of
Asaph, in particular, who had so pathetically lamented the desolation of the sanctuary, in the Seventy-fourth and Seventy-ninth
Psalms, are mentioned as having officiated in song when the
foundation of the Second Temple was laid. They were set, on
that high day, " with cymbals, to praise the LORD, after the
order of David king of Israel : and they sang one to another in
praising and giving thanks unto the LORD, saying, For He is
good, for His mercy endureth for ever toward Israel."† What
more likely than that these Levites, like their brethren the sons
of Korah, were employed by the Spirit in the composition of
new psalms—that they were psalmists as well as singers ?

Of the psalms written after the Return, a large proportion
were primarily designed for use in the Temple Service. So
strongly marked is this design, that, if they were collected into
one book, it might be entitled, " The Songs of the Second
Temple." Some of them are very short—the HUNDRED-AND-
THIRTY-FOURTH, for example :—

    1. Behold, bless ye the LORD, all ye servants of the LORD,
       Which by night stand in the house of the LORD.
    2. Lift up your hands to the sanctuary,
       And bless ye the LORD.
    3. The LORD bless thee out of Zion,
       Even He that made heaven and earth.

The HUNDRED-AND-SEVENTEENTH belongs also to this time. It

---

* 1 Chron. ix. 33 ; Ezra ii. 41.　　　† Ezra iii. 10, 11

is the shortest of all the psalms ; the shortest, but not the least weighty. It is cited in the epistle to the Romans * as celebrating beforehand the calling of the Gentiles. It invites the nations to unite with God's ancient people in worshipping Him. Since the invitation is addressed to all the nations, we may look upon it as truly a millennial song. Overleaping the intervening centuries, it anticipates the happy time when the fulness of the Gentiles shall be brought in :—

> 1. O praise the LORD, all ye nations ;
>   Laud Him, all ye peoples.
> 2. For His mercy is great toward us ;
>   And the truth of the LORD endureth for ever.
> Hallelujah !

These Temple Songs are not all short. Some of them are among the longest in the Psalter. The HUNDRED-AND-EIGHTEENTH may be named as a beautiful example. It is evidently a Temple Song ; and the critics, with great unanimity, ascribe it to the century after the Return. The precise occasion on which it was written is a point on which opinions differ ; some of the critics, like Ewald, holding that it was composed to be sung at the Feast of Tabernacles, when the remnant who returned commenced to offer again the daily sacrifice ; others, with Hengstenberg, connecting it with the laying of the foundation of the house ; while others, again, with Delitzsch, connect it with the solemnity of the dedication.† The truth seems to be that it is simply a Festal Psalm of the Second Temple, which may well have been sung on any or all of the occasions named by the critics, but is not to be restricted to any one in particular. It breathes a spirit of jubilant trust in the Lord, in the midst of infinite difficulties and perils. Its trumpet tones made it one of Luther's favourites. In the midsummer of 1530, when Melancthon was deputed to present the Confession of the Protestant Churches at Germany to the Diet of Augsburg, Luther was advised to abstain from any public appearance. Looking out from his retirement on the perils of the time, with " the sea and the waves roaring, and men's hearts failing them from fear," he found in the Hundred-and-eighteenth Psalm a word in season, and set his pen to work on an exposition of it.

---

* Chap. xv. 11.   † Ezra iii. 1-6, 8-13 ; vi. 15-22.

In the dedication, which is dated "*ex Eremo*, the first of July MDXXX.," he gives characteristic expression to his love for this portion of the Divine word. "Since I am obliged to sit here idle in the desert, and, moreover, must sometimes spare my head, and give it a rest and holiday from my great task of translating all the Prophets, I have gone back to my mine of wealth, my treasure. I have taken in hand my precious psalm, the *Confitemini*, and put on paper my meditations upon it. For it is my own psalm; which I delight in. For although the whole Psalter and the Holy Scripture is dear to me, my proper comfort and life, I have taken so to this psalm in particular that I must call it my own. Many a service has it done me; out of many great perils has it helped me, when help I had none, either from emperor, or king, or saint, or wise and prudent. I would not give it in exchange for the honour, wealth, and power of all the world, Pope, Turk, and Emperor. In calling the psalm mine own, I rob no man of it. Christ is mine, nevertheless He is the same Christ to all the saints that He is to me. Would God that all the world would challenge the psalm for their own as I do; it would be such friendly contention as scarce any unity or love could compare with. Alas, that there should be so few, even among those who might well do it, who will once say to the Holy Scriptures, or to some particular psalm, Thou art my book; thou shalt be mine own psalm!"* I make no apology for this extract. The work from which it is taken is inaccessible to the English reader; and besides, there are few things better fitted to make us feel what a treasure God has given us in the Psalms, than being put in mind of the strength and encouragement that have been ministered to saints in critical times by some of them which a person dwelling at ease might pass by.

The HUNDRED-AND-THIRTY-FIFTH and HUNDRED-AND-THIRTY-SIXTH Psalms belong evidently to the same class and period as Luther's favourite. One of them is a Hallelujah psalm; the other is remarkable for the recurrence, in every verse, of the refrain which makes itself heard so often in the songs of the Second Temple, "*for His mercy endureth for ever.*" Along with these we may class the five with which the Psalter ends. All

---

* Luther's *Saemtliche Schriften*, Walch's edition, Vol. V. p. 1704.

the five are Hallelujah psalms, that is to say, each of them begins and ends with the summons to *praise the Lord.*

Eighty years after the first band of exiles returned under Zerubbabel and Joshua, the remnant at Jerusalem had their hands strengthened by the advent of a fresh band, under the leadership of Ezra the priest. The title by which this distinguished man is constantly designated is the *Shopher,* or Scribe. When his name is first mentioned in Scripture, he is introduced to the reader as "a ready scribe in the law of Moses," who "had set his heart to seek the law of the Lord, and to do it, and to teach in Israel statutes and judgments."* He is the first well-defined example of an order of men who have never since ceased in the Church, men of sacred erudition, who devote their lives to the study of the Holy Scriptures, in order that they may be qualified to interpret them for the instruction and edification of the Church. It is significant that the earliest mention of *the pulpit* occurs in the history of Ezra's ministry. He was much more of a Teacher than a Priest. We learn from the account of his labours in the book of Nehemiah, that he was careful to have the whole people instructed in the law of Moses; and there is no reason to reject the constant tradition of the Jews, which connects his name with the collecting and editing of the Old Testament canon.† The final completion of the canon may have been—it probably was—the work of a later generation; but Ezra seems to have put it pretty much into the shape in which it is still found in the Hebrew Bible. When it is added that the complete organisation of the Synagogue dates from this period, it will be seen that the age was emphatically one of biblical study.

Of this also traces have been left on the Psalter. We see these in certain *historical* and *biblical* psalms. The age of Ezra, it is true, was not the first to be furnished with HISTORICAL Psalms. The Sixty-eighth and Seventy-eighth were written, the former by David, the latter by Asaph the Seer. But the longest of this class of compositions are undoubtedly to be traced to the century after the return. The HUNDRED-AND-FIFTH and HUNDRED-AND-SIXTH Psalms—those beautiful abridgments

---

* Ezra vii. 6-10.

† Comp. Westcott's article CANON in Smith's *Dict. of Bible* (p. 251, B).

in verse of the history of the chosen people—go together, and
the latter is wound up with the prayer,

> 47. Save us, O LORD our God,
>   And gather us from among the nations,
>   To give thanks unto Thy holy name,
>   And to triumph in Thy praise.

Of the DIDACTIC psalms we may, with much confidence,
attribute the HUNDRED-AND-NINETEENTH to the time of Ezra.   It
is throughout a meditation on the law of the Lord, the written
word.   It also is formed on a Davidic model ; for the royal
psalmist showed the way in every mode of psalmody.   The
Hundred-and-nineteenth may be regarded as an expansion of
the latter part of the Nineteenth, which is David's eulogy of the
written word.

We have followed the stream of inspired Psalmody in Israel
from Moses to Ezra, through a complete Millennium.   Did it
cease when Ezra and Malachi were gathered to their fathers ?
Or does the Psalter contain productions of the age of the
Maccabees ?   This is still a moot point among the critics.   The
question is one of very narrow dimensions, relating to not more
than three or four psalms at the utmost.   There are, no doubt,
a few critics who maintain that half the Psalter and more was
written in the Maccabean period ; but an opinion so violently
paradoxical needs no refutation here.   It would be unbecoming
indeed to reject so summarily the *whole* theory of Maccabean
psalms ; for to the limited extent just indicated, it has commended
itself to critics of the highest order, including Calvin himself.
That prince of commentators is inclined to refer the Forty-fourth,
the Seventy-fourth, and perhaps one or two more, to the persecut-
ing reign of Antiochus Epiphanes.   However, it is being more and
more felt that the grounds alleged for this are insufficient.   We
have already seen, for example, that even the Seventy-fourth (the
crucial instance) can hardly have been written after the Captivity.
And, on the other hand, there is much evidence to show that
the canon of the Old Testament must have been completed
soon after the death of Malachi.*   So strong is the presumption
on this ground against the existence of Maccabean psalms, that

---

* See the following Chapter.

nothing but positive and unequivocal proof of the existence of such psalms can countervail it; and no such proof has been adduced. We hold ourselves entitled, therefore, to conclude that the cessation of inspired Psalmody was contemporaneous with the cessation of prophecy, a coincidence in itself exceedingly probable.* When the Spirit of the Lord ceased to communicate new revelations to the Church, the harp of inspired psalmody ceased to sound. And, in this instance, the cessation was final. After an interval of four centuries, the Spirit of inspiration spoke again by the evangelists and apostles; but no Psalmist was raised up in the apostolical Church. The New Testament contains books of history, of doctrine, and of prophecy; but it contains no book of Psalms.

---

* The hypothesis of Maccabean psalms was maintained, after Calvin, by Venema, and more recently by Rosenmüller and De Wette. It was strongly opposed by Gesenius in 1816, on the ground of objections deduced from the history of the Old Testament Canon; and he has been followed not only by Hengstenberg and Keil, but by Ewald, Hupfeld, Dillmann, and others. In a much exaggerated form the hypothesis has been urged anew by Hitzig, Reuss, Wellhausen, and Kuenen, the three last-named being driven to it by the exigences of their favourite doctrine of the post-exilian origin of the Law of Moses. Comp. Steiner in Schenkel's *Bibel Lexicon*, Art. PSALMEN. There is a good resumé of the arguments *pro* and *con* in the *Speaker's Commentary*, vol. IV. p. 157.

CHAPTER VII.

*THE PSALTER AS A WHOLE, WITH ITS FIVE
BOOKS.*

THE reader who has followed with attention our sketch of
the History of Bible Psalmody can hardly fail to have
been struck with the length of the period over which the
history extends. The production of the psalms commenced
with Moses, and did not cease till the final cessation of Old
Testament prophecy—more than a thousand years after Moses
laid down his pen. This is a very wonderful fact, and one that
has scarcely received the attention it deserves. The harmony
of doctrine and sentiment from first to last is so perfect, that
one is apt to forget that the Psalms range over a space of time
not less than that which separates this year of our Lord 1886
from the year in which King Alfred set himself to translate the
Psalter out of the Latin into the vernacular of the young
English kingdom. The earlier half of the period, it is true,
made but a slender contribution. The Ninetieth Psalm was the
only one composed during the centuries between the exodus and
the anointing of David. But if we leave those centuries out of
view, there still remain other six centuries, every one of which
has left its impress on the Psalter in new songs,—a period as
long as that which separates the Europe of to-day from the
Europe of Thomas Aquinas and the Crusades—a full century
longer than the time that has elapsed since John Wyclif first set
forth the Word of God in the English tongue. "Old Hundred"
is about the oldest piece of English devotional poetry now in
use, yet the Ninetieth Psalm was more than three times as old
before the last of the psalmists fell asleep. This brings strikingly into view a feature which distinguishes the psalms from all
the other Scriptures. We call them the Book of Psalms, but it
is evident that they do not constitute a Book in the ordinary

sense of the word. They are rather a Treasury or Magazine, into which was gathered a whole literature. The Psalter is the authorised Collection of the Divine Songs of the Hebrew Church.* And how suggestive, let us note in passing, is the circumstance that, although the Psalms are the offspring of so many minds dispersed over so many centuries, there is not a jarring note in them. There is endless variety, but there is no contradiction. The feelings they utter and the views of truth that underlie them are in perfect harmony from beginning to end. This may well be taken as one proof of their divine and supernatural inspiration. In no other literature extending over centuries is so perfect a harmony found; and it would have been impossible in this, if the Psalmists had not been "men who spake from God, being moved by the Holy Ghost." †

From what has been said it is plain that, if the Psalms had been engrossed, in the order of their date, on the margin of the long roll of the Old Testament Scriptures, they would have been seen to run parallel with the rest of those Scriptures, all along, from the Pentateuch to the books of the three minor prophets who ministered in the Persian period. Some useful purposes would be served if the psalms whose dates are known were occasionally exhibited after this fashion, in juxtaposition with the contemporary annals and prophecies. An arrangement of this kind might do for the Old Testament history what the Gospel Harmonies have done for the life of our Lord. One thing it would make apparent to every eye. It would show that the *chronological* order has not been followed in arranging the Psalter. The "Prayer of Moses," which, according to the arrangement suggested, would have stood first, is in fact inserted near the middle of the collection; whereas a group of psalms which, having been written by David, would have come in among the first, are not inserted till near the end. This is a feature of the Psalter that can hardly have escaped the notice of any careful reader. It suggests the inquiry, Have the Psalms been arranged on any discoverable plan? If so, what is the plan? When were they arranged, and by whom? In a word, what

---

* "The Psalter is not (as De Wette thought) a Lyrical Anthology of the Hebrews, but the Hymn Book of the Hebrew Church, originally and primarily designed for use in the Public Worship of God."—Moll, *Der Psalter*, p. 2 (1869).
† 2 Pet. i. 21.

have the critics ascertained regarding the collection as a whole? The subject which these queries bring up presents many features of general interest, and I propose accordingly to devote to it the present chapter. Having formerly passed in review the principal facts that have been ascertained regarding the composition of the several psalms, I propose now to state as briefly as possible the facts relating to the Psalter as a whole.

The first fact that claims notice is the DIVISION OF THE PSALTER INTO FIVE BOOKS. This division has now at length been made patent to all, in the Revised Version. The gain is so obvious that one can only marvel that our older translators (and indeed translators generally) should have failed so long to bring it into view. They could not be ignorant of its existence, for it has all along been noticed by the critics, both Jewish and Christian. The ancient rabbins saw in the Five Books of the Psalter the image of the Five Books of the Law. This way of looking on the Psalms as a second Pentateuch, the echo of the first, passed over from the rabbins into the Christian Church and found favour with the early fathers. It has commended itself of late also to the acceptance of good expositors. Thus Dr. Delitzsch calls the Psalter "the congregation's five-fold word to the Lord, even as the *Thora* is the Lord's five-fold word to the congregation." * The notion is anything but a mere fancy; and its existence from ancient times shows that the five-fold division attracted early notice. Probably the neglect of it by the older translators was due to an impression that it was of no importance. The characteristics of the several books which will come before us immediately will show that in that case they were mistaken. Anyhow it is certain that the psalms are really distributed into Five Books; and the fact can be verified from any translation. The arrangement is as follows:—

Book First, Psalms i. to xli. inclusive.
Book Second, Psalms xlii. to lxxii.
Book Third, Psalms lxxiii. to lxxxix.
Book Fourth, Psalms xc. to cvi.
Book Fifth, Psalms cvii. to cl.

We shall have to notice afterwards some more recondite

---

* *Comment.* II. 382.

features of distinction among the subordinate collections. For the present, it will be a sufficient voucher for the five-fold division to point out that the compiler of the Psalter—Ezra, or whoever he was—*has appended to each book a brief doxology*, and has in this way denoted, as by a landmark, the point at which one book begins and another ends. Thus, at the end of the First Book (Ps. xli. 13) we find the following :—

> Blessed be the LORD, the God of Israel,
> From everlasting and to everlasting ;
> Amen, and Amen.

The close of the Second Book (Ps. lxxii. 18-20), besides being distinguished by a note of another kind, is adorned with the longest and most beautiful of these doxologies : —

> Blessed be the LORD God, the God of Israel,
> Who only doeth wondrous things :
> And blessed be His glorious name for ever,
> And let the whole earth be filled with His glory.
> Amen, and Amen.

A similar ascription of praise, but much shorter (at Ps. lxxxix. 52), separates the Third Book from the Fourth :—

> Blessed be the LORD for evermore.
> Amen, and Amen.

It will, of course, be understood that it was not merely to serve the purpose of landmarks that these doxologies were set down where we find them. They form an integral part of the Psalter, and were intended for use in the public worship. Possibly they were sung by themselves ; more probably they were sung along with the several psalms, very much as the *Gloria Patri* is chanted in the Churches that are accustomed to chant the psalms. We are reminded of this by the terms of the Fourth doxology (Ps. cvi. 48), where the people are invited to take part in ascribing glory to the Lord :—

> Blessed be the LORD, the God of Israel,
> From everlasting even to everlasting.
> *And let all the people say, Amen.*
> *Hallelujah !*

The Fifth Book is not furnished with a formal doxology, like the other four, which may be due in part to the circumstance that there was no need of anything to mark the end of the last book; but it is still more satisfactorily accounted for by the character of the Hundred-and-fiftieth Psalm. It is, in effect, a doxology from beginning to end. For not only does it begin and end with *Hallelujah*, but every one of the intermediate lines is an exhortation to *Praise the Lord.*

It is no small loss that in the Metrical Versions, as in the prose of the Authorised Version, the true character of these beautiful formulas of praise has been so completely overlooked. They have been translated as if they were part and parcel of the particular psalms which happen to stand last in the respective books; whereas they are not related to those psalms more than to any of the rest. For instance, the doxology at Ps. lxxxix. 52 belongs alike to all the psalms of the Third Book, and ought not to be treated as if it were merely the last verse of the psalm to which it is adjoined. It ought to be set forth in such a shape as would admit of its being sung as a separate formula of praise, or in connection with any other psalm.

The question now presents itself, WHEN AND BY WHOM WERE THESE FIVE BOOKS COLLECTED AND ARRANGED? Or, to put the question in modern phrase, Who was the Editor, and when was his work performed? This is not a vain question. It is one which the analogy of some other books of Scripture encourages us to put. It is known, for example, that the Book of Proverbs, although it is entitled *The Proverbs of Solomon, the Son of David, king of Israel*, was not put into its present shape by Solomon, or for a long while after his death. Certain chapters near the close are stated by the sacred editor to have been collected and engrossed by "the men of Hezekiah king of Judah." * Let us inquire, then, whether any similar information is forthcoming with regard to the collection and arrangement of the Psalms. What has been ascertained or reasonably conjectured on the subject?

One thing is certain, that *the Psalter must have been put into its present shape about the time of the prophet Malachi*, four hundred years or thereby before the Christian Era. Let such facts as the following be weighed. Our Lord and the

---

* Prov. xxv. 1.

Apostles were accustomed to speak of " the Book of Psalms," citing it by that title just as we do.* No well-informed person can doubt that the book they had in their hands was just the Psalter which has come down to modern times. To be sure, it is likely enough that, if we could compare the copies then in circulation with our own, there might be found some trifling discrepancies. For instance, in those ancient copies what is now the *second* psalm may have been marked the *first;* the preceding psalm being treated as a kind of preface to the whole collection. According to the reading favoured by most of the recent editors, the apostle's quotation, in Acts xiii. 33, from the Second Psalm is introduced with the words, " As it is also written in the *First* Psalm." This reading is rejected by Westcott and Hort and by the Westminster Revisers; yet the frequency of its occurrence in the Fathers seems to show that, in their time, copies of the Psalter were in circulation in which the numbering of the psalms began with the Second. Possibly there might be other discrepancies of the same kind. In this matter of enumeration, the ancient manuscripts and translations differ, here and there, both from our printed Bibles and from one another. But variations like these do not affect the substance of the sacred text; and I repeat that the Psalter of the apostolic age was just the Psalter we possess. Even in the apostolic age it bore the marks of antiquity. One proof of this, out of many, is furnished by the history of the Septuagint. That famous version of the Old Testament, executed at Alexandria in the third and second centuries before Christ, presents certain features which show that the Psalter, in its present shape, must have been an old book even in the days of the learned Alexandrian Jews.† On this and similar grounds, a large proportion of the ripest scholars of the present age, including Ewald, Hupfeld, and Bleek, as well as Hengstenberg and Westcott, are strongly of opinion that the Psalter must have been put into its present shape not later than the beginning of the fourth century before Christ. On the other hand, there are facts which forbid our going further back than the date thus reached. There is, for instance, the decisive fact, already ascertained, that a considerable number of psalms were

---

* Luke xx. 42; Acts i. 20.　　　　† See above, pp. 54 and 112.

composed by the contemporaries of Ezra the scribe.   The final
editing of the Psalter, then, may, with all confidence, be attributed to the learned scribes who are known to have flourished
among the Jews about the time of the cessation of prophecy ;
and there is no reason to doubt the substantial truth of the
Jewish tradition which ascribes the work mainly to the learned
and pious industry of Ezra himself.   Among the many items
of evidence which might be cited in corroboration of this
long-accepted conclusion, I shall mention only one.   The two
books of the Chronicles, which are the latest in date of the
historical books of the Old Testament, are understood to have
been compiled within a century or thereby of Ezra's time,—
possibly, indeed, by Ezra himself.   Even the genealogical tables
come down no later than about the close of the Persian Empire.
Now, if the reader will compare 1 Chron. xvi. 35, 36, with
Ps. cvi. 47 and the doxology which follows, he will see that
the Fourth Book of the Psalter must have been in existence,
and the termination of it marked off, as it still is, by the
doxology, *before* the Chronicles were compiled.   We hold ourselves entitled then to date the editing of the Psalter from the
age of Ezra.*

This point ascertained, other questions crowd in upon us.
Did the psalms exist only in a dispersed condition till Ezra
collected them ?   Did he find them scattered up and down
among the people, like the Proverbs of Solomon which the men
of Hezekiah copied out ?   Or, is there not reason to think that
he found in the hands of the Levites and the Congregation
minor collections of an older date ?   If so, can any of these be
identified with one or more of the Five Books, the final editing
of which was his work ?   These are questions that cannot be

---

* See 2 Maccabees ii. 13, "Nehemiah . . . founding a library [or forming
a collection of books], gathered together the writings concerning the kings, and
the writings of the prophets, and those *of David*, and the epistles of the kings
concerning the holy gifts." (The passage being unintelligible in the old English
version, I translate from the Greek, with the aid of De Wette's German.) The
information deducible from the statement here made regarding Nehemiah's biblical
labours does not amount to very much.   However, the historical data available for
the period are so scanty, and wild conjecture has been so busy, that one is glad to
get hold of any scrap of direct testimony.   One thing is plain.   The writer looks
back to the age of Ezra as a time when the sacred Scriptures, including those of
David the king, were being diligently collected." Comp. Hupfeld, 1. 43 (2nd
Edition) ; Ewald, *Dichter*, I. 264.

answered with absolute certainty; nevertheless there are materials for probable conjecture.

It will be convenient to begin with the FIRST and SECOND Books. If we may affix an early date to any, it is certainly to these; for they consist, for the most part, of psalms we owe to David and his contemporaries, and contain more than three-fourths of all that we owe to them. At this point welcome assistance is afforded by the note at Psalm lxxii. 20, "*The prayers of David the son of Jesse are ended.*" So long as the five-fold division of the Psalter was neglected, this note gave nothing but perplexity to the commentators. Augustine and his master Ambrose of Milan, finding it standing in their Psalters between the Seventy-second and Seventy-third Psalms, took it for part of the title of the latter, and tortured their ingenuity to divine its import. Calvin saw that the note is retrospective; but, not having observed its position at the end of a Book, he thought it pertained exclusively to the psalm immediately preceding, and took it to mean that that psalm embalms the last prayers of the aged king. But he was at a loss to reconcile this with the two obvious facts, that the title of the psalm ascribes it to Solomon, and that quite a different poem is elsewhere preserved as "the last words of David."* This perplexity of the great Reformer is shared by the older Commentators generally. We get rid of it at once, by simply remarking the position of the note in question. It is set down after a doxology which marks the end of the Second Book. It has no special, or, at least, no exclusive reference to the Seventy-second Psalm. It either refers to the Second Book, or, more probably, to the First and Second together.

This point settled, the meaning of the note begins to appear. It cannot mean that all David's psalms are contained in the two first Books; for the remaining Books contain eighteen that bear his name. Neither can it mean that the two first Books contain none but David's; for Asaph, Solomon, and the sons of Korah are all represented. The true explanation is to be sought in another direction. The circumstance that the psalms of David and his contemporaries were written and given out to be publicly sung in the worship of the Lord implies that there must have

---

* 2 Sam. xxiii. 1.

been some collection of them made at an early time for the use of the Levites and others.* A remarkable diversity in the use of the divine names (presently to be adverted to) divided them into two classes. The collection, accordingly, consisted of two books. These are, substantially, the first two books of the present Psalter; and the note under consideration means simply, that with it the *Collection of Divine Songs* ends. That they are styled "the Prayers of *David*" ought not to seem strange to us, who so constantly speak of the entire body of divine songs as *the Psalms of David.* The proportion of psalms strictly David's, in the two first books, is certainly much larger than in the complete Psalter. With regard to the *place* at which this note is introduced, it is to be observed that the practice of the ancients in affixing titles differed from ours.† To the Hebrews it would not seem strange to find the title of their Psalm Book at the end, in the shape of a retrospective note. The close of Job's colloquy with his three friends, the close of the prophetical discourses of Jeremiah, and the close of the Sacrificial Directory which occupies the first seven chapters of Leviticus, are all three distinguished by notes precisely similar.‡ This view of the matter is corroborated by the circumstance that the First and Second Books do not contain a single psalm that can reasonably be dated after the reign of Hezekiah; the Forty-fourth is the only one that is doubtful and, even in regard to it, the weight of evidence is in favour of an early date.

Of the Forty-one psalms contained in the First Book all but four are marked as David's; the four which do not bear his name § are all anonymous, and circumstances are not awanting which suggest that some of them also may be from the royal psalmist's pen. The Second Book is largely indebted to other pens. Eight psalms are ascribed to the sons of Korah, one to Asaph, one to Solomon; but here also the major part is David's.

---

* According to Ewald (*Geschichte d. Volkes Israel*, Vol. III. 387), a collection, of which traces are discernible in the Psalter, must have existed in Solomon's time.

† Our practice in this matter, it may be remarked, is quite modern. For several generations after the invention of printing, much of the information which it is now the custom to give on the *title-page* was given in a "colophon" at the end of the volume.

‡ See Job xxxi 40; Jer. li. 64; Lev. vii. 37, 38.

§ Psalms i., ii., x., xxxiii.

Eighteen bear his name, and of the three that are anonymous, it is probable that some are his. Respecting the *time* when this double collection was made, I will not venture on any more definite conjecture, than that it may have been under one of the earlier kings of David's house. In the history of Hezekiah's reformation, it is related that "the king and the princes commanded the Levites to sing praises unto the LORD *with the words of David, and of Asaph the seer.*" * From this we gather that there was a collection of psalms put into the hands of the Levites. The "copying out" of such a volume is exactly the kind of labour we should expect from "the men of Hezekiah." † This collection of "the words of David and of Asaph" has not unnaturally been identified by some with the First and Second Books of the Psalter. But considering the fact that these contain only one Asaph-psalm, while the next Book begins with eleven bearing that name, it is more probable that the men of Hezekiah found "the prayers of David" already collected, and that what they did was to add to them some of the psalms which now constitute the Third Book.

The distinctive features of the THIRD Book can be described in a sentence or two. It opens with a series of eleven "psalms of Asaph." ‡ Then come four Korahite psalms, with one of David's psalms § in the midst;—the only psalm bearing his name in this Book. It closes with a psalm of Ethan the Ezrahite. The Book contains several psalms that had come down from the reign of David; but the greater number belong to the reigns of the later kings or to the Captivity, and one, the Eighty-fifth, seems to be a song of the exiles who returned. These facts point to the period immediately succeeding the return from Babylon as the date of the completion of this book.

As for the two remaining books, the FOURTH and FIFTH, it seems evident that they were compiled contemporaneously, and by the same person. They are not distinguished from each other by those strongly marked features which separate them from the other three, and those three from each other. So much of a piece are they, that Ewald ‖ thinks that, from the Ninetieth Psalm to the end, there is but one book; and it must

---

* 2 Chron. xxix. 30.   ‡ Psalms lxxiii. to lxxxiii.
† Prov. xxv. 1.   § Ps. lxxxvi.
‖ *Dichter*, I. 267.

be admitted that the division into two is only justified by the
doxology between the Hundred-and-sixth and Hundred-and-
seventh Psalms. Here also we would fain know who was the
compiler, and on what principles he performed his task. A
full discussion of these points would oblige us to plunge into
the general history of the Canon, and must not be attempted.
I will only repeat what was stated before, that although the
finishing touch was certainly not given to the Old Testament
Scriptures until a good while after the death of Ezra, there
is no sufficient ground to reject the constant tradition of the
Jewish Schools, which attributes the collecting of them to that
prophet. The special work for which God raised him up was
that of the Scribe. No doubt he was something more than a
Scribe. His name is honourably enrolled in "the goodly
fellowship of the prophets," by whom God spoke to the fathers
and communicated to the Church the written word. But the
special service to which God called him was not so much the
writing of new books, as the gathering together of all the
sacred writings and the marshalling of them in fit order, with
the insertion of additional matter here and there, so as to make
the successive books dovetail into one another; in a word,
the *editing* of the Old Testament. By the good hand of his
God upon him, he happily accomplished this great task, insomuch that, when the last of the prophets fell asleep, the people
of God possessed the Hebrew Scriptures very much as they are
found in our printed Bibles.* Considering the number of the
psalms and their great variety of subject, authorship, and date,
we may be sure that Ezra found the editing of them not the
least difficult part of his task; and we have already found
reason to judge that it was finished before that of some of the
other sacred books.

The plan he pursued in this part of his work can be traced
with considerable certainty. The psalms not included in the
three previously existing books were sixty-one in number.
These were carefully arranged in various groups, and at the
head of this entire appendix was placed the Ninetieth Psalm,
the song of the Church in the wilderness. As the psalms thus
added, if written out without a break, would have made a book

---

* See Prideaux, *Connection of Old and New Testament,* I. 316–348 (at the year
449 B.C.), and the writers on the Canon.

twice as long as any of the others, they were divided into two by the doxology at the end of the Hundred-and-sixth.

Ezra's labour would be facilitated by the circumstance that the psalms which constitute the Fourth and Fifth books had been, some of them, gathered previously into minor collections. For an example, it is enough to refer to a remarkable group of psalms, eight in number, inserted near the end of the last book.* They are ascribed to David and present a marked contrast to their neighbours, both in their superscriptions and contents ; and one may reasonably conjecture that they came down from the age of David in each other's company. In several of them, particularly the Hundred-and-thirty-ninth and the Hundred-and-forty-fifth, we recognise poems wrought throughout of the finest gold of inspired psalmody, and specially dear to the hearts of all the faithful. Another group claims particular notice, the fifteen SONGS OF ASCENTS.† These undoubtedly form a class by themselves, a psalter within the Psalter. Respecting their special design, there has from the first been a singular diversity of opinion. The title common to them all, "A Song of Ascents," or " of the goings up," was no doubt meant to tell us something on the subject, but unfortunately is itself capable of diverse interpretations. According to an ancient Jewish tradition, they take their title from the circumstance that they were sung by the Levites, at the Feast of Tabernacles, on a certain " *ascent*" of fifteen steps, leading from the court of the women to the court of the men, in the Second Temple. This interpretation found considerable favour at one time, but is now set aside with general consent. There is more feasibility in another, according to which the title is descriptive of a certain *style of composition* found in these psalms, a certain gradually progressive rhythm of thought and expression. An example will bring out this peculiarity better than any description. The Hundred-and-twenty-fourth Psalm will suit our purpose as well as any other :—

> *A Song of Ascents; [a Psalm] of David.*
> 1. If it had not been the LORD who was on our side,
>   Let Israel now say ;
> 2. If it had not been the LORD who was on our side,
>   When men rose up against us.

---

* Psalms cxxxviii. to cxlv.   † Psalms cxx. to cxxxiv.

3. Then they had swallowed us up alive,
   When their wrath was kindled against us :
4. Then the waters had overwhelmed us,
   The stream had gone over our soul :
5. Then the proud waters had gone over our soul.
6. Blessed be the LORD,
   Who hath not given us as a prey to their teeth.
7. Our soul is escaped, as a bird out of the snare of the fowlers :
   The snare is broken, and we are escaped.
8. Our help is in the name of the LORD,
   Who made heaven and earth.

It would be vain to make light of a theory which is still supported by critics of such fame as Gesenius and Delitzsch ; yet it seems a fatal objection that this style, to which the title is supposed to refer, is not found in *all* the fifteen Songs of Degrees, and is found elsewhere. Ewald has revived a third explanation which was adopted by some of the early Fathers, namely, that the *goings up* to which these psalms relate were the journeyings of the exiles from the land of their captivity to the place of their fathers' sepulchres. The word is undoubtedly used elsewhere in this sense.* The Lord had promised that " His ransomed should return and come to Zion *with songs*," and it may well be believed that the bands who went up with Zerubbabel cheered the toilsome way with the music of psalms. When God brings home His ransomed, He loves to hear them sing as they go. A fourth explanation has found more acceptance than any of the rest, especially in recent times, being adopted by Herder, Hengstenberg, and Hupfeld, as well as by Mr. Perowne and a host of others at home. According to it, the psalms in question were sung by the people at the "goings up " to Jerusalem, year by year, to the solemn feasts. This explanation can very well be combined with the one last mentioned ; for the wayfarers who returned from Babylon with songs would naturally sing the psalms which had usually been sung by the companies who went up to the annual feasts. It adds a new charm to these beautiful psalms to think of them as the songs God provided for His wayfarers,—the Pilgrim Psalms.

It must be confessed that the account now given of the compilation of the Five Books of the Psalter leaves unanswered some questions we would fain put. For example, how did it come

---

* Ezra vii. 9 ; Heb., and margin of the English Versions.

to pass that so many of the earlier psalms are found in the later books ? This, it must be admitted, is not what we should have expected. Yet in some cases—in that of the Ninetieth Psalm, for example—even this admits of explanation. Examining the genealogies in the early chapters of the Books of the Chronicles, we find that, when the Chronicles were compiled (which was a considerable time after the return from Babylon), there were still extant in Israel some domestic records belonging to a period as far back as the sojourn in Egypt. Thus in 1 Chron. iv. 21-23 there is a notice regarding the family of Shelah the son of Judah, drawn from sources not extant in the earlier books of the Old Testament and which doubtless suggested the quaint note of the Chronicler, in passing, that " these are ancient things."* It is rather surprising that historical fragments which rank among the oldest in the Old Testament should have been transmitted to us only in the latest of the historical books ; but the fact being so, it ought not to seem incredible that the oldest of the Psalms should be found at the head of the latest-gathered of all the collections of psalms. Nor is the case of the psalms of *David*, found in the Fourth and Fifth books, so perplexing as it might seem. The Psalms are not arranged chronologically, but in groups of two or more, distinguished by some common character. Thus, in addition to the fifteen " Songs of the Ascents," which, it is to be observed, have been gathered together from every period of psalmody, there is a group of Songs of the Millennium ;† there is a group of *Hodu* or *Confitemini* psalms, each beginning with the invitation to " give thanks unto the Lord ;"‡ and there are two groups of *Hallelujah* psalms.§ This being the scheme according to which the Psalms are marshalled, it is not unlikely that the Psalms of David now standing in the three later Books stood originally alongside of their contemporaries in the First and Second, and were afterwards shifted to their present place, that they might stand side by side with later psalms of kindred character. This conjecture I cannot help regarding as far preferable to the theory advanced by certain critics, who, dating the psalms

---

* According to the Revised Version, " And the records are ancient."
† Psalms xcvi. to c.
‡ Psalms cv. to cvii.
§ Psalms cxi. to cxvii. and cxlvi. to cl.

according to the place they occupy in the earlier or later Books
of the Psalter, deny that any of those in the later books are
from David's pen, and cast discredit on the superscriptions
which attribute so many of them to him. It would be easy to
prove that, of these late-placed psalms, several are as certainly
David's as any in the whole Psalter.

Before concluding this account of the Fivefold distribution of
the Psalms, it will be necessary to point out CERTAIN REMARK-
ABLE FEATURES DISTINCTIVE OF THE SEVERAL BOOKS.

Foremost among these is *the variation observable in the use of
the divine names.* That the reader may be in a position to
understand what follows, I must explain that in the Hebrew of
the Old Testament the names of God most commonly employed
are two—ELOHIM, constantly rendered *God* in the English Bible;
and JEHOVAH (or *Yaweh,* for the right pronunciation is uncertain), which, except in the few places where it is left untranslated,
is uniformly rendered LORD. When so rendered, it is apt to be
confounded with another title, *Adonai,* signifying *lord,* in the
sense of *master, ruler, prince.* To obviate, in some measure
this confusion, the word LORD, when it stands for Jehovah, is
printed in capitals. It is to be noted, further, that there is
something very remarkable in the way in which these divine
names are employed in the earlier Scriptures, especially in
Genesis. Thus, in the *first* section of Genesis,* the name *God*
(*Elohim*) is exclusively used; in the *second* section, the Book
of the "generations of the heavens and of the earth,"† the two
are generally used in combination, "the LORD God" (Jehovah-
Elohim); in the *third* section, "the Book of the generations of
Adam,"‡ the two names are used indifferently; and so on, the
usage varying in the successive sections. I simply call attention to these facts; it would be too great a digression to attempt
to explain them here.

Reflecting on what has been stated, the reader will observe
with interest that a similar variation in the use of the divine
names is found in the several Books of the Psalter. Thus, in
the First Book, *Jehovah* occurs 278 times, *Elohim* only 48
times, or, including Ps. viii. 5 as rendered in the Revised

Gen. i. 1-ii. 3.   † Gen. ii. 4.   ‡ Gen. v. 1.

Version, 49 times. In this Book, the latter title occurs, for the most part, in places where the former would have been inadmissible.* In Book II. the proportion is reversed, *Elohim* occurring 198 times, *Jehovah* 33 times. In Book III. the two names are used in about equal proportions, or, to speak more accurately, the Book is made up partly of psalms in which *Elohim* predominates, and partly of psalms in which *Jehovah* predominates; in 60 places the former name is used, the latter in 45. In Books IV. and V. the name Jehovah is almost exclusively employed. To these interesting facts attention was called, apparently for the first time, by Dr. Delitzsch, in a Latin treatise which he published forty years ago.† Their importance has been universally recognised. Among other things, they go a certain way towards explaining the division into two Books of what is believed to have been the original Psalter (viz., Psalms i.-lxxii. inclusive); the former of the two Books consists of psalms in which the name JEHOVAH prevails, the latter of psalms in which *Elohim* prevails.‡

How is this remarkable way of using the divine names to be accounted for? A century has hardly elapsed since the subject, in its relation to the Old Testament generally, first attracted the attention of the learned; only forty years since the facts, in relation to the Psalter in particular, began to be carefully noted; yet theories not a few have already been elaborated, some feasible, others not feasible at all. One,

---

* For example, Psalms ix. 17; xiv. 1; xix. 1; xxii. 1, 2, 10.

† *Symbolæ ad Psalmos illustrandos isagogicæ* (1846).

‡ I am indebted to the Rev. John Urquhart for having called my attention, in an article in the *British and Foreign Evangelical Review* for April 1882, to certain errors on this subject in the former edition. It seems that, like Dr. Perowne, I had trusted too implicitly to the figures as given by Professor Delitzsch. A young friend, who is a learned and accurate Hebraist, has furnished me with the following table, exhibiting the results ascertained by a careful examination of the Hebrew :—

NAME.	BOOK I.	BOOK II.	BOOK III.	BOOK IV.	BOOK V.	SUM.
יהוה	278	33	45	112	267	735
אָדוֹן	15	18	16	3	11	63
אֱלֹהִים	48	198	60	17	28	351
אֵל	17	14	19	11	10	71

which made a great noise in this country a few years ago, is associated with the name of the late Bishop Colenso. He was of opinion that the Name which translators ancient and modern have been accustomed to veil under the more general title LORD was coined, perhaps by Samuel the prophet, shortly before David came to the throne, and that all the earlier Scriptures in which it occurs are spurious or hopelessly interpolated! The older name *Elohim* continued in use, however, for some time, and accordingly prevails in some of the psalms. After a while, it gave place entirely to the newer word. Thus the whole difficulty is resolved into an affair of chronology: the *Elohim* psalms are the earlier; the others are the later. A very simple theory, but refuted by the plain facts of the case. To name only two. The Song of Deborah in the book of Judges, the genuineness of which is recognised by nearly all the critics, of every school, celebrates the praises of God by His name JEHOVAH; whereas the Sixty-eighth Psalm, written long after and with marked allusions to Deborah's song, uses the other and less sacred title.* The theory most in vogue at present, while actuated by the same motive, takes up a position at the opposite extreme. It sees in the use of the name *Elohim* the token of a comparatively *late* date, and is inclined to rank the *Jehovah*-psalms as earlier in point of time than those in which *Elohim* predominates. This also is certainly erroneous. The key to the use of the divine names in the Psalms is not to be found in their chronological order.

Nevertheless there must be *some* reason—presumably some *wise* reason—for the usage in question. The appropriate use of the divine names in *Prayer* is an excellent aid to faith, helping the supplicant "to take encouragement in prayer from God only." It is no less excellent, we may be sure, in the kindred exercise of *Praise*. The psalmists certainly did not vary their usage by accident. It could not be by accident that David, after having given forth the Psalm as a Jehovah-psalm,

* Compare Judges v. 4, 5, "LORD, when Thou wentest forth out of Seir . . . the mountains flowed down at the presence of the LORD, even yon Sinai at the presence of the LORD, the God of Israel," with Ps. lxviii. 7, 8, "O *God*, when Thou wentest forth before Thy people . . . the heavens also dropped at the presence of *God*, even yon Sinai trembled at the presence of *God*, the God of Israel."

in giving forth a second edition of it substituted the name Elohim. Yet he has done this in the Fifty-third Psalm. And the same remark applies to the Seventieth in relation to the closing verses of the Fortieth. In all this there must have been some object; but what the precise object was, it is hard to tell. None of the explanations yet given will solve the whole problem. A partial solution is, however, to be found in the different import of the divine names. *Elohim* is the more general designation, being occasionally applied to angels, to magistrates, to heathen deities; *Jehovah* is the special and peculiar designation expressing God's covenant relation to His own Israel, and is absolutely incommunicable. This obvious diversity of import goes a considerable way towards explaining the remarkable manner in which the use of the names is varied throughout the Old Testament Scriptures generally. Thus it explains the exclusive employment of *Elohim* in Ecclesiastes, a book which, dealing with the problems lying on the border-ground between natural and revealed religion, could not so fitly use the more sacred name. It explains the repeated employment of the same title in the Fourteenth Psalm,* although it is a Jehovah-psalm. If it does not perfectly explain the existence of a whole Book of Elohim psalms, it at least furnishes a valuable contribution towards the solution of the difficulty.

There is another feature of distinction among the successive Books of the Psalter that must be noticed in conclusion. In the earlier Books *doctrine* predominates. The First and Second contain most of the psalms that embalm for our instruction the rich experience of David; and, as an introduction to these and to the whole body of sacred song, two psalms are set down which contain a kind of summary of the doctrine underlying all the rest—the First Psalm celebrating the character and blessedness of the godly, the Second the person and kingdom of Christ. In the Fourth and Fifth Books no thoughtful reader fails to remark the predominance of a certain *jubilant tone.* They contain the Millennial Psalms, the *Hodu* or Thanksgiving Psalms, and the Songs of Ascents. The Hundred-and-forty-fifth, which is entitled by way of eminence " David's Psalm of Praise," is reserved to grace the latter part of the Fifth Book; and that

---

* Thus at ver. 1, " The fool hath said in his heart, There is no *God*," it is plain the name *Jehovah* would have been inappropriate.

wonderful psalm is followed by five others which may be
described as a five-times-repeated acclaim of praise. To what
a height does this acclaim mount up in the last of the five !

> *Hallelujah !*
> 1. Praise God in His sanctuary :
>   Praise Him in the firmament of His power.
> 2. Praise Him for His mighty acts :
>   Praise Him according to His excellent greatness.
> 3. Praise Him with the sound of the trumpet :
>   Praise Him with the psaltery and harp.
> 4. Praise Him with the timbrel and dance :
>   Praise Him with stringed instruments and the pipe.
> 5. Praise Him upon the loud cymbals :
>   Praise Him upon the high-sounding cymbals.
> 6. Let everything that hath breath praise the LORD.
>   *Hallelujah !*

Is there not something instructive in this progress of thought
and sentiment in the Psalter ?   The Christian life is founded
on Doctrine. It is of indispensable necessity to the believer that
he have his mind imbued with the truth, with the whole truth
delivered by God's Holy Spirit in Scripture, above all, with the
truth respecting Christ Jesus.   But the knowledge and belief
of the truth are not the final attainment.   The heart must
be fired, as well as the understanding enlightened and the
conscience awakened.   The affections must be so thoroughly
brought under the power of the truth, so entirely captivated by
the knowledge of God and of Christ, that the soul shall soar
through the region of doctrine into the region of praise.   If I
am enabled so to profit by the doctrinal psalms that I shall,
by their help, rise to the heights of the psalms of praise, and,
with a heart all on fire, make melody to God in lofty Hallelujahs,
I shall take it for a sure token that I have known the grace
of God in truth, and that He is making me meet for the everlasting songs of the heavenly Jerusalem.

CHAPTER VIII.

THE POETICAL STRUCTURE OF THE PSALMS.

IT would be beside our present purpose to enter upon a general inquiry into the laws of Hebrew poetry. Nor is this needful. The subject has been elucidated in modern works of great merit, some of which are easily accessible. It is sufficient to mention the Prælections of Bishop Lowth, the publication of which, in the middle of last century, gave a great impetus to this kind of inquiry, both in this country and abroad. The importance attaching to the subject may be estimated by the fact that, as nearly as may be, one half of the scriptures of the Old Testament are poetical in their form. Of the poetical books, the Psalter is every way the most noteworthy. Accordingly, although the full elucidation of the characteristics of the Hebrew poetry must not be attempted in this place, the subject cannot be altogether declined. It may be possible, within the limits of a single chapter, to give such an account of the poetical structure of the Hebrew Psalms as shall convey a general conception of it to English readers, and shall aid them in appreciating the wisdom of God in the literary mould into which this portion of His word has been cast.

When a person familiar only with the classical poets or those of modern Europe takes up a volume that purports to consist of poetry, he expects to discover regular measures, rhymed or unrhymed, what Milton calls "apt numbers and fit quantity of syllables." Let it be observed, then, at the outset, that one who takes up the Hebrew Psalter with such an expectation will be disappointed. Scholars whose notions of poetry were drawn from the literatures of Europe found it so hard to understand how poems could possibly be constructed without regular measures, that it was long the favourite theory that the Hebrew poetry differed in no essential respect from that of other nations, but that, the ancient pronunciation of the language having been now irrecoverably lost, the key to the Hebrew metres was lost also.   Attempts innumerable were made, accordingly, from very early times, to show that the poetical Scriptures were written in the classical metres ; and it is not many years since learned men ceased (if they have altogether ceased) from exercising their ingenuity in the search for these familiar forms of poetical composition.   Even Lowth expresses himself doubtfully, rather inclining to the belief that, if only the true pronunciation of the language could be recovered, the measured cadences that prevail in European poetry would make themselves heard in the Hebrew Scriptures.   But the best critics are more and more settling down into the conviction that this is an error.   No doubt there is a certain harmony of sound audible in the poetical scriptures.   Imperfect as our knowledge of the pronunciation may be, there are passages which cannot be read aloud without reminding us, by their musical flow, that the prophets and psalmists are true poets—

> "Who feed on thoughts that voluntary move
> Harmonious numbers."

There are lines, here and there, which will even bear to be scanned after the manner of the classical metres.   But all this is insufficient to prove the prevalence of regular measures. Warm emotion always tends to express itself in language harmoniously modulated.   The "harmonious numbers" discoverable in the Hebrew are found quite as often in our Authorised English Version, which, of course, has no pretensions to metrical structure.   Besides being everywhere full of music, charming the ear like the chime of church bells, it occasionally falls into the measured tread of some noble metre.   In the Forty-seventh Psalm, for example, there is the fine hexameter,—

> God is gone up with a shout, the LORD with the sound of a
> trumpet :

and a little industry would bring to light many such lines.   It may be confidently affirmed that there is no more metre in the Hebrew Psalter than in the English translation.

There is another consideration, which, if it had been duly weighed, might have warned the critics that Hebrew poetry moves in an orbit of its own. So far as I have observed, the writers on this subject have failed to take note of the circumstance that the sacred volume contains specimens of the poetry of the Hebrews, in the *Greek* language. The songs in the beginning of Luke's Gospel—the Song of Mary, the Song of Zacharias, the Song of Simeon—are poems both in substance and in form ; the last notes of the Old Testament muse, uttered by way of welcome to the Sun of Righteousness, whose far-off advent she had so often foretold. It is unnecessary to decide here the controversy about the language in which they were originally delivered. An argument has been strongly urged in favour of the Greek : but, at all events, this is certain, that it is only in the Greek they have been authentically transmitted to us ; so that we must treat them as originals in their Greek dress. It is hardly necessary to add that they exhibit no vestige of measured rhythm. Their structure in the Greek is precisely what it is in the English Version.

> My soul doth magnify the Lord,
>   And my spirit hath rejoiced in God my Saviour.
> For He hath regarded the low estate of His handmaiden :
>   For, behold, from henceforth all generations shall call me
>   blessed.
> For He that is mighty hath done to me great things :
>   And holy is His name.
> And His mercy is on them that fear Him,
>   From generation to generation.
>
>   .   .   .   .
>
> He hath holpen His servant Israel,
>   In remembrance of His mercy :
> As He spake to our fathers,
>   To Abraham and to his seed for ever.

No one can fail to recognise in these lines a prolongation of the familiar notes of the poetical scriptures of the Old Testament. The *Magnificat*, although written in the language of the Greeks, is in every other respect a Hebrew poem. In its structure, as in its substance and spirit, it is an authentic specimen of the poetry of the Hebrews, as truly as the song of Hannah, from which indeed it is undistinguishable in a literary point of view. If these songs in Luke—the latest-born of the sacred poems—had been duly regarded, the learned men who have devoted so much pains to the search for metres in the poems of the Bible would not have gone off so long on a wrong scent.

Hebrew poetry, then, is destitute of metre. Are we to infer that it differs from prose merely in a certain more elevated style of thought and diction,—the lofty style into which a speaker or writer insensibly rises when his mind warms with a great and congenial theme ? That such a conclusion would be erroneous is plain, even in the case of the songs in Luke. They stand out in bold relief from the narrative in which they are imbedded. Every one reading aloud feels, on coming to the last verse of the first chapter of Luke, that it is a different sort of composition altogether from the Song of Zacharias immediately preceding ; and is sensible of a painful jolt if he have neglected to alter the tone of his voice accordingly. The songs in question differ also, quite essentially, from the lofty effusions in which the apostles and other prose writers of Scripture occasionally give vent to the reverent admiration with which the contemplation of the truth has inflamed their hearts, as, for instance in the prose poetry of the Eighth chapter of the Romans or the Eleventh of the Hebrews. Comparing the New Testament lyrics with those lofty utterances of the apostles, one feels that, much as they have in common, they nevertheless lie on opposite sides of the undefinable line which separates poetical composition from prose. There can be no doubt, therefore, of the fact, that Hebrew poetry, notwithstanding the absence of metres, can be distinguished from prose, as well as that of any other nation.

What, then, are the characteristics of Hebrew poetry ? By what features is the structure of the psalms distinguishable from the structure of European poems, on the one hand, and from prose composition, on the other ?

It is difficult to answer this question exactly, without going into inadmissible details. For our present purpose, however, it will be sufficiently correct to say, that Hebrew poetry is distinguished from prose by its *versified structure*, and from other poetry by this remarkable peculiarity, that, whereas the versification of all other nations is *verbal*, that of the Hebrews is *real*. Let the reader take up an English poem—*Paradise Lost*, for example—and mark how totally distinct is the progress of the verse from the progress of the thought. The end of the line does not necessarily represent a pause in the thought; more frequently the pause in the thought occurs somewhere else. In building his lofty measures, the musical flow of the words was the predominant consideration in the poet's mind. One who should translate *Paradise Lost* into another language would of course reproduce the sense as closely as possible, and would probably employ also the Heroic measure, but certainly he would not attempt to give line for line. In poems intended for congregational singing, a different principle no doubt comes into play. The writers of hymns and metrical psalms endeavour to introduce a pause in the thought wherever there is to be a pause in the singing; justly reckoning it a blemish if a sentence begun in one verse is carried forward into the next. But, after all allowance is made on this score, the general fact remains, that in our poetry the versification, so far from being dependent simply on the thought, is principally dependent on the words and sound. In Hebrew poetry all this is reversed. The pause in the progress of the thought determines the point at which the verse or line must end. The poetical structure fits so closely to the thought, that a Hebrew poem can be reproduced in any other language, verse for verse and line for line. This peculiarity has been well described by Bishop Jebb in the following remarks : " Hebrew poetry is universal poetry, the poetry of all languages and of all peoples : the collocation of words . . . is primarily directed so as to secure the best possible announcement and discrimination of the sense ; let, then, a translator only be literal, and, so far as the genius of the language will permit, let him preserve the original order of the words, and he will infallibly put the reader in possession of all, or nearly all, that the Hebrew text can give to the best Hebrew scholar of the present day. Now, had there been originally metre,"—he goes on to say,—" the case, it is presumed, could hardly have been such ; somewhat must have been sacrificed to the importunities of metrical necessity : the sense could not have invariably predominated over the sound ; and the poetry could not have been, as it unquestionably and emphatically is, a poetry, not of sounds or of words, but of things. Let not this last assertion, however, be misinterpreted : I would be understood merely to assert that sound, and words in subordination to sound, do not in Hebrew, as in classical poetry, enter into the essence of the thing; but it is happily undeniable that the words of the poetical scriptures are exquisitely fitted to convey the sense; and it is highly probable that, in the lifetime of the language, the sounds were sufficiently harmonious: when I say sufficiently harmonious, I mean so harmonious as to render the poetry grateful to the ear in recitation, and suitable to musical accompaniment, for which purpose the cadence of well-modulated prose would fully answer; a fact which will not be controverted by any person, with a moderately good ear, that has ever heard a chapter of Isaiah skilfully read from our authorised translation."*

We have said that the poetry of the Hebrews possesses a versified structure. This requires a few words of explanation; for those whose ideas of versification have been derived exclusively from the classics and modern poetry will no doubt be disposed to ask how there can be such a thing as verse when there is neither rhyme nor metre. The reader will by-and-by have ocular demonstration of the existence of verse in the Psalter. For the present, it will be enough to recall attention to the songs in the beginning of Luke, from which a citation has already been made. The verses quoted from the *Magnificat* were printed so as to exhibit the versification; and a glance will show that the division into verses and lines comes out, as it were, spontaneously. The point that claims special attention in this kind of versification is the relation subsisting between the several lines. In other poetry, the relation of the successive lines lies essentially in the harmony of the words; here it lies in the harmony of the ideas. The relation is in the sense, not in the sound; it is not *verbal*, but *real*, a relation not of *words* but of *things*. To express it, Lowth made use of the term *parallelism*, and perhaps a better one could not be found. It is to be observed, however, that the parallelisms are of many sorts. The two most easily described are the *synonymous* or *cognate*, and the *antithetic* parallelisms, so called because in the former the members of the verse are the synonyms, in the latter the antitheses of each other. Of the following three couplets from the *Magnificat*, the first exemplifies the *synonymous* or *cognate*; the second, the *anti-*

* Cited in Smith's *Dictionary of the Bible*, art. HEBREW POETRY.

thetic parallelism. The third exemplifies yet another sort, which occurs probably oftener than the other two put together—a parallelism which comes up in every variety of shape, especially in the more highly poetical psalmists and prophets, and which, for lack of a more definite title, has been called the *synthetic* or *constructive*.

I.

My soul doth magnify the Lord,
And my spirit hath rejoiced in God my Saviour.

II.

The hungry He hath filled with good things,
And the rich He hath sent empty away.

III.

He hath regarded the low estate of His handmaiden :
For, behold, from henceforth all generations shall call me
　　blessed.

In this exposition of the essential characteristics of Hebrew poetry, I have kept close to the track marked out by the best writers on the subject; my object being simply to exhibit, as lucidly as I could, the views now generally acquiesced in. It will, of course, be understood that everything which has been said applies as perfectly to the Psalter as to any other portion of the Scriptures. Should there be any reader who has failed to obtain a clear conception of the subject, or who is doubtful whether the view given is warranted by the facts of the case—doubtful, that is, whether the Hebrew poetry really possesses the versified structure that has been described—the most effectual way to remove all such misgivings and mis-apprehensions will be to adduce from the Psalter some well-defined illustrative examples. In doing so, I shall call special attention to the Acrostic or Alphabetical Psalms. I take these, not certainly because of any poetical superiority they may be supposed to possess over the other psalms—for, as a rule, they are the least poetical of all—but simply because their peculiar form brings out, with extraordinary distinctness and certainty, the principles that regulate the poetical composition of the Hebrews. The most remarkable of these psalms will be re-produced in English, as accurately as I can, in whole or in part. Anything further that requires to be said regarding the poetical structure of the psalms may be most conveniently presented in the way of commentary on the passages quoted.

The Alphabetical psalms—the *psalmi abcedarii*, as the Latin fathers called them—are nine in number ; * and I cannot help thinking it is a pity that, except in the single instance of the Hundred-and-nineteenth, no hint of their existence should have been suffered to appear either in the Authorised or the Revised Version. I will not take it upon me to affirm, with Ewald, that no version is faithful in which the acrostic is suppressed ; but I do think that the existence of such a remarkable style of composition ought to be indicated, even in the popular Versions, one way or another.† I believe, moreover, that useful purposes

---

* Namely, Psalms ix. and x., xxv. and xxxiv., xxxvii., cxi. and cxii., cxix , cxlv. Perhaps the two that stand first should be marked as doubtful, for the acrostic is very imperfect ; but an alphabetical arrangement is distinctly traceable, beginning with the first verse of the Ninth Psalm, and running on to the end of the Tenth, two verses generally going to each letter of the alphabet. The circumstance that the two psalms are linked together so as to form one acrostic poem will explain the fact, so unusual in the First Book, that Ps. x. is unfurnished with a super-scription. Doubtless, both psalms are from David's pen.

The Twenty-fifth and Thirty-fourth, both entitled Psalms of David, form a pair of another sort. They are identical in structure, each consisting of twenty-two verses, being one for every letter of the Hebrew alphabet, with this curious peculiarity (found in both psalms), that one letter—*Vau*—is awanting, and the number is made up by the addition of a supplementary verse, having for its initial letter *Pe*, which is thus used a second time.

The Hundred-and-eleventh and Hundred-and-twelfth constitute a third pair ; they exactly correspond, the one to the other, both in structure and sense.

The Thirty-seventh, a Davidic psalm, consists of forty verses. The acrostic is complete, two verses generally going to each letter. In the Hundred-and-forty-fifth, also ascribed to David, there are twenty-one verses—one for every letter except *Nun*, which, for some unknown reason, is lacking. The Hundred-and-nineteenth contains two-and-twenty stanzas of eight verses each. As the acrostic dominates in every verse, each letter occurs eight times over.

This acrostic way of writing is not confined to the psalms ; it is found both in the Proverbs and Lamentations. The Eulogy of the Virtuous Woman (Prov. xxxi. 10-31) is a regular acrostic of twenty-two verses. So also are the first and second chapters of the Lamentations. In the third chapter, which is likewise a long acrostic, there are three verses to each letter, making sixty-six in all. If it should seem strange that the heart-broken prophet restrained the flow of lamentations uttered because of the desolation of Zion within the limits of such an artificial kind of verse, it may be worth while to refer to our Poet-laureate's *In Memoriam.* The measure chosen seems at first intolerably monotonous for a long poem ; nevertheless the poet finds it well suited to express the sadness and desolation of his heart.

† The French Version, by Ostervald, indicates the acrostic in all cases, by setting down the names of the Hebrew letters, as our Bibles do at Ps. cxix.

are served by its being actually reproduced, at least in translations which are chiefly intended for use in the study or in Bible
classes. No doubt there are difficulties in the way. The
Hebrew alphabet differs widely from any of those now employed in Europe. Besides differences of a more fundamental
kind, the Hebrew has only twenty-two letters for our twenty-
six; and of the twenty-two a considerable number have no
fellows in ours. An exact reproduction of a Hebrew acrostic
in an English version is therefore impossible. The divergence
between the alphabets is so great that it seems vain even to
follow in English the *order* of the Hebrew letters. Dr. Delitzsch
has industriously made an attempt of the sort in his German
Version, but with little success. The only feasible method is
to omit from our alphabet the four letters that are of least
frequent use, and make the two-and-twenty that remain stand
for the two-and-twenty letters of the Hebrew.* This may not
suffice to meet the demands of a pedantic accuracy, but it will
exhibit to the English reader the structure of the original, which
is all that I propose.

It will be convenient to begin with the HUNDRED-AND-
ELEVENTH and HUNDRED-AND-TWELFTH Psalms; two very
short poems, dating apparently from the latest age of inspired
psalmody, and presenting such features of resemblance as to
leave no doubt that they came from the same pen. In structure they are identical; and this superficial resemblance is
designed to call attention to something deeper and more important. The subject of the one is the exact counterpart of the
subject of the other. The first celebrates the character and
works of *God;* the second, the character and felicity of *the
godly man.* In this connection the verses printed in italics
merit attention, exemplifying as they do the care with which the
psalmist has laboured to make the one psalm the reflection or
echo of the other. It would be doing great injustice to the
unknown writer to attribute this solely to the desire of awakening a certain pleasant surprise in the reader's mind. Literary
delight is never aimed at in Holy Scripture for its own sake.
In the present instance, the design is to illustrate the truth

---

* This is the plan followed in the volume entitled *Psalms chronologically
arranged: an Amended Version with Historical Introductions and Explanatory
Notes.* By Four Friends. Macmillan, 1867.

that the good man is the godly man—the God-like man, and thus to admonish us, that if we would shine in the beauty of true goodness, we must be ever looking on the Sun of Righteousness. It is when we, with unveiled face, behold the glory of the Lord, that we are changed into His image from glory to glory.

PSALM CXI.

Hallelujah !

1. A dore will I the LORD with all my heart :
   B oth in the meeting of the upright and in the congregation
2. C onfessedly great are the deeds of the LORD :
   D elighters in them search them out.
3. E *xcellent for honour and majesty is His work :*
   F *or evermore doth His righteousness endure.*
4. G *racious and compassionate is the Lord :*
   H is wonderful works hath He made to be remembered.
5. J ehovah hath given food to them that fear Him :
   K ept His covenant for ever.
6. L oudly hath He declared to His people the might of His deeds :
   M aking them to inherit the heathen.
7. N otable for truth and judgment are the deeds of His hand :
   O n all His commandments men may trust.
8. P *lanted firmly are they* for ever and ever :
   Q uestionless is their truth and uprightness.
9. R *edemption hath He sent to His people :*
   S *tablished for ever His covenant :*
   T errible and holy is His name.
10. U nderstanding pertaineth to all who obey the commandments :
    W isdom's beginning is the fear of the LORD :
    Y *ears without end shall His praise endure.*

PSALM CXII.

Hallelujah !

1. A ll-blessed is the man that feareth the LORD :
   B eing filled with delight in His commandments.
2. C ourageous in the earth shall be his seed :
   D escendants of upright men shall be blessed.
3. E *minent shall his house be for wealth and riches :*
   F *or evermore doth his righteousness endure.*
4. G ladsome light ariseth in the darkness for the upright :
   H *e is gracious and compassionate and righteous.*
5. J oy shall be to the man who showeth favour and lendeth :
   K nowing how to sustain his affairs with justice.
6. L o, he shall not be moved for ever :
   M emorable shall be the righteous man for ever.
7. N o evil tidings shall he fear :
   O n the LORD depending, his heart is fixed.

8. P *lanted firmly is his heart,* he shall not fear:
   Q uake shall he not, until he see [his desire] on his foes.
9. R *ichly hath he scattered: he hath given to the poor:*
   S *tand shall his righteousness for ever.*
   T ower aloft shall his horn with honour.
10. V exed shall the wicked be when he seeth it:
    W ith his teeth shall he gnash and melt away:
    Y *ea, the desire of wicked men shall perish.*

We may note, in passing, the light in which these psalms, as thus reproduced in an English acrostic, exhibit the exhortation with which they both open: " Praise ye the Lord !" In our two English Versions, the Authorised and the Revised, it stands as an integral part of each psalm ; but this cannot be reconciled with the obvious fact that in neither of them is it included in the alphabetical arrangement. The word (for it is one word in the Hebrew) occurs only in the later psalms, and would seem to have been a kind of formula with which certain Songs of the Second Temple were accompanied. It may be either translated, or simply transferred in its Hebrew form into our language. The circumstance that it is employed in the Hebrew form in the Book of the Revelation* may be urged as an argument for doing the same in the English Psalter.

Of the Bible acrostics, the most noteworthy, in every respect, is the Hundred-and-nineteenth Psalm. Its structure is exceedingly simple. The hundred-and-seventy-six verses of which it consists are alphabetical couplets, being eight for every letter ; so that there are twenty-two alphabetical stanzas, each containing eight couplets. Here also it is easy to discover the reason that led to the adoption of the alphabetical arrangement. The psalm is a meditation on God's law—the meditation of a soul, in the presence of the Lord and in communion with Him. In such a psalm, it is sententious wisdom rather than high poetry that we look for ; and a better vehicle for the aphorisms of sententious wisdom could hardly be imagined than that which is furnished by this acrostic. If, as we incline to think, it dates from the age of Ezra, it affords a welcome corroboration to the conclusion we reached on other grounds, that Ezra and his contemporary scribes were men of a very different stamp from those who bore the same title at a later period. We discern in them,

* Rev. xix. 1, 3, 4, 6.

no doubt, the familiar features of the scribe. The jots and tittles of the law are not despicable in their eyes. Raised up to edit the Old Testament Scriptures, they did the work well. But they had an eye and a heart that could appreciate the weightier matters of the law. They could look up from their studies about the letter of the word, and ejaculate to God such prayers as these, " Open Thou mine eyes that I may behold wondrous things out of Thy law ;" " My soul breaketh for the longing that it hath unto Thy judgments at all times ;" " Let my heart be perfect in Thy statutes, that I be not ashamed " (vers. 18, 20, 80).

It is curious and not uninstructive to mark the opinions expressed regarding this psalm by the modern critics. Most of them have remarked, and very justly, that, like the rest of the sacred acrostics, it seldom rises into the region of poetry ; being rather a versified meditation than a poem in the strict sense of the word. But some have gone further. Dr. Hupfeld, for example, whose Commentary on the Psalms, the fruit of the studies of a lifetime, is in many respects invaluable, ventures to charge it with " monotony and poverty of thought," and to contrast it disparagingly with the other psalms of the sententious or aphoristic order. An opinion like this is worthy of being put on record, as illustrating an observation which in these days it is very important that people should lay to heart and remember. A very able man, learned, painstaking, of excellent literary taste and honourable purpose, may nevertheless be utterly incompetent in matters lying within the domain of spiritual religion. The criticism of the learned Commentator reminds one of a remark in Augustine's preface to his Homilies on the same psalm. After mentioning that a sense of the difficulty attaching to a just exposition of this particular psalm had long deterred him from publishing anything on it, as he had done upon all the rest, he goes on to say : " Doubtless there are other psalms reputed difficult, the sense of which really is wrapped in obscurity. But then, whatever else may be difficult about them, this at least is plain, that they *are* obscure. Not so here. This psalm has an air of simplicity that might lead one to suppose that what it requires is a hearer or reader, not an expositor." Our rationalist critics, it is plain, have not mastered the difficulty so wittily pointed out by Augustine. They have not discovered that the psalm is deep. Its scope and probable history have been very well explained by Matthew Henry. "It seems to me," he observes, "to be a collection of (the psalmist's) pious and devout ejaculations, the short and sudden breathings and elevations of his soul to God, which he wrote down as they occurred, and, toward the latter end of his life, gathered out of his day book where they lay scattered, added to them many like words, and digested them into this psalm, in which there is seldom any coherence between the verses, but, like Solomon's Proverbs, it is a chest of gold rings, not a chain of gold links. And we may not only learn," he adds, "by the psalmist's example, to accustom ourselves to such pious ejaculations, which are an excellent means of maintaining communion with God and keeping the heart in frame for the most solemn exercises of religion, but we must make use of the psalmist's words, both for the exciting and for the expressing of our devout affections. What some have said of this psalm is true. He that shall read it considerately, it will either warm him or shame him." Those who have visited much among the godly in affliction will not hesitate to prefer this estimate of the Hundred-and-nineteenth Psalm to Dr. Hupfeld's. So far from being monotonous and jejune, it possesses quite a singular aptitude to refresh the souls of the weary. Its two-and-twenty clusters yield the wine of the kingdom as copiously as any to be found in all the Bible. The remark applies, although in a somewhat lower degree, to several other alphabetical psalms—the Twenty-fifth, the Thirty-fourth, the Thirty-seventh. If inferior to many others in poetical embellishment, they are inferior to none in the variety and richness of the aliment they minister to devout meditation.

The following is an attempt to exhibit in English a few stanzas of the Hundred-and-nineteenth Psalm. Those selected are the first, the second, and the last. They will suffice for illustrating the structure of the whole.

[ALEPH.]

1. **A**ll-blessed are the perfect in their way,
    Who walk in the law of the LORD.
2. **A**ll-blessed are they who keep His testimonies,
    Who seek Him with the whole heart.

3. Also they practise no iniquity:
   They walk in His ways.
4. All Thy precepts hast Thou commanded,
   That they may be kept with diligence.
5. Ah! Lord, that my ways were directed
   To observe Thy statutes!
6. Ashamed I shall not then be,
   When I have respect unto all Thy commandments.
7. At length will I praise Thee with uprightness of heart,
   When I learn Thy righteous judgments.
8. And I will observe Thy statutes:
   O forsake me not utterly.

[BETH.]

9. By what means shall a young man cleanse his path?
   By taking heed thereto according to Thy word.
10. Bending my whole heart I have sought Thee:
    O let me not err from Thy commandments.
11. Beneath the covert of my heart have I hid Thy saying,
    That I might not sin against Thee.
12. Blessed art Thou, O LORD;
    Teach me Thy statutes.
13. By my lips have I declared,
    All the judgments of Thy mouth.
14. Blessedness I find in the way of Thy testimonies,
    As much as in all riches.
15. Before mine eyes shall be Thy precepts:
    And I will have respect to Thy paths.
16. Blessed will I count myself in Thy statutes:
    I will not forget Thy word.

[TAU.]

169. Yield access into Thy presence, O LORD, to my cry.
     Give me understanding, according to Thy word.
170. Yea, let my supplication come into Thy presence;
     Deliver me according to Thy saying.
171. Yet shall my lips pour forth praise;
     For Thou wilt teach me Thy statutes.
172. Yea, my tongue shall speak of Thy saying;
     For all Thy commandments are righteousness.
173. Yield me help with Thy right hand;
     For I have chosen Thy precepts.
174. Yearned have I for Thy salvation, O Jehovah;
     And Thy law is my delight.
175. Yet to praise Thee, let my soul live;
     And let Thy judgments help me.
176. Yea, when I wander like a lost sheep, seek Thy servant:
     For I do not forget Thy commandments.

It will be admitted that the citations now made exhibit, in a clear light, several of the features mentioned as characteristic of the poetical structure of the psalms. For one thing, they make patent to every eye that the psalms, although destitute of both metre and rhyme, are regularly constructed poems, built up of distinct verses and lines. In the prose books of Scripture, the division into verses, as every one knows, was made at a late period, for the purpose of facilitating reference, and has no existence in the original structure. It is otherwise with the psalms. The 176 verses of the Hundred-and-nineteenth are marked as such in the plan of the poem. That each verse, again, is a *couplet* is equally plain, not only from internal evidence, but from a comparison of the Hundred-and-eleventh and Hundred-and-twelfth Psalms, where the acrostic is such as to distinguish the *lines* as well as the verses. The lines and the verses belong, therefore, to the original structure of the psalms. There may be room for difference of opinion regarding the expediency of printing the poetical books in the versified form, in Bibles intended for ordinary use. The Paragraph Bibles, in which this has been attempted, have not hitherto found general acceptance.* But the legitimacy of this kind of arrangement is indisputable. It is simply the exhibition to the eye of a structure which exists whether we exhibit it or not.

These Acrostics illustrate also the other characteristic of Hebrew poetry, according to which the versification is regulated by the thought rather than by the words. Let the reader look at them again, and he will find that every verse has a certain completeness in itself, and that it is constructed of two or more subordinate members, between which there prevails the parallelism formerly described. Sometimes the parallel members are synonymous or cognate, sometimes antithetic; more frequently they are related after a fashion more difficult to describe. This parallelism everywhere prevails. The lines of a Hebrew couplet are carefully constructed so as to correspond the one to the other. They are as artificially framed for that end as

---

* In the Revised Version the difficulty has been skilfully met by printing differently those parts of the Old Testament which, like Job, the Psalms, the Proverbs, and the songs found here and there in the historical books, exemplify the poetical structure in a strongly marked form, and those other parts, such as the Prophets, in which the poetical structure is more faintly marked. The former alone are printed like poetry ; the latter are printed like prose.

the several lines of an English couplet. The difference is, that in the English couplet the relation of the successive lines lies essentially in the sound of the words, whereas in the Hebrew couplet it lies in the sense.

The THIRTY-SEVENTH Psalm carries us a step further. It is an example of an acrostic of a freer order than any of the preceding.

A PSALM OF DAVID.

1. Against evil-doers fret not thyself,
   Neither be thou envious against them that work unrighteousness.
2. For they shall soon be cut down like the grass,
   And wither as the green herb.

3. But trust thou in the LORD, and do good;
   Dwell in the land and follow after faithfulness.
4. Delight thyself also in the LORD;
   And He shall give thee the petitions of thine heart.

5. Commit thy way unto the LORD;
   Trust also in Him, and He shall bring it to pass.
6. And He shall make thy righteousness to go forth as the light;
   And thy judgment as the noonday.

7. Dumb be thou before the LORD, and wait patiently for Him;
   Fret not thyself because of him who prospereth in his way,
   Because of the man who bringeth wicked devices to pass.

8. Eschew anger and forsake wrath;
   Fret not thyself, it tendeth only to evil-doing.
9. For evil-doers shall be cut off:
   But those that wait upon the LORD, they shall inherit the land.

10. For yet a little while, and the wicked shall not be:
    Yea, thou shalt diligently consider his place, and he shall not be.
11. But the meek shall inherit the land;
    And shall delight themselves in the abundance of peace.

12. 'Gainst the just the wicked plotteth,
    And gnasheth upon him with his teeth.
13. The Lord shall laugh at him:
    For He seeth that His day is coming.

.   .   .   .   .   .

The former examples furnished authentic information regarding the *verse*, with its subordinate members. This exhibits the *stanza*. In most of the recent translations printed so as to exhibit the versification, certain of the psalms will be found with the verses variously grouped into stanzas. Some commentators—Dr. Hengstenberg in particular—discover mystic allusions in the numbers (3, 7, 12, etc.) which they think predominant in these. It is a fancy which may be safely disregarded; but there is no doubt that the strophic arrangement itself rests on a firmer foundation. Hitherto, indeed, the translators have by no means reached agreement, in every instance, regarding the manner in which the verses ought to be grouped. The same psalm is arranged by one in one way, by another in another way; insomuch that the reader is apt to look with suspicion on the whole attempt, concluding that the critics have had no better guide than a lively imagination. The Thirty-seventh Psalm is valuable as showing that such a conclusion would be unwarrantable. In many cases it may be hard to decide which of several possible ways of distributing the verses into stanzas is to be preferred; but the letters of the Acrostic in this psalm are so many landmarks which, besides giving authentic indication of the division in this particular instance, favour the presumption that some similar arrangement will be found elsewhere. Among the non-Acrostic psalms there are many in which the strophic arrangement is so plain that one can hardly miss it. The Second is a good example, which I the rather quote that our illustrations may not be drawn exclusively from the Alphabetical psalms.

I.

1. Why do the nations rage,
    And the peoples imagine a vain thing?
2. The kings of the earth set themselves,
    And the rulers take counsel together,
    Against the Lord and against His Anointed, saying,
3. Let us break their bands asunder,
    And cast away their cords from us.

II.

4. He that sitteth in the heavens shall laugh:
    The Lord shall have them in derision.
5. Then shall He speak unto them in His wrath,
    And vex them in His sore displeasure:

6. Yet I have set My king
  Upon My holy hill of Zion.

III.

7. I will tell of the decree,
  The LORD said unto Me, Thou art My son;
  This day have I begotten Thee.
8. Ask of Me, and I will give Thee the nations for Thine inhe-
  ritance,
  And the uttermost parts of the earth for Thy possession.
9. Thou shalt break them with a rod of iron;
  Thou shalt dash them in pieces like a potter's vessel.

IV.

10. Now therefore be wise, O ye kings:
  Be instructed, ye judges of the earth.
11. Serve the LORD with fear,
  And rejoice with trembling.
12. Kiss the son, lest He be angry, and ye perish in the way,
  For His wrath will soon be kindled.
  Blessed are all they that put their trust in Him.

The reader will bear in mind the design contemplated in occupying so much space with the Alphabetical psalms. They are brought forward simply because of the singularly clear light in which they exhibit certain characteristic peculiarities of Hebrew poetry,—its versified parallels and its strophic arrangement. In other respects they are by no means the best examples of Hebrew poetry. The exigencies of the acrostic have in them something of the same effect which the exigencies of rhyme have in our poetry. In perusing the Hebrew, one is sensible of the same inversion of the sentences, and the same laborious seeking out of rare words for the purpose of getting the right initial letter, which hinder the easy flow of the sentences in an English acrostic. Let it be carefully observed that this feature is peculiar to the acrostics, and is therefore found only in nine out of the Hundred-and-fifty Psalms. In all the rest, the words are chosen and arranged with the single aim of clearly and vigorously expressing the sense; and the structure of Hebrew poetry is such, that a translator is able to render it perfectly into English without deviating from the natural order of the words. The Hebrew poems stand alone in all literature in this respect, that, with the partial exception of the acrostics, they can be transferred, *in their form as well as their substance,* in a literal translation, into any other language.

One may well trace in this the overruling hand and wisdom of Him who designed the Scriptures to be the fountain of spiritual light, and the rule of faith and life to all nations. Suppose the poetry of the Bible had been metrical, what would have been the effect ? One half of the Old Testament would have been to the Gentiles a fountain sealed. *Paradise Lost* turned into prose is *Paradise Lost* no more. There are literal translations of Homer and of Horace into fair English prose ; but, except for certain school-boy purposes, they are utterly useless. They convey no idea of the spirit of the Greek and Latin originals. Had the Prophecies of Isaiah or the Psalms of David been written in the classical measures or our modern rhymes, they would have fared as ill at the hands of the translators. They must have remained untranslated till some man of genius arose to execute a metrical version, which would have been but a paraphrase after all. As the case stands, David and Isaiah may be transferred, without material loss, into any language by any deft and scholarly pen. Not only their sense, but their manner and the characteristic felicities of their style, are reproduced, not unfairly, in our current English Versions.

BOOK II.

THE THEOLOGY OF THE PSALMS.

CHAPTER I.

PREDICTIONS RESPECTING OUR LORD IN THE PSALMS.

SOME of the older divines used to describe the Psalter as a Little Bible, and the title aptly denotes one of its most remarkable qualities. It possesses a certain internal completeness not found in any other single book in the sacred volume; being, indeed, a kind of lyrical and devotional reflection of the entire Bible. One consequence is, that it offers a singularly inviting field to the student who, employing the methods of modern Biblical Theology, makes it his business to collect the views of truth presented in the several portions of the divine word, and to marshal them in orderly array, according to the topics of the theological system. What is of more importance, the application of the methods of Biblical Theology may be confidently expected, in this instance, to yield results of the utmost practical value. This is evident from the very nature and design of the Psalter. It is the Book of Church Song,—the voice of the daughter of Zion, in which she utters all her heart. The diligent study of the views of truth and life that pervade such a book must needs shed a flood of light on almost every subject which is of vital importance in regard to true godliness.

What are the genuine characteristics of Scriptural piety? What influence ought it to exert on men in the various relations of life? What are the truths that constitute its proper aliment? These certainly are questions that come home to the business and bosom of every fearer of God; and where shall the materials for a satisfactory solution of them be found, if not in the authentic lyrics of the regenerate heart collected in the Psalter?

I am not sure that it would serve any valuable purpose to collect the teaching of the Psalms in regard to all the doctrines of the theological system.* At all events, the limits of the present work forbid the attempt. As the theme on which the harp of the psalmist descants most copiously is the Life of God in the soul,—not the truth respecting God, so much as the new life in man which is kindled and nourished by that truth,—I shall devote the greater part of the space at my command to the elucidation of the more salient features of Personal and Social Religion, as these are here reflected,— the religion of the Individual Soul, the religion of the Church, of the Family, of the State. No doubt the Psalms are full of truth respecting God—His being and attributes, His counsels, His works in nature, providence, and grace; and there are veins of instruction on these subjects which would richly reward a fresh exploration. On these and similar topics, however, I must limit myself to those passing notices which it may be possible to bestow while we are considering the various phases of the divine life in the soul. But there is one of the more objective or doctrinal topics so important in itself and so prominent in the psalms, as to demand a separate and most careful consideration at the threshold of these discussions. I refer to the teaching of the Psalms respecting the Lord Jesus Christ. The subject is many-sided. It will be necessary to begin with a vindication of the faith of the Church respecting the presence of Christ in the psalms. Certain important questions respecting what may be called the Theory of the Messianic psalms,—the principles, namely, according to which they are respectively to be interpreted of Christ,—will claim attention in the second place. These preliminary discussions—never more necessary than at the present time—will clear the way for our collecting into one view the whole teaching of the Psalmists regarding the Lord Jesus and His Work. Finally, considering how the sacred lyrics are, from first to last, pervaded with allusions to the Law of the Lord, it will be proper to devote a concluding chapter to

---

* The only work, known to me, in which this is attempted, is Kœnig's *Theologie der Psalmen,* Freiburg, 1857 (pp. 528); but the success is not such as to invite imitation.

the teaching of the Psalmists regarding Holy Scripture, or " the Word of God written."

That there are Psalms which are, in the strictest sense, predictive of the Lord Jesus Christ, has been the constant belief of the Church ever since the psalms were written. Till a comparatively recent period, all Commentators of note, whether Jews or Christians, accepted this belief without doubt. There might be differences of opinion as to whether this or that psalm was Messianic, differences also as to the true sense of particular passages ; but that there did exist Messianic psalms, strictly and properly so called, was assumed as incontrovertible. It is plain to every reader of the New Testament that the evangelists and apostles shared in this conviction, and that it can claim the sanction of the Lord Jesus Himself.

It might seem superfluous to discuss the grounds on which a conviction so ancient, so catholic, and so well established, rests. Yet I venture to think there is a call to do so at the present time. In common with the whole doctrine of the super- natural inspiration and divine authority of the Holy Scriptures, the belief in the existence of Messianic psalms has of late years been rejected by many. No one who looks into new books can have failed to observe, that on this subject ideas are extensively current which involve the utter rejection of the divine authority of the Psalter, and indeed of the whole Bible. These ideas are everywhere making themselves heard ; and they ought not to be left unnoticed by those who are set for the defence of the truth. I believe they can be satisfactorily dealt with. I believe, moreover, that the intelligent investigation of them will add fresh confirmation to the divine authority of both Testaments; that, in this instance, as in so many others, the overruling wisdom of God may be seen educing good out of the seeming evil ; and that He has suffered modern Rationalism to assail His Word mainly in order that He might take occasion from its assaults to shed fresh illustration on His truth. Believing this, I have a strong conviction that the discussion of the subject ought not to be confined to the Schools of Theology, but should be conducted in the audience of the entire Christian community.

The reader will kindly keep in mind the precise point in dis- pute. That in some sense there are Messianic elements in the

Psalter we need not stay to prove, nor even that there are entire psalms which, in some sense, have Christ for their subject. This is admitted on all hands. It is a fact indisputable and undisputed, that, for a long time before the birth of Christ at Bethlehem, the Jews were looking out for a Prince who was to arise to them from David's house. They were "looking for the consolation of Israel."* Many a Jew besides Simeon made it his constant prayer that he might not see death before he had seen the Lord's Christ and sung his *Nunc dimittis.* The expectation of a Redeemer and Prince had been growing in the hearts of the people ever since the Captivity, and may even be traced back through the preceding centuries as far as the accession of Rehoboam, that fatal era when the hopes of perpetual unity and dominion, which had been cherished during the brilliant reigns of David and Solomon, were extinguished by the final disruption of the kingdom. From that time till the cessation of prophecy, a long succession of predictions announced the advent of a Son of David, of the increase of whose government and peace there should be no end, upon the throne of David and upon his kingdom, to order and establish it for ever. † The last of the prophets left a charge to the people to look out for the sudden appearance, in the Temple, of the promised Prince, the Messenger of the Covenant. ‡ And the admonition so solemnly given was not neglected. When the Child Jesus was brought into the temple, Anna the prophetess could speak of Him to a company of Jews who were "looking for the redemption of Jerusalem." § It was impossible that announcements and hopes like these should fail to make themselves heard in the divine songs of the Hebrew Church. In not a few of the psalms, accordingly, the advent of the Son of David is hailed from afar, and the people are invited to expatiate on the peace and felicity which are to accrue from it, first to Israel and afterwards to the Gentiles. All this, I repeat, is not only indisputable, but undisputed. It is admitted, in substance, by the Rationalists as well as the orthodox. The infidelity of last century, standing superciliously aloof from the Scriptures, may have refused to acknowledge the existence of ancient Messianic hopes in Israel—may even have kept itself

---

* Luke ii. 25.   † Isa. ix. 6, 7.   ‡ Mal. iii. 1.   § Luke ii. 38.

in the dark regarding the existence of such hopes. But modern Rationalism moves in a different orbit. It prides itself on its scholarly acquaintance with the biblical writings ; it is loud in the praises of their literary merits ; it frankly recognises the vein of Messianic expectation that pervades their structure ; it has its own way both of explaining the origin of this rooted and steadfast hope, and of turning it to account in explaining (or explaining away) the miraculous features of the gospel narrative. Such being the present state of opinion, it is plain that a bare acknowledgment of the existence of psalms which look forward to the advent of Christ, and have in some sense been fulfilled in Him, comes far short of the acknowledgment that the Psalter contains articulate predictions respecting Christ, as the Church has always believed. At all events, it is unnecessary to spend time in demonstrating what no competently informed person, whether Jew or Gentile, would now call in question.

Christ, then, is in the psalms. But in what sense ? Is it only in the sense conceded by Rationalists? Is Christ's presence in the Psalms to be limited to this, that they gave expression to bright anticipations regarding a Prince and Redeemer, and regarding blessings to be procured by His reign for Jew and Gentile, which, in so far as they had any foundation, received their accomplishment in the Lord Jesus and the Christian religion? All this may be conceded without the recognition of the divine authority of the Old Testament, and indeed without the recognition of any such thing as a direct and preternatural revelation of the divine purposes with respect to Christ and the Church. It is, no doubt, gratifying to find that modern Rationalism has made so great an advance upon the shallow infidelity of last century, that it has awakened to some appreciation of the fine poetical feeling, the lofty ideas of personal and national duty, the high-toned and elevating hopes respecting the future destinies of the nations, with which the psalms are replete. But we cannot consent to accept its theory of the Messianic psalms as adequate or just. We believe and are sure that these psalms make representations respecting Christ and Redemption which were immeasurably above the reach of the natural hopes and presentiments of the Hebrew bards—representations of things which " eye had not seen, nor ear heard, which had not entered

into the heart of man," and which could not have been celebrated, as we see them to have been, unless they had been
supernaturally revealed by the Spirit of God—that Spirit who
" searcheth all things, yea, the deep things of God." * The
authors of the psalms were *seers* or prophets, and we believe,
with the apostle Peter, that " no prophecy ever came by the
will of man ; but men spake from God, being moved by the
Holy Ghost." † With the same apostle we believe that there
are things delivered regarding Christ in the psalms which, so
far from having been merely the bold conjectures of sagacious
men, were too high for the psalmists themselves to understand,
insomuch that they inquired and searched diligently into
the meaning of their own writings, " searching what time or
what manner of time the Spirit of Christ which was in them
did point unto, when it testified beforehand the sufferings of
Christ, and the glories that should follow them." ‡

This estimate of Old Testament prophecy the apostles learned
from their Master ; for He was accustomed to point out to
the disciples predictions concerning Himself in the law of
Moses, and in the Prophets, and in the Psalms—predictions
in accordance with which it behoved Him, as the Christ, to
suffer, and to rise again from the dead the third day.§ The
Lord Jesus having spoken thus, it may well be maintained
that the existence of true Messianic prophecy in the Psalter
deserves credit, on His testimony, from all who are not prepared
openly to reject the authority of His teaching,—would have
been entitled to claim credit, on His testimony, even if no
stringent evidence of another kind had been available. However, since we have to do with men who refuse submission
even to this pre-eminent authority, it is well to know that other
evidence is available—evidence so abundant and decisive as
to have amply warranted the conclusion that the Psalter
contains real predictions regarding the Lord Jesus, true *revelations* regarding His Person and Work, although we had not
possessed the Lord's own attestation of the fact.

To collect and marshal the whole body of available evidence
would require a volume. We must be content with two or three
of the more material items.

---

* 1 Cor. ii. 9, 10.   † 2 Pet. i. 21.   ‡ 1 Pet. i. 10, 11.   § Luke xxiv. 44-46.

I begin with the HUNDRED-AND-TENTH PSALM. I select it for many reasons,—for this among others, that there is no dispute of any consequence about the *translation.* Thus, most providentially, the considerations adducible on either side are, in this instance, of a kind regarding which any person of good sense may form an intelligent judgment.

A PSALM OF DAVID.

1. The oracle * of the LORD unto my lord,
     Sit Thou at My right hand,
     Until I make Thine enemies Thy footstool.
2. The LORD shall send forth the rod of Thy strength out of Zion ;
     Rule Thou in the midst of Thine enemies.

3. Thy people offer themselves willingly in the day of Thy power:
     In the beauties of holiness, from the womb of the morning,
     Thou hast the dew of Thy youth.

4. The LORD hath sworn, and will not repent,
     Thou art a Priest for ever,
     After the order of Melchizedek.

5. The Lord at Thy right hand
     Shall strike through kings in the day of His wrath.
6. He shall judge among the nations,
     He shall fill the places with dead bodies ;
     He shall strike through the head in many countries
7. He shall drink of the brook in the way :
     Therefore shall He lift up the head.

What, now, may we suppose is the drift of this poem ? It celebrates the majesty and prowess of some prince. Who may the prince be ? The traditional interpretation, which can be traced at least as far back as the beginning of the Christian era, refers it (as we shall see) very decidedly to Prince Messiah. This interpretation certainly does not bear on the face of it the unequivocal tokens of error ; on the contrary, it has for these eighteen hundred years and more been acquiesced in by the

---

* Or, "*Thus saith the* LORD *unto my lord.*" The phrase used is a remarkable one, found in only one other text in the Psalms (viz., xxxvi. 1), but of perpetual occurrence in the Prophets, being the formula in ordinary use for announcing a communication from God. It is important that the English reader should be apprised of this special solemnity of preface. Unfortunately, justice has not been done to it in the Revised Version.

generality of Bible readers, and thus comes before us with a presumptive token of credibility. It is totally repudiated by our modern Rationalists. The reasons which have moved them to do this, they are at no pains to conceal. It is not that the current *translations* have been found to be at fault. Nothing of the kind is alleged. The difficulties which exist do not affect the point in question. The Messianic interpretation is quite as much favoured by the version given by De Wette or Ewald, by Hupfeld or Reuss, as by our Authorised Translation. Neither is it that *some other prince* has been found to whom the words of the psalm, in their natural and obvious sense, are more applicable than to the Lord Jesus. On the contrary, the rejecters of the Messianic interpretation are unable to agree upon any other person to whom they may assign it. *The reason for rejecting the ancient interpretation is a doctrinal one entirely.* If the Lord Jesus be the person whom the psalm celebrates, the inference is inevitable that David must have known that the Son whom God had promised to raise up to him, to sit upon his throne, was a Person of super-human dignity,—his Lord as well as his Son. On the same supposition we are, in like manner, shut up to the admission that David foresaw the Sacrifice of the Lord Jesus, His Exaltation to the right hand of power, and the abrogation of the whole Levitical economy. Let it once be admitted that the oath of which the Psalmist speaks, the irrevocable oath, "Thou art a priest for ever after the order of Melchizedek," refers to the Messiah, the Son of David; and we know from the epistle to the Hebrews what will follow. The whole fabric of modern Judaism will fall to the ground. The Old Testament must be allowed to have borne witness to the cross; the Messiah behoved to suffer before He could reign; we live under a new priesthood, diverse from the Levitical and superseding it for ever. But these are conclusions as distasteful to the Rationalists as they have always been to the Jews; for, as Dr. Owen remarked with reference to the Polish and Dutch precursors of Rationalism two hundred years ago, these men "in their annotations on the Scriptures seldom depart from the sense of the Jews, unless it be where *they* are in the right." *

---

* *Exposition of the Hebrews*, i. 202 (Dr. Goold's Edition).

That there should have been a declaration of Christ's super-human dignity and everlasting priesthood, in a psalm written a thousand years before the sacrifice on Calvary, is what the Rationalists know they cannot afford to admit. Such a fact would explode the whole fortress of their unbelief. If the Hundred-and-tenth Psalm teaches what the epistle to the Hebrews deduces from it, it is a prophecy that cannot have come by the will of man ; there must have been supernatural revelations of God's mind to the Hebrew psalmists ; and there can be no more an absolute denial of the existence of Scriptures supernaturally inspired by the Spirit of God.

Let it be remembered, then, that the non-Messianic inter-pretation rests on the prior assumption that the things declared could not possibly have been known so long before the death of the Lord Jesus. They could not have been declared before-hand without a miracle ; therefore some other sense must, at any cost, be found for the psalm. Should any one think this explanation unfair or uncharitable, let him read attentively the long discussion of the point in Hupfeld's Commentary. Another argument, no doubt, is urged by that learned Com-mentator. He thinks that the martial and even vengeful acts attributed to the Prince of whom the psalm speaks—his smiting of kings and filling the countries with dead—are not in keeping with the character of our Lord, and betray an unchristian spirit. It is enough to say that the criticism applies to the Apocalypse quite as much as to the Hundred-and-tenth Psalm. The argument, therefore, needs no refutation. Indeed, it is only thrown in as a make-weight. The main pillar on which the rationalistic interpretation rests is the doctrinal assumption that a divine revelation is incredible, and that there is no such thing as supernaturally inspired Scripture. Dr. Hupfeld, who is a candid writer, frankly admits this. His words are these :—" It is certain that a prophecy of the Messias, in the *Christian* sense—that is, with the attributes which the New Testament assigns to Him on the ground of this psalm—is utterly incon-ceivable ; it cannot be reconciled with the historical and psycho-logical ideas and the hermeneutical principles which are recognised [namely, by the rationalist school of critics] in other cases. For (1) the sitting down at the right hand of the Father spoken of in the New Testament takes place in heaven, and is always connected with the resurrection and ascension of Jesus, *events of which no presentiment could have arisen in a single human heart;* (2) Christ's high-priestly or propitiatory office, as it is set forth in the epistle to the Hebrews, in opposition to the Mosaic priesthood, and as involving the abrogation of the Mosaic law, is so remote from the point of view of the Old Testament, so foreign to the Old Testament conception of the Messias, that *the thought of it could not possibly have come into the mind of any Old Testament psalmist or prophet."* I cite these remarks partly to show how directly the rationalistic doctrine contradicts that of the apostles regarding the possibility of the Holy Spirit's revealing to men things which never else could have come into their hearts, but principally that the reader may see how entirely the rationalistic interpretation of the Hundred-and-tenth Psalm has originated in a dogmatic bias.* It is proper to add that the interpretation has already been imported into this country. Dean Stanley has boldly adopted it in his *Lectures on the History of the Jewish Church,*† following in this, as in so many other particulars, the example of Ewald. It is important, therefore, that the real foundation on which it rests should be known.

The arguments by which the Messianic interpretation is sustained are mainly these three :—

1. *It is the only one that yields a tolerable sense.* Several alternatives have been proposed. For example, Herder and Ewald affirm that *David himself* is the prince to whom the psalm refers; that (like the Twenty-first Psalm) it is a prayer for the king, in which the people speak of him as their Lord, whose throne was exalted at the right hand of the Lord's throne in Zion, and whom God had invested with such honour in connection with His House, that he might be said to be a priest like Melchizedek, the ancient king of Salem. The theory can be dressed so as to wear a plausible air. But it will not bear examination. For (1) the psalm is in the title attributed to David's pen, and there is not a tittle of evidence pointing to any other writer. Would he have written of himself as "my Lord"? (2) The king is invited to sit at the right hand of

---

* Reuss's note is shorter and less outspoken, but to the same effect. (See *Psautier*, 1875, p. 337.)

† Vol. ii. 97, 98.

Jehovah, a manner of speech nowhere else in Scripture used with reference to an earthly king. The Jewish kings sat "on the throne of Jehovah," * as His representatives or vicegerents; not "at His right hand," as His fellows. (3) The people are represented as following the king in sacred attire, the beauty of holiness. That is to say, they follow him in holy sacerdotal vestments, as an army of priests;—a thing of which we find no trace in the history of David or any of the kings. It is Christ alone of whom we ever read that His "armies followed Him, clothed in fine linen, white and pure," when He went in righteousness to make war.† (4) The king is, by the oath of God, constituted a priest, "a priest for ever after the order of Melchizedek." One would think this at least cannot apply to David. But the exigencies of the rationalist theory are great, and a bold attempt must be made. Ewald, girding up the loins of his ingenuity, sets himself to show that in David's reign there was a remarkable conjunction of the royal and sacerdotal functions. How he goes to work may be gathered from the picture of David's administration which has been sketched by the elegant pencil of the late Dean of Westminster. Thus it is gravely related of the king, as if it were matter of ascertained fact, that "though not himself a priest, he yet assumed almost all the functions usually ascribed to the priestly office. He wore the priestly dress, offered the sacrifices, gave the priestly benedictions, walked round about the altar in sacred processions." ‡

---

* 1 Chron. xxix. 23.

† Rev. xix. 14.

‡ Stanley, *Lect. on Jewish Church*, ii. 96. There is a great deal more to the same purpose; indeed, the straining to make out this point gives a false colouring to page after page of the author's account of the reigns of David and Solomon. Thus, narrating the dedication of Solomon's Temple, he remarks (p. 220), "The king alone prays, sacrifices, blesses, consecrates. And, as if to keep up the memory of the day, thrice a year throughout his reign, on the three great festivals, he solemnly entered, not only the temple courts with sacrifices (2 Chron. viii. 13), but penetrated into the Holy Place itself, where in later years none but the priests were allowed to enter, and offered incense on the altar of incense (1 Kings ix. 25)." It is very doubtful whether the passage referred to in 1 Kings really means that the king burnt incense (see Keil *ad loc.*). It is certain that the law, excluding from the Holy Place all except the priest, is as old as Moses. But, not to insist on these details, it is surely too much to assume, as if it were a matter of course, that all the things the historian relates of Solomon must have been done by him in his own person. One would think that Solomon may have burnt incense in the same sense in which he slew the twenty thousand oxen; and it will hardly be con-

But all this is asserted without warrant from the sacred narrative. No doubt David is related to have "offered burnt-offerings and peace-offerings" at the bringing up of the ark; but that he did so with his own hand is no more likely than that Solomon, on a yet more solemn occasion, offered with his own hand the twenty thousand oxen and the hundred and twenty thousand sheep which he is related to have offered at the dedication of the House. David doubtless sings in the Twenty-sixth Psalm of "compassing God's altar;" but that is no more to be taken literally, than the prayer in the Twenty-seventh, that he might "dwell in the House of the Lord all the days of his life." As for the allegation that he wore the priestly dress, it is enough to say that the Ephod in which he arrayed himself at the bringing up of the ark was not the priestly robe so named; this was made of *byssus* (fine linen), whereas the king's was of ordinary linen—a sacred and festal robe, no doubt, but not peculiar to the priesthood.* This is not all. Let it be supposed, for the moment, that all these fancies about David's intromissions with the functions of the priesthood had been facts; let it be supposed that this man after God's own heart was accustomed to officiate often in rites which the law of Moses had so sacredly appropriated to the sons of Aaron, that Saul, for venturing to officiate in them on one solitary and pressing occasion,† was rejected, he and his house, from reigning over Israel; let it be supposed that he performed habitually, with high commendation, sacred offices like that for which Uzziah, when he attempted to perform it but once,‡ was sharply reproved and smitten on the spot with leprosy,—would all this have sufficed to vindicate the application to David of the oracle in the psalm? Such conduct might, perhaps, have

---

tended that he did that with his own hand. The truth is, that the only priest-like act he performed in person was the blessing of the people; and that, instead of being "the highest sacerdotal act" (p. 218), was not an exclusively sacerdotal function at all, but one which it was competent for any superior in age or station to perform.

* Samuel, although only a Levite and a mere child, wore an ephod when he ministered before the Lord as Eli's attendant (1 Sam. ii. 18). Comp. Vaihinger in Herzog's *Real-Encyclopædie*, Art. EPHOD; and the corresponding article in Smith's *Bible Dictionary*.

† 1 Sam. xiii. 9, 14.

‡ 2 Chron. xxvi. 16-21.

warranted the application of the priestly *title;* but certainly it could not have warranted the lofty and emphatic declaration: " Jehovah hath sworn, and will not repent, Thou art a priest for ever after the order of Melchizedek." The allegations so boldly made, if they had been true, would have amounted merely to this, that David exercised such priestly functions as belonged to all princes and heads of families under the patriarchal dispensation, before the Law restricted the priest- hood to Aaron and his sons—that he was a priest in the sense in which Abraham and Jacob were priests. But how far is this from answering to the grandeur of the oracle ! The king here addressed is constituted a priest *after the order of Melchizedek,* to whom Abraham, the patriarchal priest, paid tithe in token of homage, and from whom he was content to receive a benediction ; and the priesthood is confirmed by the irrevocable oath of Jehovah, and declared to be a perpetual priesthood. It shows how hard men are pressed when they can plead for the applica- tion to David of a declaration so far-reaching and magnificent.

After all, it is no wonder the rationalising interpreters fight hard for the identification of David with the priest after the order of Melchizedek—the throned priest of Zion ; for incredible as this is, it is less so than any other of the non-Messianic interpretations—than that of Hupfeld, who suggests (not without a misgiving) that the psalm celebrates *the dynasty* of David rather than any individual king; or than that of Reuss and others, who fancy that it celebrates one of the warrior- priests of the Maccabean family. The combination (so rare in history) of priestly office with warlike achievements which dis- tinguished the Maccabees lends a certain attractiveness to the last-named interpretation. But the objections to it are decisive. The psalm attributes to its hero the twofold glory of universal dominion at Jehovah's right hand and of everlasting priesthood combined with royalty. To have attributed such things to any one of the Maccabees would surely have been impious. It would have been absurd also. The Maccabees were priests by birth, and did not need to be either constituted or proclaimed priests by a divine oath. They were priests after the order of Aaron, not at all after the order of Melchizedek. Besides these interpretations, 1 do not know that there is any other worth notice, unless it be the wild notion of De Wette, that the psalm comes from the pen of some prophet who chose in this way to express his approval of King Uzziah's presumptuous invasion of the priestly functions! It is to shifts like these that learned and able men are driven when they abandon the natural sense of this great Messianic psalm.

2. *The ancient Jews unanimously understood the psalm to refer to the Messiah.* When our Lord * appealed to it to prove that David's Son was David's Lord, the Pharisees found nothing to answer, which plainly shows that, although the doctrine of the psalm may have been imperfectly apprehended, its Messianic character was universally allowed. If there had been any difference of opinion either as to David's having been the writer, or as to the Messiah's being the person whom the psalmist styles his Lord, the Pharisees would certainly have taken advantage of it to escape the edge of the question propounded to them. No doubt, when we come down to the middle ages, we find learned rabbins rejecting the Messianic interpretation; but Dr. Hupfeld states that some vestiges of it are found even among them, and that their sole motive for wishing to get rid of it was the desire to deprive the Christians of a silencing argument for the divinity and priesthood of the Redeemer. He testifies also that the interpretations they suggest are unusually far-fetched and inadmissible. It is always a presumption in favour of the Messianic interpretation of a passage in the Old Testament, if it can be shown that that interpretation prevailed among the Jews who lived prior to the birth of Christ. In the present instance, the presumption is greatly strengthened by the contents of the psalm, inasmuch as the sacerdotal character which it attributes to the Hope of Israel is not one which the Jews have shown any eagerness to attribute to Him. And it is worth remarking that, if the Rationalists were correct in thinking that the Old Testament Jews had no presentiment either of the superhuman dignity or the priestly office of the Messiah, this would simply invest with higher significance the indubitable fact of their having applied to Him the psalm in which these are so magnificently attributed to the promised King of Israel.

3. It need hardly be added that *the authority of our Lord and of the apostles* has sanctioned the interpretation we plead

---

* Matt. xxii. 43-45.

for. Not only are there quotations in the New Testament which indicate that the psalm was appealed to as a prophecy respecting the Messiah, but it so happens that this psalm is more frequently quoted and more largely reasoned from, than any other portion of the Old Testament Scriptures. Dr. Hupfeld himself remarks upon the fact, that the whole Messianic interpretation of the psalm may be collected from the places in which it is formally cited or tacitly alluded to in the New Testament.

Reference has already been made to our Lord's citation of the first verse.* It may be remarked that in calling attention to the truth taught in the psalm regarding His superhuman dignity, rather by putting a suggestive question than by a formal and explicit declaration, the Saviour was simply following His ordinary course. During His personal ministry, He dealt very sparingly in declarations regarding His Person and Sacrifice, especially in addressing mixed audiences. He chose rather to throw out remarks which set people's minds to work in the direction of the truth. Thus, in the present instance, He pointed out the remarkable circumstance that David, speaking of One who, he knew, was to be his Son, called Him his Lord. He left them to follow out for themselves the train of thought which that circumstance was fitted to suggest, and we need not doubt that some hearers would thus be prepared for the fuller declaration of the truth subsequently made. The same verse is quoted in the Pentecostal sermon of the apostle Peter : " For David ascended not into the heavens ; but he saith himself, The Lord said unto my Lord, Sit Thou on My right hand, till I make Thine enemies the footstool of Thy feet ; " and he adds, " Therefore let all the house of Israel know assuredly, that God hath made Him both Lord and Christ, this Jesus whom ye crucified." † The places in which allusion is made to the Father's invitation to Christ " to sit at His right hand till His enemies be made His footstool " are too numerous to quote. ‡

Still higher honour has been put upon the oracle in the fourth verse,—" Jehovah hath sworn, and will not repent, Thou

---

* Matt. xxii. 43 ; Mark xii. 36 ; Luke xx. 42.

† Acts ii. 34–39.

‡ The reader may refer for examples to 1 Cor. xv. 25 ; Heb. i. 13, viii. 1, x. 12, 13 ; Rev. iii. 21 ; Col. iii. 1 ; 1 Pet. iii. 22.

art a priest for ever, after the order of Melchizedek." Not only is it quoted as unquestionably an utterance of the Holy Spirit with reference to Christ, but it is a text from which the New Testament preaches, more than from any other text in all the ancient Scriptures. The central chapters of the epistle to the Hebrews—chapters more precious than gold for the elucidation they give of the Priesthood and Sacrifice of the Lord Jesus Christ —what are they but an extended commentary on this one verse?

Such are the reasons which have constrained orthodox commentators, with rare unanimity, to look upon the Hundred-and-tenth Psalm as in the strictest sense a Messianic psalm—a song which has for its theme the throned Priest in Zion, the Son and Lord of David, our blessed Propitiation and Lord, Jesus Christ. This interpretation has, from the first, been generally received in the Church; was sanctioned, in singularly express terms, by the apostles and by Christ Himself; was the only one current among the Jews prior to the Incarnation; and is not only an interpretation which the words of the psalm are fairly capable of, but is so imperatively demanded, that if it be rejected, the psalm refuses to yield any tolerable sense.

Before passing from this great Psalm, a word or two may be said regarding the *form* in which it sets forth the truth regarding Christ. It has been already remarked that, as a rule, it is not in the Psalter, but elsewhere, that we are to search for new revelations of truth—that the psalms are the authentic response of faith to God's revelations, rather than themselves the vehicle of those revelations. Such is without doubt the rule; but there are exceptions, and among these the Hundred-and-tenth Psalm is pre-eminent. Both in form and substance it is a new revelation, a prophecy respecting Christ, a divine oracle delivered in song. This is precisely what the psalm declares itself to be. Alone in the Psalter, it opens with a formula which is appropriated in Scripture to the use of prophets in publishing oracles entrusted to them by God. Justice has hardly been done to this either in the Authorised or the Revised Version. Most recent translators make the formula very emphatic—either " Jehovah's oracle to my Lord" (De Wette and Delitzsch), or "A revelation of Jehovah to my Lord" (Hupfeld).* When

---

* Comp. Dr. Cheyne's version, " *The oracle of Jehovah unto my Lord;*" and Segond's,"" *Parole de l' Eternel à mon Seigneur.*"

the Lord Jesus, in His reference to the psalm, describes David as calling Him Lord " *in the Spirit,*" there can be little doubt that He alludes to the peculiar form of this particular psalm. The contents verify the introductory formula. The psalm contains two distinct oracles—two declarations which, at the time of their publication, were revelations of new truth to the ancient Church, and not merely authentic echoes of truth elsewhere revealed. There is first, in the opening verse, the announcement of Messiah's Exaltation to the right hand of God ; and then, in the fourth verse, the memorable proclamation of His Royal Priesthood.

I have devoted what may appear a disproportionate space to the Hundred-and-tenth Psalm, because it seemed of importance to demonstrate, in one decisive instance, the existence of true Messianic prophecy within the Psalter. There is no other psalm in which the prophetically Messianic character is so unequivocally marked. Still, there are many which can be satisfactorily shown to speak of Christ ; and I know few subjects in the wide domain of biblical interpretation which better reward a serious study than that which is brought up by the questions, Which are the Messianic psalms ? and, In what sense are the respective psalms to be regarded as having Christ for their subject ? These questions will come up for careful consideration in the next chapter. Meanwhile, it may be possible, in a few sentences, to show that there are good grounds for accepting other psalms, besides the Hundred-and-tenth, as truly Messianic.

I will name three—the TWENTY-SECOND, the SECOND, the FORTY-FIFTH. These have been constantly sung in Christian congregations for these eighteen centuries ; and it may be affirmed without hesitation that if one could interrogate the faithful who have delighted to use their help in lifting up their minds to God, regarding the practical interpretation put by them upon the sacred words, they would answer with one accord, that they have been accustomed to interpret them of Christ and the Church. The arguments of rationalising critics have never been able to persuade Christian congregations that, in singing these psalms, they ought to look somewhere else rather than to Christ. Through all the centuries, devout souls have manifested a surprisingly harmonious feeling in this practical interpretation. The Twenty-second Psalm, as we learn from Augustine, was sung in the North African congregations at the Easter celebration of the Lord's Supper.   More than fourteen centuries have passed since the Vandals drowned those songs in blood; but a stranger who happens to look in upon a Scottish congregation on a communion Sabbath will be likely enough to find the psalm turned to the same holy and solemn use.   In these days of criticism, the query will be put, When the psalms are thus sung in Christian assemblies—sung by people who see in them Christ and no other—is their genuine sense preserved ?   Will the Christian thoughts that twine themselves around the words bear the scrutiny of a strict interpretation ?   The query will be put ; and, for my part, I welcome it.   There may, doubtless, be found many subordinate points in which the views of particular psalms current at particular times and in particular Churches will not bear rigid scrutiny ; but one may, without arrogance, offer to demonstrate that the Christian sense of such psalms as the three which have been named is also the genuine sense, and that no interpretation which *excludes* that sense will stand. We cheerfully admit that they may have had some other immediate reference, as, for instance, a reference to David himself, his wars and tribulations and conquests, or to Solomon in his glory.   It is well known that some commentators of excellent judgment have thought so.   I am not satisfied that, in the instance of these three psalms, any such reference can be made out.   But what I wish to remark is this, that the point is not a vital one, if, along with the immediate reference to David and Solomon, there be admitted a further and principal reference to Christ ; if, in other words, the inferior sense contended for is not held to exclude the higher Messianic one.

Of the Twenty-second Psalm, our venerable translators, following Calvin's example, remark that it is one in which "*David* complaineth in great discouragement."   But neither Calvin nor they would have thought of referring the psalm, ultimately or principally, to David.   It may well be doubted whether there is any direct reference to David at all.   It is certain that there is a reference to Christ ; that the proper design of the psalm is to set forth " the sufferings of Christ, and the glories that were to follow them."   Even rationalists like

Dr. Hupfeld have expressed astonishment at the coincidence, in minute detail, between its delineations and the circumstances of the Crucifixion.

The Second Psalm is not only applicable to Christ throughout and actually applied to Him in several New Testament texts, but was so commonly understood beforehand as having a prophetical reference to the Hope of Israel, that two of the names by which that Coming One was commonly known among the Jews were drawn from it. The title by which both the Jews and the Samaritans usually designated the expected Son of David was the MESSIAH, that is, the Christ, or Anointed One, and it was taken from this psalm. The King here celebrated is called, in the second verse, the Anointed of Jehovah—that is to say, "the Lord's Christ."* In the subsequent words, "Thou art my Son, this day have I begotten Thee," we see in like manner the Scripture which taught Nathanael to say, when he first recognised in Jesus the long-expected Christ, "Rabbi, Thou art the Son of God, Thou art King of Israel."†

The Forty-fifth Psalm is a Nuptial Song—the Epithalamium of some great King of Israel, who has set his love on a Gentile maiden, the daughter of a princely house, and is being united in marriage to her in his own palace. The glories of the King are first described, his superhuman beauty and gracious words, the everlasting stability of his throne, his martial achievements, and the mild equity of his administration. Then follows a description of the marriage. The Queen-Consort is at the King's right hand, in gold of Ophir ; she is conducted—she and her maidens—into the King's palace ; and the daughter of opulent Tyre, who has come to grace the day with her presence, brings in her hand a wedding gift. It is a song resplendent with the richest ornaments of oriental poetry. Respecting its ultimate and proper intention, there has been from the first an unfaltering consent among all devout readers. The opening verse,

My heart overfloweth with a goodly matter:
    I speak the things which I have made touching the King:
My tongue is the pen of a ready writer,

—this verse, I say, in their judgment, is strictly parallel to that of the apostle, "This is a great mystery : but I speak concerning Christ and the Church."‡ There are, no doubt,

---

* Luke ii. 26.   † John i. 50.   ‡ Eph. v. 32.

differences of opinion in regard to what may be called the *theory* of the psalm ; some understanding it to refer to Christ and the Church, directly and exclusively, while others think there is an immediate reference to Solomon (or some other Hebrew king) and his Gentile wife.   But this difference is immaterial, so far as our present purpose is concerned ; for those who think there is an immediate reference to an earthly marriage agree with the others in holding that there are many things in the psalm which, in their full and proper sense, apply only to Christ, and that it was designed from the first to lead men's thoughts to Him.

Is this received interpretation just ?   Certainly, if external authority is to be accepted as decisive in the matter, it cannot be called in question ; for, besides the general consent of the Christian Churches, the mystical interpretation is known to have been the one that prevailed among the Jews before the Christian era, and it is unequivocally sanctioned by the New Testament.*   But the same reasons which oblige the rationalising critics to impose some other than the Messianic construction on the Hundred-and-tenth Psalm find place here also ; and they endeavour, with one consent, to make out that this glorious Nuptial Song is nothing more than an earthly Epithalamium, the memorial of the marriage of a Jewish king with a Gentile princess.   How untenable this interpretation is might be shown by many arguments.   In the first place, there is much in the psalm that cannot, without violence, be applied to any one but Christ.   Take the sixth verse, for instance :

> Thy throne, O God, is for ever and ever:
> A sceptre of equity is the sceptre of Thy kingdom.

Surely the epistle to the Hebrews puts the most natural construction on these words when it cites them as having been spoken "unto the Son."   In answer to this, it used to be alleged that "God" (Elohim) is a title communicable to creatures, that it is repeatedly applied to magistrates, and might well be given to Solomon as a king.   The reply was not far to seek.   The title in question is never applied to any creature, whether man or angel, except in such a connection as excludes the possibility of misapprehension, certainly never in the unqualified

---

* Heb. i. 8, 9.

way in which it is used here. That device, accordingly, is now laid aside, and the Messianic sense is evaded by altering the translation. It is made to run thus, " Thy throne of God (or, thy God's-throne) is for ever and ever ; " according to which the meaning would be, " Thy throne, which is the throne of the Lord, on which thou sittest as His vicegerent, is for ever." So far as grammar is concerned, the translation is possible, and it is far from excluding the Messianic reference ; but it is harsh, and all the old Versions, from the Septuagint downwards, are against it. Dean Stanley—who, as usual, favours the non-Messianic interpretation—alludes to the verse as if it said of the king that "his throne is *like* the throne of God ; " * but that is a sense which none of the translations will yield.

Another consideration deserves to be mentioned. There is no example in the Psalter of a purely secular song. Church Songs alone are here in place. Not even David's name could procure for his Lament for Saul and Jonathan admission into the sacred collection. If the Forty-fifth Psalm celebrates the wedding of a Jewish king, and nothing else, it is the solitary exception to the rule—the only one of all the hundred-and-fifty psalms that is not a devotional composition. This is frankly acknowledged by Ewald, and involves him in great perplexity. Again and again, in the course of his learned disquisitions, the glaringly exceptional song comes in his way, and he does not know what to make of it. In one place, he throws out the desperate conjecture that it may have got into the Psalm Book by some oversight of an editor or transcriber ; but, finding no rest in this, he comes back to the supposition that the allegorical interpretation may be as old as Ezra's time, and that this may have led to the insertion. Why not take one short step more, and acknowledge that the allegorical interpretation is the true one ? Does not this, besides its other high recommendations, best accord with the lofty terms in which the Psalmist announces that his theme is to be "a goodly matter," and declares that it has so taken possession of his heart that his tongue is like the pen of a ready writer ? No other psalm is introduced after the same fashion. Is it credible that the one secular song in the Psalter should be adorned above all the rest with such a preface of eulogy ?

* *Lect. on Jewish Church,* ii. 199.

CHAPTER II.

A CLASSIFICATION OF THE MESSIANIC PSALMS.

THE epistle to the Hebrews opens with the statement that God's speaking to the fathers by the prophets took place " by divers portions and in divers manners ; " and to no part of the Old Testament does the remark apply better than to the Messianic Psalms. They all celebrate the Hope of Israel, but not after one and the same manner. There are some which, as we have seen, are in the strictest sense predictions regarding our Lord ; but there are others which cannot be so described, inasmuch as, although they speak of Him, He is neither their exclusive nor primary subject. The Eighteenth Psalm, for instance, is undoubtedly Messianic. Apostolic authority concurs with internal evidence in showing that the Person who speaks in it is Christ. Yet we know for certain that it is not predictive of Christ in the same high and exclusive sense as the Hundred-and-tenth. It was written by David in thankful commemoration of the kindness of the Lord, in delivering him " from the hand of all his enemies, and from the hand of Saul." Not only is there a superscription to that effect, but the whole poem is inserted in the history of David's reign,* as a document relative to the period. Such having been the origin and primary intention of the poem, the question will be asked, On what principle do you refer to Christ a song in which, as you admit, David speaks of himself, his dangers, his marvellous escapes, the eventual establishment of his throne and wide extension of his sway ? This is a perfectly fair question. Since it is a question, moreover, which crosses the path of every careful student of the Bible and is apt to cause serious perplexity, the discussion of it cannot be declined,

---

* 2 Sam. xxii.

although it brings up some points which are amongst the most difficult in the whole domain of biblical theology.

When we classify the Messianic psalms, according to the "divers manners" in which they severally speak of Christ, they arrange themselves into three principal groups. First, there is a large group, consisting of those in which Christ is present in the person of David or some other type ; then there is a smaller one, consisting of psalms which relate to Him directly and exclusively ; lastly, there is a group of undefined extent, consisting of psalms in which the person who speaks is "Christ mystical," the whole Church, the Head and the members together.

I. It will be convenient to begin with the psalms in which Christ is spoken of in the person of David or some other type : THE TYPICALLY MESSIANIC PSALMS.

It has often been observed that God's most perfect works are never accomplished by a sudden extemporised stroke of power. He delights to unfold His purpose in successive portions. This is seen in Nature. The geologist traces a constant progress, from the rudimentary forms of animal and vegetable life which have left their traces on the early sedimentary rocks, to the perfect forms which are the contemporaries of man. The human body, so fearfully and wonderfully made, in respect of which man is "the paragon of animals," was not altogether a novelty in creation on the day that the Lord God formed man from the dust of the ground. We can imagine that the only thing which an angelic observer would take notice of as altogether new was the lodgment of a soul—a personal intelligence—in a material tenement. Of the tenement itself all the leading features had been seen before, in one or other of the pre-existing animals. Those animals were therefore the *types* or *figures* of the race which was predestined to exercise lordship over them. This principle of progressive development pervades God's administration in the work of Redemption, not less extensively than in the material universe. Long before He sent His Son into the world, to offer up the great sacrifice and establish His kingdom, He had familiarised men's minds with the leading features of His Person and Work. During the centuries from the creation of Adam to the incarnation of Christ, the events which form the subject of the sacred history were so ordered as to be a gradual unfolding of the divine purpose respecting the predestined Redeemer.

This unfolding was accomplished by the twofold machinery of facts and oracles, the latter with the occasional accompaniment of symbolical institutions. On the one hand, there were divine Oracles,—direct and formal revelations of the mind and purpose of God. Such was the promise of the seed of the woman who should bruise the serpent's head. Such was also the promise of the seed of Abraham, in whom all nations should be blessed; the Ruler out of Judah; the Prophet like unto Moses. This succession of great oracles culminated at length in the promise made to David, that the Hope of Israel was to be his Son and the Inheritor of his throne. Running parallel to these oracles and their accompanying institutions, we can trace a long succession of Providential Events, which were a kind of real predictions concurring with the verbal predictions in the disclosure of the divine counsels. Thus the redemption from Egypt was designed to familiarise men's minds (and did familiarise them) with the idea of God's Israel as a community of emancipated bondmen,—bondmen who are emancipated, not by their own prowess but by the favour of God, that they may be a holy people to the Lord. To this day, when the Christian attempts to describe what he was by nature and what grace has made him, he insensibly makes use of forms of speech that originated with the exodus. The Old Testament is full of prefigurations of this kind,—precursive representations of the truth respecting Christ by means of analogous personages and dispensations. The types, then, were events, institutions, persons, so ordered by the providence of God as to bring out, clearly and impressively, the leading features of the eternal purpose which was one day to be realised in the person and work of the incarnate Son. It was by means of these types, quite as much as by the more direct and explicit medium of verbal revelations, that the mind of God was made known to the ancient Church, and presentiments of good things to come were awakened within its bosom.

All this bears directly on the problem before us in the Messianic psalms. For David, who was, by way of eminence, the Psalmist of Israel, was also, as we have seen, in his personal history and in his kingdom, the most distinguished of the types of Christ. In him men beheld the image of a just and wise prince, who, having grown up in an obscure town, was afterwards filled, in an admirable measure, with the spirit of kingly wisdom, and counsel, and might; a captain who, although he had been anointed by a prophet to be king over God's Israel, was detained for long years in the school of bitter humiliation, but who, when he was at length brought to the throne, achieved for his people deliverance from their enemies on every side, and subjugated the nations from the Euphrates to the border of Egypt. How distinctly, in these and a hundred other features, David and his kingdom prefigured Christ and His kingdom, and awoke presentiments regarding them in the hearts of God's people, no reader of the Bible needs to be told. His history, from first to last, was a kind of rehearsal of the sufferings and glory of Christ. When it is remembered that every step in David's chequered career finds its lyrical expression in the Psalter, it will be at once apparent that the Psalter must be full of Christ. One who gives a faithful description of the shadow must needs describe the substance which casts the shadow. The Paschal lamb having been a divinely ordered prefiguration of the Lamb of God, the law which ordained that a bone of him should not be broken is cited in the Gospel as a prophecy which spoke of Christ and which was fulfilled in the manner of His death.* The Psalms are full of prophecies of this sort regarding Christ—passages which, although, in the first instance, they speak of David and his kingdom, carry forward the mind to the person and kingdom of David's Son. Nor do these typically Messianic passages speak of Christ only by way of such unconscious and unnoticed prefiguration as took place in the offering of the Paschal lamb. There is no reason to suppose that Moses, when he wrote the law of the Passover, thought of anything but the literal ordinance. At least, there is no reason to attribute to him a distinct foresight of the manner of Christ's death, which he so exactly described. But it was otherwise with David. He knew that Christ was to be born of his seed and was to be a King after the manner of David, as well as a Priest after the manner

---

* Exod. xii. 46; John xix. 36.

of Melchizedek.   Accordingly, we find that, in the psalms which unfold his own experience, he is sometimes lifted above himself, and speaks in terms which, although they may perhaps admit of being applied to himself, are much more easily and naturally applicable to our Lord.   Thus the Eighteenth Psalm, the great song of thanksgiving for the mercies of his life, rises at the close into this strain :—

> 49. Therefore I will give thanks unto Thee, O LORD, among the
>   nations,
>   And will sing praises unto Thy name.
> 50. Great deliverance giveth He to His king ;
>   And showeth lovingkindness to His Anointed,
>   To David and to his seed, for evermore.

When these verses are quoted in the epistle to the Romans,[*] as a declaration, on the part of Christ, of His purpose to publish God's name among the Gentiles, the apostle is not to be understood as applying the words to Christ, by way of arbitrary accommodation.   No doubt the words are David's, and express his purpose to indite songs in which all nations might one day sing praise to the God of Abraham.   But, in the character in which he speaks throughout the psalm, he so exactly prefigured Christ that the whole is applicable to Christ as truly as to himself ; and in these concluding verses, he is moved by the Holy Spirit to utter words which, although true of himself, were much more perfectly fulfilled in Christ.   And this is what we mean when we entitle his song of thanksgiving a *typically Messianic* psalm.

To the same class belong such Psalms as the Thirty-fifth, the Forty-first, the Fifty-fifth, the Sixty-ninth, the Hundred-and-ninth ; a cycle which will come before us again in connection with the subject of the Imprecations which impart to them such a terrible character.   They are all from David's pen, and were written with reference to the implacable enemies of his kingdom and of the cause of God in Israel. They are so distinctly typical as to partake more or less of the predictive character also.   Christ and Judas are present in them as truly as David and Ahithophel.   There are other psalms of David that might be ranked in this typical group, but

---

* Chap. xv. 9.

I will not attempt to enumerate them ; for, indeed, it is hardly possible to draw a line of separation between the psalms which look no farther than David and those which have an ulterior reference to Christ. When the psalmist writes in his kingly character he is ever ready to look beyond himself and his own age, to the future glories of his house and to its promised Heir. The Twenty-first and Sixty-first Psalms, for example, although they might seem to relate entirely to the temporal kingdom, utter hopes with respect to it which are distinctly Messianic. " Thou wilt prolong the king's life : his years shall be as many generations ; he shall abide before God for ever." " He asked life of Thee, Thou gavest it him ; even length of days for ever and ever."*

When Solomon came to the throne, it was his honourable ambition to govern so that his reign might be remarkable for righteousness, benignity, and peace. Hence his prayer at Gibeon. Hence also the tenor of the SEVENTY-SECOND Psalm, in which he has put on record the hopes and aspirations of his golden prime. It was the people's interest, as well as his own, that he might be enabled to reign justly, and might be blessed with peace. He associates them, therefore, with himself in the prayer.

1. Give the king Thy judgments, O God,
   And Thy righteousness unto the king's son.
2. He shall judge Thy people with righteousness,
   And Thy poor with judgment.
3. The mountains shall bring peace to the people,
   And the hills, in righteousness.
4. He shall judge the poor of the people,
   He shall save the children of the needy ;
   And shall break in pieces the oppressor.

Solomon is certainly here. The psalm is the joint prayer of prince and people, entreating that the new reign may be wise and just, long and happy. But we cannot read it to the end without feeling that, even when it was first sung, the thought of every reflective Israelite must have been carried beyond the young king, who had just entered upon the government, with such honourable aspirations and such a rich dower of

---

* Ps. lxi. 6, 7 ; xxi. 4.

wisdom and diversified accomplishment. In Hebrew, the optative and future run so much into each other that it is hard to say whether the psalm ought to be translated throughout as a prayer, or ought not rather to be thrown, in the latter part, into the form of a prediction, as it is in the English version. Some, like Hupfeld, make it a prayer throughout, and read it thus :

> 10. Let the kings of Tarshish and the isles render gifts,
>   Let the kings of Sheba and Saba offer presents.
> 11. Yea, let all kings bow themselves down before him,
>   Let all nations serve him.
> 12. For he delivereth the poor when he crieth,
>   And the afflicted who hath no helper.*

But even thus rendered, the terms would have been too fulsome for a Bible psalm if the scope of it had been limited to the person and reign of Solomon. He could not modestly have asked his people to unite with him in offering to God requests of such extensive and glorious import unless he had intended them to be offered in behalf of THE KING in the most comprehensive sense of the term, as including the House of David for ever, and especially the greater Son of David who was promised to succeed upon the throne. The reference to Christ is, of course, still more pointed and obvious if (as seems preferable)† the latter part of the psalm be rendered as a prediction. And if those who first made use of the psalm may be presumed to have looked beyond Solomon, what shall we say regarding those who lived to see the kingdom divided and the house of David represented by men like Rehoboam ? The psalm, let it be remembered, was not a mere Coronation Anthem, sung once and then forgotten. It was a fresh addition to the Church's Psalter, and continued thenceforward to be sung in divine worship. We may be sure, therefore, that even if it could be supposed that the people, in the bright morning of Solomon's reign, fixed their hopes on him as they sang the psalm, they would cease to do so when their hopes from him and his were so cruelly disappointed. The type would more and more recede from their

* Canon Perowne's translation.
† The predictive rendering is given in the Septuagint, the Vulgate. and Jerome ; in the Genevan, the Authorised, and the Revised English Versions ; by Venema, by Hengstenberg, and (as regards the second half of the psalm) by Delitzsch.

view, as the temporal glory of David's house waned ; and they would come to sing the psalm, very much as we do, with an entire concentration of the thoughts on the Prince of Peace.*

The Hundred-and-thirty-second Psalm, written, apparently, with reference to the dedication of the Temple, and the Eighty-ninth, which seems to be a wail on account of the disruption of the kingdom, are two other well-defined examples of the typically Messianic class. The promise of perpetuity given to David's house is celebrated in both ; and in both the terms are carefully framed, so as to admit and invite the thought of Him in whom the promise has received its complete and ultimate accomplishment. The Hundred-and-eighteenth is another example, from a later age. It is a song of the Second Temple ; and, under the type of the advancement of a despised stone to be the head stone of the corner,—the advancement of the feeble remnant of God's Israel to be the honoured depositaries of His ordinances, —it celebrates the advancement of the Man of Sorrows to be the glorified Head of the Church.†

The EIGHTH Psalm, although it is mentioned last, has a certain title to the foremost place amongst those which hold forth Christ under the veil of some type. For, in this instance, the type under which Christ is presented is the oldest of all the types, being no other than the common progenitor of the race. Adam was "a figure of Him that was to come."‡ He prefigured Christ in this very notable respect, that as he was the Head and Surety of the entire race, insomuch that in his fall they fell, so Christ is the Head and Surety of the entire Church, insomuch that by His obedience they are constituted righteous. "For since by man came death, by man came also the resurrection of the dead : for as in Adam all die, so also in Christ shall all be made alive."§ The primary scope of the Psalm is to celebrate the condescending bounty of God displayed in endowing our nature, in the person of Adam, with such a rich heritage of privilege ; crowning it with glory and honour, making it to have dominion over the works of His

---

* Compare Delitzsch, vol. i. 537, 538.

† Fairbairn's *Typology of Scripture*, Fourth Edition, vol. i. 436–440. A work of authority on this whole subject of the Bible types.

‡ Rom. v. 14.

§ 1 Cor. xv. 21, 22.

hands, and subjecting all things to its rule. " Excellent endowments (some one may say) ; but is it not mockery of our fallen condition to ask us to celebrate them now, after they have been forfeited by our apostacy from God ? " The answer is, that they were forfeited, but are now restored. And the restoration is made in a way exactly corresponding to the manner of the original endowment. It is made to God's people in the person of their common Head and Surety, by whose blood the lost heritage has been redeemed. The grant first made to the race in Adam is made the second time to the Church in Christ, the second Adam. Hence the remarkable way in which the epistle to the Hebrews* cites the psalm, as if it had been a prediction regarding Christ. It celebrates the second Adam and His dominion, under the type of the first Adam and the dominion with which he was crowned at the creation.

II. It was Calvin who first applied the principle of types, with distinguished success, to the interpretation of the Messianic psalms. Before his time, indeed, devout men, as they listened to David's harp, were sensible of the presence of a greater than David, and their devotional use of the psalms was, from the first, animated and governed by the conviction that Christ was in them of a truth. But when the problem arose how to reconcile this conviction with the plain rule that, in interpreting an author, particular expressions must be read in the light of the context and must have no meaning imposed on them which the context refuses to share, they found themselves at a loss. Here were psalms of which some parts evidently related to David and not to Christ ; was it allowable to interpret other parts as if they were prophetical of Christ ? Being unable to work out a satisfactory answer, and being at the same time perfectly confident that the sentiment of their hearts which testified to Christ's presence in the psalms was well founded, they fell upon the way of handling them which is so familiar to all who have looked into the patristic writings. It is well exemplified in Augustine. That great divine was certainly neither ignorant of the rules of exact interpretation, nor unaware of the importance of applying them to the Messianic Psalms.† But not having a clear conception of the nature of a type,—as distin-

---

* Chap. ii. 6–8   † See *De Civ. Dei*, lib. xvii. c. 15.

guished from a prediction, on the one hand, and from a mere emblem or allegory, on the other,—his expositions drift perpetually into a style of allegorising by which any sense that may happen to be desired can be extracted from any passage. It was not the least of the many services rendered to the cause of truth by the Reformers, and especially by Calvin, that they, for the first time, reconciled the sentiment of devout readers as to the ultimate reference of the Messianic psalms with the principles of exact interpretation.

But, as often happens, the great Reformer, having got hold of a valuable principle, went to an extreme in the application of it. In no psalm except the Hundred-and-tenth did he find Christ set forth without some intervening type. In the Second Psalm he thinks there is an immediate reference to David, and in the Forty-fifth to the nuptials of Solomon; and in this he has been followed by many commentators of the highest standing. But the interpretation in both instances is, I venture to think, without solid foundation. It is difficult, no doubt, to draw a line between the psalms which relate exclusively to Christ and those in which He is seen through the veil of some type. The Seventy-second, although typical, approaches to the character of a direct prediction; the Second and Forty-fifth, on the other hand, so largely borrow from the reigns of David and Solomon the poetical imagery in which they celebrate Christ, that they have a good deal of the look of typical psalms. But this borrowing of imagery is by no means inconsistent with the strictly prophetical character. There are passages in Isaiah (the ninth and eleventh chapters, for example) in which Christ and His reign are celebrated in imagery wholly taken from the kingdom of David, yet no one regards them as anything but direct predictions. There is no reason to deny the same character to the Second and Forty-fifth Psalms. To expound them as having a primary reference to David or Solomon is simply to introduce confusion and embarrassment.

There is yet another psalm for which I would claim a place amongst those that are directly prophetical of Christ. I mean the TWENTY-SECOND. The majority of the best commentators, I must admit, regard it as referring throughout to David, and so rank it in the typical class. But the objections to that view are many, and, I think, unanswerable. For one thing, David's biography contains nothing corresponding to the account the Sufferer here gives of his tribulations.* His enemies never "parted his garments among them or cast lots upon his vesture." Indeed, so inapplicable is the description to any Bible saint, that some who reject the direct reference to Christ are fain to attribute the psalm—contrary to all existing evidence—to " some afflicted person, otherwise unknown to us, during the Captivity." Besides, even if it had been possible to find in the life of David or of some other saint a time of such sufferings as the psalm describes, those who see a primary reference to him would still have had to explain the remarkable hopes expressed in the latter part of it. The Sufferer, rising above the sense of his present sorrow, rejoices in the confident persuasion that, as the fruit of what he is now enduring, all the families of the earth shall one day be moved to return to the Lord, and to bow themselves down before Him. This is a feature which so evidently points to the Man of Sorrows, that the great Jewish critics have betaken themselves to the same explanation by which they seek to get quit of the testimony of the Fifty-third chapter of Isaiah to the cross of Christ. In both cases, they labour to make out that the sufferer described is the nation of Israel during the Babylonish captivity, and that the blessing so confidently anticipated to spring out of the sorrows of the chosen people was no other than that diffusion of the true religion which resulted from the dispersion of the exiles among the nations. The theory is ingenious, and it has been eagerly appropriated by the Rationalists. But there are things both in the prophecy and in the psalm that conclusively refute it. Thus, in the former, the Lord's righteous Servant whose sufferings are pourtrayed, instead of being identified with the people of Israel, is expressly contrasted with them.† In the psalm, there is not only the same contrast,‡ but, from beginning to end, the terms in which the Sufferer's condition is described are too strongly individual to admit the hypothesis of personification. The only adequate and natural interpretation of the psalm is that which sees in it a lyrical prediction of "the sufferings of Messiah and the glories that were to follow." No sufferer but One could, without presumption, have ex-

---

Vers. 14–18.   † Isa. liii. 4-6.   ‡ Vers. 22, 23.

pected his griefs to result in the conversion of nations to God.

Moreover, it is not a vague description of a good man's sufferings which this great psalm sets forth. It goes into many details, and these so exactly correspond to the sufferings of Christ that the whole reads like a poetical version of the gospel history. (1) The scene pourtrayed is a *crucifixion*, and just such a crucifixion as was witnessed at Calvary. The Sufferer cannot obtain the solace of retirement. He is encompassed by scornful men, who load him with reproaches. They deride the profession of his hope in God, and do so in terms which startle us by their identity with those actually employed by the crowds who encompassed the Lord's cross. All the dreadful accompaniments of crucifixion are seen ;—the strength dried up like a potsherd—the bones out of joint—the burning thirst, making the tongue cleave to the jaws—the piercing of the hands and the feet*—the bones projecting so that one might count them— the parting of the garments by lot amongst the executioners. Surely the cross of Christ is here, and without the intervention of any type. (2) Not only is the psalm cited by the evangelists as having been fulfilled in the Crucifixion, but the Lord employed it Himself† in expressing the anguish of His soul. " About the ninth hour He cried with a loud voice, saying, Eli, Eli, lama sabachthani ? that is, My God, My God, why hast Thou forsaken Me ? " Taking all the circumstances into account, it is a fair construction of this exclamation to understand it, with Augustine,‡ as equivalent to saying, The psalm was written concerning Me. (3) There is in the psalm a singular alternation of deep dejection under present sorrow and of solemn joy in the prospect of the blessings that are to accrue to all the nations. And this very alternation of conflicting sorrow and joy was seen in Christ, both on the cross and during the week preceding His death.§ (4) In one respect, the

---

* This remarkable expression in ver. 16 is rendered by many of the modern critics, according to the Massoretic punctuation and the Jewish interpreters, " like a lion my hands and my feet ; " but the usual translation is supported by all the ancient Versions, and yields the better sense. Indeed, the other yields no tolerable sense at all. Compare Canon Perowne's note.

† Matt. xxvii. 46.

‡ *Enarratio* II. in Ps. xxi. (xxii.) sec. 3.

§ John xii. 20–33.

psalm stands alone in the Scriptures, and indeed in all religious literature. It is a cry out of the depths,—the sorrowful prayer of one who is not only persecuted by man, but seems to himself, for the time, to be utterly forsaken of his God. Yet there is no confession of sin, no penitent sorrow, no trace of compunction or remorse. This distinguishes the psalm, not only from ordinary psalms of complaint, but from those in which Christ speaks in the person of David His type. The complaints found in them are never unaccompanied with confessions of sin. If David, or any other ancient saint, had written the Twenty-second Psalm, as the expression of his own griefs and hopes, there would certainly have been audible in it some note of penitence.*

On the whole, then, we hold ourselves entitled to set down as Psalms *directly* Messianic, not only the Hundred-and-tenth (in regard to which there is no difference of opinion among those who heartily accept the Scriptures as supernaturally inspired), but also the Second, the Forty-fifth, and the Twenty-second. If any think the Seventy-second ought to be added, I shall not object.

To the same class belong also the psalms which—like the Eighty-seventh, the Ninety-sixth, the Ninety-eighth, the Hundredth, the Hundred-and-seventeenth—although they make no mention of the Person of Christ, celebrate the glorious advancement which awaits the Church in the latter days. I merely name these at present; for they will afterwards claim careful notice in another connection.†

---

* Canon Perowne (4th Ed. p. 238), after quoting the above paragraph, adds, "The remark is of value, but the inference based on it is refuted by reference to the Forty-fourth Psalm, where, in like manner, there is not only the sorrowful complaint without any confession of sin, but the strong sense and assertion of righteousness." The resemblance between the two psalms is, I confess, noteworthy. Yet, I think, there is an important difference also,—important, I mean, in relation to the point in hand. The Forty-fourth Psalm is the prayer of the Congregation, rather than of an individual sufferer; and in appealing to the Searcher of hearts to be witness of their integrity, what they assert is not sinless rectitude, not righteousness in the strict sense, but entire loyalty to the Lord. They claim to be perfect as the heart of Asa (for example) is said to have been "perfect with the Lord all his days" (1 Kings xv. 14). They had "not forgotten God nor dealt falsely in His covenant." They had not stretched forth their hands to a strange god. It was not for apostasy from God that they were being so sorely oppressed. On the contrary, it was "for the Lord's sake that they were killed all the day long" (vers. 17, 20, 22).

† See Chap. ix. of this Book.

III. There are psalms demonstrably Messianic which cannot well be assigned to either of the two classes we have surveyed. They are neither directly predictive of Christ, nor yet do they speak of Him through some type. The two most prominent examples of this class are the Sixteenth and the Fortieth ; and its characteristic features will be best illustrated by examining one of these. For various reasons I select the Fortieth :—

> 5. Many, O LORD my God, are the wonderful works which
>   Thou hast done,
>   And Thy thoughts which are to us-ward :
>   They cannot be set in order unto Thee ;
>   If I would declare and speak of them,
>   They are more than can be numbered.
> 6. Sacrifice and offering Thou hast no delight in ;
>   Mine ears hast Thou opened ;
>   Burnt-offering and sin-offering hast Thou not required.
> 7. Then said I, Lo, I am come ;
>   In the roll of the book it is written of Me ;
> 8. I delight to do Thy will, O my God,
>   Yea, Thy law is within my heart.
> 9. I have published [glad tidings of] righteousness in the great
>   congregation :
>   Lo, I will not refrain my lips,
>   O LORD, Thou knowest.

This is applied to Christ, in the most unqualified way, in the epistle to the Hebrews. "It is impossible that the blood of bulls and goats should take away sins. Wherefore when He cometh into the world, He saith, Sacrifice and offering Thou wouldest not, but a body didst Thou prepare for Me. . . . Then said I, Lo, I am come (in the roll of the book it is written of Me) to do Thy will, O God. . . . He taketh away the first, that He may establish the second. By which will we have been sanctified, through the offering of the body of Jesus Christ, once for all."* There is no mistaking the view here taken of David's words. So plainly is the Messianic interpretation laid down, and so strongly is the argument of the epistle built upon it, that many eminent divines† conclude that Christ must be the direct and exclusive subject of the psalm. The fatal objection to that view is, that the psalm contains one of those

---

* Heb. x. 4–10.

† Calovius in *Pool's Synopsis;* Owen on the Hebrews, at chap. x. 5 ; J. Pye Smith, *Scripture Testimony to the Messiah,* i. 205.

sorrowful confessions of sin the absence of which from the
Twenty-second Psalm has just been commented upon.

> 12. For innumerable evils have compassed me about;
>   Mine iniquities have overtaken me, so that I am not able
>   to look up :
>   They are more than the hairs of mine head, and my heart
>   hath failed me.

In explanation of this, it is urged that Christ, though He knew
no sin, was made sin for us ; so that He was, in a very true
sense, a sinner before God.   This explanation is an old one.   It
is thus put by Augustine :—" He made our offences His offences,
that He might make His righteousness our righteousness.
Why should not He who took upon Him the likeness of the
sinner's flesh take upon Him also the likeness of the sinner's
voice ? "*   There is force in these suggestions, and they go far
to explain the fact (to which we shall revert immediately), that
in one and the same psalm we hear the voice both of the sinless
Saviour and His sinning people.   But it is pressing them too far
to urge them as a reason why we should attribute to Christ
words which, in their natural sense, are a sorrowful and shame-
stricken confession of personal sin before God.   The psalm is
certainly not of the directly Messianic order.

Shall we set it down therefore among the typically Messianic
class ? This is a very common interpretation. According to
it, David is the person who speaks, but he speaks as a type of
Christ, and therefore his words are attributed to Christ by the
epistle to the Hebrews.   But neither is this view satisfactory.
David was not a type of Christ in His Priesthood and Sacrifice ;
and it is of these only, and not at all of the kingdom, that this
psalm speaks.   The Person who here comes forward and
declares his purpose to do the will of God puts such a value
on His obedience, as neither David nor any mere man could,
without presumption, have claimed for theirs.   The true key to
the psalm is to be found, not in the doctrine of the types, but
rather in that of the Mystical Union between Christ and the

---

* *Enarratio* II. in Ps. xxi. (xxii.) sec. 3 ; in Ps. xlix. (l.) sec. 5. It is plain
that, however hazy or defective may have been the views of the early fathers
regarding the doctrine of justification, they knew and prized the doctrine of the
imputation of our sins to Christ and of Christ's righteousness to us, which underlies and sustains that great article of the Reformed Theology.

Church. It is a MYSTICALLY MESSIANIC psalm. This is the view taken by the ancient fathers, and especially Augustine. That great divine was penetrated with a sense of the unity which, through the grace of God, subsists between Christ and all His people, even the humblest and feeblest in the company of the saints. He is never weary of reminding his hearers how, when the obscure disciples of Christ in Damascus were persecuted, the Lord Jesus resented it as a wrong done to Himself, and thundered in the ear of the oppressor, " I am Jesus whom thou persecutest ; " and how, when any poor saint is visited or fed, Christ takes the kindness as done to Himself.* And he makes perpetual use of the doctrine of the Mystical Union in endeavouring to open up the Messianic element in the Psalter. The pages of his *Enarrationes* are thus made fragrant with the savour of the Bridegroom's name. Few will deny, indeed, that he presses the principle too far. He applies it to many places which can only be successfully explained on the typical principle. Nevertheless, the principle is a sound one and is of great value in the interpretation of Scripture.

The difficulty to be explained, in the class of psalms under consideration, is the seeming incongruity involved in the attributing of different parts of one and the same song to different persons,—one part to Christ, another part to His people,—while there is nothing in the context to indicate a change of subject. The mystical hypothesis explains it by pointing out, that there is such a union between Christ and His people as warrants their being thus conjoined with Him in the same song. That He and they are conjoined in a real fellowship of life is most certain. " For as the body is one, and hath many members, and all the members of the body, being many, are one body ; so also is CHRIST. For in one Spirit were we all baptised into one body, whether Jews or Greeks, whether bond or free."† The CHRIST here named is not the individual person of our Lord, but He and the Church together, Christ Mystical, *totus Christus, caput et corpus.* This mystical union is reflected in many parts of Scripture. Thus, throughout the prophecies of Isaiah, one and the same title, "The Servant of the Lord," is used to denote, sometimes the Lord Jesus Himself; ‡ some-

---

* Acts ix. 5 ; Matt. xxv. 40.　　† I Cor. xii. 12, 13; comp. Gal. iii. 16
‡ Chap. xlii. I ; liii. II.

times His people;* sometimes the whole mystical body, including Him and them together.† This no doubt wears an
appearance of incongruity. But something of the kind is
always found when diverse elements are conjoined in an
intimate union. I sometimes speak of myself as an immortal
creature, sometimes as a dying man. Why? Because my
nature is not simple but composite. By my soul, I am
immortal; it is a "deathless principle:" by my body, I am
subject to corruption. Just so is it with the Church. The
Lord has taken His people into a union with Himself, more
intimate than that even of body and soul. He and they constitute one Christ. *And of that one Christ the Psalter is the
Voice.* If in some psalms it is the members who speak and in
others the Head, there are others, again, in which we can
distinguish the speech of both. This seems to furnish the only
satisfactory explanation of the remarkable conjoining of Christ
and the Church in the Sixteenth and Fortieth Psalms. In the
case of the latter, the explanation is frankly accepted by Calvin,
although he was as little tolerant of subtleties in the interpretation of Scripture, as can well be imagined. "David (he
observes) is not speaking here in his own name only, but is
pointing out generally what is common to all God's children;
but when he thus bringeth in the community of the Church, we
must ascend to Him who is the Head."

It is related in the gospel that the Lord Jesus joined with
the disciples in singing the paschal Hallel; ‡ and there is no
reason to suppose that His voice was ever mute when the psalms
were sung in the synagogues of Nazareth or Capernaum on the
Sabbath days. He lifted up His soul to God in " the praises of
Israel;" § and He did not deem it necessary to refrain His voice
when the melody descended to notes of contrite confession.
There was no impropriety or untruthfulness in His thus making
use of words which, in their letter, were inapplicable to His
case. There is hardly a psalm but contains things which are
applicable only to some in the congregation; yet all who are
present take part in the song. We do not enjoin the little

children to be silent when the Seventy-first Psalm is sung although it is the song of old age, nor the aged men to be silent when the Twenty-seventh is sung, although it is properly the prayer of one who is still young. The psalms are Church Songs, and all who belong to the Church are to sing them. " Both young men and maidens, old men and children, let them praise the name of the Lord."* The ripe believer, who can triumph in the steadfast hope of God's glory, is to lend his voice to swell the song of the Church when she cries to God out of the depths ; and the penitent, who is still sitting in darkness, is not to refrain his voice when the Church pours out in song her sense of God's love. The whole Church has fellowship in the psalms. And from this fellowship the divine Head does not turn away. There are sentiments, here and there, in which He cannot perfectly participate. Nevertheless, the psalms are the voice of the body of which He is the Head, and therefore He joins in them. This simple fact, that the Lord Jesus sang the psalms,—how vividly does it bring home to us the truth of the Mystical Union ! When we sing the psalms, especially those in which the voice of Christ makes itself so distinctly audible as it is in the Sixteenth and Fortieth, it may well affect our hearts to think, that we are, in effect, sitting beside Christ, as the disciples did in the guest chamber in Jerusalem, and are singing along with Him out of the same book.†

---

* Ps. cxlviii. 12, 13.

† The partnership which Christ and the Church have in the psalms is strikingly brought out in Heb. ii. 11, 12, where the words of Ps. xxii. 22 are quoted as words spoken by Christ. " He that sanctifieth and they that are sanctified are all of one : for which cause He is not ashamed to call them brethren, saying, I will declare Thy name unto My brethren ; in the midst of the Congregation will I sing Thy praise." On which Bengel observes that " Christ sings in the Church *tanquam dux chori.*" Calvin's note is to the same effect : " Hæc doctrina acerrimi stimuli vice nobis est quo ferventiore studio feramur ad laudandum Deum, quum audimus Christum nobis præcinere, et primum esse hymnorum modulatorem."

CHAPTER III.

THE CHRISTOLOGY OF THE PSALMS.

TILL the Lord Jesus died and rose again, a certain veil obscured the meaning of those prophecies of the Old Testament which spoke of the sufferings of the Messiah and the glories that were to be His reward. The prophets were themselves sensible of this obscurity; for the Holy Spirit revealed to them that it was not properly to themselves, or to the men of their time, that they ministered the divine oracles regarding Christ and redemption, but rather to us who belong to the Christian dispensation.* So late as the eve of the Crucifixion, we find the Lord saying to the disciples that they could not yet bear the full disclosure of the truth. Three days later, this incapacity was gone; the Lord had suffered and risen again; the crisis of the world's history was past. Accordingly, the first discourses of the risen Saviour were devoted to the exposition of the things that were written concerning Himself. The last chapter of Luke's Gospel contains accounts of two several discourses of this kind, with which the disciples were favoured on the very day of the resurrection. The first was spoken, on the road to Emmaus, to the two friends who were returning home from the Paschal solemnity. It must have been a long exposition; for the evangelist mentions that, after joining himself to their company and hearing them express the sorrowful perplexity into which they had been cast by the events of the past week, the Lord first of all showed them that the tragical death of their Master was just what it behoved the Messiah of the Scriptures to endure before entering into His glory; and thereafter went on to unfold in detail what we should now

---

* Comp. I Pet. i. 10-12.

call the Christology of the Old Testament. " Beginning from Moses and from all the prophets, He interpreted to them in all the Scriptures the things concerning Himself."* A second discourse, to the same purpose, was spoken in the evening, at the meeting of the infant Church in Jerusalem. The two brethren to whom the risen Saviour had made Himself known at Emmaus had just come in, and, forgetting the fatigue of their double journey, were reporting what they had seen and heard, when the Lord Himself stood in the midst and resumed the subject by which He had made their hearts to burn within them by the way. The tenor of this second discourse is thus described by the evangelist : † " He said unto them, These are My words which I spake unto you, while I was yet with you, how that all things must needs be fulfilled, which are written in the law of Moses, and the Prophets, and the Psalms, concerning Me." It is added, " Then opened He their mind, that they might understand the Scriptures ; and He said unto them, Thus it is written, that the Christ should suffer, and rise again from the dead the third day : and that repentance and remission of sins should be preached in His name unto all the nations."

The question has sometimes been asked, not without surprise and disappointment, Why did the evangelists omit to give a full report of these great sermons of the risen Lord ? They must have shed a flood of light on the most interesting passages of the ancient Scriptures. It is plain that the disciples hung upon the Preacher's lips. Why, then, are the precious words not recorded ? What Christian is there who would not be well content to endure, like those disciples, the Saviour's loving reproofs, and even to be called " fool, and slow of heart to believe," if so be he might with them hear Christ Himself proving from the Scriptures that it was necessary He should suffer the things He did suffer, and should rise from the dead the third day ? The desire is a natural one, and may be entertained without rebuke. Nevertheless, it is a mistake to suppose that the Saviour's expositions have perished, or that, in collecting THE CHRISTOLOGY OF THE PSALMS, we must forego the assistance which would have been

---

* Luke xxiv. 27.   † Luke xxiv. 44-47.

furnished by His authoritative declaration of "the things that were written in the Psalms concerning Him." The eleven faithful apostles were among the auditors; the discourses were treasured in their memories, and they have been careful to embody the substance of them in their sermons and epistles. It may be difficult to explain why the teaching of Christ during the Forty Days from the resurrection to the ascension has, for the most part, been left to be gathered from the apostolic Scriptures, instead of having been set down in the four Gospels, like that which went before; but of the fact there can be no doubt. There are many passages in the sermons and epistles of Peter, which one cannot read without feeling that the apostle is availing himself of the expositions he had heard Christ deliver in the upper room at Jerusalem. The discourse he preached on the day of Pentecost is largely made up of quotations from the Messianic prophecies of the Old Testament, and especially of the Psalter. He quotes first the Sixteenth Psalm and then the Hundred-and-tenth; in both instances opening up and vindicating the true interpretation. So largely is the same thing done in all the subsequent discourses and writings of the apostles who heard Christ at Jerusalem, and in those of the Apostle Paul, to whom Christ made similar communications afterwards,* that it would be difficult to name one Messianic psalm that is not cited or commented upon in one place or another. In these apostolic expositions of the psalms, what we hear is just the echo of the expositions that had been delivered by the risen Saviour Himself.

I am very sensible that the attempt to exhibit the Christology of the psalms is an arduous one, and that complete success is not to be expected. The views of the truth respecting Christ which pervade this part of the Scriptures are inexpressibly high and deep. The greatest of the Church-fathers mentions in his *City of God*, that although his friends were expecting him to undertake the task of opening up David's predictions regarding the Lord Jesus Christ and His Church, he felt himself constrained to decline it; "not because he had too little to say, but because he had too much." † The design of

---

* Comp. 1 Cor. xv. 3.

† "Copia quam inopia magis impedior."—August., *De Civitate Dei*, Lib. xvii. c. 15.

the present chapter is the more humble one of setting forth such a general view of the subject as may indicate the extraordinary richness of the field, and afford both an impulse and guide to Bible readers in the further exploration of it. And I am sure we may hope to prosper in this design, if we (the writer and his readers together), while thankfully availing ourselves of the authoritative expositions which Christ has delivered to us by the apostles, ask and receive that "opening of the mind to understand the Scriptures" which He gave to the disciples at Jerusalem, and which it is the office of His Spirit to give to disciples still.

Respecting the PERSON of Christ, the testimony of the psalms is copious and sufficiently distinct. For one thing, it is everywhere assumed that He is the Kinsman of His people. The Christ of the Old Testament is one who is to be born of the *seed of Abraham* and *family of David*. The modern Rationalists, in common with the unbelieving Jews of all ages, refuse to go further. They will not recognise in Him more than man, maintaining with great confidence that superhuman dignity is never attributed to the Messiah, either in the Law, or the Prophets, or the Psalms. It would be strange indeed if the fact were so. The disciples were slow of heart to receive any truth that happened to lie out of the line of their prior expectations,—any truth of which the faithful who lived before the Incarnation had had no presentiment; yet we know that they readily accepted the truth that Jesus was more than man. The Cross of Christ was long an offence to them. It was not without a long struggle that they were constrained to acknowledge the abrogation of the Mosaic law and the opening of the door of faith to the Gentiles. But there is no trace of any similar struggle in regard to Christ's *superhuman dignity.* The moment Nathanael recognised in Jesus of Nazareth the expected Redeemer, he cried out, "Rabbi, Thou art the Son of God;" * and, long before the close of the public ministry, Peter, in the name of all the rest, made the articulate profession of faith, "Thou art the Christ, the Son of the living God." † They believed Him to be the Son of God, in a sense in which it would have been blasphemy to affirm the same of any mere

---

* John i. 49.   † Matt. xvi. 16 ; comp. John vi. 69.

man.   Instead, therefore, of deeming it a thing incredible, or
highly improbable, that intimations of Christ's superhuman
dignity should be found in the psalms, we think it every way
likely that they will be discoverable on a diligent search.   In
truth, they are neither few nor recondite.   Take these three
verses :—

> Thy throne, O God, is for ever and ever :
>   A sceptre of equity is the sceptre of Thy kingdom.*

> The LORD said unto me, Thou art my Son ;
>   This day have I begotten Thee.†

> Thus saith the LORD to my lord,
>   Sit Thou at My right hand,
>   Until I make Thine enemies Thy footstool ‡

I do not forget the attempts that have been made to put a
lower sense on each of these passages.   I do not think they are
successful.   But suppose it were admitted to be just possible to
put on each of them, separately, a meaning that would come
short of the ascription of superhuman dignity to the Son of
David, we should still be entitled to deduce an argument in
favour of our interpretation, from the fact that, in so many
separate places, He is spoken of in terms which most naturally
suggest the thought of a superhuman Person.   From the exclamation of Nathanael it is evident that this thought did suggest
itself to Jewish readers, before the veil of unbelief settled down
upon their hearts in the reading of the Old Testament.   The
truth is, that, if a man reject the eternal Godhead of Christ, he
must either lay the psalms aside or sing them with bated breath.
The Messiah whom they celebrate is fairer than the sons of
men ; He is One whom the peoples shall praise for ever and ever.§
The ancient Jews understood the particular psalms just quoted
to refer to the Messiah ; and no one who heartily believes in the
inspiration of the Psalter, will be at a loss to discern in it more
testimonies to the proper divinity of the Hope of Israel than
could well have been discovered, before His incarnation and death
had lighted up so many dark places of the ancient Scriptures.
It will be sufficient for our purpose to indicate a single example.
The coming of Jehovah to establish a reign of righteousness in
all the earth is exultingly announced in several lofty psalms.

---

* Ps. xlv. 6.   † Ps. ii. 7.   ‡ Ps. cx. 1.   § Ps. xlv. 2, 17.

It may very well be doubted whether the ancient Jews were able to link these to the person of the Messiah ; but we are enabled to do it. We know on good grounds that it was of Him that the Spirit spoke in them from the first. The announcement is thus made in the Ninety-sixth Psalm :—

11. Let the heavens be glad, and let the earth rejoice ;
    Let the sea roar, and the fulness thereof ;
12. Let the field exult, and all that is therein ;
    Then shall all the trees of the wood sing for joy ;
13. Before the LORD, for He cometh ;
    For He cometh to judge the earth :
    He shall judge the world with righteousness,
    And the peoples with His truth.

We know whose advent this is. No Christian can doubt that the proper response to the announcement is that furnished by the book of the Revelation, " Amen. Even so, come, Lord Jesus."

It is undeniable that, in the recoil from Arian and Socinian error, Christ's people have sometimes failed to give due prominence in their thoughts to the truth of His *Humanity*. Not that they deny or altogether forget such a cardinal article of the faith ; but they have too often been unwilling to accept all that it implies, and have failed to appreciate the store of consolation treasured up in it for the many brethren of whom He is the First-born. The Eternal Word truly came in the flesh. The Son of God became man, taking to Himself at once a true body and a rational human soul, with all the sinless infirmities proper to such a soul. The great Protestant divines have not hesitated to hold and teach that the Child Jesus was really a child, a child in the unfurnished immaturity of His sinless mind, as well as in the imperfect stature of His body ; that there was room for instruction, and for advance in knowledge and wisdom, as well as for growth in bodily strength : nor have they hesitated to take in its natural and obvious sense His own declaration, that, even after His measureless baptism of the Holy Spirit, He remained ignorant of the day of final judgment.* From error, Christ was always and absolutely exempt ; but His human soul was not omniscient. And His soul was subject to other human infirmities. It was not impassible. On the

---

* See, for example, Calvin on Mark xiii. 32 and Luke ii. 40, 52.

contrary, it shrank from pain and death with the reluctance
of an unsophisticated human nature. The Romish divines *
have been accustomed to charge the teaching of the Reformers
on this subject with a tendency to Arianism, and have laboured
hard to explain away the texts which attribute to our Lord
nescience and the infirmity which shrinks from suffering. But
their error, although it might seem to be "on the safe side,"
has yielded fruits which show that there is no such thing as
a safe side in error, least of all in error touching the Person of
Christ. Explaining away the truth of Christ's Humanity, they
have affrighted trembling souls from His presence, and driven
them to resort to the Virgin and the saints, in the hope to find
in them intercessors "who can be touched with the feeling of
their infirmities, having been in all points tempted like as they
are." †

I mention these things here, although they may seem to be
a digression, because I think they go far to illustrate the wonderful wisdom of God in the Christology of the psalms. These
divine songs never swerve from the just line of truth in their
representations of the Person of Christ. We have seen how
copiously and loftily they celebrate His superhuman dignity,
how unqualifiedly they crown Him with the incommunicable
name of God, how reverently they offer to Him divine worship.
Let the reader now remark how copiously they celebrate the
other aspect of the Saviour's Person. It was from one of them ‡
that He took the title of Son of Man, which was so constantly on His lips when He was on the earth. What is of more
importance, they bring Him near to us. Without the slightest
touch of that offensive familiarity which has sometimes tainted
uninspired hymns in celebrating the Incarnation and Humanity
of the Lord, the psalms present to us the Man Christ Jesus
with a boldness that has never been approached. In singing
them, we are permitted, like the doubting apostle, to satisfy
ourselves, as by actual contact, that the Son of God has truly
come in the flesh. We are permitted to handle the Holy One,
to touch the print of the nails and the pierced side; we are
even suffered to feel the throbbings of the human heart within.

How wonderful, how inexpressibly wonderful, in this connec-

---

* Bellarmine, *De Christi Anima*, chap. I.   † Heb. iv. 15.   ‡ Ps. viii. 4.

tion is the Twenty-second Psalm! It is the voice of our Joseph, as with tears and sobs He makes Himself known to His brethren! We learn from the Gospel that, although the sentiment of Christ's heart from first to last was always the same, " Lo, I come, to do Thy will, O God,"—although He never, even for a moment, refused to do, or to suffer, any part of the Father's will, but kept His commandment,—there was yet the shrinking of human infirmity from the agony and the death that were appointed to Him. When the hour of His agony approached, He sought the company and sympathy of the disciples, earnestly pressing them to watch with Him. When the great eclipse shrouded His soul in darkness on the cross, He expostulated with the Father on account of the hiding of His face. We learn from the Gospel, moreover, that, in the midst of His sufferings, the mind of Christ was much occupied with thoughts about the joy that was set before Him in the salvation of souls, and that the sure hope of that joy lent Him support under His heavy cross. A day or two before He died, He was heard to exclaim, " Now is My soul troubled, and what shall I say ? Father, save Me from this hour. But for this cause came I unto this hour. Father, glorify Thy name. And I, if I be lifted up from the earth, will draw all men unto Myself."* These things, I say, are all related by the evangelists. But it is in the Twenty-second Psalm that Christ brings us nearest to Himself, and, withdrawing the veil from His heart, shows us the conflicting emotions of fear and hope, of human shrinking under present grief and of superhuman resolution to finish the work that was given Him to do. It is a sight not to be contemplated without tears, nor without adoring admiration of the love which made Him who was in the form of God willing to take on Him the form of a bondman and to become obedient to this death.

1. My God, my God, why hast Thou forsaken me ?
   Why art Thou so far from helping me, and from the words of my roaring ?
2. O my God, I cry in the day-time, but Thou answerest not ;
   And in the night season, and am not silent.
3. But Thou art holy,
   O Thou that inhabitest the praises of Israel.

---

* John xii. 27, 32.

4. Our fathers trusted in Thee :
     They trusted, and Thou didst deliver them.
5. They cried unto Thee, and were delivered :
     They trusted in Thee, and were not ashamed.
6. But I am a worm and no man ;
     A reproach of men, and despised of the people.
7. All they that see me laugh me to scorn :
     They shoot out the lip, they shake the head, saying,
8. Commit thyself unto the LORD ; let Him deliver him :
     Let Him deliver him, seeing He delighteth in him.

Where shall we find another such picture of the Man of Sorrows ?   Where shall we find such a vivid expression of the conflicting emotions which agitated His soul during the closing days of the week on which He was offered up ?   It is common to say that the psalm sets forth Christ on the Cross ; but a comparison with the narrative of the evangelists will show that its scope is more extensive—that it expresses also the varying exercises of His soul during the days which preceded the Crucifixion.   It exhibits traits which are either omitted or more faintly given in the Gospel, as when the Divine Sufferer calms His agitated soul by looking up and adoring the Holiness of the Father who was putting Him to grief, and by calling to remembrance how the Old Testament saints, when they cried to God in trouble, were delivered and found reason to encompass the throne of the Lord with the incense of their praises.   If I do not greatly err, this affords us a deeper insight into the truth of our Lord's human nature than anything which the evangelists themselves have recorded, and more feelingly persuades us that we have an High Priest who is able to sympathise with our human infirmities, having been tried just as we are, except that He had no sin.

If the first part of this great Psalm delineates with incomparable vividness the Sufferings of Christ, the latter part brings before us with a vividness not much inferior His steadfast anticipation of the Glories that were to follow.

22. I will declare Thy name unto my brethren :
     In the midst of the congregation will I praise Thee.
23. Ye that fear the LORD, praise Him ;
     All ye the seed of Jacob, glorify Him ;
     And stand in awe of Him, all ye the seed of Israel.

24. For He hath not despised nor abhorred the affliction of the
    afflicted ;
    Neither hath He hid his face from him ;
    But when he cried unto Him, He heard.
25. Of Thee cometh my praise in the great congregation :
    I will pay my vows before them that fear Him.
26. The meek shall eat and be satisfied :
    They shall praise the LORD that seek after Him ;
    Let your heart live for ever.
27. All the ends of the earth shall remember and turn unto the
    LORD :
    And all the kindreds of the nations shall worship before Thee.
28 For the kingdom is the LORD'S :
    And He is the Ruler over the nations.
29. All the fat ones of the earth shall eat and worship :
    All they that go down to the dust shall bow before Him,
    Even he that cannot keep his soul alive.
30. A seed shall serve Him ;
    It shall be told of the Lord unto the next generation.
31. They shall come and shall declare His righteousness,
    Unto a people that shall be born, that He hath done it.

Passing from the Person of Christ to His WORK, we find that
respecting this also the psalms minister abundant aliment to
faith. The mediatorial office is not, indeed, mentioned in express
terms ; the psalms are poetical compositions, and formal definitions of doctrine would be out of place in them ; but it is in the
character of Mediator, the Father's righteous Servant, that
Christ is everywhere spoken of. The correspondence, in this
respect also, between the Christ of the Psalter and the Christ
of the Gospel, is perfect. In the gospel of John a saying is
preserved in which the Lord gives compendious expression to a
sentiment that runs through all His sayings and discourses :
" I am come down from heaven, not to do Mine own will, but
the will of Him that sent Me ; and this is the will of Him
that sent Me, that of all that which He hath given Me I should
lose nothing, but should raise it up at the last day."[*] Christ's
advent took place in virtue of His being sent by God ; His death
also took place in virtue of the Father's commandment that He
should lay down His life and so bring home the children of
God that were scattered abroad. Such is the tenor of Christ's

---

[*] John vi. 38, 39.

language in the Gospel.　Let His language in the Fortieth Psalm be compared with it.

> 6. Sacrifice and offering Thou hast no delight in;
>   Mine ears hast Thou opened:
>   Burnt offering and sin offering hast Thou not required.
> 7. Then said I, Lo, I am come;
>   In the roll of the Book it is written of me:
> 8. I delight to do Thy will, O my God;
>   Yea, Thy law is within my heart.

This, without doubt, is the voice of the Beloved.　Here, just as in the Gospel, He represents Himself as coming, not to offer the sacrifices which could never take away sins, but to do the will of God, to fulfil the commandment He has received of the Father.　The words might indeed have been used, in a certain sense, by David and the other godly kings.　There were things written for them in the roll of the Book of the Lord—commandments which it behoved them to obey.　But they apply far more perfectly to Christ.　His whole mediation, culminating in His death, was a course of obedience to the will of the Father and of compliance with the prophecies of the Scripture. "I lay down My life," He said; "this commandment received I from My Father."* And we have already remarked that, after His resurrection, He was accustomed to say, "Thus it is written, that the Christ should suffer."† The general conception of Christ's work, therefore, is identical in the New Testament and in the Psalms.

Even in regard to the details, the correspondence is remarkable.　It would not be easy to name a single function of our Lord's office to which the harp of David is a stranger.　From the earliest ages of the Christian Church, it has been customary for divines to distribute Christ's work into the three categories of Priesthood, Royalty, and Prophecy.　It will be profitable to take notice how copiously all the three have been celebrated in the psalms.

The PRIESTHOOD of Christ, as it is here set forth, claims special attention.　The great oracular announcement in the Hundred-and-tenth Psalm attributes this office to Him more expressly than any other part of Scripture written prior to the

---

* John x. 17, 18.　　　　　† Luke xxiv. 46.

Crucifixion. The Messiah of the psalms is " a Priest for ever after the order of Melchizedek." As a Priest He must, of course, have somewhat to offer. Of what, then, is His sacrifice to consist ? Do the psalms give any help in answering that question ? The verses quoted above, from the Fortieth, furnish a partial answer. They teach that the sacrifice to be offered by Him was to be of a different order from those the smoke of which went up, year by year, continually, from the altar of burnt-offering on Zion. And this inference from one psalm is corroborated by those others which intimate that He was to be the Son of David, and was therefore to spring out of Judah, "as to which tribe Moses spake nothing concerning priests." * His sacrifice was to consist in obedience to the Father's commandment, as it was prescribed in the roll of the Book.

The doctrine of the Priesthood and Sacrifice of Christ, since it plainly includes the idea of a Suffering Saviour, is more strenuously denied than anything else included in the Christology of the Psalms. The cross of Christ is still what it was at first, "to the Jews a stumbling-block and to the Greeks foolishness." A Messiah who shall conquer and reign, the Jews have always been ready to welcome ; a Messiah who is a Priest and a Propitiation for sins, they will not hear of. This rooted prejudice of the Jews has been inherited from them by the modern Rationalists. They are ready enough to go a certain length in acknowledging the existence of psalms which express hopes regarding Christ as the King of Israel ; but the existence of psalms predictive of His sufferings, they will by no means allow. This denial of predictive announcements of Christ's sacrifice is, so far as I know, universal on the part of the modern Jews and Rationalists. On the other hand, the existence of such announcements is constantly affirmed both by the apostles and by Christ Himself. The gospel which the apostles preached declared not merely the fact that Christ died for our sins, but that He did so " according to the Scriptures."† They maintained that in preaching the cross they were "saying nothing but what the prophets and Moses did say should come : how that the Christ must suffer, and how that He first by the resurrection of the dead should proclaim light both to the

---

* Heb. vii. 14.   † 1 Cor. xv. 3.

people and to the Gentiles." * The reader will remember that this authoritative exposition of the drift of Old Testament prophecy has been already shown to be capable of the most thorough vindication on the ordinary principles of exegesis. The Hundred-and-tenth Psalm is demonstrably inapplicable to any one but Christ ; and it declares, in so many words, that He is a Priest ; a Priest for ever ; a royal Priest after the order of Melchizedek. From that one text, the writer of the epistle to the Hebrews is able to establish the whole substance of the Christian doctrine of our Lord's vicarious death.

How far the Old Testament saints were able to penetrate the meaning of such psalms as the Hundred-and-tenth, it is hard to say. It was not till after the Crucifixion that the disciples began to understand these Scriptures perfectly. But care must be taken not to make too much of the imperfect conceptions of the ancient Jews on this vital subject. The amount of truth laid up in the Psalter is not to be measured by the amount of truth which readers were able to bring out from it before Christ died. We must hold rather by the principle stated by the Apostle Peter, that it was to us, rather than to their contemporaries, that the holy men who wrote certain of the ancient Scriptures ministered the truths there revealed. There are many things in the Psalter which the Psalmists themselves found it difficult to understand ; many things, especially, respecting Christ, which were set forth, not so much for the use of the Hebrew Church, as for that of the Church universal. Reading these in the light furnished by their fulfilment in Christ, we do not hesitate to connect the Twenty-second Psalm with the Hundred-and-tenth. It may be true that, as some affirm, the ancient Jews failed to perceive the connection of the Sufferings of Christ, spoken of in the former, with the Priesthood attributed to Him in the latter. What of that ? It would certainly be to our shame if we failed to understand those ancient predictions better than the saints who lived prior to their fulfilment. Both psalms delineate the same Saviour, and we are now in a position to combine them into one picture. From the Twenty-second we learn that it behoved the Son of David to suffer the hiding of the Father's face, the scorn

---

* Acts xxvi. 22, 23 ; comp. Luke xxiv. 46; 1 Pet. i. 11.

of foes, and the ignominy of the cross ; and that the fruit of His sufferings was to be the conversion to God of the ends of the earth and the providing of a feast for all nations, both for the opulent of the earth and for the neediest of those who descend to the dust. Let that prediction be well weighed, and it will furnish a key to the oracle in the Hundred-and-tenth Psalm, regarding the Priesthood. Let the two psalms be taken together, and they will yield the whole substance of the doctrine of Christ's Priesthood and Sacrifice. Every time we sing them, we are to call to remembrance " how that Christ died for our sins according to the Scriptures," and to animate one another to cordial faith in the atonement thus accomplished.

Add the Sixteenth Psalm to those two, and there will be a commemoration of the other great article of our faith regarding Christ—" that He rose from the dead the third day, according to the Scriptures." It is a psalm of David, and expresses the faith which possessed his soul in the prospect of death ; but he looks beyond himself when he sings,—

8. I have set the LORD always before me ;
    Because He is at my right hand, I shall not be moved.
9. Therefore my heart is glad, and my glory rejoiceth :
    My flesh also shall dwell in safety.
10. For Thou wilt not leave my soul to Sheol ;
    Neither wilt Thou suffer Thine holy one to see corruption.
11. Thou wilt show me the path of life :
    In Thy presence is fulness of joy ;
    In Thy right hand there are pleasures for evermore.

The Apostle Peter, it will be remembered, quoted this psalm on the day of Pentecost, as an undoubted testimony to the resurrection of Christ.* We may place by the side of it that verse of the Hundred-and-eighteenth to which the same apostle referred in his speech before the Sanhedrim, a few days later :— " The stone which the builders rejected is become the head of the corner." † In the beginning of the Passover week the daughter of Zion saw her King coming to her, in meek state, riding upon an ass. He thus made a solemn offer of Himself to Israel. But the builders rejected Him. Thereupon, God, raising Him from the dead, made Him the head of the corner ; and the day on which He rose, the first day of the

---

* Acts ii. 25-31.　　　† Ps. cxviii. 22 ; comp. Acts iv. 11.

week, was thenceforward consecrated to be the *Lord Christ's day*,[*] the weekly memorial of His finished work. "This is the day which the Lord hath made; we will rejoice and be glad in it."

The KINGLY office of Christ is celebrated in very many psalms. The harp of David was oftener occupied with it than with either the Priestly or Prophetical office. It will not be necessary, however, to say much on this head. Christ's proper kingdom is the Church; and most of the particulars relating to the Kingly office will demand consideration when we proceed to elucidate the doctrine regarding the Church as it is set forth in the Psalter. The following points, however, claim notice here:—

In the first place, the psalms enable us to perceive that the Kingdom of Christ is founded on His Sacrifice. He must die before He can gather into one the children of God that are scattered abroad. The Cross comes first, then the Crown. Because of the suffering of death He is crowned with glory and honour.[†] This is implied in the relation which the latter half of the Twenty-second Psalm sustains to the former half. The preaching of repentance and the remission of sins among all nations in the name of Jesus, which is so glowingly predicted in the one, is consequent upon the sufferings described in the other. The same connection is intimated even in the Hundred-and-tenth Psalm; for the people of the throned Priest in Zion are described as crowding to Him "in the beauties of holiness." They follow Him to the field in sacred priestly attire, even the righteousness of saints. Their King is a Priest, and they are themselves a kingdom of priests, whom He has redeemed to God by His blood.

It is equally evident, from the psalms, that Christ's kingdom must always reckon on encountering violent opposition. The decree is, "Rule Thou in the midst of Thine *enemies*." Never yet did Christ find men His friends. Inexperienced persons, who have newly come to know the grace of Christ, the excellence of His salvation, and the pleasantness of His ways, have always been ready to indulge the generous anticipation that, when the gospel is plainly set before men, they will at once welcome it

---

[*] Rev. i. 10.   [†] See John xi. 52; Heb. ii. 9.

to their hearts. The picture of the advancement of Christ's kingdom which Christian poets have commonly drawn represents it as a peaceful Progress along a way strewn with flowers —the holiday march of a royal train. Church history has a very different tale to unfold. Its pages are crowded with the record of a warfare that has never slept since the Church was sent forth on its mission. And it will not do to blame the historians for this, as if they had mistaken the accessories for the essential facts. The pencil of the Holy Spirit, describing in the Apocalypse the fortunes of the Church during the Christian centuries, discloses to our sight, in like manner, a series of conflicts, fierce, often bloody, always trying to faith and patience. And when we go back to the Psalms, we find that they everywhere present the same view of things. They are the songs of a Militant Church. The prescient Spirit of inspiration has framed them so as to harmonise with the predestined fortunes of the kingdom of Christ. Thus the Second Psalm describes the nations and their rulers as taking counsel against God and His Christ, scornfully refusing to be bound by His law, and bringing down on themselves in consequence His iron rod. Even the Forty-fifth Psalm, although it is a Nuptial Song and, for the most part, redolent of peace, contains a prayer to the King to gird His sword on His thigh and ride forth to conquer His enemies.

The psalms, nevertheless, celebrate Christ with peculiar complacency as *the Prince of Peace.* His sword wounds that it may the more surely heal. If He rides forth like David, His right hand teaching Him terrible things, it is that, like Solomon He may rule in peace over a willing people. His arrows are sharp in the heart of His enemies, in order that He may reconcile them to God. The strifes and revolutions which follow the entrance of the gospel into a community, and which attend every notable advance it subsequently makes, have for their object the overturning of throned iniquities and the gradual introduction of a reign of justice, in order that at length " the mountains may bring peace to the people, and the hills in righteousness." *

The PROPHETICAL office of Christ is not overlooked in the

---

* Ps. lxxii. 3.

Psalter.   Thus, in the Fortieth Psalm, Christ Himself, speaking
by the mouth of David, declares :—

> 9. I have published (glad tidings of) righteousness in the great
>   congregation ;
>   Lo, I will not refrain my lips,
>   O LORD, Thou knowest.
> 10. I have not hid Thy righteousness within my heart ;
>   I have declared Thy faithfulness and Thy salvation :
>   I have not concealed Thy lovingkindness and Thy truth from
>   the great congregation.

These remarkable words of the great Prophet received a partial
accomplishment in His earthly ministry, in such sermons, for
example, as the one which filled with astonishment the towns-
people of Nazareth, amongst whom He had grown up.   But that
was only the beginning of their accomplishment.   The proper
and full accomplishment is that which they are still receiving,
generation after generation.   In the gospel of Christ, " the
righteousness of God is revealed to faith." *   Wherever that
righteousness is faithfully declared, it matters not who the
preacher may be, the message is Christ's, and it is to be received
as His.   In this connection, also, I may cite the classical text
from the Twenty-second Psalm (ver. 22) :—

> I will declare Thy Name unto my brethren :
>   In the midst of the congregation will I praise Thee.

Our Lord had these words in His heart when He said in the
guest chamber, " I have declared unto them Thy name, and will
declare it." †   They are a compendious summary of all He taught
the disciples, and of all that He still continues by them to teach
all generations.   The scope of Christ's teaching is evermore *to
declare to men God's name;* in other words, to convey into
their minds and hearts the truth concerning God.   But the
peculiar glory of the psalmist's declaration of Christ's prophetical office lies in the golden words, " *My brethren.*"   Christ
teaches in the midst of the Church, not with the dazzling
majesty of the Godhead, but in the milder radiance of the
First-born of the many brethren.   The words of the psalmist
suggest, by contrast, the manner in which God's name was
declared from Horeb, in the audience of the mighty congregation

---

* Rom. i. 17.   † John xvii. 26.

which filled the plain below. It was with thunder-peals, out of the thick darkness. The people found the weight of the glory insupportable, and entreated that Moses, their brother, might be constituted an internuntius to bear to them the word of the Lord. It was in allusion to that entreaty that, when Moses afterwards delivered the prediction respecting Christ, in which, for the first time, mention is made of His prophetical office, it ran in these terms, "The Lord thy God will raise up unto thee a Prophet, from the midst of thee, of thy brethren, like unto me;"*—of thy brethren, so that His voice will not affright thee, any more than mine has done. In the psalm, the Prophet thus announced takes up the promise, and repeats it in His own person, when He says, "I will declare Thy name unto My brethren."

One who would thoroughly enter into the fulness of these words must look beyond the formal teaching of the Lord Jesus —beyond those manifestations of the Father which took place by means of His sayings and discourses. No doubt, the grace of Christ's personal teaching is very precious. Listening to it, we appreciate the glowing description in the epistle to the Hebrews, "Ye are not come unto a mount that might be touched, and that burned with fire, and unto blackness, and darkness, and tempest, and the sound of a trumpet, and the voice of words; which voice they that heard entreated that no word more should be spoken unto them. . . . But ye are come unto Mount Zion, and unto the city of the living God, the heavenly Jerusalem, . . . and to Jesus the Mediator of a new covenant." † Still, it was not by verbal declarations only, nor by them principally, that Christ manifested the Father. Rather, it was by showing Himself. He is the Incarnate Son of the invisible God; and, wherever He went, they who had eyes to see saw in Him the glory of the Only-begotten of the Father, and, in that glory, the glory of the Father Himself. All effective, all saving knowledge of God is derived from this declaration of Him which has taken place in the Person of Christ,—in His incarnation, and life, and sufferings, as well as in His spoken words. One who would know God's name must fix his gaze on Christ. Christ on Olivet, weeping over Jeru-

---

* Deut. xviii. 15.   † Heb. xii. 18, 19, 22, 24.

salem, is a more perfect declaration of the mind and heart of God in relation to lost men, than could possibly have been made in words. He affirms of Himself, "He that hath seen Me hath seen the Father."* With such a fulness of meaning could He say, by the mouth of David, "I will declare Thy name unto My brethren."

The Psalter, which sets forth so much truth respecting the Person and Work of Christ—truth more precious than gold, and sweeter than the honey-comb—is not silent respecting the bond subsisting between Him and His people, THE MYSTICAL UNION BETWEEN CHRIST AND THE CHURCH. When a prince sets his affections on a woman of lowly rank and takes her home to be his wife, the two are so united that her debts become his, his wealth and honours become hers. When a branch of wild olive is engrafted into a good olive stock, the two are so conjoined that the rich juices of the stock circulate through all the veins of the branch and enable it to yield fruit, not after its own inferior kind, but after that of the more generous stock. Now, that there is formed between Christ and the Church,—between Christ and every soul that will consent to receive Him,—a connection of which these most intimate of all natural relations are the analogues and types, we have already found to be not only taught in the psalms, but implied in the very structure of many of them. He takes His people's sins upon Him, and they receive the right to become the sons of God; the same Spirit of God wherewith He was baptised without measure dwells in them according to the measure of the grace that is given them. I will only add further, that this union, besides being implied in so many places, is expressly set forth in one most glorious psalm—the Forty-fifth—the Nuptial Song of Christ and the Church—which has for its proper theme the home-bringing of Christ's elect, that they may be joined to Him in a union that will survive the everlasting hills.

> 10. Hearken, O daughter, and consider, and incline thine ear;
>   Forget also thine own people, and thy father's house:
> 11. So shall the King desire thy beauty:
>   For He is thy Lord; and worship thou Him.

· · · · · · · · ·

---

* John xiv. 9.

13. The King's daughter within the palace is all-glorious:
     Her clothing is inwrought with gold.
14. She shall be led unto the King in broidered work:
     The virgins her companions that follow her
     Shall be brought unto Thee.
15. With gladness and rejoicing shall they be led:
     They shall enter into the King's palace.

CHAPTER IV.

GOD AND THE SOUL.

A THOUGHTFUL person on taking up a religious auto-biography or a volume of sacred poetry, especially if it have come from a foreign country or a distant age, finds it a profitable and very interesting study to mark the distinctive features of the religious life expressed in it. In all ordinary cases, books of this sort furnish a more vivid and trustworthy representation of the piety of a given age and place, than works of a formally didactic character. In this connection also, the Psalter possesses a singular value. In other parts of Scripture we are told much about godliness—its essential characters, the dangers to which it is exposed, the truths which are its proper aliment; in this book we see godliness itself in living and powerful exercise. It is to be noted, moreover, that the devotional poetry here collected, while it obviously expresses the genuine feelings of the several writers, was written by the special direction and inspiration of the Holy Spirit; so that it is at once a just record of what godly men have felt and an authentic intimation of the mind of God with respect to the feelings which we ought to cherish. The value thus communicated to the psalms is altogether incalculable. "Next to a sound rule of faith there is nothing of so much consequence as a sober standard of feeling in matters of practical religion." *

Seeing, then, that we possess in the Psalms an authentic expression of genuine religion in all its manifold phases, I propose to devote some chapters to the illustration of the more salient features of the piety here set forth for our imitation. From this one portion of Scripture, it will, I think, be possible to collect information with regard to every stage in

---

* The weighty sentence of Mr. Keble, in the *Advertisement* prefixed to *The Christian Year.*

the momentous history of Religion in the Soul. It will prepare the way for what is proposed if we first take pains to ascertain certain fundamental principles which underlie the whole subject.

lxxiii. 25. Whom have I in heaven but Thee?
    And there is none upon earth that I desire beside Thee.
    26. My flesh and my heart faileth:
    But God is the strength of my heart, and my portion for ever.

These heavenly words briefly express the kind of Personal Religion which has always animated the faithful. The sentiment uttered in them lies at the root of all genuine piety. Considering them attentively, we perceive that they proceed on the assumption of two doctrines, which must therefore be regarded as pertaining to the foundation of all living and effective religion. The one doctrine relates to the nature of God, the other to the nature of man. The one may be styled the doctrine of God's Personality; the other, the doctrine of the Divine Similitude in man. These two are, in the Psalter, what the two pillars that Samson grasped were, in the temple at Gaza. On them the whole fabric rests. They are correlative principles; they stand or fall together; and there is not a psalm but implies them both. It will greatly facilitate our subsequent progress if we can attain a clear conception of them.

I. The doctrine of the DIVINE PERSONALITY is briefly this, That the Living God, the Infinite Mind, is a Being who can say I WILL, and to whom His creatures may reasonably say THOU WILT —a Being to whom it is not a vain thing for us to speak, as a man will speak to a friend whom he knows to be near. A very simple truth, level to the capacity of a child; so simple that it may seem trifling to announce it as one of the main pillars of Scriptural piety. For who is there (it may be said) that needs to be taught that personality belongs to the nature of God?

The doctrine, blessed be God, is simple, and to those who have known the Scriptures from their childhood may well seem trivial. Nevertheless, a little reflection will show that it possesses all the significance we have claimed for it. It is a doctrine which, although so evidently agreeable to the light of nature, has never been able to retain its hold on men's minds apart from the Scriptures, and especially (may I not add?) apart from the Psalms. Those who have made the religious systems of the world their study know that the personality of God finds no place in modern heathenism. The hoary systems which hold in bondage the educated minds of China and India are thoroughly pantheistic. Their god—if one ought not rather to say the vast company of their gods—is just another name for the universe. The soul of man is identified with the divine nature ; it is the divine nature in a self-conscious state. It is deemed absurd, therefore, to speak of holding communion with God, as a man may hold communion with his neighbour. Thus Personal Religion is annihilated. Among the ancient Greeks and Romans, this deadly leaven of Pantheism had not yet suppressed the traditions of a purer faith, but it was everywhere at work. The best of the philosophers spoke of *the god,* or *the Deity,* in a vague impersonal way. Their god was a nebulous abstraction,—not a Personal Being, whom one could speak to, whom one could love, into whose ear the burdened soul could pour its griefs. I the rather call attention to these facts inasmuch as, even amongst ourselves, the philosophical systems continually gravitate towards the same vague and distant notion of God. So long as the human heart "dislikes to retain God in its knowledge," * Materialism and Pantheism will continue to make themselves heard in our schools of philosophy, and will make their influence felt far beyond, in the deadening of the sense of a personal God.

It would be instructive to mark how carefully the prescient wisdom of the Holy Spirit has framed the Scriptures to be, in all their parts, a powerful witness to the divine personality. The first sentence of the Bible is a proclamation of the truth that the world had a personal Creator ; and the following verses explain the sense in which that announcement is to be understood. God created the heaven and the earth *by His Word.* " He *spake,* and it was done ; " † so that the creatures were not emanations from the divine nature, but effects of the divine will, —the fruits of intelligence, and design, and counsel. It would be too wide a digression to follow out this line of remark here. I hasten, therefore, to observe, that the Psalter is the portion of Holy Writ in which the testimony to the divine personality is delivered with the most impressive force. The Psalms are the

---

* Rom. i. 28.   † Ps. xxxiii. 9.

voice of the Church, addressing her Lord and pouring out her heart before Him.   Every one of them partakes of the nature of a prayer—a deliberate address to God, craving pardon, expressing gratitude, seeking light and help.   In every one of them there is, therefore, a distinct profession of faith in God, as One who heareth prayer.   Besides all this, the Psalter abounds in intimations of the divine personality, so boldly expressed, that, in the hands of uninspired writers, they could scarcely have failed to pass over into irreverent familiarity.   Some striking examples of this will be cited immediately ; in the meanwhile the reader may be referred to these :—

xxxiii. :3. The LORD *looketh from heaven;*
    He beholdeth all the sons of men.
  15. He that fashioneth the hearts of them all,
    That *considereth* all their works.
  18. Behold, *the eye of the Lord* is upon them that fear Him,
    Upon them that hope in His mercy.

xxxvii. 23. A man's goings are established of the LORD ;
    And *He delighteth* in his way.
  24. Though he fall, he shall not be utterly cast down :
    For the LORD *upholdeth him with His hand.*

lxxviii. 38. But He, *being full of compassion,* forgave their iniquity,
    and destroyed them not :
    Yea, many a time turned He His anger away,
    And *did not stir up all His wrath.*
  39. And He *remembered that they were but flesh ;*
    A wind that passeth away, and cometh not again.

xl. 17. I am poor and needy ;
    Yet the Lord *thinketh upon me :*
    Thou art my help and my Deliverer ;
    Make no tarrying, O my God.

The boon bestowed on the Church in such texts as these is quite inestimable.   It is not merely that they teach the doctrine of the Divine Personality.   They do much more than teach doctrine.   They take us by the hand, conduct us into God's presence, and encourage us to speak to Him.

The class of texts of which a few specimens have been given exemplify a remarkable feature of the Scriptural representations of God.   I refer to what divines have been used to call the *anthropopathy* of Scripture,—that is to say, the free ascription to the Most High of human thoughts and feelings.   This mode of representation, being peculiarly frequent in the psalms, claims notice in this place, especially since a handle is often made of it by the impugners of the Scriptures. Anger, grief, scorn, jealousy, disappointment, gladness, the relentings of fatherly love, exultation in the successful accomplishment of great enterprises,—these are feelings which, as they are found in us, are attended with inward tumult. They always betray infirmity, and are often attended with poignant suffering. Now it is most certain that there is no infirmity in the Almighty, no grief in the supremely Happy One, the blessed * and only Potentate. How, then, are we to account for the fact that these human feelings are, constantly and in the boldest way, attributed to Him by the psalmists? That they are so, can hardly have escaped the notice of any reader. Not to revert to the texts already cited, how common are such statements as these :—

lxxviii. 58. They *provoked Him to anger* with their high places,
　　　　　And *moved Him to jealousy* with their graven images.
　　　59. When God heard this, He *was wroth,*
　　　　　And greatly abhorred Israel :
　　　60. So that He forsook the tabernacle of Shiloh,
　　　　　The tent which He placed among men.
　　　65. Then the Lord *awaked as one out of sleep,*
　　　　　Like a mighty man that shouteth by reason of wine.

　ii. 4. He that sitteth in the heavens *shall laugh :*
　　　　　The Lord shall have them in derision.

lxxxi. 13. Oh that My people would hearken unto Me,
　　　　　That Israel would walk in My ways !
　　　　　I should soon subdue their enemies !

xliv. 23. *Awake, why sleepest Thou,* O Lord ?
　　　　　Arise, cast us not off for ever.
　　　24. Wherefore *hidest Thou Thy face,*
　　　　　And *forgettest* our affliction and our oppression ?

It is not difficult, I think, to perceive the design of the Holy Spirit in adopting so freely this boldness of speech respecting

---

* ὁ μακάριος δυνάστης, "the Happy Potentate" (1 Tim. vi. 15). One can understand the reasons which deterred our Translators and have again deterred their Revisers from applying to God an epithet apt to suggest the incongruous notion of *hap* or *good luck.* Yet it is surely unfortunate that the English *blessed* should have to represent two Greek words so distinct in meaning as μακάριος and εὐλογητός—the *ever-felicitous* and *ever-praised.* Better describe God as " the happy and only Potentate," than hide the fact that there is ascribed to Him supreme felicity.

the divine nature. Nothing short of it would have sufficed to serve the purpose, which was to establish and maintain in men's hearts a real and effective belief in the living God. The only personal intelligences that are familiarly known to us are our fellow-men. We believe, indeed, in the existence of persons of a higher order than ourselves—the angelic spirits, "whose dwelling is not with flesh ;" but we have the same difficulty in realising their existence as we have in realising that of God. We cannot attain a vivid conception of an angelic person, except by clothing him in the garb of our own nature. It is plain, therefore, that when the Most High condescends to show Himself "in fashion as a man" (and this is precisely what He does in the texts in question) He adopts the only effectual way of enabling us to conceive of Him as a Person, and to speak to Him as such. It is easy to stigmatise the language of the psalmists as rude, unphilosophical, unworthy of the divine majesty ; but history proves that when men reject the guidance of this Scriptural mode of speech, they are obliged to forego all real salutary belief in God, all living communion with Him.

I can imagine that this consideration may fail to satisfy some. They may say, "Utility is one thing; truth is another. You do not believe that God ever grieves, or laughs, or changes His mind, or falls asleep. Why, then, do you sing psalms that represent Him as doing so ? You have claimed for this manner of representation the merit of utility ; but an honest man will not deal in falsehood in the hope that good may come out of it. From erroneous representations of the Godhead only mischief can come in the end." That is a way of looking at the subject which, I rather think, is not uncommon. How is it to be met ?

We might call attention, in the first place, to the obvious fact that the same Scriptures which attribute to God the feelings of a man are careful to intimate the qualification with which this is to be understood. If the Forty-fourth Psalm calls upon God as if He were asleep, the Hundred-and-twenty-first reminds us that " He that keepeth Israel shall neither slumber nor sleep ; " and it is only captious readers who omit to read the one text in the light of the other. However, I will not insist on this consideration, reasonable and just as it is. We are entitled to take higher ground. We hold that the representations of God which impart so much vividness and power to the psalms rest

on a far deeper wisdom, a far truer philosophy, than the
supercilious deism which ventures to condemn them. We hold
that the reason why they are, in fact, so useful is just because
they are, in their principle, profoundly true. We admit, of
course, that the Most High is infinitely superior to the infirmities of human nature. It is certain, nevertheless, that there
must be in the divine mind thoughts and feelings analogous to
those of which we are conscious in ourselves. Paley's famous
argument, in which, from the traces of design in nature, he
demonstrates the existence of an all-wise Designer, leads inevitably to this conclusion. The aptitude to be angry at the sight
of base injustice, to relent over the tears of a sorely-chastised
child, to rejoice in the successful accomplishment of great works,
is no blemish in human nature, but a part of its glory. It is
not the symptom of a morbid condition of our faculties, but
rather the token of their healthful play. The Author of our
nature must therefore be One who sympathises with such
feelings ; and we ought not to think it strange to find the
psalmists declaring that He " rejoiceth in His works ; " that
" like as a father pitieth his children, so the Lord pitieth them
that fear Him ; " that He " hateth all workers of iniquity."*

It will surprise some to be told that this very argument is
urged in the Psalter itself. It is very powerfully stated in a
psalm—the Ninety-fourth—which may most probably be
ascribed to the age of the later kings, when righteousness was
oppressed, and the oppressors pleased themselves with the
thought that there was no Eye above to see, nor Hand to smite
them. How does the psalmist deal with the atheistical imagination?

> 6. They slay the widow and the stranger,
>   And murder the fatherless.
> 7. And they say, The LORD shall not see,
>   Neither shall the God of Jacob consider.
> 8. Consider, ye brutish among the people :
>   And, ye fools, when will ye be wise ?
> 9. He that planted the ear, shall He not hear ?
>   He that formed the eye, shall He not see ?
> 10. He that chastiseth the nations, shall not He correct,
>   Even He that teacheth man knowledge ? †

---

* Ps. civ. 31 ; ciii. 13 ; v. 5.
† Our English Versions have been unfortunate in their rendering of the last

As the mechanism of the telescope bears witness to the skill of the optician who devised it, so the eye and the ear bear witness, in their curious structure, to the existence of an intelligent creative mind—a mind that can see and hear. In like manner, the ethical faculty in man, his "knowledge" of evil and of good, concurs with the moral purpose discernible in the providential government of the nations, in bearing witness to the existence in God of a mind that hates all workers of iniquity and that will not fail to punish their evil deeds. Let this argument be duly prosecuted, and it will lead to the conclusion that the bold anthropopathy of the Psalms rests on a profoundly true conception of the Divine Nature. The nature of God is the prototype of our own; so that the fittest language for expressing His mind is that which is furnished by the analogy of our own thoughts and emotions. By boldly making use of this language, the Psalter rescues from neglect and brings to bear upon the conscience a whole world of truth respecting God, which quite escapes the notice of those who have impugned it as unphilosophical.

There is yet another light in which this subject may be viewed, and it is, in some respects, the most satisfactory of all. The Lord Jesus, although He was in the form of God, took upon Him the form of a servant, and was found in fashion as a man. And He teaches us to regard His human nature as the truest and most adequate representation of God that our minds are capable of apprehending. "He that hath seen Me hath seen the Father." * Let that one saying of our Lord be duly

---

verse of this passage. In the Prayer-book Version it is sadly mangled, standing thus, "Or He that nurtureth the heathen ; it is He that teacheth man knowledge, shall not He punish?" The Authorised Version (following in this the Genevan) is more faithful to the Hebrew, but is marred by an ill-advised addition. "He that chastiseth the heathen, shall not He correct? He that teacheth man knowledge, *shall not He kno u ?*" The point of the psalmist's argument is thus missed. The tenth verse is not a mere iteration of the argument of the ninth. It carries the argument forward to another and more advanced point. The ancient Versions (the Septuagint, Vulgate, and Jerome's translation from the Hebrew) give the correct rendering.—So I wrote in the former Edition. The amended translation has since been adopted in the Revised Version. Nevertheless I retain the note, as it may serve to elucidate the argument of the psalm, and also because some readers will be none the worse for being reminded again of the debt which all students of the English Bible owe to the Old Testament Company of Revisers.

* John xiv. 9.

considered, and it will be found to cast a flood of light on the psalmists' habitual ascription to God of thoughts and feelings which might seem peculiar to human nature. It is true, the Incarnation did not take place till long after the psalms were written; but that is no reason why we should refuse to read them in the light of the recorded life of the Incarnate Word. It was ever in the Person of the Son that God made Himself known to the ancient saints. The appearances vouchsafed to the patriarchs and prophets took place in the likeness of the nature which was afterwards to be assumed. Thus the minds of God's people were familiarised with the notion of an Incarnation, long before the birth at Bethlehem; and we have already found, in the psalms themselves, distinct references to the union of the two natures in Christ. Of this I am sure, that, when, at any time, misgivings arise in the heart respecting the legitimacy or trustworthiness of the representations of God in the Psalter, the effectual way to remove them is to call to remembrance the Christ of the Gospels. A believer in the Son of God, when he remembers the burning invective which Christ launched against the Scribes and Pharisees, and the tears He shed on Olivet over the doomed city which was about to crucify Him, will not find it hard to believe that the Most High is such an One as the psalmists describe, that He regards His proud enemies with anger, and that, when those to whom He has made overtures of reconciliation will not be reconciled, there is room in His heart for the thought, "Oh that My people had hearkened unto Me!"*

From what has been said, we may gather a lesson with respect to the practical use of the Psalms. Care ought to be taken not to yield to the dread of criticism from the side of "philosophical thinkers," so as to begin to explain away, or even to tone down, the passages which attribute anger and hope, grief and joy, to the Most High. That there is a difficulty in understanding how feelings of this kind can have a place in Him is undeniable. But the life of Christ admonishes us that, in some shape, they are found in God; for He was touched with hope and anger, with joy and grief, and when we have seen Him we have seen the Father. There must be in

---

* Ps. lxxxi. 13.

the mind of God something analogous to the sentiments of a good man, thoughts and feelings which, although a perfect and adequate comprehension of them is beyond our reach, can be truly and profitably known to us from what passes within our own hearts, and from what is related of our Blessed Lord.

II. From these remarks on the Divine Personality, it is an easy transition to the kindred doctrine of the DIVINE SIMILITUDE IN MAN.

This also is a main pillar in the temple of scriptural devotion. It is plain that, when I lift up my heart to God in such songs as those of David and Asaph, there is a reciprocation of thought and feeling between Him and me. I am admitted into His presence; I have "access unto the Father." He vouchsafes to speak to me, and my heart is emboldened to respond. This is well brought out in the Twenty-seventh Psalm, "Hear, O LORD, when I cry with my voice. When Thou saidst, Seek ye My face; my heart said unto Thee, Thy face, LORD, will I seek. Hide not Thy face from me; put not Thy servant away in anger." This (as it has been already remarked) involves a certain assumption regarding the divine nature; for there can be no personal communing with God unless He is a Personal Intelligence. Let it be now remarked, that there is a certain assumption regarding the Human Nature also. It is assumed that we, by our souls, are of kin to God,* so of kin to Him as to be capable of knowing Him and reciprocating His thoughts and feelings. The psalm in question, and all the psalms, are built upon the truth which Paul preached to the Athenians on Mars' Hill, that men are the offspring of God.

It will not be a digression from our purpose to linger a while on this topic.

It deserves to be noticed that the Bible, in its very first mention of man, announces this doctrine of the God-like quality of human nature. I refer, of course, to the remarkable record in the beginning of Genesis,† "And God said, Let us make man in our image, after our likeness . . . And God created man in

---

* "They that deny a God destroy man's nobility; for certainly man is of kin to the beasts by his body; and if he be not of kin to God by his spirit, he is a base and ignoble creature" (Bacon's *Essays*, xvi.).

† Chap. i. 26, 27.

His own image, in the image of God created He him." It is to
that primitive record that the evangelist Luke * carries us back
when he closes the genealogy of our Lord with the statement
that Adam "was the son of God." In the work of the days
many glorious creatures were formed: the sun, moon, and stars
that adorn the heavens; the firm land and the ever-restless
sea; the manifold forms of vegetable life that cover the naked-
ness of the earth, from the grey lichen, scarce distinguishable
from the rock it grows upon, to the stately cedar; last of all,
the innumerable tribes of living creatures which people the sea
and the dry land. But when God surveyed all those creatures
of His hand, He saw that there was not one capable of recognis-
ing the wisdom and the power by which they were framed. All
were fair and good of their several kinds, but not one was
sufficiently of kin to Himself to be capable of knowing Him, or
of maintaining conscious intercourse with Him. Seeing this,
He pronounced His creative work incomplete, and said, Let us
form a creature with whom we may have fellowship; a creature
which may join this lower world to our throne by the bond of
intelligent homage and free obedience. "Let us make man in
our image, after our likeness."

This natural image of God in which man was created, and
which is an indestructible property of the human soul, includes
the fourfold capacity of knowing God, of having intelligent
communion with Him, of freely serving Him, and of enjoying
Him. And the possession of such nobility of nature, the possession of a nature endowed with such high capacities, implies
that it is not a matter of indifference whether they are exercised
upon their appropriate object or prostituted to the service of some
creature. On the contrary, it is our chief end and felicity to
seek God. "Man's Chief End is to glorify God, and to enjoy
Him for ever." Of the manifold excellences that have endeared
the Westminster Shorter Catechism to so many churches on
both sides of the Atlantic, I am disposed to reckon this among
the greatest, that it opens with such a solemn announcement of
the nobility of our human nature. I know no other catechism
that opens so grandly.† And it is interesting to observe (I do

---

* Chap. iii. 38.

† The same fine chord is, no doubt, struck in the opening questions of the

not know whether the authors of the Catechism had adverted to the circumstance) that this opening statement holds forth the very same idea of our nature as is expressed in the passage just quoted from the beginning of Genesis. The truth thus announced is worthy of the place it occupies at the threshold both of the Bible and the Catechism; for it is the key to the whole scriptural doctrine of Sin and Redemption, of Heaven and Hell. We have been so framed that God alone is the adequate portion of our souls. In Him alone can we find enjoyment for ever. It was a keen sense of this which drew from the greatest of the Church-fathers the oft-quoted exclamation, "Thou hast made us for Thyself, and our heart hath no rest until it rest in Thee." * As the eye was formed for the light, the ear for sound, the palate for taste, the intellect for truth; and as those faculties can find satisfaction only in their respective objects; so the soul was formed by God for Himself, and can never know real or abiding enjoyment except in Him.

If the doctrine of the Divine Similitude in man is the keynote of the entire Bible in its teaching respecting sin and salvation, it is emphatically the key-note of the Psalms. Nothing, it is true, can exceed the humility which these lyrics breathe. The mind in which they admonish us to approach the Throne is a mind clothed with the profoundest reverence. "When I consider Thy heavens, the work of Thy fingers, the moon and the stars which Thou hast ordained; what is man, that Thou art mindful of him? and the son of man, that Thou visitest him?"† These expressions of reverent humility are so framed, however, as to show that the Psalmist holds fast the confident persuasion that man *is remembered* and *is visited* by his Maker,—that the little children of Zion, the very babes and sucklings, may without presumption expect God to listen to their praises and take pleasure in them. In the immediate context, moreover, there occurs one of the boldest declarations of the divine similitude in man, "Thou

---

Catechism drawn up by Calvin for the Genevan Church; and the Westminster divines probably had these in view. But their imitation (if it be such) is a great improvement on the original.

* "Fecisti nos ad te, et inquietum est cor nostrum donec requiescat in te" (August., *Confess.* I. cap. i.).

† Ps. viii. 3, 4.

hast made him but little lower than God,* and crownest him with glory and honour" (ver. 5). The Psalms, as we shall see, bear terrible witness to the poisonous malignity with which our nature has become tainted, and the guilt resting on us in consequence ; but they never deal in contemptuous disparagement. On the contrary, they admonish us of our original dignity and invite us to seek its restoration ; and they have ever been one of the principal levers by which the Holy Spirit has raised men's thoughts and affections out of the dust, and directed them heavenwards.

These remarks on the two doctrines which sustain the devotional fabric of the Psalter may be profitably followed up by calling attention to one or two passages, in which they stand forth with special prominence.

I invite the reader's attention, in the first place, to the latter part of the Seventy-third Psalm. This is one of the twelve which bear the name of Asaph, and we have seen reason to conclude that it came from the pen of Asaph the seer, the great contemporary of David. The theme of it is one to which the prophets and psalmists often revert—the mystery of God's providence towards the righteous and the wicked. Asaph's faith staggers at the sight of the prosperity of the wicked. They get on in the world. Their forgetfulness of God seems no bar to their success. Beholding them, the saint is tempted to exclaim, "My pains have been thrown away ; verily I have cleansed my heart in vain, and washed my hands in innocency."

* So it is in the original, and the literal rendering is preferred, not only by Jerome (in his valuable translation from the Hebrew) and by all the modern critics, but also by Calvin and the Genevan (English) translators. The Revised Version also has returned to it. Calvin explains that the reference is to "the creation of man in God's image." The less exact rendering given by the Seventy, and adopted from them in the Vulgate and our Authorised Version, is adopted also in the epistle to the Hebrews, chap. ii. 7, "Thou madest him a little lower than the angels." But it has been justly observed, that "nothing in the way of argument is built (by the Apostle) on the difference between that version and the original ; and the sentiment it expresses, so far as used by the Apostle, would not have been materially affected by a more literal translation" (Principal Fairbairn, *Typology*, vol. i 465). Besides, Kœnig is no doubt right in thinking that "the word *Elohim* (God) must be taken here in that general sense in which it denotes the *Godhead* abstractly—the *divine*—and thus *the supermundane* generally " (*Theologie der Psalmen*, p. 326).

He is only restrained from venting these dark atheistic doubts by the apprehension that he may thereby undermine the dearest hopes of some whom he knows to be the generation of God's children. Such is his temptation. He recovers himself in some measure when, retiring from the din and glitter of the world, he goes into the sanctuary of God, and contemplates things as they appear in the serene light that shines there. He now perceives, what he had before failed to observe, the goal to which the prosperity of the wicked tends ; how they are brought into desolation, as in a moment ; how their felicity passes away like a dream and gives place to consuming terrors. But the consideration which banishes all envy from his heart is not that of the sad end of the ungodly. It is by a loftier thought that his heart is purged of the perilous stuff with which it is overcharged :—

> 23. Nevertheless, I am continually with Thee :
>   Thou hast holden my right hand.
> 24. Thou shalt guide me with Thy counsel,
>   And afterwards receive me to glory.
> 25. Whom have I in heaven but Thee ?
>   And there is none upon earth that I desire beside Thee.
> 26. My flesh and my heart faileth :
>   BUT GOD IS THE STRENGTH OF MY HEART AND MY POR-
>   TION FOR EVER.
> 27. For, lo, they that are far from Thee shall perish ;
>   Thou hast destroyed all them that go a-whoring from Thee.
> 28. But it is good for me to draw near unto God :
>   I have made the Lord GOD my refuge,
>   That I may tell of all Thy works.

What a high estimate of the soul underlies these words with which the saint emerges from the cloud of his temptation ! It is as if he had said, " Why should I envy because of the prosperity of the foolish ? Why should my faith stagger because a full cup of temporal felicities is occasionally bestowed on them ? Wealth, health, honour—these are not the objects in which it was ever intended that my soul should find rest and supreme enjoyment. God Himself is my soul's fit portion. Seeing then that I have, in the Lord's great mercy, been made heir of that portion, I will make my boast in Him, whatever my earthly lot may be. I rejoice in the sure hope that I shall be satisfied with His likeness." It is thus that God would have us arm ourselves against unbelieving thoughts. It is well to be restrained from uttering unworthy suspicions of God by consideration for the faith and comfort of our Christian acquaintances; it is better to curb envious thoughts by recollecting that godless prosperity is only a smooth road to perdition; but it is best of all to be raised above the reach of Satan's fiery darts by the assured persuasion that we possess in God's favour a portion that is richer than a thousand worlds.

Much akin to these exercises of Asaph are those of David in the Seventeenth Psalm. Here again the theme is the mystery of God's providence. But there is this difference between David's temptation and Asaph's, that while Asaph's was caused merely by the sight of the prosperity of the ungodly, David's came in the sharper form of cruel treatment at their hands. The proud ungodly men of whom he speaks were his " deadly enemies." It is unnecessary here to trace the whole conflict of his faith under this trial : the closing verses will bring out the truth of which we are in quest :—

> 13. Arise, O LORD,
>   Confront him, cast him down :
>   Deliver my soul from the wicked, by Thy sword;
> 14. From men, by Thy hand, O LORD,
>   From men of the world, whose portion is in this life,
>   And whose belly Thou fillest with Thy treasure :
>   They are satisfied with children,
>   And leave the rest of their substance to their babes.
> 15. As for me, I shall behold Thy face in righteousness :
>   I shall be satisfied, when I awake, with Thy likeness.

What a world of meaning lies in these few words! They suggest views respecting God and the soul which have elicited expressions of astonishment even from rationalising critics.* Let it be observed that David is not here *complaining* of the prosperity of the wicked which he so graphically describes. He has been lifted up to a height whence he can look on it with calm indifference. It is with commiseration, rather than envy, that he contemplates the gay abundance of his scornful enemies. For, after all, what is their condition? They are "men of the world;" "their portion is in this life." Their

---

* Compare Hupfeld, *Die Psalmen*, vol. i. 450, 2nd edition ; and Ewald, *Die Psalmen*, p. 243, 3rd edition.

portion is a lean and hungry one at the best, a portion that may fill the hand but cannot fill the heart ; and, such as it is, when they die they shall have to part with it for ever. How different the condition of the righteous ! They are not "men of the world ;" their citizenship lies elsewhere. Their portion is not an earthly and temporal one. God Himself is their portion,—the true and only adequate inheritance of souls created in the divine likeness. They live in the assured expectation of beholding His face in righteousness, and of being satisfied with His image when they awake from the sleep of the grave.

The Sixty-third Psalm is a sunnier one, although it comes from the darkest period of David's life. It embalms, for the solace of God's people, the thoughts which sustained the Psalmist's heart when Absalom's revolt drove him into the wilderness of Judah. In the day of his distress, his soul turns to God as his true portion, and he finds ineffable enjoyment in communing with Him.

1. O God, Thou art my God ; early will I seek Thee:
   My soul thirsteth for Thee, my flesh longeth for Thee,
   In a dry and weary land, where no water is.
2. So have I looked upon Thee in the sanctuary,
   To see Thy power and Thy glory.
3. For Thy lovingkindness is better than life ;
   My lips shall praise Thee.
4. So will I bless Thee while I live:
   I will lift up my hands in Thy name.
5. My soul shall be satisfied as with marrow and fatness ;
   And my mouth shall praise Thee with joyful lips ;
6. When I remember Thee upon my bed,
   And meditate on Thee in the night watches.
7. For Thou hast been my help,
   And in the shadow of Thy wings will I rejoice.
8. My soul followeth hard after Thee:
   Thy right hand upholdeth me.

How vividly does the psalmist realise the presence of God, of a personal God, to whom he can speak, and whom his heart can trust ! How entirely is he persuaded that he may behold, and has often beheld, God's power and glory ; and that this beholding of "the beauty of the Lord" is the proper felicity of his soul. It ought not to be thought to derogate from the sincerity

or value of this profession of faith, or of the similar professions
uttered in the psalms formerly cited, that they were elicited by
sharp afflictions and temptations. When we are surrounded
with the lights of a city, the stars are unseen or unheeded ; but
when those nearer lights are extinguished, the stars shine out
and fill the eye with a superior delight. It is just so with
God's people. In a prosperous time, earthly enjoyments are
apt so to occupy the thoughts and affections as to turn them
aside from God. He is wont, accordingly, to send on His
people afflictions and temptations, in order to drive them in
upon their proper portion and thus to fill their souls with the
deep and tranquil enjoyment which it alone yields.

It will sometimes happen—such is the perverseness of our
nature—that when persons of a contemplative turn of mind
ruminate long on these two doctrines which we have found
underlying the devotional exercises of the Psalter, they get
entangled in the meshes of a mischievous error. It would not
be difficult to recall the names of persons of undoubted piety
who, reflecting on the truth that the soul was made for God
and that He is its proper portion, have dreamt of a kind of
mystical absorption in Him. It may be well, therefore, to mark
the corrective which the divine wisdom has provided against
that error. The psalms, while holding forth God as the soul's
portion, never fail to keep us in mind of the truth that He is
also the soul's Ruler and Judge. " His eyes behold, His eyelids try, the children of men." * David was not suffered to
dream of mystical absorption. He was taught by the Spirit to
know and feel his position as a moral subject of the Lord, who
had violated His law, and whose only hope was in the mercy of
his Judge. " I acknowledge my transgressions : and my sin is
ever before me. Against Thee, Thee only, have I sinned, and
done that which is evil in Thy sight : that Thou mayest be
justified when Thou speakest, and be clear when Thou
judgest." †

---

* Ps. xi. 4.   † Ps. li. 3, 4.

CHAPTER V.

THE PROGRESS OF RELIGION IN THE SOUL.

IT was not without a purpose that a greater number of minds, and these of greater diversity with respect to age, and gifts, and experience, were employed in the composition of the Psalter, than were set to work upon any other portion of the Divine Word. The people of God were to be furnished with songs expressive of the immense variety of their religious experience; a variety much greater than was ever embraced in the life of one individual, or even in the collective experience of a generation. And this purpose has been admirably accomplished. It would be difficult to point out any phase of true religion, any crisis or notable passage in the divine life, which has been altogether overlooked. This feature in the Psalter, which has so well fitted it to be the manual of devotion for the universal Church, has made it also a glass in which we can study the whole course of the religious life from its origin to its consummation—the Rise and Progress of Religion in the Soul.

This, accordingly, is what is now to be attempted,—not certainly to collect the whole doctrine of the Psalter on the subject of Personal Religion, for that would require a commentary on something like the half of the psalms, but to collect and illustrate the principal topics, with the view of bringing out the information respecting them that is furnished by this part of the Divine Word. Personal Religion being the specialty of the Psalter, its primary and characteristic element, we may be sure that the materials available under this head will be abundant and diversified.

I. For obvious reasons, it will be convenient to begin with the subject of SIN. It is a topic on which men have seldom wished to hear much said, but on which, for that very reason,

God has taken care that all who come within the reach of His Word shall be plainly told the truth. The Law promulgated at Sinai had for its primary and characteristic design the declaration of the mind of God in regard to it. " Through the law cometh the knowledge of sin." * The oracles and ordinances communicated by Moses ; the Ten Words spoken in the audience of the whole congregation from the flaming top of Horeb ; the forty years' discipline to which the people were subjected in the wilderness ; the terrible office committed to them when they were made the executioners of the divine vengeance on the Canaanites—all had, for their chief intention, the instruction of the Church in the knowledge of sin. By all these things God laboured to show the people, and make them feel, the nature of sin, its turpitude, its hatefulness to Him and its certain fatality to them. Now, the Psalms are the Church's response to God's revelations. If, in the Law, God teaches the people the truth about sin, in the Psalter the people give expression to the convictions and feelings which that teaching has produced in them.

What, then, do we find on turning to this book ? Long familiarity makes it a little difficult for us to distinguish its most characteristic features ; but I rather think that one of the earliest to strike a thoughtful person, on first becoming acquainted with it, would be the deep sense of sin which is everywhere perceptible. I am sure that in this respect it presents a marked contrast to all secular literature. Men of the world try to forget that there is such a thing as sin. This cannot, indeed, be easily done. In such a world as ours, the existence of moral evil forces itself on every one's notice. It confronts us wherever we turn ; and no man can help seeing it, or avoid the frequent mention of it. But men of the world, if they cannot overlook it altogether, try to forget it in its relation to God. They will speak of *vice*—that is, of moral evil considered as a violation of one's own nature. They will speak of *crime*—that is, of moral evil considered as an offence against society. Moral evil, in its relation to a man's self, and in its relation to his fellow-men, or to the society of which he is a member, they may be induced to look at ; but moral evil,

---

* Rom. iii. 20.

in its relation to God, they resolutely ignore. The word SIN, just because it denotes the Godward aspect of moral evil, branding it as the transgression of divine law, is excluded from the vocabulary of certain philosophical schools and is seldom heard from the lips of worldly men.

The depth of feeling that pervades the Bible on this subject comes out in many ways. It has left its impress on the very vocabulary of the Hebrew language. Students of the science of language observe, that in proportion as any particular set of ideas has laid hold of the mind of a nation, the national vocabulary will be found to have been enriched with terms expressive of the various aspects in which those ideas present themselves on being carefully considered. Now it is a fact, well known to the Hebrew student, that the vocabulary of the psalmists is extraordinarily copious in terms relative to sin, —terms expressive of its vile nature, its folly, its guilt; and that this copiousness extends also to the terms which denote its pardon, its subjugation, and the removal of its stain. Modern translators find it no easy business to discover, even in the most copious languages of Christendom, terms to match those of the Hebrew original. Thus the most modern of the historical sciences is able to read, in the assortment of words that are found marshalled in the Hebrew Dictionary, an impressive testimony to the truth that, by the Law, the Holy Spirit had effectually convicted the Jewish Church of sin.

A more obvious token of the same thing is seen in the frequency with which the subject comes up. Sin, either as a present burden weighing down the soul, or as a burden that has been removed by the mercy of God, is a theme of perpetual recurrence. We everywhere meet with notes such as these,

cvi. 6. We have sinned with our fathers,
     We have committed iniquity, we have done wickedly.

cxliii. 2. Enter not into judgment with Thy servant :
     For in Thy sight shall no man living be justified.

xxxii. 1. Blessed is he whose transgression is forgiven, whose sin is
       covered.
    2. Blessed is the man unto whom the Lord imputeth not iniquity,
       And in whose spirit there is no guile.

And it is to be observed that, while the other aspects of

moral evil are by no means forgotten or made light of, its Godward aspect is so earnestly contemplated that the others seem occasionally lost to view. Every other consideration is swallowed up in the thought that it is a wrong done to the majesty and loving-kindness of God. What a touching example of this is furnished by the Fifty-first Psalm! In his great transgression, David had sinned against the nation, against his own family, against Uriah and Bathsheba, against his own body ; and the thought of those aspects of his great offence would often come up in his mind, and swell the torrent of his anguish ; but in the first agony of his repentance, every other thought was swallowed up in this, that he had sinned against God.

> 1. Have mercy upon me, O God, according to Thy lovingkindness :
>   According to the multitude of Thy tender mercies blot out
>   my transgressions.
> 3. For I acknowledge my transgressions :
>   And my sin is ever before me.
> 4. Against Thee, Thee only, have I sinned,
>   And done that which is evil in Thy sight :
>   That Thou mayest be justified when Thou speakest,
>   And be clear when Thou judgest.

This is the inevitable consequence of that living recognition of a Personal God which (as we have seen) is such a characteristic feature of the psalms. When God, instead of being absent from all our thoughts, comes to be feelingly remembered, the effect will assuredly be, that in us, as in the psalmists, the aspect of moral evil which we are naturally most inclined to forget will so occupy our minds as to cast every other into the shade.

And this, let it be noted by the way, furnishes a criterion by which true repentance may be distinguished from its many counterfeits. There is a certain feeling of remorse or shame which detected sin always produces. But there is nothing divine or gracious in that feeling, nothing that ensures salvation from the sin. It may be only " the sorrow of the world which worketh death." The saving grace of repentance has always chief respect to God. It is well described by the apostle [*] as " godly sorrow," " sorrow in relation to God." It utters itself

---

[*] 2 Cor. vii. 10.

in words like those of the prodigal,* " Father, I have sinned in Thy sight."

As a rule, it will be found that it is actual transgressions—these as distinguished from corrupt habits of soul—which the psalmists have in view when they speak of their sins. Their conscience is principally occupied with the thought that they have, by innumerable transgressions, violated the law, and have thus incurred its just condemnation. But, occasionally, we see them going deeper into the matter, and lamenting the deep corruption of nature out of which their transgressions flow as from a bitter poisonous fountain. They not only confess themselves to be sinners, in the superficial and obvious sense which must be admitted by all in whom the belief in God is not utterly dead; but they distinctly acknowledge that their very nature has been, from their birth, infected with a deep malignity. This doctrine of Original Sin is one that has been as often rejected and as bitterly reviled, as any in the circle of revealed truth. That human nature has, in all men, become depraved; that this depravity is total, insomuch that men, in a state of nature, are disabled from doing anything spiritually good; above all, that this total depravity has been the common property of the race ever since the day that Adam fell, and that it is a heritage transmitted to all mankind as the penal consequence of their apostacy from God in the person of their progenitor and representative—these articles, which together make up the orthodox doctrine of Original Sin, have been regarded with special hostility by the enemies of revealed truth, and have generally been among the first to be explained away or repudiated by individuals and Churches whose love of the doctrines of apostolic Christianity has become cold. Even among those who sorrowfully admit that " all have sinned, and fall short of the glory of God," † there are many who look upon sin as consisting only in particular transgressions or, at most, in bad habits that have gradually grown out of those transgressions. Total depravity they will not admit; and as for the doctrine that sin is in the nature, that it is born with us, being an heirloom which the whole human family inherit from their first head,—the scorn with which they reject it has no

---

* Luke xv. 18. † Rom. iii. 23.

bounds. They rail upon it as a dogma, woven in the loom of the Schoolmen or of the early Fathers, but destitute of solid support in Scripture and repudiated by the enlightened conscience. It would, of course, be too long to set forth the Bible proof of the doctrine in this place; but I think it important to observe that in the Psalter it is quite distinctly acknowledged.

It is not meant, of course, that the doctrine of Original Sin is anywhere formally stated or reasoned out in this book. The Psalms are not doctrinal treatises. There is no express mention either of the first transgression, or of the manner in which the fortunes of the race were affected by that act of apostasy. Curiously enough, the name of Adam is scarcely once mentioned in the Old Testament * after the first five chapters of Genesis, so that we need not marvel at its absence from the psalms. But the whole substance of the doctrine of inborn depravity finds here an articulate echo. Whatever else God's people failed generally to understand and receive, there was plainly no failure either to perceive the drift of His testimony regarding our fallen state or to acknowledge its truth. It is remarkable that when the Apostle sets himself, in the epistle to the Romans, to collect and exhibit the Bible texts which bear witness to the lost and helpless condition of mankind, by reason of sin, the proofs he cites are, with one exception, taken from the Psalms.† He had a purpose in resorting to this book, in particular, for arguments in support of the truth in question. No doubt, texts even more explicit in their testimony might have been found in other parts of the Old Testament; but the Apostle seems to have felt that a singular importance attached to those he cites from the psalmists. Nor is it difficult to discover the reason of the selection. What we hear in the psalms is the voice of the Church, as well as the voice of God's Spirit. Accordingly, when the subject about which they bear witness happens to be one belonging to the domain which lies open to

---

* It is found in our English version in four texts only : Deut. xxxii. 8, Job xxxi. 33, Hosea vi. 7, and 1 Chron. i. 1. In the last of these, the name merely stands at the head of the long genealogical table ; and, in the three others, it is doubtful whether the word is really the proper name, or ought not rather to be translated "man," as it usually is in the Old Testament. It is certainly surprising that the name and history of the father of the race should not have been oftener mentioned in the Hebrew Scriptures.

† Rom. iii. 10-18 ; compared with Psalms xiv. 1-3, v. 9, cxl. 3, x. 7, xxxvi. 1.

the observation of men's own consciousness, the testimony of the psalms is not one but manifold. Borrowing the language of a well-known text,* one might say that in the case supposed, " the Spirit beareth witness along with the spirit of God's people." Double weight attaches, therefore, to the affirmations made in the psalms respecting our sinful and lost condition, for in them the truth is affirmed by the concurrent testimony, first, of the Spirit of inspiration speaking in the holy psalmists, and then, of the innumerable multitude of the godly who, during so many generations, have appropriated the confessions of the psalmists, and addressed them to God as the expression of their own heartfelt conviction.

The apostle's longest quotation is from the FOURTEENTH Psalm, which I shall therefore set down here entire :—

1. The fool hath said in his heart, There is no God.
   They are corrupt, they have done abominable works ;
   There is none that doeth good.
2. The LORD looked down from heaven upon the children of men,
   To see if there were any that did understand,
   That did seek after God.
3. They have all gone aside ; they are together become filthy ;
   There is none that doeth good, no, not one.
4. Have all the workers of iniquity no knowledge ?
   Who eat up My people as they eat bread,
   And call not upon the LORD.
5. There were they in great fear :
   For God is in the generation of the righteous.
6. Ye put to shame the counsel of the poor,
   Because the LORD is his refuge.
7. Oh that the salvation of Israel were come out of Zion !
   When the LORD bringeth back the captivity of His people,
   Then shall Jacob rejoice, and Israel shall be glad.

It is the first three verses that are cited by the apostle in support of the doctrine that " both Jews and Greeks are all under sin," and that "the whole world is brought under the judgment of God." And certainly the terms applied by the psalmist are quite as universal in their sweep as those of the apostle. Indeed, this very fact, that the terms are so sweeping, has been urged as a reason why some construction less severe should be put on the psalm. " The psalmist (it is argued) can-

---

* Rom. viii. 16.

not mean that all men, without exception, are such as he describes. For we know that, in fact, they are not so. There is a congregation of the righteous. In the worst times, God has His seven thousand who abide faithful to Him. And even beyond that circle there is much virtue to be found, much civil righteousness, much beautiful natural affection." The facts alleged, blessed be God, are patent, and are not to be gainsayed; nevertheless the apostle's interpretation is the only one that will stand. No doubt there is a congregation of the godly on earth. But they are what they are, not by nature, but by the grace of God; so that their godliness does not avail to mitigate our judgment regarding fallen human nature. And as for the natural virtues that still adorn the world and claim the admiration of men, they are vitiated before God by this, that there is no regard in them to His will. The gravamen of the psalmist's indictment against natural men is, that " they do not seek after God."

This one passage is sufficient to demonstrate Original Sin. For if all men, everywhere and always, turn away from God till His grace recover them, there must be some reason for their doing so. A constant event indicates a law of nature. There must be in mankind a certain malignity of nature, an inborn ungodliness of heart. The existence of this innate depravity is more distinctly asserted in the Fifty-eighth Psalm :

3. The wicked are estranged [turn aside] from the womb:
    They go astray as soon as they be born, speaking lies.
4. Their poison is like the poison of a serpent:
    They are like the deaf adder that stoppeth her ear;
5. Which hearkeneth not to the voice of charmers,
    Charming never so wisely.

It is not easy to make out whether these words are spoken of mankind in general, or only of the worse sort of men. But, in either case, their testimony is unequivocal, to the effect that there is such a thing in men as inborn depravity, corruption of nature, a headlong tendency to sin brought from the very womb.

There is a feature, I confess, in the severe testimonies we have quoted which makes it comparatively easy for any one to say Amen to them. They are in the third person. A man may, with a dry cheek and unbroken heart, confess other people's sins, or even the inborn depravity of the race ; and there is too much confession of sin that goes no further. But the Psalter contains other and more trying testimonies. Thus the anonymous Hundred-and-thirtieth Psalm opens with a cry that comes from the very heart : "Out of the depths have I cried unto Thee, O LORD. Lord, hear my voice ; let Thine ears be attentive to the voice of my supplications. If Thou, LORD, shouldest mark iniquities, O Lord, who shall stand ?" Here the penitent expresses the heartfelt conviction that there is on every soul of man such a burden of sin as only God's mercy can remove ; and this he speaks, not in mitigation of his own share in the general sin, but as the aggravation of his dismay. The Fifty-first Psalm is another of the same class, and the most remarkable of them all. We know well both who the writer was and the occasion on which it was composed. Notice has already been taken of the way in which it brands sin as an offence committed against the majesty of God. That was the royal penitent's first thought. From it he was led on to look into his heart—to scrutinise it by the light which his glaring transgression had thrown into its depths. The result of the scrutiny he records, first, in the sorrowful confession, "Behold, I was shapen in iniquity ; and in sin did my mother conceive me," and then in the prayer that follows, "Create in me a clean heart, O God ; and renew a right spirit within me." He saw that his transgression sprang from the root of a depraved nature. It is possible that, in some sense, he knew the doctrine of original sin before. He had meditated much, as this very psalm proves, on the spiritual import of the rites prescribed in the Law ; and he can scarcely have failed to decipher the testimony to inborn depravity which the wisdom of God had inscribed on some of these. The ordinance of Infant Circumcision signified not obscurely that children, even the children of God's people, are, by nature, uncircumcised in heart ; and that intimation was made more emphatic by the law which debarred the Hebrew mother from the sanctuary for eight days after her child was born, and prescribed lustrations for the removal of the taint contracted in child-bearing. * However, to discover a doctrine in the Bible is one thing ; to find the truth of it in one's own heart is another. The Fifty-first Psalm shows that

---

* Lev. xii.

David had been enabled to do both. The humbling doctrine of Original Sin, which he had read before in the Law, was, through his fall, certified and illustrated to him by the testimony of his own conscience. He got such a sight of human depravity—of depravity inherent in the very nature, born with the man into the world, and so radical as to render necessary the creation of a new heart—that it came upon him with the force of a new discovery. And a hundred generations of God's people have repeated his confession, as a just and sober expression of what they have found to be true of themselves.

Before passing from this topic, I am anxious to observe that there is an intimate, although much-overlooked, connection between it and the doctrine of the Divine Similitude in Man, elucidated in the preceding chapter. I do not hesitate to say that a principal cause of some men's unwillingness or inability to accept the plainly revealed doctrine regarding our hereditary and total corruption of nature is to be found in the wretchedly low idea they have formed respecting the proper dignity of man. I am well aware that this is not their own way of explaining the matter. On the contrary, they imagine themselves peculiarly the advocates of human nature, and continually deride the low, unworthy, uncharitable views of it which (as they suppose) characterise those who adhere to the old evangelical opinions. Nevertheless they are mistaken. The real difference between them and us relates to the answer to be given to the question, What is the chief end of man? What is the true *idea* of human nature? With what intention did God make man? They do not attempt to answer that question; but their whole way of thinking is based on the assumption that man's chief end is to be found in the practice of the social virtues; that if a man be just in his dealings, if he be a kind neighbour, a generous friend, warm-hearted and dutiful in the circle of his own family, he is entitled to be looked upon as a good man and is well-pleasing to God. It may be freely conceded that if that *idea* of human nature had been the right one, the doctrine of Original Sin might reasonably enough be discarded. Judged by that standard, human nature is not utterly depraved. There is much civil righteousness amongst natural men, much neighbourly kindness, much domestic affection. But the standard is false, and false because base. It falls infinitely short of the true *idea* of our nature. The psalmists believed that man is of kin to God, and that his chief end is to know, and serve, and enjoy God. It was precisely because their minds were possessed with such a lofty conception of God's intention in making man, that they felt so keenly the guilt, the degradation, the helpless impotence of their fallen condition. Let a man once be awakened to a just sense of his chief end, and nothing more will be needed to make him feel, like the psalmists, that he has sinned and fallen short of the glory of God, and that alienation from God is rooted in his very nature.

II. Passing from the subject of sin, let us consider what the Psalter teaches respecting the DIVINELY PROVIDED REMEDY.

1. It distinctly, and with assured persuasion, celebrates the truth that "there is mercy with the LORD, and plenteous redemption." These are the words in which one of the psalmists invites Israel to "hope in the LORD;" and before giving utterance to them he makes a profession of his own faith in the comfortable truth on which he encourages others to lay hold: "There is forgiveness with Thee, that Thou mayest be feared."* These are very simple statements; but they are more precious than gold and sweeter than the honey-comb. Among the heathen there were of old, and there still are, instances of individuals smitten with convictions of sin, fallen into the depths, and crying out for light and deliverance. But they possessed no articulate revelation of God's willingness to forgive,—no such revelation of divine grace as might have enabled them to find rest in the persuasion expressed in the psalmist's words. Being "separate from Christ, and strangers from the covenants of the promise," the heathen "had no hope, and were without God in the world."†

---

* Ps. cxxx. 4, 7.

† Eph. ii. 12. The hymns of the Rig Veda, as translated by Max Müller, remarkably illustrate both parts of the above statement. There are touching confessions of sin and a certain "feeling after God," but there is no assured knowledge of pardon. (See the specimens given in Müller's *Chips from a German Workshop*, I. pp. 39-41.) The same remark applies to the Babylonian and Accadian hymns quoted by Dr. Cheyne (*Book of Psalms:* Introd. pp. viii, ix.). Beautiful and touching as these are, they at no point exhibit that articulate hope in God's sin-forgiving mercy which characterises the Bible psalms, and of which one may surely venture to affirm that it can spring only from the knowledge of God's Name.

It would be interesting to inquire by what means the Psalmists reached the clear discovery of God's willingness to forgive which they manifestly had made. I believe that the true explanation is the one suggested by the terms used by the apostle, in that description of the heathen world from which I have just quoted. The psalmists belonged to the commonwealth of Israel, whom God had chosen to be the depositaries of His oracles and ordinances, and therefore, unlike the heathen, they possessed "the covenants of the promise" and were not "separate from Christ." They were familiar with the Name of the Lord, which was proclaimed in the hearing of Moses on the Mount : "The Lord, the Lord, a God full of compassion and gracious, slow to anger, and plenteous in mercy and truth ; keeping mercy for thousands, forgiving iniquity, and transgression, and sin ; and that will by no means clear the guilty."* Knowing that joyful sound, they walked in the light of God's countenance. They had diligently weighed the promise respecting the seed of the woman, the Redeemer of Israel. Moreover, they witnessed continually those sacrifices and manifold lustrations which were performed in the Temple, by God's command ; and might well perceive that the intention of them was to represent the making satisfaction for sin, the propitiating of God's just anger, the forgiving of men's offences, the purification of their souls from the taint of evil. No doubt, the purpose of God in the Levitical ordinances was constantly overlooked or misconstrued by the unawakened and self-satisfied multitude. The example of the Pharisees and of the Sadducees shows how impenetrable the secret of the Law was to persons of a self-righteous or a coldly secular spirit ; and many seem to think that the Hebrew Church was made up of Pharisees and Sadducees. But the psalms tell another tale. They show that, from generation to generation, the Spirit of God went on convincing men of sin ; and that, when men were brought to repentance, the divine oracles and ordinances were seen to be radiant with evangelical light. It would have been a pleasant study, if our space had permitted, to gather up the covert allusions to Levitical rites or ancient predictions which are scattered up and down in the psalms, and to mark the success with which the psalmists have

---

* Exod. xxxiv. 6, 7.

been enabled to penetrate the mind of God in them. The following may serve for specimens of the kind of allusions I have in view :—

> li. 2. Wash me throughly from mine iniquity,
>   And cleanse me from my sin.
>
>   7. Purge me with hyssop, and I shall be clean :
>   Wash me, and I shall be whiter than snow.
>
> lxv. 3. Iniquities are too strong for me :
>   As for our transgressions, Thou shalt make atonement for them.*

2. If the Psalter is unfaltering in its recognition of the truth of redemption, it is no less so in what it teaches respecting the manner in which the sinner becomes interested in that redemption. It is told of Luther, that one day being asked which of all the psalms were the best, he made answer, " Psalmi Paulini," and when his friends pressed to know which these might be, he said, " The Thirty-second, the Fifty-first, the Hundred-and-thirtieth, the Hundred-and-forty-third. For they all teach that the forgiveness of our sins comes, without the law and without works, to the man who believes, and therefore I call them Pauline Psalms ; and when David sings, ' There is forgiveness with Thee, that Thou mayest be feared,' this is just what Paul says, ' God hath concluded them all in unbelief, that He might have mercy upon all' (Rom. xi. 32). Thus no man may boast of his own righteousness. That word, ' That Thou mayest be feared,' brushes away all merit, and teaches us to uncover our heads before God, and confess *gratia est, non meritum ; remissio, non satisfactio ;* it is mere forgiveness, not merit at all." † This judgment of the great Reformer is just. There are psalms that breathe the very gospel which Paul loved to preach. The term " faith " may hardly be found in the Psalter : one may search in vain for such a formula as that which the great apostle so much delighted to employ, " By grace have ye been saved, through faith ; not of works, that no man should glory." ‡ But the sentiment which finds its dogmatic

---

* Ps. lxv. 3. In this text I retain the translation given in the first edition. I observe that the American company of Revisers have put an equivalent translation in the margin, *Thou shalt expiate them.* The allusion, of course, is to the Levitical expiations.

† The *Table Talk*, as cited by Delitzsch (at Ps. cxxx.).

‡ Eph. ii. 8, 9.

expression in that formula pervades the whole of the psalms, and is especially prominent in those deeply experimental ones which Luther enumerates. It would not be difficult to set forth, in the form of a collection of texts gathered out of them, a complete answer to that question of questions, What must I do to be saved? and it would be found to correspond in its whole substance to the answer which the apostles were wont to give.

cxliii. 2. Enter not into judgment with Thy servant;
    For in Thy sight shall no man living be justified.

  li. 16. Thou delightest not in sacrifice; else would I give it;
    Thou hast no pleasure in burnt offering.
    17. The sacrifices of God are a broken spirit.

cxxx. 4. There is forgiveness with Thee,
    That Thou mayest be feared.
    5. I wait for the LORD, my soul doth wait,
    And in His word do I hope.

xxxii. 5. I acknowledged my sin unto Thee, and mine iniquity have
    I not hid;
    I said, I will confess my transgressions unto the LORD;
    And Thou forgavest the iniquity of my sin.

Could words more persuasively express the way of a sinner's acceptance with God? When the sinner, deeply convinced of sin, makes the discovery that there is mercy for sinners in God and plenteous redemption, and is thus moved to repair to Him with humble confession and hope in His mercy, his sin is forgiven; and if the inward assurance of his acceptance be not immediately vouchsafed, he is encouraged to wait for it,—to wait for it with hopeful, ardent expectation, as the watcher waiteth for the morning.

III. It remains that we consider the view which the Psalter gives of THE CONDITION OF THOSE WHO HAVE EMBRACED THE DIVINELY PROVIDED REDEMPTION. In other words, What are the characteristics of God's people, and how does religion accomplish its progress in their souls? It is on this head that the testimony of the psalms is especially copious. They are the songs of God's redeemed, and furnish the most perfect reflection of the whole life of faith. The rays of light which they reflect on the condition of the soul without God, and even those which they throw on the great spiritual revolu-

tion in which the sinner, smitten with repentance and turning
to the covenant, embraces the promise, confesses his sin, and
finds mercy, are not to be compared to the flood of illustration
they shed on the condition and manifold experience of the
forgiven and regenerated soul. I can only touch on the more
prominent and important particulars.

1. God's people are justified by their faith. The great evangelical doctrine of justification by faith, the central doctrine of
the gospel which the apostles preached and the reformers set
forth afresh, underlies all those psalms (and they are many)
in which the saints express their tranquil assurance of God's
favour. It was because they were justified by faith that they
had peace with God and were able to rejoice in hope of His
glory. But it is not by implication only that this cardinal
truth is taught. When the apostle, in the epistle to the
Romans, collects the testimony of the Old Testament to his
doctrine, the second passage he brings forward is taken from
a Psalm, and it is one of the four which Luther so felicitously
entitled the *Psalmi Paulini:* "To him that worketh not, but
believeth on Him that justifieth the ungodly, his faith is
reckoned for righteousness. Even as David also pronounceth
blessing upon the man unto whom God reckoneth righteousness
apart from works, saying, Blessed are they whose iniquities are
forgiven." * The quotation is from the Thirty-second Psalm :—

1. Blessed is he whose transgression is forgiven, whose sin is
   covered :
2. Blessed is the man unto whom the LORD imputeth not iniquity,
   And in whose spirit there is no guile.

The apostle's way of interpreting the text is remarkable.
Finding David celebrating the *non-imputation of iniquity,* he
construes this to mean the *imputation of righteousness.* Some
have made bold to challenge the legitimacy of the construction,
and have contended that the apostle quotes David's words by
way of accommodation. But the interpretation is strictly
correct. For what are the sins whose non-imputation is so
gratefully celebrated ? Are they the man's positive transgressions only ? his sins of commission ? That cannot be.
For in that case the non-imputation would still leave the man

* Rom. iv. 5, 6.

under the ban of God's holy law.   A sin of omission may sink a soul in perdition as surely as a sin of commission.   " Inasmuch as ye did it *not*," will be the word of condemnation to many in the great day.*   It must therefore be the non-imputation of all sins, of either kind, that David celebrates.   Now, if God impute to a man neither his transgressions of the law, nor his omissions of duty, He treats him as a man who has fulfilled all righteousness, which is just to say, that He imputes to him righteousness without works.†

And this brings out very clearly the nature of the benefit which the Scriptures celebrate under the title of Justification. It is forgiveness; and it is something more.   When a pardon comes down from the Crown to some condemned felon, it cancels the sentence and opens the prison door; but there its effect ceases.   It does not restore the wretch to his former standing in society.   He is a marked man for life.   Very different is the effect of the pardon God bestows on those who, trusting in His mercy, confess their sins.   By their faith they are *justified*.   For Christ's sake they are treated as righteous persons, as persons who had perfectly obeyed the law.   God imputes to them righteousness, the righteousness of Christ, in whom they trust.   The ground of justification is not plainly declared in the Psalms.   It could not be plainly declared till Christ died.   Nevertheless, the doctrine of justification itself is distinctly revealed.   And, as already stated, this truth, which comes up in the shape of a clear articulate statement in the Thirty-second Psalm, underlies all the rest of the psalms. The voice which makes itself heard in the songs of God's Israel is not the voice of a prodigal who has been forgiven merely, and has been suffered to take a place among the bondservants of his father's house.   It is the voice of a son, rejoicing in all the inexpressible joys of sonship and compassed about with songs of deliverance.   Thus David sings in the Hundred-and-third Psalm :—

  1. Bless the LORD, O my soul;
       And all that is within me, bless His holy name.
  2. Bless the LORD, O my soul,
       And forget not all His benefits :

---

* Matt. xxv. 45.
† Compare Chalmers, *Lectures on Romans*, at chap. iv. 6.

3. Who forgiveth all thine iniquities ;
   Who healeth all thy diseases ;
4. Who redeemeth thy life from destruction ;
   Who crowneth thee with lovingkindness and tender mercies :
5. Who satisfieth thy mouth with good things ;
   So that thy youth is renewed like the eagle.

.   .   .   .   .

10. He hath not dealt with us after our sins,
    Nor rewarded us after our iniquities.
11. For as the heaven is high above the earth,
    So great is His mercy toward them that fear Him.
12. As far as the east is from the west,
    So far hath He removed our transgressions from us.
13. Like as a father pitieth his children,
    So the LORD pitieth them that fear Him.

2. God's people are held forth in the psalms as regenerated also. A clean heart has been created in them ; a right spirit has been put within them. The feelings which everywhere find utterance are redolent of holiness as well as peace, and correspond at every point to those of the spiritual man whom the apostles contrast with the natural man. The reader will recollect the passages in which we have seen the Psalmists spurning the earth, turning with eager expectation heavenwards, and seeking God's face ; the passages also in which they abjure the fellowship of the "men of the world, whose portion is in this life," and declare their desire to possess God for their portion. He will remember, moreover, the multitude of places in which the saints are described as " delighting in the law of the Lord, and meditating in His law by day and by night ; " as delighting to trace God's hand in the works of nature and the vicissitudes of providence ; and as desiring, above all, to dwell in the house of the Lord all the days of their life, to behold His beauty, His loving-kindness and tender mercy, as they are manifested in the appointed ordinances of His worship. From these classes of texts no quotation need be made ; they lie on the surface, and are patent to every reader. Their meaning may be summed up in this : that God's people are persons who have come to know what is their chief end, whose minds have been opened to know and feel that their felicity lies in God, and who make it, therefore, their paramount object in life to " seek after God."

Such is the general cast of the piety which distinguishes

God's redeemed, as their heart is laid open in the psalms. Some subordinate features claim notice in connection with it.

(1) The Psalter so pourtrays the faithful as to show that they are not yet made perfect. Although God's law is the law of their minds, being seated securely on the throne of their affections, there remains another law, in their members, warring against that better law. Every day they need both pardon and strength. This need is urgent not only in their days of back-sliding and darkness, but in their best and brightest days. At the very time when they are filled with the assured confidence that they are God's servants and that their transgressions are expiated, they are fain to pray God not to enter into judgment with them, and are constrained to confess that their iniquities are too strong for them.* The life of faith is accordingly held forth as a militant life, a warfare in which there is no discharge on this side the grave. The sanctity which pours out its heart before God in the psalms has nothing in common with the sanctity of the Pharisee, who, when he comes into the Temple, has no penitent confession to offer, but only proud thanks that he is not as other men are.

(2) At the same time, the Psalter shows no taint of morbid humility. On the contrary, there is much in it which has seemed to some not unlearned readers to savour of self-righteous-ness. How boldly does David, for example, in the Seventeenth Psalm, assert his integrity, and call on the Lord to pronounce judgment on his character!

> 1. Hear the right, O LORD, attend unto my cry ;
>   Give ear unto my prayer, that goeth not out of feigned lips.
> 2. Let my sentence come forth from Thy presence ;
>   Let Thine eyes look upon equity.
> 3. Thou hast proved mine heart ; Thou hast visited me in the night ;
>   Thou hast tried me, and findest nothing ;
>   I am purposed that my mouth shall not transgress.
> 4. As for the works of men, by the word of Thy lips
>   I have kept me from the ways of the violent.
> 5. My steps have held fast to Thy paths,
>   My feet have not slipped.

---

* Ps. cxliii. 2 ; lxv. 3.

What can be the meaning of this appeal? Has David forgotten how he elsewhere deprecates God's entering into judgment with him? Has the leaven of the Pharisees corrupted his humility? No such thing. The explanation must be sought in another quarter. The psalm was written during Saul's shameful persecution of him. David was treated as a malefactor by the rulers of his country; whereas in relation to them he was blameless. Yet the Lord seemed to forget this and to leave him in their hand. Hence his appeal to the judgment of the King of kings. The psalm reminds us that from man's injustice and misconstructions there always lies an appeal to God, and it certifies us that He is well-pleased to hear His people making the appeal. This kind of appeal and protestation of integrity is quite consistent with a deep sense of sin before God. The same apostle who confessed that in his flesh dwelt no good thing, and that sin tainted his best deeds, resolutely asserted his integrity and boasted of his services, when his personal uprightness and apostolic authority were called in question. Job not only made a similar profession of integrity, but exceeded bounds in asserting it; yet the Lord commended him as having spoken better than his friends. God's people, if they are such indeed, can with truth affirm, like David, that they are the same before God when He visits them by night as they are before men by day; and He is not displeased to find them showing even a keenness and heat of jealousy when their sincerity is called in question.

(3) The piety delineated in the Psalter, although it soars to heaven and its life is hid in God, never omits the assiduous cultivation of the lowly duties of every-day morality. The Church has always been infested with a sort of people whose religion is all expended on the first Table of the law; who, along with a great show of contrition, and faith, and spiritual joy, and delight in God's worship, are ill-natured in the domestic circle, censorious and unfriendly neighbours, unsafe men to deal with in business. It may be questioned whether the duties of common life are always so faithfully inculcated in the evangelical pulpit as they ought to be; but of this I am sure, that the psalms do full justice to the perfect law of God in this matter. Whatever may be the quarter whence the Antinomian perversion of the gospel may derive its aliment, certainly it is not from them.

What a fine portrait the Fifteenth Psalm, for example, draws of the godly man! He loves God's tabernacle and holy hill; his heart is there. And when he goes out into the world he does not leave his religion behind. He shows the influence of the fear of God in all he does. "He walketh uprightly, and worketh righteousness, and speaketh truth in his heart." His tongue utters no malice. When he falls in with a vile person, he despises him, although his house may be a palace and his wealth untold; but " he honoureth them that fear the Lord," be they ever so poor. He is a man of his word. He will not make gain of his neighbour's necessity; nor will he, for any consideration, join in condemning one whom he knows to be innocent. These are the true fruits of faith unfeigned. " He that doeth these things shall never be moved."

(4) It remains to be added, that the Psalter shows the sky of God's people brightened with the Hope of the heavenly Glory. But this opens up an extensive and much-agitated question, which deserves and will reward separate consideration.

CHAPTER VI.

THE DOCTRINE OF THE FUTURE LIFE.

IS it indeed true, that the Personal Religion which finds its undying expression in the Psalter is nourished by the spring of a firm hope of eternal life, and that that hope filled and cheered the hearts of God's people from the first age of the Church ? The question is one to which contradictory answers have been given. Not that the general sentiment of devout readers of the Scriptures has wavered much on the point. On their part, it has all along been the prevalent opinion that the hoary fathers of the Church,—the patriarchs, and prophets, and psalmists,—when they came to die, fell asleep in the tranquil expectation of an awakening in glory. The contrary opinion has been pretty much confined to narrow circles of learned men, and may be ranked among the paradoxes of the Schools. Still the point is, on many accounts, too important to be passed by. Certainly, if the hope of eternal life be absent from the psalms,—much more, if there be found in them words which exclude or repel that hope,—they are not suited to be the manual of praise for the Christian Church, the Church of that Prince of life who, by His resurrection, has begotten His people to the living expectation of the glory of God.

It is undeniable that there do occur, in certain psalms, words which have the appearance of excluding the hope of eternal life.* And it may be freely admitted that, if nothing could be brought forward on the other side, we should be shut up to the darkest conclusions regarding the feelings with which the Old Testament saints looked forward to their dissolution. These psalms, accordingly, are much referred to for the purpose of making out one of two things ; either that the Old Testament

---

* Psalms vi. 5 ; xxx. 9 ; lxxxviii. 10-12 ; lxxxix. 47 ; cxv. 17.

saints were utterly ignorant of a future life, or that their minds were possessed with heathenish notions of it, as a state of darkness and of distance from God.   The right interpretation of the texts in question is not without its difficulties.   But many circumstances concur to show that we are by no means shut up to conclusions so widely different from those which have found general favour with simple-minded students of the divine word.

I. It is to be observed that, with one exception, the passages referred to occur in psalms of complaint ; and, in fact, are cries of distress lifted up to heaven in seasons of darkness and trouble. A moment's reflection will make it manifest that words spoken in such circumstances are not to be so severely construed as if they occurred in a calm dispassionate confession of a man's faith.   Let the Eighty-ninth Psalm be taken for example.   It was written by Ethan the Ezrahite when he witnessed the collapse of the glory of David's house, and the Lord's seeming breach of covenant with David and with Israel.*   The over-turn was so complete as to forbid the hope that the psalmist or any of his contemporaries should ever again, while they lived, behold the good of Jerusalem as they had seen it in the golden reigns of Solomon and his father.   This was a bitter reflection to one who so dearly loved Zion ; and, when he poured out his heart before God, he could not refrain from a passionate complaint because of the brevity of human life.   God's promise to David, his faith assured him, would yet be fulfilled ; but what comfort was there in that to one who knew that he should be dead long before the fulfilment came ?

46. How long, O LORD, wilt Thou hide Thyself for ever ?
    How long shall Thy wrath burn like fire ?
47. O remember how short my time is :
    For what vanity hast Thou created all the children of men !
48. What man is he that shall live and not see death,
    That shall deliver his soul from the power of Sheol ?

This undoubtedly sounds like the voice of one who knows no hereafter.   The psalmist speaks as if all his hopes were bounded by the grave, as if the overthrow of the united kingdom of Judah and Ephraim had bereft him of all his joy, and as if he

---

* Compare Book I. chap. v. (p. 82).

knew no future kingdom to compensate him with its hopes.
But it would be doing cruel injustice to take him thus at his
word. What we hear is the language of passion, not of sedate
conviction. This is well expressed by John Howe in a famous
sermon. " The expostulation (he observes) was somewhat
passionate, and did proceed upon the sudden view of this dis-
consolate case, very abstractly considered, and by itself only ;
and the psalmist did not, in that instant, look beyond it to a
better and more comfortable scene of things. An eye bleared
with present sorrow sees not so far, nor comprehends so much
at one view, as it would at another time, or as it doth presently
when the tear is wiped out and its own beams have cleared it
up."* It would be unwarrantable, therefore, to infer from
Ethan's expostulation, that the saints who lived under the early
kings were strangers to the hope of everlasting life. I am inclined to go further, and to point to this very complaint as
affording a presumption that there was in their hearts an irre-
pressible sentiment of immortality. The bird that frets and
wounds itself on the bars of its cage shows thereby that its
proper home is the free air. When inveterate sensuality has
quenched in a man's heart the hope of a life beyond the
grave, the dreary void which succeeds utters itself, not in
solemn complaints like Ethan's, but in songs of forced mirth,
—dismal Anacreontic songs : " Let us eat and drink, for to-
morrow we die." †

> " 'Tis time to live if I grow old,
> 'Tis time short pleasures now to take,
> Of little life the best to make,
> And manage wisely the last stake." ‡

2. It deserves notice, moreover, that several of the psalms
which seem so void of hope were written under deep impres-
sions of sin and an awful sense of God's displeasure. What we
hear in them is the cry of hearts smitten with the fear that they
are unforgiven, and that God's wrath abides upon them. It is
no marvel if, in such a state of mind, the blackest views of
death and of the world beyond are seen to predominate. An

---

* *The Vanity of Man as Mortal*, p. 2.
† 1 Cor. xv. 32.
‡ Anacreon's *Age*, as translated by Cowley.

instance of this occurs in the Sixth Psalm, the earliest of the class known as " The Penitential Psalms."* It is David's sorrowful prayer for mercy at a time of deep affliction,—affliction inexpressibly aggravated by the thought that he had brought it upon himself by his crimes, so that he could not but see in it the wrath of an offended God.

> 1. O LORD, rebuke me not in Thine anger,
>   Neither chasten me in Thy hot displeasure.
> 4. Return, O LORD, deliver my soul;
>   Save me for Thy lovingkindness' sake.
> 5. For in death there is no remembrance of Thee:
>   In Sheol who shall give Thee thanks?

Dr. Delitzsch observes very justly † that the Christian need have no difficulty or scruple about appropriating these words, although he knows very well that in the world to come God is both remembered and praised continually; for we may quite legitimately take what the psalmist has written regarding the invisible world generally, and apply it in our minds to the place of torment. We are sure that in the lake of fire there is no more any thankful commemoration of God, no singing of sweet psalms. I would go a step further, and attribute this meaning to the psalmist himself. At the time when he uttered his cry for mercy, David feared that he was unforgiven, that his afflictions were the rod of an angry Judge, not of a loving Father. Is it any wonder if, under that apprehension, he takes a very black view of death? To a man who is unforgiven, death is just what the psalm declares it to be,—the final separation of the soul from God, its banishment into a region where His name is no more recorded. This is the explanation of the psalm given by Luther and Calvin, amongst others; and they knew from experience something of the inward conflict which it unfolds. I will add, that these penitential psalms, dark and full of unbelief as they may at some points appear to be, are not the least precious of the songs we owe to the harp of David. The hopeful exultation with which they usually close encourages the penitent to trust that, if he will only pour out his complaint at the throne of grace, his soul will be disburdened. And surely

---

* Psalms vi., xxxii., xxxviii., li., cii., cxxx., cxliii.
† *Commentar*, vol. ii. 422 (*Allgemeiner Bericht*, chap. 10).

we may see God's love in the circumstance, that He not only invites us to pour out our hearts before Him, but puts into our mouths words in which we may give utterance to our anguish and fear.

3. Yet another consideration is suggested by the fact (it is a very significant one), that the psalms in question all express an earnest solicitude for the glory of God. If death is deprecated, it is in order that the Lord may not lose the glory, nor His Church the service, which a life prolonged might furnish. This is well exemplified in the Hundred-and-fifteenth, which I the rather cite because, being the sole exception to the rule that the dark views of death are found in psalms of contrition and deep sorrow, it is the only psalm to which the preceding observations are inapplicable. It is a tranquil hymn of praise, and may be rendered as follows :—

17. The dead are not they who praise the LORD;
　　Neither any that go down into silence,
18. But WE * will bless the LORD
　　From this time forth and for evermore.
　　Hallelujah !

The psalm thus closed was one of the Songs of the Second Temple. What we hear in it is the voice of the Church, rather than of an individual soul. And this may assist us in perceiving its harmony with faith in the heavenly glory. The honour of God requires that there be continued, on the earth, a visible Church, in which His name may be recorded from generation to generation. The function is one which cannot be performed by the dead. Since, therefore, the uppermost desire of the Church ought ever to be that God's Name may be hallowed, His Kingdom advanced, and His Will done on the earth, it is her duty to pray for continued subsistence here, on the earth, to witness for God. And it is to be carefully observed, that not only in this passage, but in all the parallel texts in

---

* The pronoun is emphatic in the original. The English Versions (the Authorised and the Revised) fail to bring out sufficiently the point of the contrast instituted between the dead and the living. It is well brought out in Ewald's *nicht die todten loben Jah . . . aber wir—wir segnen Jah.* So Professor Alexander, Dr. Cheyne, and all the recent German translators. Comp. Jerome's Version from the Hebrew, *Non mortui laudabunt Dominum . . . Sed nos benedicemus Domino.*

which the psalmists seem to speak doubtfully or disparagingly of the state of the departed, it is in connection with the interest of God's cause on the earth.   The thought that is uppermost in their hearts is, that "in death there is no commemoration" of God—no recording of His name for the salvation of men.   This single circumstance might, I think, suffice to put the reader on his guard against a precipitate fastening on them of a meaning which would exclude the hope of eternal life.   It goes far to show that what the psalmists deprecate is not death simply considered, but premature death.   Their prayer is, "O my God, take me not away in the midst of my days." *   And I do not hesitate to say, that there are men so placed in stations of eminent usefulness, that it is their duty to make the prayer their own.   No one will attribute to the Lord Jesus either darkness or hesitation of mind with respect to the future state or the blessedness of that state to the righteous ; yet He spoke of His life on the earth as His " day," a day that was soon to be swallowed up in a night wherein there should be no more power to work. †   We have every one a day's work appointed us by God ; and if we have reason to suppose that our day's work is not done, we may well join with the psalmists in deprecating the coming on of " the night when no man can work."

I have thought it right to begin our inquiry into the doctrine of the Psalter respecting the Future Life with a notice of the passages which seem to make most strongly against our belief that this part of the Divine Word glows with the hope of eternal glory.   It may be admitted that some of the passages disclose a state of painful darkness, and are hardly of the sort that would command ready entrance into a modern collection of sacred poetry.   Nevertheless they are worthy of the place assigned to them by the Spirit.   Experience testifies that not seldom the way of God's pilgrims lies through the Valley of the Shadow of Death, as well as over the Delectable Mountains ; and if the Psalter lets us hear the lamentable cry of Christian in the valley, as well as his joyful shout on descrying the walls of the heavenly city, we ought to accept the fact

---

* Ps. cii. 24.   † John ix. 4.

as a new proof, that it is indeed the authentic utterance of the whole heart of God's children in their entire pilgrimage.

The number of psalms in which there is an expression of faith and hope regarding the Future Life is very considerable. They may be grouped in three classes.

I. There are some in which the Psalmists profess their hope by appropriating to themselves the confession of the patriarchs, that they were strangers and sojourners on the earth. The history of Abraham, Isaac, and Jacob contains nothing more interesting or affecting than the recital of the circumstances in which they witnessed this good confession. After Abraham and Sarah had dwelt together long, as joint-heirs of the grace of life, it pleased the Lord to take away from the patriarch's side the wife of his youth, the dear partner of his life, and he was fain to solicit from the sons of Heth a sepulchre in which he might bury her dust. He prefaced his request with the words, " I am a stranger and a sojourner with you." * The same confession was made by Jacob, many years after, when he stood before the king of Egypt. Being asked how old he was, he replied, " The days of the years of my pilgrimage are an hundred-and-thirty years." † Thus he too confessed he was a pilgrim as his fathers had been. The confession thus made by those venerable saints was often repeated by their descendants. ‡ It means much more than some hasty readers perceive. It is often quoted in a way that shows it is taken to mean no more than that the patriarchs knew and acknowledged that they were mortal men, frail creatures, whose days on earth were a fleeting shadow. But if that had been all, it was a confession that might have come quite as well from the sons of Heth as from Abraham, from Pharaoh as from Jacob. We must seek some worthier interpretation. Jacob's confession was not one that Pharaoh could have made. Pharaoh was not a stranger and sojourner in Egypt. Egypt was his home, the only home he knew or desired. With Jacob it was not so. He had no home on the earth. His home lay in a better country. His eye had never seen it ; he had never set foot upon it ; nevertheless he looked for it, and was content, for its sake, to sojourn

---

* Gen. xxiii. 4. † Gen. xlvii. 9.
‡ Exod. ii. 22 ; 1 Chron. xxix. 15.

as a stranger on the earth. This is the interpretation which the epistle to the Hebrews puts on the patriarchs' confession. "They that say such things make it manifest that they are seeking after a country of their own. And if indeed they had been mindful of that country from which they went out, they would have had opportunity to return. But now they desire a better country, that is, a heavenly : wherefore God is not ashamed of them, to be called their God : for He hath prepared for them a city." *

Bearing this interpretation in mind (and it is the only one which a serious consideration of the words will allow), how instructive it is to find the Psalmists witnessing the same confession ! David does so in the Thirty-ninth Psalm, which is a complaint because of the frailty and vanity of human life :—

> 12. Hear my prayer, O LORD, and give ear unto my cry;
> Hold not Thy peace at my tears :
> For I am a stranger with Thee,
> A sojourner, as all my fathers were.

In the literal sense of the words, David was *not* a stranger and sojourner in the land, as the patriarchs had been. Judah was the place of his nativity ; and from the roof of his palace at Jerusalem his eye might daily visit the fields about Bethlehem where his boyhood had been spent. It is plain, therefore, that in appropriating the patriarchs' confession, he put the same construction upon it as the writer of the epistle to the Hebrews has done. Walking in the steps of the faith in which his godly progenitors had lived and died, he set his face towards the better country and declared that his true citizenship was in heaven. One of the later psalmists, also, witnesses the same good confession, and urges it as a plea in enforcement of the prayer, that the Lord would vouchsafe him a deeper insight into His law : "I am a sojourner in the earth; hide not Thy commandments from me." † As if he had said, " This earth is not my home : I find nothing in it worthy to be my soul's portion. Thou art my portion, my dwelling-place, my exceeding great reward. O hide not from me, therefore, the knowledge of Thy commandments. How but by their help can

---

* Heb. xi. 14–16.   † Ps. cxix. 19.

my soul raise itself to Thee ? It breaketh for the longing it
hath unto them at all times."

II. There are not wanting professions of belief in the future
life of a more explicit and striking kind.

Some of the places where these occur have already come under
our notice, especially in connection with what was said in a
previous chapter respecting the doctrine of the Divine Similitude. For it is evident that that doctrine—especially when
taken in connection with the relative doctrine of the federal
relation of the saints to God—carries the sure hope of a
blessed immortality in its bosom. It implies that men may
claim an interest in God of a kind from which the lower
creatures are debarred. God has said to the believing soul, " I
am thy God ; " and the soul may without presumption reply,
" Thou art my God." These are plain words ; but who can
fathom the thought they express ? When the Sadducees came
to Christ thinking to perplex Him with their cavilling
objections against the doctrine of eternal life, He silenced them,
to the admiration of the multitude, by quoting the text in
which the Lord proclaimed Himself to be the God of the
patriarchs. " As touching the resurrection of the dead, have ye
not read that which was spoken unto you by God, saying, I
am the God of Abraham, and the God of Isaac, and the God of
Jacob ? God is not the God of the dead, but of the living."*
The argument is this. The Lord would not have described
Himself to Moses as the God of the patriarchs if He had done
nothing more than minister to their support during the few and
evil days of their mortal life. To be Abraham's God is something more than to be Abraham's Guide through a few troubled
and changeful years.† This argument is stated in the epistle
to the Hebrews, with a force that is almost startling : " God is
not ashamed of them, to be called their God (the God of
Abraham, and of Isaac, and of Jacob) ; for He hath prepared for
them a city."‡ God would have been ashamed of them, would
have deemed it unworthy of Himself to be called their God, if all
that remained of them when they died had been the mouldering

---

* Matt. xxii. 31, 32.
† Comp. Bengel's *Gnomon* on Matt. xxii. 32.   ‡ Heb. xi. 16.

bones at Machpelah,—if He had not prepared for them, and duly gathered them into, a city of habitation.   It is incredible that God should have put His grace into men's hearts, and received them into such affectionate intimacy as is implied in His being *their God*, if He had not prepared for them a city in which they might dwell with Him for ever.   Who will venture to impugn this way of interpreting the Old Testament ?   It is Christ's way of interpreting His own Word ; the way He practised Himself, and which the apostles learned of Him ; and it is infinitely to be preferred to the lean, and blind, and barren way taught in some arrogant Schools.   If our eyes were but opened, we should behold many such wondrous things out of places in God's law which, to our dim sight, seem comparatively meagre.

I have not forgotten that it is the doctrine of the Psalter, and not of the Old Testament as a whole, that is the matter in hand.   To look back, as we have been doing, is no digression from our proper task.   No man can do justice to the Psalms who does not study them in connection with the earlier Scriptures, and especially with the Law of Moses.   The Pentateuch was the Bible of the Psalmists.   They studied it with inexpressible ardour, and its chimes ring through their songs.   The light in which they viewed the texts on which we have just seen Christ and the apostles building the doctrine of eternal life was the same in which Christ and the apostles have presented them.   We see, accordingly, that when their meditations turn upon the privilege of communion with God into which His grace has admitted them, they are insensibly led on to profess a joyful hope with respect to the future world. This is exemplified in almost all the passages that were quoted in illustration of the doctrine of the divine similitude in man. Thus in the Seventy-third Psalm, Asaph, when the sight of prosperous ungodliness leads him to think of the more excellent portion his soul possesses in God, finds pleasure in reflecting that this portion is Eternal.

24. Thou shalt guide me with Thy counsel,
    And afterward receive me to glory.
26. My flesh and my heart faileth :
    But God is the strength of my heart and my portion for
    ever.

Thus also David, in the Seventeenth Psalm, when his faith is subjected to a trial of the same sort as Asaph's, finds comfort in the same thought which had proved so helpful to him. Turning away from the "men of the world, whose portion is in this life," he makes this lofty profession of his hope :—

15. As for me, I shall behold Thy face in righteousness ;
I shall be satisfied, when I awake, with Thy likeness.

The strength of these testimonies to the faith of the psalmists does not lie within the scope of a merely grammatical inter- pretation. The expressions made use of do not, by themselves, absolutely compel us to reject the lower and temporal meaning, which accordingly is advocated by some commentators of great eminence. But, standing where they stand, they naturally raise the mind to the higher meaning ; and have done so in the vast majority of serious readers ever since they were penned. Those words of David, for instance, in which he describes his enemies as " men of the world, whose portion is in this life,"—do they not by plain implication hold forth the godly as men who are *not* of this world and whose portion is in another life ? The words are exactly parallel to those of the Apostle in which, contrasting himself with many " whose end is perdition, whose god is the belly, who mind earthly things," he declares that " our citizenship (that is to say, our country, the commonwealth to which we pertain) is in heaven."* This being the psalmist's meaning, is it for a moment to be supposed that when he goes on, as he does in the words that follow, to profess his faith in God with respect to the future, the jubilant hope he utters is bounded by the grave ? Is it to be supposed, that this soul, conscious of the divine image, of present communion with God, and of an interest in His love as its proper portion,—is it to be supposed, I say, that such a man has no better hope to utter than that, ere he finally quits the world, ere he bids farewell to the sun, and the fair face of nature, and the sweet companion- ships of the earth, ere he passes to a land of darkness, and silence, and deep forgetfulness, where the light of God's face will never shine, he shall be satisfied with some transient gleams of the divine favour ? Can this be all that David means in comforting himself

---

* τὸ πολίτευμα ἡμῶν (Phil. iii. 19, 20).

with the hope of a bright awakening, when he shall behold the face and be satisfied with the likeness of God ?*

Another passage belonging to this class has been already cited from the Sixteenth Psalm. It is much appealed to by the apostles as bearing witness to the resurrection of Christ. Whatever view may be taken of the principle according to which the psalm is to be interpreted,—whether it is regarded as having a direct and exclusive reference to the Lord Jesus, or as expressing, in the first instance, the faith of David and of the Church,—on either supposition, it is evident that the hopes so plainly uttered must have been within the reach of Old Testament believers. What, then, are those hopes ?

9.   —My flesh also shall dwell in safety.
10. For Thou wilt not leave my soul to Sheol;
        Neither wilt Thou suffer Thine holy one to see corruption.
11. Thou wilt show me the path of life:
        In Thy presence is fulness of joy,
        In Thy right hand there are pleasures for evermore.

The grave does not terminate either the existence or the felicity of God's people. Beyond it, there is for them a path of life, an entrance into God's presence, where their joy shall be full and their pleasures everlasting. There is, moreover, to be a resurrection of the body, a glorious resurrection, in the hope of which the faithful may well resign their dust to the grave without dismay.

It is certain, therefore, that the Personal Religion set forth in the psalms was pervaded with a steadfast expectation of the glory of God. The holy men who wrote them, although their views of the heavenly state were more obscure than those to which the resurrection of Christ has admitted us, were partakers of a hope that was the same in kind as ours. The hope in God that there shall be a resurrection of the dead was a hope to which " the twelve tribes, earnestly serving God night and day," steadfastly looked forward,† even as we do ; and it filled them with the kind of exhilaration which the early traveller feels when the sky before him begins to brighten with the promise of the coming day.

---

* Compare the weighty observations of Hupfeld on Ps. xvii. 14 (vol. i. p. 450).

† Acts xxvi. 7.

Among the psalms which assert the hope of eternal life, an eminent place belongs to the FORTY-NINTH. Both in form and substance, it is a didactic poem ; and it deals expressly with the subject in question, from beginning to end.

1. Hear this, all ye peoples ;
   Give ear, all ye inhabitants of the world :
2. Both low and high,
   Rich and poor together.
3. My mouth shall speak wisdom ;
   And the meditation of my heart shall be of understanding.
4. I will incline mine ear to a parable ;
   I will open my dark saying upon the harp.

5. Wherefore should I fear in the days of evil,
   When iniquity at my heels compasseth me about ?
6. They that trust in their wealth,
   And boast themselves in the multitude of their riches ;
7. None of them can by any means redeem his brother,
   Nor give to God a ransom for him :
8. (For the redemption of their soul is costly,
   And must be let alone for ever :)
9. That he should still live alway,
   That he should not see corruption.
10. For he seeth that wise men die,
    The fool and the brutish together perish,
    And leave their wealth to others.
11. Their inward thought is, that their houses shall continue for ever,
    And their dwelling places to all generations ;
    They call their lands after their own names.
12. *But man abideth not in honour :*
    He is like the beasts that perish.

13. This their way is their folly,
    Yet after them men approve their sayings.
14. They are appointed as a flock for Sheol ;
    Death shall be their shepherd :
    And the upright shall have dominion over them in the morning ;
    And their beauty shall be for Sheol to consume, that there
    be no habitation for it.
15. BUT GOD WILL REDEEM MY SOUL FROM THE POWER OF
    SHEOL :
    FOR HE SHALL RECEIVE ME.
16. Be not thou afraid when one is made rich,
    When the glory of his house is increased :
17. For when he dieth he shall carry nothing away ;
    His glory shall not descend after him.

18. Though, while he lived, he blessed his soul,
        And men praise thee, when thou doest well to thyself,
19. He shall go to the generation of his fathers;
        They shall never see the light.
30. *Man that is in honour, and understandeth not,*
        Is like the beasts that perish.

The psalms which are introduced with a formal preface are few in number; and they are all psalms of principal note, in their several kinds.* The circumstance that the one before us is thus introduced may be taken as an intimation that it is of great weight, and claims more than ordinary attention. And this is confirmed by the farther circumstance, that the introduction, instead of being addressed (like that of the Seventy-eighth) to the Hebrew Church, as the public for whose instruction it was primarily intended, is expressly and emphatically addressed to the Church catholic, to "all peoples," even "all the inhabitants of the world." It is plain that, in this instance, the Holy Spirit had very specially in view the ages during which the psalm, instead of being "recited, in one nation, in the synagogue of the Jews, should be recited in all Churches, throughout the whole world." † And such being the case, it is certainly a mistake to think that the psalm expresses a type of doctrinal sentiment and religious feeling proper only to the darkness of the preparatory dispensation and now rendered obsolete by the resurrection of the Lord Jesus. Although indited by a Hebrew pen, it is a Christian psalm and was from the first inscribed to the Christian Church. The particular exercise of faith which it holds forth will never become obsolete while the world lasts.

The theme is the same as we have seen elucidated in the Seventeenth and Seventy-third Psalms—the mystery of God's providence towards the righteous and the wicked; and the aim of the psalmist is the same, namely, to encourage God's people to take "for a helmet the hope of salvation," ‡ when they are shaken in mind at the sight of prosperous ungodliness. The grand lesson intended to be inculcated is worked out in each of

---

* See Psalms xlv. 1 and lxxviii. 1–8, and compare the remarks on the former in chap. i., and on the latter in chap. x. of this Book.
† Augustine : *Enarratio* i. in Ps. xlviii. (xlix.).
‡ 1 Thess. v. 8.

the two stanzas of which the body of the psalm consists. In the first it is worked out partially, in the second more perfectly. The psalmist has himself been perplexed by the problem to which he summons the attention of the world. Like Asaph in the Seventy-third Psalm, he has been shaken in mind by seeing vile men rich, powerful, prosperous. Reflecting on that sight, the first consideration impressed on his mind is the vanity of riches. These men trust in their wealth. They boast themselves as if they were a kind of gods on the earth. Yet how helpless are they! When Death knocks at their door and they would fain have him depart, will their wealth bribe him away? When a brother is laid down with sickness, will their wealth avail for a ransom-price? Can they buy him off, so that he shall still live and not see corruption? No, no. Death prevails over all; wise men and brutish fools,—all die; and their wealth passes into other hands. The redemption of a man's life is too precious to be accomplished with silver and gold. The attempt is vain. It must be let alone and cease for ever! Thus the Psalmist is conducted to the sentence with which the first stanza is wound up, " *Man abideth not in honour; he is like the beasts that perish.*" The reflection is a salutary one : fitted to arm the rich against pride and the poor against envy. Death visits the palaces of the rich as surely as the cottages of the poor, and all the wealth in the world cannot persuade him to pass by. It is, I repeat, a salutary reflection; but it is not a strengthening or consolatory one. There is no glory of heavenly hope upon it. Heathen poets were as familiar with it as the psalmist. It is useful, so far as it goes; but it does not go far towards enabling the heart to acquiesce cheerfully in the allotments of God's providence. It may enable a man to look with stoical contempt on worldly grandeur; but stoical contempt is a heathenish virtue, and stops far short of the soul-tranquillising thought that God doeth all things well.

The verses that follow lift us up beyond these clouds into a serener air. The sentence into which the argument of the first stanza was gathered up is set down a second time at the close of the psalm. But this time with an important variation. Here it is the man that, being in honour, " *understandeth not,*" who is compared to the beasts that perish. We are thus re-

minded that there are some who, by God's grace, do understand ;
men who " fear the Lord, which is wisdom ; and depart from
evil, which is understanding." Their case is not to be confounded with that of the ungodly. Death does not separate
them from their soul's portion, does not extinguish their felicity.
They do not perish like beasts, but are taken up into God's
presence to dwell there like angels. What is thus taught by
implication, in the refrain, is set forth explicitly in the body of
the stanza. Two statements claim special attention here.
After describing the death of the ungodly as their being driven
by the stern shepherd, Death, into the unseen world, like sheep
that are driven unwillingly into a pen, the psalmist declares his
belief that a day is coming,—a bright Morning,—in which the
saints shall have dominion (ver. 14) : an announcement which
carries forward the mind to the morning of the resurrection, when
" the saints shall judge the world." * Then, coming home to his
own case, he makes profession of his hope in words of strong
assurance : " *God will redeem my soul from the power of Sheol ;
for He shall receive me.*" The former part of this profession of
the psalmist's faith is best illustrated by the parallel text in
Hosea, " I will ransom them from the power of the grave," or
rather (for the Hebrew is the same as it is here in the psalm)
" I will redeem them from the power of Sheol ; I will redeem
them from death : O death, where are thy plagues ? O grave,
where is thy destruction ? "† The believer has faith in God
that, when he dies, he shall not be shut up in darkness,
but shall be received into the presence of God, and be raised
up in glory at the last day. That victory over death, which
the worldling's wealth cannot purchase for his dearest friend,
is made sure to every one who puts his trust in God. The
words that follow, " for He shall receive me," correspond to
those of Asaph, " Thou shalt guide me with Thy counsel, and
afterwards receive me to glory ; " and, in both places, there is an
allusion to the language of the sacred history in relating the
translation of Enoch, how " he was not, for God took (or
received) him."‡ Not that Asaph or the writer of the Forty-
ninth Psalm expected to be translated like Enoch ; but the
" taking up " of the antediluvian saint suggested to their minds

* I Cor. vi. 2.　　† Hos. xiii. 14.　　‡ Gen. v. 24.

a world of precious truth respecting the future life, and strengthened in their hearts the hope of eternal glory in the presence of God. We have before us, therefore, in this psalm a clear and strong declaration of hope ; for, indeed, what more can the believer say even now ? The highest attainment our faith can reach in the prospect of dissolution is to lay hold on the promise of Christ and say, " Thou comest again, Lord Jesus, and wilt receive me to Thyself, that where Thou art, there I may be also ; " and what is this but to repeat the profession of hope that is embedded in the Forty-ninth Psalm ?

Hitherto the testimonies cited have been such as must have been understood, by the psalmists themselves and by the faithful of their time, in the sense contended for. In order to complete our view of the subject it is right to add, that there are other texts, many in number, which, although it may be impossible to prove that they were penned with a conscious reference to the future life, have been framed by the Spirit to admit and suggest the thought of that life. * Thus, when it is said † that " the wicked shall not stand in the judgment, nor sinners in the congregation of the righteous," the words may not have carried the mind of the Old Testament reader beyond the thought that, even in this present world, the Lord will, by sifting dispensations of His providence, bring to light the worthlessness of the ungodly and separate them from the company of His true people. It is just possible that this may be all that the words signified to Hebrew readers. But they are obviously capable of a much higher reference ; and I do not doubt that they were purposely framed by the Spirit to be the vehicle in which we, who live under the New Testament, may give expression to our belief, that a time is coming when the Lord will " sever the wicked from among the righteous," and "gather out of His kingdom all things that cause stumbling, and them that do iniquity."‡ The closing verse of the Twenty-third Psalm furnishes another example of the same sort. There may be room for difference of opinion as to the thought that was in David's mind when he wrote, " Surely goodness and mercy shall

---

* Delitzsch has some judicious remarks on this aspect of the subject in the Appendix to his Commentary, vol. ii. 422 (3rd Ed., vol. i. 57).

† Ps. i. 5.

‡ Matt. xiii. 41-49.

follow me all the days of my life ; and I will dwell in the house
of the Lord for ever." Some excellent interpreters maintain
that the hope with which the psalmist solaces himself is simply
that of enjoying communion with God through a long serene
evening of life. If this interpretation is preferred, I will not
contend about it ; nevertheless I am sure that it is no arbitrary
accommodation of the words when we, in singing them, think
of the heavenly Temple and cheer ourselves with the hope of
dwelling there for ever. This is a sense the words easily
admit; which they inevitably suggest; and of which, I do not
doubt, they were framed to be the vehicle. And the number
of such passages in the psalms is very considerable.

The Psalter, then, is certainly misinterpreted by those who
represent it as destitute of articulate intimations respecting the
Future Life. It would have been a strange thing, indeed, if
intimations of the kind had been wanting in such a book. We
should have been shut up to the inference that the thoughts of
the chosen people were tied down to the earth and this temporal
life by tighter bonds than were laid on any of their heathen
neighbours.* It is well known that the Egyptians, in whose
wisdom Moses was educated and whose civilisation was the
cradle in which the Hebrew Church was nursed, were a people
who speculated exceedingly about the world beyond the grave.
The thought of it was never long absent from their minds. It
coloured their entire religious system and social life. It is
hard to believe that a Church which, in addition to its peculiar
heritage of primitive revelation, had been indoctrinated in the
wisdom of the Egyptians and subjected to the discipline of the
Mosaic law, was, nevertheless, so chained to the present
world and so much a stranger to the thoughts which soar into
eternity, that its sacred poetry contains no distinct expression
of the bright and joyous hope of future glory. But in truth
there is, as we have ascertained, no ground whatever for such a

* Max Müller observes, that in the Vedas, the Sacred Books of the
Ancient Hindoos,—" we find what is really the *sine qua non* of all real
religion, a belief in immortality, and in personal immortality." And he
adds that, "without a belief in personal immortality, religion surely is like
an arch resting on one pillar, like a bridge ending in an abyss." (*Chips from a
German Workshop*, I. p. 45).

paradoxical conclusion. The Psalter glows everywhere with a brightness which nothing could have imparted except a deep presentiment of Eternal Life ; and in several places that presentiment shapes itself into a strong articulate hope.

Another side of the question claims a short notice before we pass on. Admitting that the hope of the heavenly glory is found in the psalms, it may be asked how we are to explain the comparative *paucity* of the instances in which it is expressed. The texts that are perfectly clear and explicit are few in number. It would be difficult to muster so many as half-a-dozen. In the rest of the psalms, the hope is present, at the best, in the shape of a diffused brightness. This circumstance, and the reason of it, were well brought out by the late Isaac Taylor. After referring to the fact that there are some psalms which "contain allusions, not obscure, to that better world,—that 'more enduring substance,'—that 'inheritance unfailing,' upon which the pious in all times have kept the eye of faith steadily fixed," he calls special attention to the Hundred-and-nineteenth, and remarks :—

" But now in all the 176 couplets of this psalm, there are not more than two or three phrases, and these of ambiguous meaning, which can be understood as having reference to the Future Life, and its blessedness ; and so it is in other psalms of this same class. One such expression, susceptible of an extended meaning, there is in the 23rd Psalm, none in the 25th, nor in the 30th, where it might naturally be looked for, nor in the 32nd, the 42nd, the 63rd, the 84th, the 103rd ; and these are the psalms which might be singled out from the class which they belong to, as samples of the deepest utterings, the most intense yearnings, of individual devotion—the loving communion of the soul with God. Can any explanation be given of this apparent defectiveness in the instances adduced, which seem to demand the very element that is *not* found in them ?

" We are not called to seek for an explication of this difficulty among groundless conjectures concerning what might be the divine intention in thus holding back from these devotional odes the element which might seem the most eminently proper to find a place among them : what we have before us is the incontestable fact, that these psalms—and these by preference —have actually fed the piety of the pious, have sufficed for giving utterance to the deepest and most animated religious emotions, throughout all time, since their first promulgation; and it has been as much so since the time of the Christian announcement of immortality, as before it; we might say, much more so. During all these ages, these many generations of men who have sought and found their happiness in communion with God, there has been in use, by the divine appointment, a liturgy of the individual spiritual life, which, abstinent of all the excitements of immortal hope, unmindful of, almost, as if ignorant of, the bright future, takes its circuit, and finds its occasions, in and among the sad and changeful and transient experiences of the present life. Here is before us a daily ritual of fervent, impassioned devotion, which, far from being of an abstracted or mystical sort, is acutely sensitive towards all things of the passing moment. This metrical service of daily prayer, praise, intercession, trust, hope, contrition, revolves within the circle of the every-day pains, fears, and solaces of the religious man's earthly pilgrimage. Pilgrimage it is, for the devout man calls himself 'a stranger, a sojourner on earth;' and yet the land whereunto he is tending does not in any such manner fill a place in his thoughts, as that it shall find a place in the language of his devotions!

" What is the inference that is properly derivable from these facts? Is it not this, that the training or *discipline* of the soul in the spiritual life—the forming and strengthening of those habits of trust, confidence, love, penitence, which are the preparations of the soul for its futurity in a brighter world—demands a concentration of the affections upon the Infinite Excellence—undisturbed by objects of another order? If this be a proper conclusion, then we find in it a correspondent principle in the abstinence, throughout the Christian Scriptures, of descriptive exhibitions of the 'inheritance' that is promised. The eternal life is, indeed, authentically propounded; but the promise is not opened out in any such manner as shall make meditation upon it easy. Pious earnestness presses forward on a path that is well assured; but on this path the imagination is not invited to follow. The same purpose here again presents itself to notice— a purpose of *culture*, not of excitement.

" There can be little risk of error in affirming that the New Testament itself furnishes no liturgy of devotion, for this reason, that a liturgy, divinely originated, had already been granted to the universal Church ; and it was such in its subjects, and in its tone, and in its modes of expression, as fully to satisfy its destined purposes. Devout spirits, from age to age of these later times, since 'life and immortality were brought to light,' have known how to blend with the liturgy of David the promises of Christ, these later distinguished from those long before granted to Patriarchs and Prophets more by their authoritative style and their explicit brevity, than by any amplifications that might satisfy religious curiosity."*

This explanation is as just as it is eloquently propounded ; and accordingly we must recognise the wise hand of God in the comparative abstinence of the Psalmists from those detailed contemplations of the promised glory which have always abounded in the devotional poetry of uninspired writers. There is a way of dilating on the heavenly felicities which tends to foster the Antinomian perversion of the gospel, and which is scarcely less mischievous in its effects than the practice (so apt to attend Ritualism) of annexing the hope of heaven, and of a speedy admission into its joys, to services which are obviously compatible with habitual ungodliness of mind. What our hearts need to be taught is, not so much that heaven is a very glorious place and exceedingly to be desired, as that without holiness no man can enter into it. This is what the Holy Spirit seems to have designed in impressing on the psalms the feature under consideration. The future glory is never held forth except with accompaniments which compel the reader to associate with it the thought of God and of holiness. We have seen that the delineations of the heavenly state are so framed, that it has been possible to interpret them, not without plausibility, as merely descriptive of the life of faith on the earth. The design, I have no doubt, was—as the effect certainly is—to render it impossible for any to employ the psalms for nourishing in their minds the hope of the heavenly glory unless they are willing to use them also for assistance in a course of present communion with God.

* *The Spirit of the Hebrew Poetry.* 1861. Pp. 177-180.

CHAPTER VII.

THE IMPRECATIONS.

OF all the features which characterise the style of Personal Religion unfolded in the Psalms, there is none that has given rise to so much unfavourable comment as the vindictive spirit which some of them appear to breathe. It is not to be denied, that in a very considerable number of places the desire is expressed, in one form or another, that God would pour out the vials of His wrath on the enemies of the Psalmist himself or of Zion ; that He would not forgive their iniquity, but give them the due reward of their deeds. Besides isolated and minor examples of prayers of this kind, there are, in at least three psalms,—the Thirty-fifth, the Sixty-ninth, and the Hundred-and-ninth,—long and terrible imprecations of evil. Thus in the SIXTY-NINTH we read :—

21. They gave me also gall for my meat ;
    And in my thirst they gave me vinegar to drink.
22. Let their table before them become a snare ;
    And when they are in peace, let it become a trap.
23. Let their eyes be darkened, that they see not ;
    And make their loins continually to shake.
24. Pour out Thine indignation upon them,
    And let the fierceness of Thine anger overtake them.
25. Let their habitation be desolate ;
    Let none dwell in their tents.
26. For they persecute him whom Thou hast smitten ;
    And they tell of the sorrow of those whom Thou hast wounded.
27. Add iniquity unto their iniquity ;
    And let them not come into Thy righteousness.
28. Let them be blotted out of the book of life,
    And not be written with the righteous.

The Psalms of this class have been subjected, especially in modern times, to unmeasured condemnation as the offspring of a "savage spirit."* Not only have the enemies of divine revelation made a handle of them for their purposes, but some Christian interpreters have been betrayed into a style of remark which, if it could be justified, would necessitate the removal of the Psalter from the place which it has hitherto occupied in the worship of the Church. On this account, therefore, as well as on account of the embarrassment often felt by persons the most devout and loyal in their allegiance to God's Word, the subject claims attention here.

In a question of this kind, it is expedient to begin by making a careful survey of the facts belonging to the case. Much of the offence that has been taken can be traced to sheer misunderstanding. Even in regard to those points which remain obscure and difficult after the most careful survey, the labour will not be lost ; for an intelligent and circumspect consideration of the whole matter will at least exclude the presumptuous dogmatism into which some of the critics have fallen. What then are the facts ?

The first circumstance that claims notice is the rather significant one that, with a few unimportant exceptions, the psalms in question come from the pen of David. This is significant in several respects. For one thing, David was about as devoid of vindictiveness as any public character who can be named. His conduct in relation to Saul, from first to last, displayed a singularly noble spirit, far removed from anything like the lust of vengeance ; and the meekness with which he endured the bitter reproaches of Shimei bore witness to the same spirit after his accession to the throne. His dying charge to Solomon with regard to Joab and Shimei has been cited as a set-off against the better passages of his life. But this is hardly just. Regarding Shimei our information is scanty ; yet we know that David acted towards him, in the first instance, with extraordinary forbearance.† As regards Joab, there can be little doubt that the motive which dictated the king's bequest was something very different from the cruel, implacable, and cowardly remembrance of personal affronts, which is all that some are willing to see in it. Joab had repeatedly " shed the blood of war in peace," and the dying king felt that he ought to have been put to death long

---

* Stanley, *Lectures on the Jewish Church*, ii. 153.
† 2 Sam. xvi. 10-12 ; xix. 21-23.

ago. But he was a formidable person. As the king's nephew, the captain of the host, and one of the ablest men in the nation, he was not so much David's subject, as his partner and rival in the sovereign power,—a man too high for the sword of justice to reach during David's unsettled reign. In the well-founded anticipation that Solomon's throne would be firmer than his own had ever been, the king bequeathed to him the duty of executing vengeance for an offence which would otherwise be a stain on the government, and might bring down the judgment of God on the royal house. When David's whole career is intelligently and fairly reviewed, it leaves on the mind the impression of a man possessed of as meek and placable a temper as was ever associated with so great strength of will and such strong passions. Even in the heats of sudden resentment, he was not apt to be hurried into deeds of revenge. Such being the case, it would certainly have been a strange and unaccountable thing if he had shown himself less the master of his own spirit in poems composed in seasons of retirement and communion with God, especially since these very poems express a keen sense of the heinousness of the sin that has been laid to his charge. He can affirm regarding his implacable enemies,

xxxv. 13. As for me, when they were sick, my clothing was sack-
cloth :
I afflicted my soul with fasting ;
And my prayer returned into mine own bosom.
14. I behaved myself as though it had been my friend or my
brother :
I bowed down mourning as one that bewaileth his mother.

vii. 3. O Lord, my God, if I have done this ;
If there be iniquity in my hands ;
4. If I have rewarded evil unto him that was at peace
with me ;
(Yea, I have delivered him that without cause was mine
adversary :)
5. Let the enemy pursue my soul, and overtake it ;
Yea, let him tread my life down to the earth,
And lay my glory in the dust.

Surely one ought to think twice before putting on the impreca-tions an interpretation which would make them utterly incon-gruous with these appeals, uttered almost in the same breath.

This suggests a second circumstance of great importance. Examination shows that the imprecations are not the utterance of resentment for private injuries, or of a base desire to see personal enemies laid low. Sometimes, as in the wish expressed for the destruction of Edom and Babylon in the Hundred-and-thirty-seventh Psalm, the objects of the imprecation are the nations which have cruelly wronged the people of God. At other times, if the psalmist seems to call down the divine vengeance on personal foes, it will be found that the person who speaks is always David, and that he speaks in his public character, as the chosen servant of the Lord and anointed King of Israel; and that he has in view, not his own particular foes, but the enemies of the cause of which he is the representative,— the cause of God, and of truth and righteousness in Israel. To forget David's singular position in the nation, and to read these psalms of his as if they were the utterances of some private individual in reference to neighbours who had done him a private wrong, is to leave out of account the principal element in the case. It was not David who sought the throne, but the Lord who set him apart for Himself,* and He chose and anointed him to the kingdom, in order that, in his reign, the seed of Jacob might exhibit the most perfect representation the world had yet seen of the predestined kingdom of the Lord Jesus Christ. His enemies,—whether the unprincipled servants of Saul, like Doeg, who plotted his destruction before he obtained the crown; or the conspirators who, like Ahithophel, sought to pluck the crown from his head by the hands of his own children,—were men whose hatred of David arose out of, and derived its peculiar character from, a hatred of the cause of which David, with all his faults, was the champion and embodiment. We see, accordingly, that the evil deprecated by the Psalmist is not so much the reproach and wrong which he and his people suffer, as the dishonour done to the name of the Lord. So long as his enemies prosper in their wicked counsels, they can plausibly say "God hath forgotten; He hideth his face; He will never see it." † They can even please themselves with the thought that "there is no God." ‡ What he desires is that God would no longer sleep,—that He would arise and lift up His hand, so

---

* Ps. iv. 3.   † Ps. x. 11.   ‡ Ps. xiv. 1.

that all should be constrained to take notice of it. His fear is
that if God give him over to the power of his enemies, a fatal
wound will be inflicted on the faith of afflicted saints in ages to
come. They will be tempted to say: David was raised up by
God to be His servant; yet He forsook him, so that he sank
beneath the malice of those who hated him for the sake of his
piety. Hence his prayer is, " Let not them that wait on Thee
be ashamed through me, O Lord God of hosts: let not those that
seek Thee be brought to dishonour through me, O God of Israel."*
The motive of the imprecations is not to be sought in a sense
of private wrong or of wounded honour, nor in selfish vindictiveness, but in a holy regard to the glory of God, trodden
in the dust and given over to contemptuous blasphemy. If the
psalmist startles us with the vehement exultation with which
he looks forward to the hour (which, his faith tells him, will soon
arrive) when God will come forth from His place and show Himself to His affrighted enemies, it is not to be forgotten that the
thing which yields him so much joy is not the vengeance itself,
or the fearful destruction of his enemies, but the public vindication of the divine justice, the unequivocal demonstration of
the reality and power of the divine government. " The righteous
shall rejoice when he seeth the vengeance: he shall wash his
feet in the blood of the wicked. So that men shall say, Verily
there is a reward for the righteous; verily, there is a God that
judgeth in the earth." †

Yet another fact must be mentioned. The frequency with
which the Old Testament Scriptures are cited by our blessed
Lord and the writers of the New Testament, and the marked
deference with which the citations are made, have always, and
justly, been regarded as a strong testimony to the plenary
authority of the ancient Scriptures. This being so, the fact is
remarkable that the psalms under discussion have been counted
worthy of an eminent share in this honour. The Sixty-ninth,
for example, which bears more of the imprecatory character

---

* Ps. lxix. 6.

† Ps. lviii. 10, 11. Comp. Kurtz, *Zur Theologie der Psalmen* (Dorpat,
1865), p. 169. The whole chapter devoted to the Imprecatory Psalms is
thoughtful and valuable, much superior to the rest of the little treatise, which, as
a whole, is scarcely worthy of the learned author. Comp. also the note in the
same writer's *Lehrbuch der heiligen Geschichte*, sec. 84.

than any other except the Hundred-and-ninth, is expressly quoted in five separate places, besides being alluded to in several places more. Among all the psalms, only three or four others can be named that have been so largely quoted by Christ and the apostles ; and they are all great Messianic hymns.*
The *nature* of the quotations is even more significant than their number. It would seem that our Lord appropriated the psalm to Himself, and that we are to take it as a disclosure of thoughts and feelings which found a place in His heart during the course of His ministry on the earth. In the Guest Chamber, He quoted the words of the fourth verse, "They hated me without a cause ; " and represented them as a prediction of the people's hatred of the Father and of Himself.†
When He drove the traffickers from the Temple, John informs us that " His disciples remembered that it was written, The zeal of Thine house shall eat Me up,"‡ which implies that those words of the psalm expressed the very mind that was in Christ. When Peter, after mentioning the crime and perdition of Judas, suggested to the company of the Hundred and twenty that they ought to take measures for the appointment of a new apostle to fill the vacant place, he enforced the suggestion by a quotation : " For it is written in the Book of Psalms, Let his habitation be made desolate, and let no man dwell therein ; and, His office let another take "§—manifestly on the supposition that this psalm and the Hundred-and-ninth (for they are both quoted) were written with some kind of reference to Judas. In the epistle to the Romans, the duty of pleasing, every one of us, our neighbour for his good, is enforced by the Apostle with the argument that " Christ also pleased not Himself; but, as it is written, The reproaches of them that reproached Thee fell upon me," ‖ an argument which has no weight if David alone is the speaker in the psalm,—if Christ be not, in some real sense, the speaker in it also. Finally, we are taught in the same epistle to recognise a fulfilment of the psalmist's most terrible imprecations, in the judicial blindness which befell the body of the Jewish nation

---

* Psalms ii, xxii, cx, cxviii, are the four most frequently quoted in the New Testament.

† John xv. 25.
‡ John ii. 17.

§ Acts i. 20.
‖ Rom. xv. 3.

after the crucifixion of Christ.*   All this proves that, if we are
not to reject the authority of the apostles and of Christ Himself,
we must take this imprecatory psalm as having been spoken by
David as the ancestor and type of Christ.   I do not say that
the circumstance that these psalms are so unequivocally
endorsed and appropriated by our blessed Lord is sufficient,
by itself, to explain the difficulty they involve.   But I am sure
that the simple statement of it will constrain disciples of Christ
to touch them with a reverent hand, and rather to distrust their
own judgment, than to brand such Scriptures as the products of
an unsanctified and unchristian temper.

Coming now to the great question brought up by these
Imprecatory Psalms, are we in a condition to throw any light
upon it?   It is the undoubted law of Christ that we should
love our enemies, bless them that curse us, do good to them
that hate us, pray for them that despitefully use us and
persecute us.   Can we explain how the language of the
psalmists can be reconciled with the sentiments and conduct
enjoined in that command?

In some instances, the reconciliation is easy.   Take, for
example, the prayer with which the Hundred-and-fourth Psalm
concludes, "Let sinners be consumed out of the earth, and
let the wicked be no more."   The psalm is a meditation on
God's works in nature, and has excited the admiration of the
historians of Natural Science as the fullest and brightest
expression of that sympathy with nature and appreciation of its
unity in which the sacred poets so remarkably excelled all the
pagan writers.†   At first sight it seems unaccountable that such
a sunny joyous ode should be wound up with a petition for the
rooting out of wicked men.   So stern a prayer sounds like a
jarring note in the song in which the Church expresses her participation in the joy of her Lord over this fair world, the product
of His beneficent wisdom.   But, in truth, the prayer is both in
harmony with the song and necessary to its completeness.   An
anecdote will explain my meaning.   It fell to my lot several
years ago to undertake a walk of some miles, on a summer
morning, along a sea-shore of surpassing beauty.   It was the
Lord's Day; and the language of the Hundred-and-fourth Psalm

* Vers. 22 and 23, compared with Rom. xi. 9, 10.
† Humboldt's *Kosmos*, vol. ii. 413 (Bohn's Ed.).

rose spontaneously in my mind as one scene after another unfolded itself before the eye. About half-way to my destination the road lay through a dirty hamlet, and my meditations were suddenly interrupted by the brawling of some people, who looked as if they had been spending the night in a drunken debauch. The psalmist (I thought with myself) must have had some such unpleasant experience. He must have fallen in with people, located in some scene of natural beauty, who, instead of being a holy priesthood to give voice to nature in praise of her Creator,—instead of being, in the pure and holy tenor of their lives, the heavenliest note of the general song,—disturbed it with a harsh discord. His prayer is the vehement expression of a desire that the earth may no longer be defiled by the presence of wicked men,—that the wicked may be utterly consumed, and may give place to men animated with the fear of God, just and holy men, men that shall be a crown of beauty on the head of this fair creation. If this be the right explanation of the Psalmist's prayer, it is not only justifiable, but there is something wrong in our meditations on nature if we are not disposed to join in it.

With respect to the more difficult Imprecations, there is an explanation which has found a good deal of acceptance among recent critics. It lays great stress on the difference between the Old Testament and the New, on the " defects of the Jewish system," and the alleged "vindictive spirit of the ancient dispensation." * Sometimes this explanation is urged in a spirit of undisguised hostility to the Old Testament, by persons who, although they do not venture to make a direct assault on apostolic Christianity, hope to wound it through the prior dispensation. But it is sometimes urged also in good faith, by divines who desire to hold fast their allegiance to the whole Word of God. Deeming it vain to justify the imprecations, they endeavour to save the divine authority of the Scriptures by insisting on the inferiority of the Jewish economy. They call attention to the obvious and admitted facts that many things not consistent with the rule of eternal justice were "suffered" to the Jews "because of the hardness of their hearts ; " and that the Advent of Christ, and the Mission of the Comforter, have ministered assistance to Christ's people in the

---

* Stanley, *Jewish Church*, ii. 153.

cultivation of a higher style of holiness than prevailed under the former dispensation : and they argue that it is no disparagement to the Scriptures if some of the ancient psalmists are occasionally betrayed into the utterance of vindictive feelings, irreconcilable with the Christian temper.* Of the explanation, as urged in this guarded way, I would speak with all respect. It is most certain that faith in the divine authority of the whole Bible does not oblige us to defend all that the ancient saints said or did ; and there is no doubt that the people of God have been elevated, under the gospel, to a general level of religious attainment, higher than was reached by the faithful under the law. Nevertheless, the explanation must be rejected, even in its most guarded and qualified form. Prayers which were not only offered by particular saints, but which God by His prophets taught the Church to offer in the perpetual service of song, are not to be charged with any taint of sinful passion.

Besides, it occurs to ask what foundation there is for attributing to the Old Testament the "vindictive spirit" of which it is the fashion to speak so confidently ; whether there is really any ground for making such a difference between the two dispensations, with respect to this particular sentiment. Certainly, there is no lack in the Law of Moses of precepts identical in their tenor with the much-quoted words of our Lord in the Sermon on the Mount ; precepts which, for the charitable spirit they breathe, are not surpassed by anything in the Christian Scriptures. " If thou meet thine enemy's ox or his ass going astray, thou shalt surely bring it back to him again. If thou see the ass of him that hateth thee lying under his burden and wouldest forbear to help him, thou shalt surely help with him."†   " Thou shalt not hate thy brother in thine heart : thou shalt surely rebuke thy neighbour, and not bear sin because of him. Thou shalt not take vengeance, nor bear any grudge against the children of thy people, but thou shalt love thy neighbour as thyself. I am the LORD."‡ The defensive attitude which the Church had to assume towards the nations, prior to the giving of the Spirit at Pentecost, rendered necessary a line of action, in some respects, which may be plausibly represented as

---

* Perowne, *Book of Psalms*, vol. i. pp. 73–75 ; also on Ps. xxxv., vol. i. 159.
† Exod. xxiii. 4, 5.
‡ Lev. xix. 17, 18.

expressing "a hateful particularism;" but, from the first, the kindly and charitable spirit enjoined in the Mosaic precepts was known and felt to be obligatory on the people of God towards their neighbours foreign and domestic. Thus Job in his eloquent protestation of integrity does not forget this point of duty:—

> If I rejoiced at the destruction of him that hated me,
> Or lifted up myself when evil found him:
> Yea, I suffered not my mouth to sin
> By asking his life with a curse. *

The New Testament does not profess to add one jot to our knowledge of the will of God in this matter. When Christ, in the Sermon on the Mount, commands us to love our enemies and to pray for them which despitefully use us and persecute us, He does this, not in the way of setting forth a new commandment, as so many have strangely supposed, but rather in the way of rescuing the old commandment from the perverse glosses of the scribes, and setting it forth anew with His endorsement. We find accordingly that the Apostle, in dissuading his readers from taking vengeance, sends them back to the law of Moses, and fetches from it his decisive argument: "Avenge not yourselves, beloved, but give place unto wrath; for it is written, Vengeance belongeth unto Me; I will recompense, saith the Lord." †

If the explanation under review thus errs in depreciating the Old Testament, it errs no less in the one-sided view it presents of the mind of Christ, the genuine Christian temper. That temper has another aspect besides the one presented in the Sermon on the Mount. The New Testament may not contain any imprecations so awfully emphatic, reiterated, and specific as those which are to be found in two or three Psalms; but imprecations are by no means absent. The apostles of Christ occasionally used language with reference to their opponents which, in point of principle, cannot be distinguished from that of David. Thus Peter, in rebuking Simon Magus for his heartless hypocrisy, expressed the wish that he might perish, he and his money along with him.‡ This, it may be argued, was spoken in great heat,—the heat of what was doubtless a just

---

* Job xxxi. 29, 30.   † Rom. xii. 19; Deut. xxxii. 35.   ‡ Acts viii. 20.

anger, but in heat nevertheless; and ought therefore to be taken with some abatement. But what shall we say to the imprecation of Paul against Alexander the coppersmith, that " the Lord might reward him according to his works " ? * The wish was uttered by the Apostle in the heavenliest of all his writings, the serene epistle in which he sent his farewell to his own son in the faith. Nor is it only on this side the grave that Christ's saintly servants have uttered such words. There is a vision in the Revelation which plainly warrants us to attribute similar imprecations to the saints who, having " come out of the great tribulation," are now before the throne : " I saw underneath the altar the souls of them that had been slain for the word of God. . . . And they cried with a great voice, saying, How long, O Master, the holy and true, dost Thou not judge and avenge our blood on them that dwell on the earth ? " † Whether we can account for such sentiments or not, one thing is clear, that the difficulty raised by the imprecations is by no means peculiar to the Psalms. If the psalmists are condemned, a measure of the same condemnation must be extended to the apostles of Christ. And, this, in fact, is done by some of the rationalising divines. ‡

It is sufficiently plain, therefore, that even if the Imprecatory Psalms had not received a special endorsement from Christ and the apostles, it would have been idle to seek the explanation of them in the diverse characters of the Old and New Testaments. To curse an enemy is just as severely forbidden in the Old Testament as in the New; and passages are to be found in the New Testament which bear the imprecatory character quite distinctly, although not in such a strongly marked form, as those in the Old. In this matter, both Testaments stand or fall together; and we must look to some other quarter than their differences (whatever these may be) for the explanation of the difficulty under review.

---

* 2 Tim. iv. 14. The Revised Version substitutes the *future* for the *optative:* " The Lord will render to him according to his works." Critics are by no means agreed on the point. (See Ellicott's *Past. Epistles, in loc.*) And even according to the milder interpretation, the sense is not materially altered ; for it still remains true that the apostle feels a certain satisfaction in looking forward to the doom which he foresees.

† Rev. vi. 9, 10.

‡ Hupfeld, *Die Psalmen,* at Ps. lxix. 23–29.

In looking round for light on a question of this kind, it is always well to bear in mind that there are dark places in God's Word, the perfect elucidation of which is not to be hoped for in the present life. From the circumstance that the Imprecations, after all that has been written about them these many centuries, still give rise to much embarrassment and anxious discussion, it is sufficiently evident that they present a real difficulty. And it is anything but a proof of strong faith in the divine inspiration of the Scriptures to be afraid to acknowledge the existence of such a difficulty. If there had been no difficulties in the Bible, it would not have been like its Author. If, in its teachings, there had been nothing too deep for my understanding to fathom, nothing embarrassing to the feelings of my heart, I might well have presumed that it was of merely human origin, and that the thoughts unfolded in it were only the thoughts of fallible men like myself. The revelation that God has made of Himself in *Providence* is certainly not devoid of difficulties. On the contrary, we may say of it what the Apostle Peter remarked of the Pauline epistles, that in it "are some things hard to be understood, which the ignorant and unsteadfast wrest unto their own destruction."* God's way is often in the sea, and His path in the great waters, and His footsteps are not known. A sense of this made one of the psalmists exclaim, "How great are Thy works, O LORD! Thy thoughts are very deep."† The "thoughts" thus reverently adored are those to which God has given expression in His works; for every act of God's Providence is the embodiment of a thought of His heart. God's Providence, I repeat, shows many a dark passage. We often find it hard to discover what His meaning is; too often, moreover, when He makes His meaning plain enough, our hearts rebel against it. It ought not therefore to be thought surprising if we find in the Imprecations of the Psalter some things which remain hard to be understood, and liable to be wrested by men to their own destruction.

But, without professing to be able to dissipate every shadow, or to set the whole matter in a clear light, I think it will be possible to indicate the direction in which a satisfactory solution of the main difficulty is to be found.

---

* 2 Pet. iii. 16.   † Ps. xcii. 5.

Let these two considerations be duly weighed :—(1) However dreadful the evils may be which the psalmists imprecate,—and they are dreadful beyond expression,—there is not one of them which God does not, in fact, send on wicked men. Let them be translated into the language of history, and the truth of the imprecations will at once be recognised. " Destruction cometh upon the wicked at unawares ; his net that he hath hid catcheth himself ; into that very destruction he falleth. . . . Their eyes are darkened that they see not, and their bones are made continually to shake. The Lord poureth out upon them His indignation, and the heat of His wrath overtaketh them. The Lord addeth iniquity unto their iniquity, and suffereth them not to come into His righteousness. They are blotted out of the book of the living; and with the righteous they are not written." I suppose no person ever reads the Sixty-ninth and Hundred-and-ninth Psalms, attentively, without being reminded of Judas Iscariot and of the Jews who crucified the Lord of glory; indeed, the latter psalm used to be denominated, in the ancient church, "the Iscariot Psalm." * When the Apostle, in the epistle to the Romans, describes that judicial hardening of his Jewish kinsmen which was going on before his eyes, and in which he saw the sure token of their impending destruction, he brings in the words of the Sixty-ninth Psalm as the fittest for his purpose : " David saith, Let their table be made a snare, and a trap, and a stumblingblock, and a recompense unto them. Let their eyes be darkened that they may not see, and bow Thou down their back alway."† It is worthy of notice that the Apostle's account of what God was doing, in his time, to the Jews, calling some of them by His grace and hardening others,—his simple statement of the facts as they were taking place before his eyes,—has given rise to the very same sort of hostile criticism as we are familiar with in regard to the imprecation of them by the Psalmist. This goes far to show that the real difficulty lies *in the facts themselves*, rather than in the language of the sacred writers with reference to them. Such things as David imprecates, and Paul records, are not to be spoken of but with fear and trembling. Nevertheless, it is certain that they take place, and that they enter into the

---

* *Psalmus Ischarioticus.* See Delitzsch (at Ps. cix.).
† Chap. xi. 9, 10.

plan of the Divine Government; and who will dare to affirm that God is unrighteous who thus taketh vengeance on bold presumptuous sinners ? Vengeance belongs to His prerogative; and His terrible acts in executing it are not to be challenged by any creature.

(2) Not only are these dreadful judgments, in fact, poured out by God on those who proudly reject His grace and persecute His people; but we are bound to take notice of His hand in such dispensations, and even to express acquiescence in what God has done—acquiescence, not light-hearted, indeed, but rather chastened with awe and tears. When John saw in the Apocalypse the vials of God's wrath poured on the earth, and the sea, and the rivers and fountains of water, he " heard the angel of the waters saying, Righteous art Thou, which art and which wast, thou Holy One, because Thou didst thus judge : for they poured out the blood of saints and prophets, and blood hast Thou given them to drink : they are worthy." * In like manner, when he saw Babylon fall, he heard this exhortation, " Rejoice over her, thou heaven, and ye saints, and ye apostles, and ye prophets ; for God hath judged your judgment on her." †

Thus far, there can hardly be any difference of opinion among those who receive the Scriptures as the Word of God. And the considerations adduced indicate the light in which the Imprecatory Psalms are to be read. Commentators like Matthew Henry and Bishop Horne, whose sole object is the edification of their readers, have been used to say that David's words are to be understood, not as expressing desire, but as predicting the doom of the enemies of God. If this explanation be offered as the strict interpretation of the words, it must be rejected. It is certain that the psalmist speaks in the *imperative*, not in the *future* merely. Nevertheless, I as little doubt that the explanation contains much truth, and comes nearer the mark than those that are offered by some more ambitious interpreters, who see nothing in the words but private vindictiveness. Imprecations which were uttered in the Spirit, by one whom God had constituted the living representative of the cause of truth in the world, were, in effect, predictive denunciations of

---

* Rev. xvi. 5, 6.   † Rev. xviii. 20.

the doom of those against whom they were spoken, and are to be read as such. This principle did not escape the observation of Augustine, and he has unfolded it with characteristic power and wisdom. "In the words of the Psalmist (he observes) there is indeed the expressing of desire; but the language is figurative, and is to be understood as denoting the prescience of one who foretells. For as it is the manner of prophetical Scripture, in predicting things yet future, to narrate them as if they were already past, even so certain things are spoken, as it were by way of *prayer*, while yet they who rightly understand the words perceive in them rather *the intuition of a prophet*. Thus the prophet, speaking of Judas the traitor, as it were, desires for him the doom which he foretells as awaiting him. Nor is it without reason that things future are spoken of as if already accomplished. For to God they are so certain, that they may be esteemed already done; and the prophet seems to express, by way of desire, that which he foresees will certainly come to pass; *the intention, so far as I can see, being nothing else but to teach us that the counsel of God, His fixed and immovable determination, ought not to be displeasing to us.*" *

This view of the matter, in itself most reasonable, is powerfully enforced by the circumstance already adverted to, that Christ is in these psalms as well as David, and that they were spoken with a prophetic reference to His betrayers and murderers. They were applied by Christ to the unbelieving Jews, when (with evident allusion to the Sixty-ninth Psalm) He foretold that their house was about to be left unto them desolate! † They were expressly applied, as we have seen, by one apostle to Judas Iscariot, and by another to the general body of the nation.‡ Many divines of great eminence, like Augustine and Luther, apply these psalms (especially the Sixty-ninth and Hundred-and-ninth) exclusively to Christ and His betrayers. That is probably an extreme view: they seem plainly to express the sentiments of David, in the first instance. Nevertheless, I do not doubt that the remoter interpretation indicated by the New Testament quotations is the one on

---

* *Augustini Sermones*, xxii., Ed. Benedict.
† Matt. xxiii. 38. Comp. Ps. lix. 25.
‡ Acts i. 20; Rom. xi. 9.

which the mind ought principally to rest in the devotional use of the psalms; and that our aim ought to be to avail ourselves of their assistance in reverently adoring the justice of God when He takes vengeance on the incorrigible enemies of Christ.

One other point has yet to be noticed. It cannot be denied that, like the imprecations of the apostles and of the souls under the altar, the language of the Psalmist has reference not only to judgments already executed, but to judgments which are viewed as still future and in suspense. It brings up the question, What ought to be our sentiment with respect to such judgments?

In reply to this question, I do not hesitate to say that, as a rule, our duty is to *deprecate* them, and not to *imprecate* them. Even although we see reason to conclude that they are surely coming, we ought to cry aloud for mercy to be shown to the transgressors. The Lord Jesus prayed for His murderers; and we ought to do likewise. To make the Imprecatory Psalms the vehicle of maledictions against personal enemies is a frightful abuse of God's holy Word. Calvin mentions, as a fact notorious in his time, that certain monks,—the Franciscans especially,— made a trade of this detestable sacrilege. If any one had a mortal enemy and wished him destroyed, he would hire one of those wretches to curse him, day by day, in the words of the Hundred-and-ninth Psalm. The Reformer adds that he himself knew a lady of rank in France who hired certain Franciscans to imprecate perdition in this way on her only son.* Matthew Henry, after mentioning these shameful facts, makes this reflection, that "greater impiety can scarcely be imagined, than to vent a devilish passion in the language of sacred writ; to kindle strife with coals snatched from God's altar; and to call for fire from heaven with a tongue set on fire of hell." Those who are capable of such daring profanity (one may surely trust that it has never shown its head in any Protestant Church) would not be dissuaded by any argument of ours; but it may not be useless to observe that it would be a dangerous and overbold employment of these psalms to recite them even against those who are our enemies in some good and holy work. When James and John proposed to imitate Elijah by commanding fire

---

* Commentary on Ps. cix. 6.

to come down from heaven and consume certain Samaritans who opposed their passage to Jerusalem, the Lord "turned, and rebuked them, and said, Ye know not what manner of spirit ye are of." *

This, I repeat, is the rule by which we are to walk. We are to bless them that curse us, and to pray for them that despitefully use us, and persecute us. But there are exceptions even to this rule. One of these is pointed out by the loving disciple, in a quarter where, but for his intimation, we might well have deemed the rule absolute. " If any man see his brother sinning a sin not unto death, he shall ask, and God will give him life for them that sin not unto death. There is a sin unto death : not concerning this do I say that he should make request " † And there are other exceptions. It is plain that civil society and its officers are not to walk by the letter of the commandment about forgiving trespasses and rendering to no man evil for evil. The Civil Magistrate is neither obliged, nor at liberty, to forgive those who trespass against him. "He is a minister of God, *an avenger for wrath* to him that doeth evil." ‡ It is at his peril if he refuse or neglect to perform this office ; and all private persons whose minds have not been corrupted by a false sentimentality will concur with him in the execution of his stern duty. When a foul crime has been perpetrated, tender-hearted Christian women, who would not touch a hair of their enemy's head but would rather feed him, will express keen resentment, and will be disquieted in mind till they hear that the perpetrator has been convicted and duly punished. They will imprecate condign punishment on the offender. It is their hearty desire and prayer that the violated majesty of the law may not remain unrevenged. Facts like these, if they were fairly considered, would be felt to throw much light on the Bible imprecations. If we had more of the Psalmist's consuming zeal for the cause of God ; if we were as much concerned for the honour of the divine government as every virtuous citizen is for the honour of the national laws, the imprecations would sound less strange and harsh in our ears. This has been well pointed out by an eminent foreign divine, who observes that " David is the Old Testament type of the inviolable majesty of

---

* Luke ix. 55.   † 1 John v. 16.   ‡ Rom. xiii. 4.

Christ; and therefore his imprecations are prophetic of the final doom of all the hardened enemies of Christ and His Church : and in this sense the Christian appropriates them in prayer. Thus turned to account, they are a wholesome antidote to the religious sentimentality of our time, which shuts its eyes to the truth that God's wrath against impenitent despisers of His grace is at once necessary and salutary ;—necessary, because demanded by the divine justice ; salutary, because conducing to the victory and consummation of the kingdom of God. As such, they are simply an expansion of the prayer, Thy Kingdom come. For the kingdom of God comes not only by the showing of mercy to the penitent, but also by the executing of judgment on the impenitent." *

I will not maintain that the Imprecatory Psalms are to be the Christian's habitual song. Many godly persons, who would be the last to charge them with sin, are accustomed to omit them, for the most part, in the regular consecutive singing of the Psalms. Certainly, they ought never to be sung but with fear and trembling. Nevertheless, at fit seasons, they may and ought to find a place in our service of praise. It has been justly said that " in a deep sense of moral evil, more perhaps than in anything else, abides a saving knowledge of God." † There is " a hatred of them that hate God," which is the invariable accompaniment and indispensable token of the love of God in the heart. ‡ And sin is to be looked upon not only as a disease to be loathed, but as a violation of law which calls for punishment. As powerful witnesses for the truth that sin is hateful to God and deserving of His wrath and ever-lasting curse,—a truth which the world would fain forget,—the Imprecatory Psalms must be accounted worthy of their place in the divine Manual of Praise.

---

* Kurtz, *Zur Theol. d. Psalmen*, p. 173.
† Dr. Arnold's life, p. 662.
‡ Ps. cxxxix. 21, 22.

CHAPTER VIII.

THE CHURCH, OR ISRAEL OF GOD.

THE voice which rises to the Throne of God in the Psalms is the voice of the Church rather than of the individual believer. Not that the individual is suffered to lose himself in the crowd—the single believer in the community of the faithful. We are never suffered to forget that we are, each one of us, to hold personal and particular communion with God, even as we are each to give in an account at the final judgment. The Church is composed of Individuals who have, every one, a distinct history; who have been brought to God one by one; and to whom it is of vital necessity that they be each sanctified, and guided, and guarded, and received into glory. When the Church assembles for the worship of God, if all its heart is to be poured out in song, the hymns that are used must deal much with the personal aspects of religion; and this is done so abundantly in the Psalms, that we have found it possible to collect from them alone something like a complete view of the history of religion in the soul.

Nevertheless, there can be no doubt that the Psalter is properly the book of Church Song. In this respect it differs remarkably from other collections of religious poetry. In them, the personal aspects of religion are the well-nigh exclusive theme; whereas in it, although the personal aspects receive their due place, the social aspects are equally prominent. There is something remarkable in the equal balancing of these two elements. Let the Hundred and fifty psalms be distributed into two columns,—the one containing those in which the personal element predominates, the other those that are characteristically social,—and it will be found that the two columns are, as nearly as may be, of equal bulk. An accurate distribution is, indeed, impossible. There is not a psalm that can be called private or personal in such a sense as to preclude its use in public worship; and there are few, if any, that are social in such a sense as to preclude their use in private devotion. There are not a few which might equally well be set down in either class. In some instances, moreover, it is hard to distinguish between the voice of the individual and the voice of the community. The use of the singular pronoun does not determine the point; for, not seldom, the person who speaks in the singular is the collective Church, the Daughter of Zion. Besides, it is instructive to mark how private prayers—prayers which are meant to make the individual worshipper feel himself, as it were, alone with God—will occur, as by way of interjection, in the midst of public psalms; and how, conversely, private psalms will rise into intercession for the public cause. An example, in either kind, will illustrate this. The Hundred-and-sixth is one of the great Historical Psalms; it is a lyrical commemoration of " the mighty acts of the Lord" performed in behalf of the nation during the long centuries of its history, from the Exodus to the Captivity; yet, ere it is well begun, the Psalmist throws in the prayer,—

4. Remember *me*, O LORD, with the favour that Thou bearest unto
      Thy people;
    O visit *me* with Thy salvation:
5. That I may see the prosperity of Thy chosen,
      That I may rejoice in the gladness of Thy nation,
      That I may glory with Thine inheritance.*

The other example is furnished by the Fifty-first Psalm, † "Do good in Thy good pleasure unto Zion; build Thou the walls of Jerusalem." There is no ambiguity about this psalm; it is the most intensely personal that was ever penned. David has sinned. The Lord has convinced him of his sin; and he now cries for mercy, pleading with the importunity of a man who knows he is pleading for his life. If ever there was a time when a man might have been expected to be absorbed in the thought of his own salvation, and utterly oblivious of the general interests of religion and the Church, surely it was the time when David passed through the crisis of which this psalm

---

* There is another example in Ps. xlviii. 14 ; compare the remarks on it above, at p. 86.

† Ver. 18.

is the memorial. How instructive, then, to see that, even in this hour of his anguish, he is led to look beyond himself! First, the thought arises in his heart, " If God would but show me mercy, O what a preacher of His grace I should be ! I would declare His name with tongue and pen ; and in me there should be seen such a monument of mercy as might waken hope in the breast of despair itself. Let God restore unto me the joy of His salvation ; then will I teach transgressors His ways, and sinners shall be converted unto Him !" Then, as light begins to dawn upon him, solicitude for the welfare of God's Israel,—the Church, which has been so deeply wounded by his sin,—stirs his soul again, and he utters the prayer that the Lord would, in His good pleasure, do good unto Zion and build the walls of Jerusalem.

This blending of the personal and social elements of religion is very instructive. It admonishes us that a similar blending ought to find place in our devotions. And this inference is remarkably corroborated by the circumstance that the Lord's Prayer exhibits the same careful conjunction and balancing of the two diverse elements. In three of the petitions of that divine form of prayer, we are taught to set forth our personal wants ; in the other three we are admonished to look, not on our own things only, but every one also on the things of others, especially on the general interests of God's glory in the earth ; and the three public petitions are set down first. We are thus admonished that in our more solemn and stated prayers we ought to seek first that God's Name may be hallowed, that His Kingdom may come, and His Will be done on the earth ; and that petitions with respect to our personal concerns are to come after. It is not meant, of course, that this order is to be uniformly observed, or that God's children may never resort to Him with petitions which wholly relate to their private and personal affairs. The rule is simply intended to indicate, in a general way, the kind of things that are to be asked of God, and the relative prominence they ought to receive in our more solemn prayers. The coincidence in this matter between the Psalter and the Lord's Prayer is, I think, profoundly significant.* True religion is always

---

* I do not know whether Luther had observed the coincidence referred to. Probably not. I do not remember to have seen it taken notice of anywhere. It is all the more interesting to remark how sensible the Reformer was of a certain

personal ; but it is something more. It begins at home ; but it does not end there. It embraces in its solicitude the whole interest of God's glory and the good of men.

When we set ourselves to study the social aspects of religion, as these are delineated by the pencil of the Holy Spirit in the psalms, the society which first and chiefly calls for notice is the CHURCH OF GOD. The Psalter everywhere gives it a large and prominent place ; expatiating on its past History, its contemporary Fortunes, and the bright Future which awaits it in the latter days. These are great and far-reaching subjects, and ought to possess a deep interest for every one who has been admitted into the household of God.

A word or two must be said, in the first place, regarding the view which the psalmists take of *the nature and constitution of the Church.* Not that we are to expect to gather from them very precise information on these much-controverted topics. Detailed and exact definitions would be out of place in poetry, and especially in lyric poetry. Nevertheless, I believe that even from the Psalms some valuable suggestions may be gathered, particularly with respect to the more fundamental and vital points.

If one were asked to explain *of whom this Church of God consisted* which is so affectionately celebrated by the psalmists, it would be a fair reply to say that it consisted of " the seed of Jacob,"—the children of Abraham in the line of Isaac and Israel. For wise reasons, God was pleased, under the Old Testament, to make a *nation* the depositary of His oracles and ordinances, the covenant society within which He chose to dispense the benefits of salvation. This is just to say, in other words, that under the Law the Church of God was Jewish, not Catholic. This, I repeat, is a true account of the matter, so far as it goes. However, it is important to observe that, even under the Old Testament and while the Church was still in its national form, care was taken to guard men against the hierarchical notion of the Church,—the notion which, identifying the visible and invisible Church, and making connection with a particular polity the

deep and most pleasant harmony between these two divine Manuals of Devotion. See his Preface to the Psalter of 1545, inserted below (Book III., Chap. 3).

sole and sufficient bond of union with the true Church, would
exclude from the ordinary ministration of God's saving grace
all who are outside the charmed circle of that polity, and would
teach those who chance to be within the circle that they
are certainly the people of God, the vessels of His mercy, and
heirs of His kingdom. Considering that the Law of Moses set
up many ordinances which were so strictly national that they
could not be celebrated except by a people living under one
external government, it is plain that the narrow theory of the
hierarchists might very plausibly have been maintained under
the Old Testament. In fact, the Pharisees and all the carnally
minded Jews held what was in substance that very theory ; and
the error was, in their circumstances, far more excusable than
it is now, under the Gospel, when all the local and national
rites have been abrogated, and the ordinances of Christian
worship are so framed that every one of them can be observed
in a hundred distinct and independent communities.* It is,
therefore, all the more remarkable that the theory is tacitly
rejected by the Psalmists. One fact of great interest in this
connection came under our notice, in tracing the history of
Psalmody under the later kings, when the children of Israel
were divided into two rival kingdoms. In Temple Songs
written long after the division of the kingdom, Ephraim and
Manasseh are named with fraternal affection and commended to
the grace of God.† It is plain that the faithful in Judah
recognised their northern brethren as still embraced in the
covenant society, and that they perceived the significance of the
fact that the Lord, although the capital of Judah was the chosen
and exclusive seat of His solemn worship, had never ceased to
raise up within the Ten Tribes also a succession of faithful
prophets. With regard to that part of the hierarchical theory
which makes membership in the visible Church identical, for
all practical purposes, with membership in the Church invisible,
it is tacitly refuted in places without number. The true citizen
of Zion is not the man who can merely show his descent from
Jacob, but "the man that walketh uprightly, and worketh
righteousness, and speaketh truth in his heart." "He that
hath clean hands, and a pure heart ; who hath not lifted up

---

* Amesius, *Medulla Theologiæ*, chap. xxxviii. sects. 36, 37.
† Ps. lxxx. 1-3. See above, pp. 87-89.

his soul unto vanity, and hath not sworn deceitfully : he shall receive a blessing from the Lord. . . . This is the generation of them that seek after Him." * What do texts like these teach but the Protestant and apostolic doctrine that there is an all-important distinction between the visible and invisible Church ; that the true Church and the professing Church, although they are so closely connected that the eye of man cannot draw a line of separation between them, are by no means coincident :—that " he is not a Jew which is one outwardly ; neither is that circumcision which is outward in the flesh : but he is a Jew which is one inwardly ; and circumcision is that of the heart, in the spirit, not in the letter ; whose praise is not of men, but of God " ? †

We must beware, indeed, of running into the anarchical extreme of treating matters of external Church Order as if they were of no account. There is a right and a wrong even in them. Under the Old Testament, for example, it was the will of God that His people should subsist in the form of an organised and visible Unity, resorting annually to the solemn feasts in the one sanctuary at Jerusalem. The tribes were commanded to go up to Jerusalem : " the tribes of the LORD, for a testimony unto Israel, to give thanks unto the name of the LORD." ‡ The will of God in this matter could not be disobeyed without sin and loss. Nevertheless, even under the Old Testament, the breach of external and organic unity did not necessarily separate either party from the covenant society. Nothing can be more certain than that Elijah and Elisha, although they had no external fellowship with the altar of the Lord in Zion, belonged to the Israel of God and were no strangers to the covenants of promise. They did not live and die beyond the pale of the true Church. These are patent and undisputed facts. Their significance in relation to the question of eccles-

---

* Ps. xv. 2 ; xxiv. 4-6.

† Rom. ii. 28, 29. Comp. Kœnig, *Theologie der Psalmen,* pp. 79-81. This Roman Catholic writer,—Professor of Theology in Freiburg,—although he avoids the terms " visible and invisible Church," clearly teaches the doctrine they express. He does full justice to the distinction made by the psalmists between the natural posterity of Jacob and the true people of God who are to inherit His salvation. Quoting Rom. ix. 6, " They are not all Israel which are of Israel," he justly remarks that it is simply a restatement of " an Old Testament doctrine."

‡ Ps. cxxii. 4.

iastical unity is not hard to make out. It is admitted that
under the Old Testament, at least, there was a divinely appointed Church order.   But we are not therefore warranted to
leap to the inference that only those who lived in subjection to
that order enjoyed communion with the Lord and were to be
reckoned as belonging to the covenants of promise.   The facts
are such as to exclude any such inference.   Subjection to the
divinely appointed frame of Church order was neither indispens-
ably required in order to connection with the true Church, nor, on
the other hand, did it necessarily infer that connection.   If the
matter stood thus under the Old Testament, much more may we
expect to find it so under the more spiritual and catholic economy.
There is no one frame of Church order that includes all, or nearly
all, God's true people.   And, on the other hand, valuable as
connection with a well-ordered society undoubtedly is, something
more is necessary in order to prove a man to be a true member
of the general assembly and Church of the first-born whose
names are written in heaven, the company of the true people
of God who shall inherit the kingdom.   Not Gentiles only, like
Hobab or Rahab or Ruth, but born Israelites also, were taught
in the psalms to pray that they might have an inheritance in the
true Israel,—that the Lord would " remember them with the
favour He beareth to His people, so that they might see the
prosperity of His elect, and be glad in the gladness of His
nation ; " * and there is not a member of any Church on earth
this day but has, at least, equal need to offer continually that
admirable prayer.

The *Ends for which God has instituted His Church* (besides
the godly nurture of the children of His people—a subject
which will come before us at a later stage) are mainly these
two : the edification of the faithful by joint attendance on
religious ordinances, and the holding forth of a testimony for
God in the view of the world.

1. With regard to the former, it is to be observed that the
psalms lay great stress on Social Worship.   It would have been
strange had they not done so ; for the social principle is strong in
our nature, and it might well have been expected that the Author
of our nature would take care to turn the principle to account in

---

* Ps. cvi. 4, 5.

promoting His people's edification. It is an old and just remark that Christ taught us to say, not *My Father,* but *Our Father,* in order that we might be admonished to pray with and for one another. With like reason, it is to be inferred from the social quality of the Psalms that we ought deeply to feel the relation which binds us to " the congregation of the Lord," and to take delight in being associated with His people in His worship. We are admonished that the ideas expressed in such phrases as these, " the seed of Abraham," " the Israel of God," " the congregation of the righteous," " Mount Zion," " the daughter of Jerusalem," ought to receive a large place in our hearts. The more we imbibe the spirit of the psalms, the less shall we be inclined to fall into a cold, selfish, unbrotherly isolation. We shall more and more rejoice in the thought on which the apostle of the Gentiles so much delighted to expatiate, that God has, even on the earth, a numerous people, who have all been, by one Spirit, baptised into one body ; and that, if we are believers indeed, we are members of that body and united in the fellow-ship of life to all other believers. That Pauline doctrine is not expressly laid down in the psalms, but it underlies them. Hence the delight with which the faithful are seen resorting to the public worship of God. They " serve the LORD with gladness, and come before His presence with singing."* They sing with David† :—

1. Behold, how good and how pleasant it is
   For brethren to dwell together in unity !
2. It is like the precious oil upon the head,
   That ran down upon the beard,
   Even Aaron's beard ;
   That came down upon the skirt of his garments;
3. Like the dew of Hermon,
   That cometh down upon the mountains of Zion:
   For there the LORD commanded the blessing,
   Even life for evermore.

The ordinances that were celebrated in the Temple were, for the most part, of a kind little fitted in themselves to convey spiritual refreshment to the worshippers. They were " weak and beggarly rudiments,"‡—soon to be removed, that they might give place to better means of grace. Nevertheless, *inasmuch as*

---

* Ps. c. 2.   † Ps. cxxxiii. ; comp. p. 47, above.   ‡ Gal. iv. 9.

they had been appointed by God, the faithful knew that so long as the divine appointment remained in force, the ministration of the Spirit would accompany and fructify even those barren rites, and that the place where the congregation waited on them would thus become all that its name imported, —a true " Tent of Meeting." The Lord had promised that in every place where He recorded His name He would come to His people and bless them,* The ancient believers came expecting the fulfilment of the promise ; and so far was their expectation from being disappointed that the psalms in which they expressed the holy satisfaction they experienced in attending on God's worship remain, to this hour, the truest and most adequate expression of the feelings awakened in the souls of Christian worshippers, when their hearts are made to burn within them by the tokens of Christ's presence in their assemblies.

> 1. How amiable are Thy tabernacles,
>   O LORD of hosts !
> 2. My soul longeth, yea, even fainteth for the courts of the
>   LORD ;
>   My heart and my flesh cry out unto the living God.
>
>   .　.　.　.　.　.　.　.　.
>
> 4. Blessed are they that dwell in Thy house :
>   They will be still praising Thee.
>
>   ..　.　.　.　.　.　.　.
>
> 10. For a day in Thy courts is better than a thousand.
>   I had rather be a doorkeeper in the house of my God,
>   Than to dwell in the tents of wickedness.†

2. The Church was instituted not only for the comfort of the faithful, but to maintain a testimony for God in the view of the world, from age to age. We find, accordingly, that the piety unfolded in the Psalms is largely imbued with what may be called, in modern phrase, a *public spirit.* It is assumed that, wherever true religion has found entertainment in the heart, there will be a lively interest in the cause of God. There are men, called by the Christian name, who take no interest in the Churches of Christ. However deeply religion may be wounded in their sight, they feel no wound in their heart ; and they witness the prosperity of Zion without any thrill of joy. Certainly such persons are strangers to the mind of Christ ; for

---

* Exod. xx. 24.　　　　　† Ps. lxxxiv

He could say that "the zeal of God's house had eaten Him up;" and I am sure they can neither pray the Lord's Prayer nor sing the Psalms. The spirit which utters itself in the songs of Zion is the very opposite of theirs. It is that which the exiles expressed, in the Hundred-and-thirty-seventh Psalm when they hung their harps on the willows of Babylon :

> 5. If I forget thee, O Jerusalem,
>   Let my right hand forget her cunning.
> 6. Let my tongue cleave to the roof of my mouth,
>   If I remember thee not ;
>   If I prefer not Jerusalem
>   Above my chief joy.

This consuming zeal for the house of God is common to all the psalms. So many of them are either lamentations over the reverses of Zion or songs of thanksgiving because of her prosperity, and so distinctly do they thus reflect her contemporary fortunes, that the careful student of the national history finds little difficulty in affixing to many of them the date at which they were composed and first sung. One consequence is, that God has thus provided songs adapted to every variety of condition in which the Church can be placed. Another consequence scarcely less important is, that the faithful are admonished to raise themselves out of that selfish isolation,—that entire absorption in the concerns of their own personal wellbeing,—into which even good men are apt to fall. I believe that the lesson just named is one which very many God-fearing people have sadly failed to lay to heart. They can sing that half of the Psalter which expresses the various exercises of *personal* piety ; but the other half, which summons them *to remember Zion*, calls forth little sympathy from their hearts. Even in the interest of personal piety itself, this is to be lamented. Job's captivity was turned when he prayed for his friends ; and it has many a time been found that believers, who before were troubled with weakness and perpetual fears, have been lifted up into a higher and brighter and serener region when, looking no more on their own things only, they have become absorbed in labours and prayers in behalf of some grand Christian enterprise. The Lord will not fail to "remember His Davids and all their affliction,"—their anxious labours for His house and kingdom. David's own faith in this matter was strong; and in one of the songs of ascents he encourages God's people to pray for the peace of Jerusalem, by reminding them that "they shall prosper that love her."*

While manifesting such a lively interest in the varying fortunes of Zion in their own time, the psalmists do not confine their view to one generation. They dwell much on THE HISTORY OF THE CHURCH IN FORMER TIMES. They look back, as well as around; and live much in communion with the generations that have long passed away. I have not attempted to compute the relative space given to the historical element in the Psalter, but it must be very considerable. Several of the longest of the psalms are historical from beginning to end. The Sixty-eighth, although it is brightened with an ultimate reference to Christ and the gospel times, is, in the first instance, a glowing recital of the march out of Egypt and the conquest of Canaan. The Seventy-eighth, the Hundred-and-fifth, and the Hundred-and-sixth, all traverse the same field. In the Seventy-eighth, Asaph, taking up his "parable," teaches the people to read the dangers and the duties of their own time in the light of the history of the nation between the Exodus and the reign of Solomon. In the Hundred-and-fifth, one of the later psalmists taking the materials furnished by the same history, builds them up into a lofty Ode of thanksgiving, that so the Lord's name may be hallowed in the continual commemoration of His mighty acts. The Hundred-and-sixth, which is also from the later period of psalmody, partakes of quite a different character. It is a sorrowful confession of the sins by which the nation had brought dishonour on the name of the Lord and provoked Him to anger, in every period of its long history. These are the most prominent of the Historical Psalms. Others of less note will occur to the reader's memory; and there are, besides, historical allusions in very many of the rest.

This historical quality of the Psalter deserves more consideration than it has commonly received. It proceeds upon the great principle of the unity of the Church in its successive generations. The events of the past are celebrated, not as matters foreign to the men of the present generation, but as matters in which they are vitally interested. They are admo-

---

* Ps. cxxii. 6.

nished not only to identify themselves, generally, with the older generations of their people, but even to humble themselves in the retrospect of *sins* long past, and to say, like Daniel, " O Lord, to us belongeth confusion of face, to our kings, to our princes, and to our fathers, because we have sinned against Thee." * They are invited also to commemorate, with thanksgiving, the years of the right hand of the Most High,—the times when the Lord revived His people and prospered the work of their hands. By a curious coincidence it happens that each of the three longest of the Historical Psalms is introduced with certain prefatory stanzas ; and these are worth looking into, not only for their own sakes, but as indications of the scope of the respective psalms. The following are the Prefaces to the Hundred-and-fifth and the Hundred-and-sixth respectively :—

1. O give thanks unto the LORD, proclaim His name : †
   Make known His doings among the peoples.
2. Sing unto Him, sing praises unto Him :
   Talk ye of all His marvellous works.
3. Glory ye in His holy name ;
   Let the heart of them rejoice that seek the LORD.
4. Seek ye the LORD and His strength ;
   Seek His face evermore.
5. Remember His marvellous works that He hath done ;
   His wonders and the judgments of His mouth ;
6. O ye seed of Abraham His servant,
   Ye children of Jacob, His chosen ones.

Hallelujah !
1. O give thanks unto the LORD ; for He is good :
   For His mercy endureth for ever.
2. Who can utter the mighty acts of the LORD,
   Or show forth all His praise ?
3. Blessed are they that keep judgment,
   And he that doeth righteousness at all times.
4. Remember me, O LORD, with the favour that Thou bearest
   unto Thy people ;
   O visit me with Thy salvation :

---

* Dan. ix. 8.

† This, rather than "call upon His name," is the correct rendering, both here and in Gen. iv. 26, xii. 8, etc. Comp. Exod. xxxiii. 19 ; xxxiv. 5, where the correct rendering is given in the Authorised and Revised Versions. So Luther, *prediget seinen Namen ;* and Ainsworth, *proclaim,* i.e. *preach His name.* Dr. Cheyne's rendering is to the same effect : *celebrate His name.*

5. That I may see the prosperity of Thy chosen,
   That I may rejoice in the gladness of Thy nation,
   That I may glory with Thine inheritance.
6. We have sinned with our fathers,
   We have committed iniquity, we have done wickedly.

Running through these and many other passages there is a sentiment of national continuity, analogous to that of personal identity. I know I am the same person I was twenty years ago ; and, believing as I do that all the events of my life are governed by the provident wisdom of God, I feel it to be my duty carefully to keep in memory, and often to meditate upon, the way He has led me and tended me from my youth. I know it would be both a dereliction of duty and a forfeiture of inestimable benefits were I to forget the errors of my youth or the dispensations of God's providence in ordering my lot. How often in times of perplexity or sorrow has the believer found the strongest comfort in calling to remembrance instances in which God heard his prayer and sent him help, in years gone by ! The Psalmists recognise a similar identity,—a corporate identity,—as pertaining to the Church, and linking together its successive generations. Accordingly, they represent the Church of any given time as having very much the same interest in its prior history which an individual has in his infancy or childhood ; and, in their hands, the principle is wonderfully fruitful both of admonition and comfort. How admirably is it applied, for example, in the Seventy-seventh Psalm ! In a time of deep distress, a dark and cloudy day, the daughter of Zion is at the point of despair : " Will the Lord cast off for ever ? and will He be favourable no more ? Is His mercy clean gone for ever ? doth His promise fail for evermore ? Hath God forgotten to be gracious ? Hath He in anger shut up His tender mercies ? " How does her faith obtain the victory in this conflict ? It is by reverting to her own history in better days, and calling to remembrance God's doings of old. " I said, This is my infirmity : but I will remember the years of the right hand of the Most High. I will make mention of the deeds of the LORD ; for I will remember Thy wonders of old. I will meditate also upon all Thy work, and muse on Thy doings." This, accordingly, is what she proceeds to do throughout the verses that follow. She meditates on the mighty acts of the

Lord in the redemption of Israel from Egypt, till the clouds pass away and her confidence is restored.

The principle involved in all this is set forth in a remarkable way in the Preface to the Seventy-eighth Psalm :—

1. Give ear, O my people, to my law :
   Incline your ears to the words of my mouth.
2. I will open my mouth in a parable ;
   I will utter dark sayings of old :
3. Which we have heard and known,
   And our fathers have told us.
4. We will not hide them from their children,
   Telling to the generation to come the praises of the LORD,
   And His strength, and His wondrous works that He hath done.

The announcement with which Asaph opens his song calls for a word or two of explanation. He promises that he will set forth "a parable" and "dark sayings ;" yet when we look into the psalm it seems to be merely a poetical rehearsal of the marvellous story of the exodus, the forty years' sojourn in the wilderness, and the stormy period of the Judges. Where then, it may be asked, are the parable and the dark sayings that were promised ? The truth is that the facts of the history are viewed, not as mere *events*—things that fell out in those old times—but rather as divine dispensations, the judgments of the Most High, each of which, since it embodied a thought of God's heart, was full of instruction for the generations following. This is the view which the apostle teaches us to take of the history of God's ancient people ; for the things which befell them, he writes, "happened unto them by way of example : and they were written for our admonition, upon whom the ends of the ages are come." * As Christ during His personal ministry instructed the Church with *spoken* parables, so during the long centuries of the Old Testament He instructed it with *acted* parables. It is impossible to estimate the profit, in the shape both of doctrine and reproof and correction and instruction in righteousness, which has been got by contemplating the events of the history of which so large a portion of the Psalter is the lyrical memorial.

Unbelievers will, of course, sneer at this account of the Historical Psalms. They see in these nothing but national

---

* I Cor. x. II.

songs. If there be any lyrical faculty in a nation, it naturally applies itself to the celebration of the national heroes and the most memorable passages of the national history ; and what more reasonable than to attribute to this source the historical poems of the Bible ? The explanation can be dressed so as to captivate the unwary. But it will not stand. Not to dwell upon the fact that all the psalmists are careful to testify, either explicitly or by clear implication, that, in their judgment, the national history is a " parable," that it is everywhere replete with religious significance, and that their design, in making it the burden of their song, is to spread abroad the lessons it was meant to teach—not to dwell, I say, on that fact, it is enough to remark that there is no glorifying either of the nation itself or of its great men. This is quite fatal to the notion that these psalms are national songs and nothing more. That the lyrical genius of the Hebrew bards was quite capable of celebrating great men and chivalrous deeds is sufficiently proved by David's lament for Saul and Jonathan. Yet the Psalter does not contain one song of that order. There is not a single ode in praise of any national hero, Abraham or Joseph, Moses or Joshua or Samson. If David seems to be an exception, the explanation is to be found in the singular place he occupies in the history, as the ancestor and type of Christ. When the Psalter extols him, it is not as a national hero, but as the Anointed of the God of Jacob ; and the praise is intended for the royal office and the Divine Antitype. When David, in his individual person, comes before us, it is not as a hero at all, but in the totally different character of a sinner saved by grace. As for that glorifying of the nation which is the habit of every other lyrical literature, there is no trace of it in the Scriptures. On the contrary, the ordinary drift of the Historical Psalms is to inculcate on the people the remembrance of their sins, and to make them feel that in no respect were they intrinsically better than their neighbours. Let any one who doubts this read the Hundred-and-sixth Psalm. The key-note is that sorrowful confession with which, as we have seen, it begins : "We have sinned with our fathers, we have committed iniquity, we have done wickedly," and the same penitential tone is maintained to the close. The poets of other nations have never written in this humbling strain. The world does not contain another instance of a collection of national lyrics so totally devoid of everything that could inflame national vanity, so redolent of a sense of the unworthiness of the nation and of the marvellous grace of the Most High.

One other remark before quitting this topic. The feature of the Bible Psalmody on which I have been commenting, —the large space occupied by odes which invite the godly to take notice of and expatiate upon the intimate relation which unites them, in a fellowship of life, to the whole people of God on the earth, and to the Church of all preceding times,—does it not impressively teach us that the humblest believer is crowned with a dignity which casts the honours of the earth into the shade? He is a citizen of no mean city. God has enrolled him in the citizenship of the heavenly Jerusalem, in the general assembly and congregation of the first-born. On one occasion, when John Knox had expressed somewhat freely his judgment respecting certain affairs of state, the Queen scornfully asked what he had to do with such matters: "What are ye within this commonwealth?" "A subject born within the same, Madam," was the Reformer's intrepid reply.* Those noble words have sometimes been recalled to my mind by the bold and public-spirited way in which the psalmists offer petitions and remonstrances respecting the high affairs of the kingdom of God, and invite us to do the same. To a secular mind it seems a vain thing when some believer, it may chance a person in a very humble station, not only manifests a zealous interest in great public questions vitally affecting Church and Commonwealth, but ventures to offer prayer respecting them, in the hope of thus contributing something towards the promotion of divine truth and public justice. I suppose that among those who have made conscience of labouring in prayer that God's Kingdom may come and His Will be done in the earth, there are few who have not themselves been troubled with misgivings and doubts respecting the likelihood of their being able to accomplish anything by their prayers. I can well imagine that when Daniel set apart a day for special supplication with respect to the captive Church and its predicted return, even he might be momentarily shaken in mind by sceptical doubts insinuating themselves

---

* Knox's *History of the Reformation*, ii. 388 (Edin. 1848).

in the guise of humility.   I can fancy him arguing thus with
himself, " What am I in this great Kingdom of God, that I
should presume to make my voice heard in its high affairs ?
Would it not better consist with modesty were I, when I pray,
to confine myself to my own personal concerns,—my sins, my
necessities, the mercies I have received, the hopes I cherish ?
Am I not overbold thus to deal with God for my people, con-
fessing their sins and seeking their good ?   Is it not a fond
conceit to imagine that my poor prayers shall avail anything in
bringing about those great imperial revolutions which are to
break the fetters of my people and restore them to the place of
our fathers' sepulchres ? "   Misgivings like these will arise in
the hearts of God's people and weaken their hope as they pray
for the coming of Christ's kingdom, or might have done so,
if God had not Himself filled their mouths with songs which
invite them to cherish a self-forgetting zeal for His glory, to
remember their rights and responsibilities as the citizens of His
Jerusalem, and to cherish the steadfast hope that when the
Lord shall build up Zion and appear in His glory, " He will
regard the prayer of the destitute, and not despise their
prayer." *

* Ps. cii. 16, 17.

CHAPTER IX.

THE FUTURE GLORIES OF THE CHURCH.

IN common with the whole Scriptures, the Psalms predict the ultimate extension of the Church of Christ over all the earth, and the universal prevalence of truth and holiness, of justice and peace. They invite us, accordingly, to launch into the unvisited seas of the future, that, by the help of that faith " which is the assurance of things hoped for," we may expatiate on the glorious things that have been spoken concerning the City of God.

Nothing can well exceed the plainness, directness, and precision with which the conversion of the nations is announced.

> lxxxvi. 9. All nations whom Thou hast made shall come and worship before Thee, O Lord ;
> And They shall glorify Thy name.
> 10. For Thou art great, and doest wondrous things :
> Thou art God alone.
> xxii. 27. All the ends of the earth shall remember, and turn unto the LORD ;
> And all the kindreds of the nations shall worship before Thee.

There is no mistaking the meaning of these announcements. They are as unambiguous as anything that can be spoken by the most sanguine advocate of Christian missions in this nineteenth century. Yet they come from the age and the pen of David. By him the Holy Spirit has, for eight-and-twenty centuries, been bearing witness that God's visible Church is destined to embrace all the nations whom God has created on the face of the whole earth. A day is coming when they shall all resort to the Lord's throne, and bow themselves down before Him. They have long forgotten Him, although He made them ; but they shall one day call to remembrance His claims upon them and will turn to Him again, even in the uttermost parts of the earth.

The presence of announcements like these in the Bible, and specially in the Psalter, which is the throbbing heart of the Bible, is a fact worthy of being pondered. It imparts to the Scriptures, and has from the first imparted to the piety which has been kindled and nourished from the Scriptures, a character of hopefulness and consequent moral strength nowhere else to be found. It has often been remarked that, in regard to this, there is a wonderful contrast between the Holy Scriptures and scriptural piety, on the one hand, and the literatures and religions of paganism, on the other. Amongst all nations, the poets have sung much of a golden age ; for even the light of nature discloses enough to suggest that the world, as we now see it,—so full of confusion and darkness,—comes far short of ideal perfection, and to awaken a certain sentiment of a better and nobler order of things. * But, while the poetry of the nations which have not enjoyed divine revelation places the golden age in the past, when the human race was young, the poetry of the Bible places it in the future, under the millennial reign of Christ. When a thoughtful heathen looked wistfully into the future, he was filled with gloomy forebodings ; for it seemed to him as if the world ever grew the longer the worse. God's people, on the contrary, although in forecasting the future they have been no strangers to the sorrowful apprehension of coming judgments, have been enabled to descry a serene heaven beyond the clouds, so that the immediate prospect has not reduced them to despair. They have been able to sing with the captive Church, "Thou shalt arise and have mercy on Zion," and to add, " We may not see the happy time, but its advent is sure, and our children will see it ; this shall be written for the generation to come, and a people which shall be created shall praise the LORD." † This sentiment pervades the whole Psalter. Its songs are the most hopeful in the world, and, because

---

* According to Bacon, a sentiment of this sort is one of the chief fountains of grave and lofty song. " If the matter be thoroughly considered, a strong argument may be drawn from Poesy, that a more stately greatness of things, a more perfect order, and a more beautiful variety delights the soul of man than anyway can be found in nature since the fall." (*Advancement of Learning.* Book II. chap. xiii.)

† Ps. cii. 13, 18.

hopeful, wholesome and helpful also. They comfort the heart with the sure persuasion that they who fight on the Lord's side,—whose sword, like Christ's, is drawn "in behalf of truth, and meekness, and righteousness,"*—fight on the winning side, and may well be steadfast and unmovable, always abounding in the work of the Lord, forasmuch as they know that their labour and conflict shall not be in vain in the Lord.

The tide of hope which runs so strong in this portion of the Divine Word is significant in many ways. It bears witness to a catholicity of feeling scarcely to be expected under the Mosaic institutions. Whatever judgment may be formed regarding the matter in controversy between Augustine and the Donatists, the great Church-Father was undoubtedly right in maintaining, as he so often does, that men whose sympathies are restrained within the limits of some provincial sect are in no condition to sing the Psalms of David. The catholicity of these songs is so wide, that it not only embraces in its sympathy God's people all the world over, but refuses to give Him rest till He have filled the whole earth with the knowledge of His way. This, I repeat, is very significant. It gives an interesting glimpse into the state of men's minds under the Old Testament with respect to the Gentiles. If a people's heart burn with desire to embrace some neighbouring community in the loving fellowship of a common faith, it may hate the ways of that community and may shun their familiar society so long as they remain unconverted, but it will not regard them with scornful disdain. Now, it is to be remembered that the Psalms were the utterance, not of individual feeling only, but likewise of the common mind of the Hebrew Church. As Church Songs, they were in perpetual use in public worship. They must be accepted, therefore, as indubitably attesting the existence in Israel of a tone of sentiment in relation to the Gentiles very different from what has often been imagined. It has long been the fashion in some quarters to speak disparagingly of the religion of the Old Testament; ascribing to it a certain "hateful particularism"—a bitter, scornful antipathy to the Gentiles. It is not difficult to understand how some learned persons have been led into this estimate of

---

* Ps. xlv. 4.

the Hebrew Church.   If men will take the Pharisees for the
genuine representatives of Old Testament piety, and confine
their attention to those parts of the law which the Pharisees
(reading them apart from the general drift of the Scripture)
abused to the encouragement of their unholy pride, they can
reach no other conclusion.   The estimate, nevertheless, is just
about as mistaken and unfair as ever men of learning fell into.
No doubt, God did separate the seed of Abraham to be a peculiar
people to Himself, and imposed on them a system of rigid and
exclusive ordinances to be a wall of separation between them
and the Gentiles.   But the barrier thus reared was intended
for *defensive* purposes alone.   Its use was to ensure the con-
servation of the true faith and the pure worship of the living
God in the bosom of the chosen people, not to debar the
surrounding nations from participating in the benign influences
which that faith and worship never fail to diffuse.   The
wall of partition was built to shut heathenism out, not to
shut the truth in.   The purpose it was meant to serve may
be compared to that served by the glass walls of a con-
servatory, which are set up, not to make the rest of the
garden cold, but to protect the border where tender flowers
and herbs are to be cherished till the summer comes round.
Nothing can be plainer than that the Hebrew Church was
taught to look forth from Zion upon the blinded heathen, not
with pride and scorn, but with commiseration and earnest desire
that the Lord would make known to them also His salvation.*

Since it is certain that, as a rule, the Psalms are not so much

---

* Some observations on the subject here touched upon will be found in a
singularly eloquent sermon, *The Mission Hymn of the Hebrew Church,* by my
honoured friend the Rev. Dr. Goold (Edinburgh, 1866).   Speaking of the Sixty-
seventh Psalm, he remarks, that " it was not some rare and sudden elevation to
which our poet rose on the wing of a special inspiration.   It was designed to
embody the hope. the desire, the prayers of the whole Hebrew Church, that Church
which some delight to paint as so rigid in its forms, so narrow in its beliefs, so
morose in its spirit, that our relation to it is only that of contrast, if not positive
antagonism. . . . We would have hailed it had it been some tiny stream of
holy music issuing from the tower of David in his night watches, when the moon
was sleeping on Olivet, and no other voice joined him in the rapt minstrelsy
expressive of his individual and peculiar hope.   But it comes to us a Church's
Hope, a Nation's Song, in one swelling volume of glorious melody, ringing from
every arch of the temple, and reverberating to this hour in echoes that will never
die, ' Let the peoples praise Thee, O God ; let all the peoples praise Thee' "
(pp. 2, 3).

the vehicle of new revelations as the authentic response of the Church to revelations elsewhere delivered, it becomes an interesting question, Where are the revelations which we may suppose the Holy Spirit to have employed in filling the psalmists with the hopes they utter respecting the conversion of the nations? So far as the later psalmists are concerned, the explanation is sufficiently easy. They had listened to the predictions of Isaiah; and we can distinctly hear his tones ringing through their songs. But how shall we account for the equally explicit language of David and his contemporaries?

The question admits of a satisfactory answer. The Pentateuch contains several distinct intimations of God's purpose to manifest Himself to the Gentiles, as when He announced to Moses,* "All the earth shall be filled with the glory of the LORD." What is more remarkable, the earlier Scriptures are framed according to a plan which must have been intended to awaken, in thoughtful readers, just those catholic hopes which animated the heart of the Hebrew Church. Thus the opening chapters of Genesis, recording as they do the creation of the earth and of man, by the word of God, announce the very truth with which the apostle startled the Athenians, when he said that " God hath made of one every nation of men for to dwell on all the face of the earth." † I will not affirm of that single truth (so generally forgotten by the heathen) that it would of itself have sufficed to awaken hopes respecting the nations; yet when David writes, " All nations *whom Thou hast made* shall come and worship before Thee;" ‡ and when another psalmist, addressing the Gentiles, exclaims, " Make a joyful noise unto the LORD, all ye lands. Know ye that the LORD He is God: *it is He that hath made us, and we are His:* " § it is plain that they have perceived great and prophetic significance in the history of the creation. They feel that the existing condition of things, in which the vast majority of God's rational creatures on the earth live and die in utter oblivion of their Maker, is monstrous and intolerable; so that if, in spite of it, God's Providence preserves and blesses the world, the reason must be that He desires to fill it yet with His glory.

And what shall we say of the Calling of Abraham as it is

---

* Num. xiv. 21.　　　　‡ Ps. lxxxvi. 9; and comp. Hengstenberg *in loc.*
† Acts xvii. 26.　　　　§ Ps. c. 1, 3.

recorded a little farther on in Genesis? Doubtless, it had an aspect of wrath towards the Gentiles. They were to be left to their own ways, which was, in effect, to deliver them over to unbelief and dishonour. Accordingly, the carnally minded Jews afterwards took occasion from it to justify their proud exclusiveness. Were they not Abraham's seed, and therefore entitled to look with scorn upon "sinners of the Gentiles"? But they might have observed, that the same record which commemorates the call of Abraham intimates that, in electing him, the Lord had a loving eye to the ultimate salvation of the Gentiles. The oracle which conveyed to Abraham the intimation that the Lord had chosen him and his seed to be the covenant society spoke of a time when the Gentiles should be likewise blessed, and intimated that the blessing in store for them should arise from the seed now promised to him. The sacred historian relates, that on four different occasions the patriarchs received the promise, that "in their seed all the nations of the earth should be blessed." * In the covenant with Abraham there was therefore an intimation of goodwill to the Gentiles. If he and his seed were separated from the nations and peculiarly blessed, it was in order that, in God's good time, all the families of the earth might share in the blessing. The Hebrew Church carried the hope of the Gentiles; so that when our Lord declared that many should come from the east and west, and should sit down with the patriarchs in the gospel kingdom, it was not a novel announcement He made. He simply recalled attention to an announcement coeval with Abraham.

One who would do full justice to this promise of a blessing to be given to the Gentiles, in the latter days, by the mediation of the seed of Abraham, must read it in connection with the remarkable Table of the Nations which fills the Tenth chapter of Genesis. It is, I think, a most significant circumstance that, immediately before proceeding to relate how God turned His back on the nations and made choice of the seed of Abraham to be His peculiar people, the sacred historian carefully engrosses in his narrative a catalogue of the families by which the whole earth began to be peopled after the flood. May we not discern in this an intimation that, although the nations were to be

---

* Gen. xii. 3 ; xviii. 18 ; xxii. 18 ; xxvi. 4.

suffered to walk in their own ways, it was to be only for a season? Their names are engrossed in Genesis—are solemnly inscribed on the walls of the porch of sacred Scripture, in token that, although they may forget the Lord, His purpose is to keep His eye on them and one day to reassert His right to the homage of their hearts. The Table of the Nations, we may be sure, was not set down in the Tenth of Genesis merely to guide the researches and gratify the thirst of our modern archæologists. It shone from the first with a deep religious significance for the people of God, and kept them from forgetting the Lord's interest in the nations.

These intimations of mercy in store for the Gentiles do not perhaps lie quite on the surface of the early Scriptures; and it is likely enough that, in every generation, there would be many among the children of Israel who overlooked them, and, like the Pharisees, took occasion from the covenant with Abraham to despise the Gentiles, instead of learning from it to take an affectionate and prayerful interest in them, and to look forward in hope to a time when they should be enrolled among the fearers of the Lord. But we must not do the Old Testament Church the injustice of supposing that all its members were so blind and carnal. Here, as in so many other particulars, the Psalms enable us to vindicate the faith of the ancient saints. They show that the intimations we have pointed out were neither overlooked nor forgotten. The Church's *missionary work,* it is true, did not begin under the Old Testament dispensation; nor indeed did it begin till the day of Pentecost; for even Christ Himself was not sent save to the house of Israel. Till the full time came for the great sacrifice to be offered up and the Comforter to be sent forth, there was no commission given to the Church to go unto all nations, preaching repentance and the remission of sins. The Hebrew Church was neither called nor qualified to be a missionary society. But it never ceased to desire and hope for the conversion of the nations. This is seen in those passages in which the Psalmists betray a consciousness that they shall one day have all the world for auditors. How boldly does David exclaim, "I will give thanks unto Thee, O Lord, among the peoples; I will sing praises unto Thee among the nations."*

---

* Ps. lvii. 9.

In the same spirit, a later psalmist summons the Church to lift up her voice, so that all the nations may hear her recital of the Lord's mighty acts: "O give thanks unto the LORD; proclaim His name: make known His doings among the peoples."* The full import of this class of texts has hitherto been much hidden from the English reader by the circumstance that King James' Translators hardly ever used the word *people* in its plural form. Twice, in the Revelation, they ventured to write *peoples;* but it seems to have been a new-fangled word in 1611, so that, except in the two places referred to, the singular form has to do duty for both numbers. The consequence has been that, in passages almost innumerable relating to "the nations," the sense has been greatly obscured to those unable to refer either to the original or to other versions.† In the Psalms, in particular, the mention of the Gentiles is more frequent than the English reader has hitherto been made aware of. It is to be observed, moreover, that in addition to this strain of indirect prediction, the conversion of the world is articulately celebrated in many glorious psalms.‡ Indeed, so numerous are these, and so generally distributed over the centuries between David and Ezra, that it would seem that at no time during the long history of inspired psalmody did the Spirit cease to indite new songs in which the children of Zion might give utterance to their world-embracing hopes.

It does not fall within the scope of this work to go into detailed exposition of particular Psalms; and the number of those which, in one way or another, celebrate the Church's future glory, is so great as to make such exposition peculiarly inadmissible in the present instance. It may, nevertheless, be both possible and useful to call attention to some of the more salient features of the Church's future, as it is celebrated in these divine songs. The general fact that there is an element of millennial prophecy in the Psalter can hardly have escaped the notice of any who read the Bible at all; but few are aware how rich and various is its teaching on this fascinating subject.

---

* Ps. cv. I.

† See the Old Testament Revisers' *Preface.*

‡ Psalms ii., xviii., xxii., xlv., xlvii., lxvi., lxvii., lxviii., lxxii., lxxxvii., xcvi., xcviii., c., cxvii. Compare Psalms lxv. 2, lxxxii. 8, lxxxix. 25, cx. 2, cxlviii. 11, etc.

1. The point which claims notice, in the first place, is the care with which the ultimate glorious extension and prosperity of the Church are connected with the Person and Office of Christ. We are thus put on our guard against a prevalent and injurious misconstruction of the predicted progress of the kingdom of God. It requires little faith now, in this nineteenth century of the Christian era, to affirm confidently that Christianity is destined to embrace the world, and that all the nations whom God has made shall come and bow themselves down before Him. Even the dull eye of the worldling can perceive that things are now tending to this issue, all the world over. Christendom already embraces the whole living civilisation of the globe. But, if the matter be carefully looked into, it will be found that not seldom, when men speak about the spread of Christianity, God and His Christ have no place in their thoughts. It is the natural growth of a Reign of Justice they are dreaming of ; as if the truth were destined to prevail and make conquest of the world by its own natural force, apart altogether from the supernatural power and grace of Christ. The Psalter presents the matter in a different light. The progress of Christianity is held forth as the progress of a Kingdom—the widening reign or domination of a Mighty Prince, who, having girded His sword upon His thigh, rides prosperously forth in behalf of truth and meekness and righteousness. It assumes, indeed, that the Truth is the grand instrument by which men's minds are brought into willing subjection. The conversion of "the peoples" is to be accomplished by the "proclamation of God's name, the declaration of His mighty acts."* The Word of God is the sword of the Spirit. But a sword does not wound unless it be grasped by a strong hand. Our blessed Lord, when He went away to the Father, left with His disciples not only the gospel message, but the promise of the Spirit,—the promise that He would Himself be with them, in the power of the Spirit, even to the end of the world. The presence of Christ, really and truly in the midst of His people, is that which alone can secure the victory of the truth. The Psalter, accordingly, does not permit us to dissociate the progress of the Church from the person of her ever-present Lord.

---

* Ps. cv. 1.

cx. 1. Thus saith the LORD unto my lord, Sit Thou at My right hand,
Until I make Thine enemies Thy footstool.
2. The LORD shall send forth the rod of Thy strength out of Zion :
Rule Thou in the midst of Thine enemies.

ii. 7. I will tell of the decree :
The LORD said unto Me, Thou art My son ;
This day have I begotten Thee.
8. Ask of Me, and I will give Thee the nations for Thine inherit-
ance,
And the uttermost parts of the earth for Thy possession.
9. Thou shalt break them with a rod of iron,
Thou shalt dash them in pieces like a potter's vessel.

In like manner, the Seventy-second Psalm holds forth the felicities of the millennial period as the benign fruits of the reign of the Prince of Peace ; and it is quite unwarrantable to explain this away, as if it meant no more than that the blessing is to be wrought out by the pacific doctrine and institutions with which Christ endowed the Church eighteen centuries ago. Invaluable as these are, they could of themselves accomplish among men nothing more than a superficial amelioration of manners. It is the presence of Christ and the supernatural power of His Spirit which makes them mighty to the conquest of souls. The Church spreads, because her "God is in the midst of her." * When at any time she has forgotten her dependence on the invisible intercession of her Head and the gracious energy of His Spirit, she has found herself shorn of the locks of her great strength, and has become the laughing-stock of the Philistines.

Nor is it only on the Intercession and almighty Reign of Christ that the psalmists teach us to ground our hope of the conversion of the world. They teach us to seek its ultimate foundation in the Sacrifice He offered on the cross. The connection between Christ's cross and His universal mediatorial dominion is wonderfully exhibited in the Twenty-second Psalm. Of the two strongly contrasted parts of which the long poem is composed, the first has the Cross for its theme, the second the Crown. This is the only explanation that can be given of the fact that a Psalm which opens with the cry, *Eli, Eli, lama 'azabhthani,* ends with a shout of triumph over a world won to God.

* Ps. xlvi. 5.

27. All the ends of the earth shall remember and turn unto the
   LORD :
   And all the kindreds of the nations shall worship before
   Thee.
28. For the kingdom is the LORD'S ;
   And He is the Ruler over the nations.
29. All the fat ones of the earth shall eat and worship ;
   All they that go down to the dust shall bow before Him,
   Even he that cannot keep his soul alive.
30. A seed shall serve Him ;
   It shall be told of the Lord unto the next generation.
31. They shall come and shall declare His righteousness
   Unto a people that shall be born, that He hath done it.

2. The Psalter indicates the means by which the universal
prevalence of Christ's kingdom is to be brought about. It
would be unreasonable to look to it, or indeed to any other
portion of the Old Testament, for detailed instructions with
respect to the missionary enterprises of the Church. For
instructions of that kind, one must turn to the New Testament,
especially to the Acts of the Apostles and the Pauline epistles.
It is in the Apostolical Scriptures that the Holy Spirit has laid
up all necessary information respecting those institutions, and
precedents, and counsels by which the Christian missionary
must be guided in his operations. They are the parts of
Scripture which are meant to be to him what the " working
plans" of an edifice are to the builder. But the builders of
God's Zion need something more than " working plans " of the
edifice. The Church needs something more than practical
directions regarding the fit manner of carrying on her Lord's
work on the earth. In their own place, these are, doubtless,
both indispensable and invaluable. But, although they yield
guidance, they furnish little motive power. We stand in need,
therefore, of such general views of the enterprise and its results
as will fire the imagination and warm the heart ; and for
these we are chiefly indebted to the Prophets and the
Psalmists. Missionary sermons are generally preached from Old
Testament texts. The best missionary hymns that ever were
written,—those which have the power of keeping abreast of
every new generation,—are the Hymns in the Psalter. It is
certainly a remarkable fact, that although the Old Testament
Church was not a Missionary Church, the flame of its piety

was fed with missionary hymns; and that the Psalter anticipated, by much more than the space of two thousand years, that efflorescence of evangelistic song which has of late shed a new glory on our modern poetry.

What then do the Missionary Psalms teach or suggest with regard to the means by which the conversion of the Gentiles and the millennial glory are to be brought about? We have already ascertained that the principal instrument is to be *the declaration of the truth,*—" the truth as it is in Jesus." That is the rod of Christ's strength, sent out of Zion, whereby He is to achieve for Himself dominion in the midst of His enemies. *Gold* also has a place assigned it. Because of His temple at Jerusalem, kings are to bring presents to the Lord, and of the peoples every one is to submit itself with pieces of silver.* To the Prince of Peace there is to be " given of the gold of Sheba," while prayer is made for Him continually.† These two—gifts and prayers—must go together. The gold is not likely to avail much that has not been dedicated with prayer; and, on the other hand, there is something wrong about the prayers which are unaccompanied with gifts proportioned to the suppliant's ability,—something wrong about that man's professed submission to Christ who does not find his heart moved to give of his substance to promote Christ's work. However, the principle most earnestly inculcated is, that *the world is to be brought to God by means of the prayers and labours of a revived Church.* There must be preaching, and praying, and the giving of men's substance; yet the Lord's effectual blessing will not attend these if they are only the constrained offerings and mechanical services of a dead Church. The blessing will be sent to crown the hearty services of a Church whose heart is fired with love to God, with zeal for His house, with gratitude for His mercy, with Christ-like compassion for souls. Prayer for revival at home and prayer for a blessing abroad ought always, therefore, to go hand in hand. This is brought out in the Sixty-seventh Psalm—the Missionary Hymn of the Hebrew Church :—

1. God be merciful unto us, and bless us,
   And cause His face to shine upon us:
2. That Thy way may be known upon earth,
   Thy saving health among all nations.

---

* Ps. lxviii. 29, 30.   † Ps. lxxii. 15.

3. *Let the peoples praise Thee, O God;*
   Let all the peoples praise Thee.
4. O let the nations be glad and sing for joy;
   For Thou shalt judge the peoples with equity,
   And govern the nations upon earth.
5. *Let the peoples praise Thee, O God;*
   Let all the peoples praise Thee.
6. The earth hath yielded her increase:
   God, even our own God, shall bless us.
7. God shall bless us:
   And all the ends of the earth shall fear Him.

How admirably balanced are the parts of this Missionary Song! The people of God long to see all the nations participating in their privileges, "visited with God's salvation, and gladdened with the gladness of His nation."[*] They long to hear all the peoples of the world giving thanks to the Lord, and hallowing His name; to see the face of the whole earth, which sin has darkened so long, smiling with the brightness of a second Eden. This is not here a vapid sentiment. The desire is so expressed as to connect with it the thought of duty and responsibility. The faithful are not suffered to dissociate the expectation of the Church's vast extension from the thought of their own duty in relation to it. They have learned that the extension of Christ's kingdom is to be brought about by means of a general diffusion of "the knowledge of God's way," the spreading abroad of the truth regarding the way of salvation. They are sensible, indeed, that for the present they are not in a condition to set about the evangelising of the nations. But they long and pray to be delivered from this disability. They cry for a time of quickening. What is very remarkable, they draw encouragement in this prayer from a quarter where we should not have expected them to find it. They recall the terms of the Aaronic Benediction, and find in it an encouraging promise. As if they had said, " Hast Thou not commanded the sons of Aaron to put Thy name upon us and to say, The LORD bless thee and keep thee; the LORD cause His face to shine on thee and be gracious to thee ? Remember that sure word of Thine ! God be gracious unto us, and bless us, and cause His face to shine upon us. Let us be thus blessed, and we shall, in our turn, become a blessing. All the families of the earth shall,

---

[*] Ps. cvi. 4, 5.

through us, become acquainted with Thy salvation." Such is
the Church's expectation.   And who shall say it is unreasonable ?   If the little company of one hundred and twenty disciples
who met in the upper chamber at Jerusalem, all of them persons
of humble station and inconspicuous talents, were endued with
such power by the baptism of the Holy Ghost, that within three
hundred years the paganism of the Empire was overthrown,
one need not fear to affirm that, in order to the evangelisation
of the world, nothing more is required than that the Churches
of Christendom be baptised with a fresh effusion of the same
Spirit of power.

   3. In celebrating the happy age that awaits the Church, the
Psalmists use language which implies that the old distinction
between Jew and Gentile is to be finally done away.

   In three remarkable chapters of the epistle to the Romans,
the series of the divine dispensations toward Jew and Gentile,
from first to last, is sketched with a wonderful sweep and comprehensiveness of vision, the Apostle being careful to describe
not only the dispensations themselves but the true design of God
in them.   After the primitive ages, during which the distinction
between Jew and Gentile was yet unknown, there came the *Abrahamic or Old Testament period,* during which the literal seed of
the patriarch constituted the covenant society, and the Gentiles
were excluded.   The arrangement, no doubt, admitted some
exceptions ; a few Gentiles, like Rahab and Ruth, were incorporated with the chosen seed, and some Israelites were
suffered to fall away into heathenism; but the rule was as I
have described.   The Abrahamic period has been succeeded by
the *pre-millennial Christian period,* during which the body of
the Jewish people are excluded from the covenant society, and
their place is taken by the first-fruits of the Gentiles.   Lastly,
there is to come *the period of the Church's millennial glory,*
when the Jews are to be engrafted again into their own olive
tree, and to flourish in it side by side with the Gentiles.   This
plain didactic exposition of the successive periods furnishes
the key by which we are to open the obscurer oracles of the
poetical Scriptures ; and it enables us to interpret them with
a precision beyond the reach of Old Testament readers.   Applying it to the Psalms, what do we find ?

   It is the ordinary manner of the Prophets, when they predict the conversion of the Gentiles, to describe it figuratively as their subjugation to the sceptre of the house of David, or as their being moved to resort to Jerusalem to pray before the Lord of Hosts. This manner of representation abounds in the Psalms, and occasionally is found in a shape which might suggest to the unwary the idea of carnal conquests. Thus, in one place, the Church is taught to say, "The LORD Most High is terrible; He is a great King over all the earth: He shall subdue the peoples under us, and the nations under our feet."* Let us note, however, by the way, that in the verse immediately preceding, the Gentiles themselves are thus addressed, "O clap your hands, all ye peoples; shout unto God with the voice of triumph,"—an invitation which plainly implies that the subjugation announced is not a carnal one, but the gaining of men's minds and hearts for God. However, it is evident that the psalms of this class, excellent as they are, and perfectly in harmony with what we now know to be the true nature of the Gospel Church, did not press the true conception of Messiah's kingdom on the attention of the Hebrew reader. They did not furnish him with a more adequate conception of the Gospel dispensation than the one which so long clung to Christ's disciples; and they (we know) looked upon the new order of things as intended to be a continuation of the Jewish system, with this difference only, that there was to be a larger resort of Gentile proselytes to Jerusalem than ever was seen of old in the Temple of Solomon.

There are other psalms which hold forth a much higher conception of the Gospel Church. Let the reader mark how the Eighty-seventh, for example, dilates on the glorious things that are spoken concerning the City of God :—

> 4. I will make mention of Rahab and Babylon as among them
>   that know me :
>   Behold Philistia, and Tyre, with Ethiopia;
>   This one was born there.
> 5. Yea, of Zion it shall be said, This one and that one was born
>   in her;
>   And the Most High Himself shall establish her.
> 6. The LORD shall count when He writeth up the peoples,
>   This one was born there.

Thus the Gentiles, far and near, are to be incorporated, along

---

* Ps. xlvii. 2.

with the Jews, into the one commonwealth of the Israel of God, and are, equally with the seed of Abraham, to have their names inserted in the register of the born citizens of Zion.   It is a picture in which the Spirit of prophecy foreshadows the truth taught by the apostle of the Gentiles when he writes, that " in one Spirit were we all baptized into one body, whether Jews or Greeks, whether bond or free." *   In the Church of Christ there is no distinction to be made between Jew and Gentile, any more than between rich and poor, or between bond-men and free-men.   The middle wall of partition is now thrown down.   All the kindreds of the peoples are to come into the courts of the Lord and to take part without fear in the most solemn duties of His worship, on the same terms as the children of Israel.   Trophimus the Ephesian has the same right to tread the Temple courts as Barnabas the Levite, or as Saul of Tarsus the Hebrew of the Hebrews.   How spiritedly is this declared in the Ninety-sixth Psalm !

1. O sing unto the LORD a new song :
   Sing unto the LORD, all the earth.
2. Sing unto the LORD, bless His name ;
   Show forth His salvation from day to day.
3. Declare His glory among the nations,
   His marvellous works among all the peoples.
4. For great is the LORD, and highly to be praised :
   He is to be feared above all gods.
5. For all the gods of the peoples are idols :
   But the LORD made the heavens.
6. Honour and majesty are before Him :
   Strength and beauty are in His sanctuary.
7. Give unto the LORD, ye kindreds of the peoples,
   Give unto the LORD glory and strength.
8. Give unto the LORD the glory due unto His name :
   Bring an offering, and come into His courts.
9. O worship the LORD in the beauty of holiness :
   Tremble before Him, all the earth.

This joyous psalm belongs in part to a class which carry the mind forward to a time still future, inasmuch as they not only predict the millennial glory, but are themselves Songs of the Millennium.   Not content with hailing the happy time from afar, they transport us into the midst of it and celebrate its joys as present realities.   It is a striking fact, worthy to be

* 1 Cor. xii. 13.

pondered by those who are haunted with the notion that the Psalms are somehow antiquated, and that we must part company with them if we would keep abreast of the age—it is, I say, a striking fact, that there are found in the Psalter hymns which are far in advance of any time the world has yet seen, insomuch that the faithful will never be able to sing them with an entire appropriation and unqualified delight, till the earth is covered with the knowledge of the Lord. The Hundredth Psalm is an example of this class, as are also the Hundred-and-seventeenth and the Ninety-eighth. The two former were cited in an earlier chapter. The Ninety-eighth bears so directly on the point in hand that it must be quoted here. The scope of it is well indicated in our old Translators' prefatory note, "The psalmist exhorteth the Jews, the Gentiles, and all the creatures, to praise God." It belongs to the last and brightest of the three periods sketched in the epistle to the Romans, and is properly a song of the mighty congregation of the Lord which will fill the earth with the voice of rejoicing and salvation, when all Israel shall have been recovered to the faith of Abraham, and, the fulness of the Gentiles shall have been brought in.

1. O sing unto the LORD a new song :
    For He hath done marvellous things ;,
    His right hand, and His holy arm, hath wrought salvation for Him.
2. The LORD hath made known His salvation :
    His righteousness hath He openly showed in the sight of the nations.
3. He hath remembered His mercy and His faithfulness toward the house of Israel :
    All the ends of the earth have seen the salvation of our God.
4. Make a joyful noise unto the LORD, all the earth ;
    Break forth, and sing for joy, yea, sing praises.
5. Sing praises unto the LORD with the harp ;
    With the harp and the voice of melody.
6. With trumpets and sound of cornet
    Make a joyful noise before the King, the LORD..
7. Let the sea roar, and the fulness thereof ;
    The world, and they that dwell therein.
8. Let the floods clap their hands ;
    Let the hills sing for joy together ;
9. Before the LORD, for He cometh to judge the earth :
    He shall judge the world with righteousness,
    And the peoples with equity.

Is not this indeed a Millennial Anthem? "It accords with the condition of the world when Christ shall sit enthroned in the willing loyalty of our race. The nations join in an acclaim of praise to Him as their rightful Judge and King. There is a unanimity in the song, as if it ascended from a world purged into a temple of holiness, and whose inhabitants were indeed a royal priesthood, with one heart to make Jesus King, with one voice to sound forth one peal of melody in praise of the name above every name." *

4. From the quotations now made, it will be seen that the Psalter is much occupied in celebrating *the benign fruits which Christ's reign is to yield* in all the earth. Christ's reign will be a reign of HOLINESS. This is its proper and distinctive nature. Under it, the ends of the earth will fear God and rejoice in His salvation. It will likewise be a reign of JUSTICE. Under it, the wars and oppressions and cruelties, the unequal laws and iniquitous institutions, that have so long vexed and cursed the world, will find a place no more. This happy reformation is usually foretold (as in the psalm just quoted) in the form of a proclamation that the Lord is coming "to judge the earth." It is important, therefore, to keep in mind the true sense and intention of that oft-repeated proclamation. It does not refer, as a cursory reader might suppose, to the judgment of the Great Day. There is no terror in it. The psalms that have it for their principal burden are jubilant in the highest degree. The design of the proclamation rather is to announce Christ in the character of a Peaceful Prince coming to administer equal laws with an impartial hand, and so to cause wrong and contention to cease in the earth. This is Christ's manner of judging the earth. What He has already done in this direction enables us to form a conception of what He will yet set Himself to do. When He designs to accomplish great and salutary reforms in the political and social institutions of a people, He begins by dislodging false principles from men's minds and planting true and equitable principles in their stead; by purging evil passions from men's hearts, and baptising them with the Spirit of truth and justice, godliness and loving-kindness. A sure foundation having thus been laid for a better order of things, He will by some storm of controversy or of revolution sweep away the

---

* Dr. Goold's *Mission Hymn of the Hebrew Church*, p. 5.

institutions in which injustice has entrenched itself, and will thus make it possible for righteousness to have free course. What a store of comfort for the downtrodden, the enslaved, the needy, is laid up in the announcement that the Lord is coming to be the Avenger of all such! Well may all the creatures be invited to clap their hands for joy at the thought that He has taken this work in hand; that He sitteth upon the floods; and that the storms which agitate the nations are the chariot in which He rides, to take possession of the earth and make it an abode of righteousness and peace! What a pleasant scene unfolds its tranquil beauty in the Seventy-second Psalm, as Solomon "the Peaceful" describes the justice and benignity with which David's greater son, the true Prince of Peace, will reign over the whole earth in the latter days!

6. He shall come down like rain upon the mown grass:
   As showers that water the earth.
7. In His days shall the righteous flourish;
   And abundance of peace, till the moon be no more.
8. He shall have dominion also from sea to sea,
   And from the River unto the ends of the earth.
9. They that dwell in the wilderness shall bow before Him;
   And His enemies shall lick the dust.
10. The kings of Tarshish and of the isles shall bring presents:
    The kings of Sheba and Seba shall offer gifts.
11. Yea, all kings shall fall down before Him:
    All nations shall serve Him.
12. For He shall deliver the needy when he crieth;
    And the poor that hath no helper.
13. He shall have pity on the poor and needy,
    And the souls of the needy He shall save.
14. He shall redeem their soul from oppression and violence;
    And precious shall their blood be in His sight.
15. And they shall live; and to Him shall be given of the gold
    of Sheba:
    And men shall pray for Him continually;
    They shall bless Him all the day long.
16. There shall be abundance of corn in the earth upon the top
    of the mountains;
    The fruit thereof shall shake like Lebanon:
    And they of the city shall flourish like grass of the earth.
17. His name shall endure for ever;
    His name shall be continued as long as the sun:
    And men shall be blessed in Him;
    All nations shall call Him happy.

Such being the fruits with which Christ's reign will bless the world, who would not join in the prayer of Asaph and say, " Arise, O God, judge the earth : for Thou shalt inherit all the nations " ? *　Even so, come, Lord Jesus ! come quickly !

* Ps. lxxxii. 8.

CHAPTER X.

THE FAMILY AND THE COMMONWEALTH.

WITH a divine comprehensiveness, the Psalter touches human life at every point. As there are Psalms for the Individual and Psalms for the Church, so there are Psalms for the Home and Psalms for the Commonwealth. If either the Family or the State had been overlooked in the Book of Praise, the omission would have been painfully felt; for they are the primitive forms of society, divinely ordained, and all-pervading in their influence. They differ from the Church in this respect, that, having their foundation in nature, they derive their authority from the law of nature; whereas the Church is wholly founded in grace, and derives its authority from the supernatural institution and law of Christ. The distinction is very important; but care must be taken not to exaggerate its importance. It is not to be imagined that, because the Family and the State spring out of the primitive constitution of human nature and are competent to the heathen, they are therefore to be set down either as institutions which owe no allegiance to God's law, or as institutions upon which the dominion and law of Christ have no claim. Families and nations, if they are to answer the ends of their existence, must be in intelligent and willing subjection to the Most High, and must take His law for their rule. Now it is certain that, in our fallen world, this loyal subjection to God cannot be realised except in connection with the redemptive work of our Lord Jesus Christ. It was His design, in undertaking our redemption, that the effects of His mediation should extend to all the relations that had been debased by sin; and the all-important relations of the Family and the State were certainly not overlooked.

In this doctrine of Christ's relation to the two primary

forms of human society lies the explanation of the place they occupy in the Psalter. There are schools of political philosophy which have much to say in praise of what they style " the atheism of the State ; " but the Psalms reject that doctrine, and recognise both Family and State as institutions which ought to be neither without God nor without Christ. While giving the foremost place to the Church,—as it was fit that lyrics of the spiritual life should do,—they look with a kindly eye on the two more primitive institutions. The significance of this was long overlooked even by wise and holy men. The early Fathers were haunted with the notion (since so prevalent in the Church of Rome) that Domestic and Political life are essentially profane, insomuch, that one who would lead a religious life must come out and be separate from them. " Nor was it till the Reformation, and its assertion of the dignity of the family and the nation against the Papacy, which made war upon them both, that the letter of the Old Testament, with its record of an elect family and chosen nation, came to its full rights and honour in this matter." *

The Romish disparagement of the family and nation has now (one may hope) been finally banished from the minds of intelligent Christians. It is not necessary, therefore, to expend words in elucidating the testimony to their dignity that can be gathered from the Psalms. But there are other and still more important purposes that will be served by a careful study of those views of Domestic and National Life which pervade the Psalter.

I. I begin with the FAMILY, which is the nation in embryo.

Of the fifteen Songs of Ascents, two are pictures of domestic life ; and they are both replete with instruction on the point in hand. One of them, the Hundred-and-twenty-eighth Psalm, is anonymous ; and we have no materials for forming so much as a probable conjecture regarding its author and date.

1. Blessed is every one that feareth the LORD,
   That walketh in His ways.
2. For thou shalt eat the labour of thine hands:
   Happy shalt thou be, and it shall be well with thee.

---

* Archbishop Trench, *Augustine as an Interpreter of Scripture*, p. 64.

3. Thy wife shall be as a fruitful vine, in the innermost parts
   of thine house :
   Thy children like olive plants, round about thy table.
4. Behold, that thus shall the man be blessed
   That feareth the LORD.
5. The LORD shall bless thee out of Zion ;
   And thou shalt see the good of Jerusalem all the days of
   thy life.
6. Yea, thou shalt see thy children's children.
   Peace be upon Israel.

The Domestic Institution had its birth in Eden, before sin
had tainted our nature with its foul breath. In sparing to the
world this relic of Paradise, the Lord meant not only that it
should mitigate the evils which have come in by sin, but that,
in the hands of God-fearing men and women, it should import
into this life something that might recall the memory of the
Paradise that has been lost, and both stir up yearnings after,
and minister to our preparation for, the Paradise that is
regained by the Son of God. All this crowds in upon the
mind in thoughtfully listening to the music of the psalmist.
His ode is like a Zephyr laden with the fragrance of the
garden of God. It is the picture of a happy home. God has
blessed the land with peace. The husband goes forth to his
toils, not sparing himself that he may provide for his house ;
and God is pleased to bless his industry. He eats the labour
of his hands. When the sun declines to the western sea, he
intermits his toil and returns to enjoy the solace of a home
made bright and musical with the presence and the voices of
wife and children. The domestic pieties run in a full stream,
for they are fed from heaven. It is not a scene of mere earthly
or secular enjoyment that the prophet delineates. Above this
home, heaven is open and the angels of God ascend and descend.
Never a day passes over the family but they lift up their eyes
to Him that dwelleth in the heavens, and wait on the Lord
their God until that He have mercy upon them. They love
Zion. When the great congregation praises the Lord, they
take part in the song, " both young men and maidens, old men
and children ; " and out of Zion the Lord sendeth them His
salvation from day to day. Their mutual love and their table
mercies are made the sweeter to them, by being enjoyed in the
fear of the Lord.

The Psalmist's description is a very bright one, and it has been often realised in the homes of the godly. The Family sometimes presents another side. Domestic life has its share of the sorrows and anxieties belonging to this sin-stricken world. The birth of children not seldom is itself the occasion of anxiety ; for how are the new-comers to be fed and clothed ? Another Family Song has, accordingly, been provided to meet this case. The Hundred-and-twenty-seventh Psalm is the complement of the Hundred-and-twenty-eighth. It was cited before in our notice of Solomon's psalms, but may well be introduced again in this place.

1. Except the LORD build the house,
      They labour in vain that build it :
   Except the LORD keep the city,
      The watchman waketh but in vain.
2. It is vain for you that ye rise up early, and so late take rest,
      And eat the bread of toil :
   For so He giveth unto His beloved sleep.
3. Lo, children are an heritage of the LORD ;
      And the fruit of the womb is His reward.
4. As arrows in the hand of a mighty man,
      So are the children of [a man's] youth.
5. Happy is the man that hath his quiver full of them :
      They shall not be ashamed,
   When they speak with their enemies in the gate.

Children are the Lord's gift ; and parents may trust in Him that, if they do their duty, He who sends mouths will send meat to fill them. Prudent industry ought not to be suffered to degenerate into unbelieving anxiety about the future.

These domestic psalms caused sore perplexity to the early church-Fathers. For the notion already referred to, that conjugal life is essentially earthly in its spirit and incompatible with a high style of godliness, early came to prevail, and engendered that false and dangerous estimate of celibacy which ultimately brought forth its fruit in the monastic institutions of the Greek and Latin Churches. Even Chrysostom and Augustine were not superior to this weakness. The latter divine, in expounding the psalms before us, laboriously explains away the natural sense of the words and turns the whole into an allegory. The *wife* is the Church ; for is not the spouse of Christ a vine from Egypt—a fruitful vine ? The *olive plants* are the children of Zion ; and so forth. Much can be said, no doubt, in extenuation of the error of these great men. It was an error, nevertheless, and wrought much mischief. Of the many services which the world owes to the Reformers, not the least valuable was their reinstating of the Family in its long-forgotten honours. Luther, in particular, vindicated the truth of God on this subject with incomparable power. His marriage was a protest against the doctrine which attributed a peculiar sanctity to single life, and a solemn declaration of his belief that the wedded life of Christians is holy ; and the testimony was not thrown away. Of the four bas-reliefs which adorn the great Luther-Monument at Worms, one perpetuates the memory of the day on which the Reformer gave his hand to Catherine von Bora, and expresses the sense entertained by the German nation of the value of the example which he then set to his countrymen and to all Christendom. It deserves to be mentioned that Luther's high estimate of the dignity of the Family was not a little fortified by his study of the Psalms, especially of the two which we have just quoted. He wrote separate commentaries on them, in which he did ample justice to their true and natural sense. Thus men's minds were opened to perceive that the monastic idea of a religious life is a very different one indeed from that of the holy prophets and psalmists.

The Family is honoured in the Psalms, because it has an honourable place assigned it in God's economy of salvation. Christian families are ordained to be nurseries for heaven. Not that the grace of God can be made an heirloom in any line of natural descent. It is not transmissible by man. Every child of Adam who is saved must have been the subject, in his own person, of a radical change, by the special grace of the Holy Spirit. But it is plain that we are not left altogether withou information with regard to the quarters in which the ministration of the Spirit is ordinarily vouchsafed ; and both Scripture and experience bear witness that God is wont to pour out His quickening Spirit especially on the seed of true believers. "The promise is to them and to their children."* Under the Old Testament, as under the New, the initial Sacrament, which

---

* Acts ii. 39 ; compare Isa. xliv. 2-4.

was the "seal of the righteousness of faith," * was appointed to
be administered to believers and to their seed along with them ;
and thus it was intimated that the children of those who are
members of the covenant society are members along with them.
That this is the principle underlying the domestic element which
receives such honourable prominence in the Psalter, is plain
from such passages as the following, in the Hundred-and-third
Psalm :—

15. As for man, his days are as grass ;
    As a flower of the field, so he flourisheth.
16. For the wind passeth over it, and it is gone ;
    And the place thereof shall know it no more.
17. But the mercy of the LORD is from everlasting to everlasting
    upon them that fear Him,
    And His righteousness unto children's children ;
18. To such as keep His covenant,
    And to those that remember His precepts to do them.

This promise respecting children and children's children is
intended, like every other, to be a stimulus to duty, not a
pillow for sloth. The duty resting on parents and the special
function God devolves on them, in nurturing for Him those
whom He claims as, in a peculiar sense, His own children, † has
never been more instructively declared than in the prologue to
the Seventy-eighth Psalm. The people of God (for it is in
their name that Asaph writes), calling to remembrance the
precious heritage of truth they had received from the ancient
times, vow that they will not suffer it to fall into oblivion in
their hands. The things "which we have heard and known,
and our fathers have told us ; we will not hide them from their
children ; telling to the generation to come the praises of the
LORD, and His strength, and His wondrous works that He hath
done." Let the reader take notice of that phrase, "their
children." It is as much as to say, "Our children are our
fathers' children. In the battles they fought, in the institutions
they reared, they had an eye to the good of their children's
children in all coming time. God forbid that the inheritance
they laboured to entail in their families should be forfeited in
our hands. Our children are our fathers' children ; duty to our
fathers obliges us to train their children for God ; and, if we

---

* Rom. iv. 11.   † Ezek. xvi. 20, 21.

neglect the task, they will rise up against us in the judgment."
This is not a mere stroke of the poet's fancy : it is a point in
regard to which the Lord has confirmed the dictate of nature
by a positive command ; and it is upon that command that the
Psalmist builds the doctrine he labours to enforce. Having
spoken of the "dark sayings from the ancient time," he
adds :—

4. We will not hide them from their children,
    Telling to the generation to come the praises of the LORD,
    And His strength, and His wondrous works that He hath
        done.
5. For He established a testimony in Jacob,
    And appointed a law in Israel,
    Which He commanded our fathers.*
    That they should make them known to their children :
6. That the generation to come might know them, even the chil-
    dren which should be born ;
    Who should arise and tell them to their children :
7. That they might set their hope in God,
    And not forget the works of God,
    But keep His commandments :
8. And might not be as their fathers,
    A stubborn and rebellious generation ;
  A generation that set not their heart aright,
  And whose spirit was not steadfast with God.

This ordinance of domestic instruction, which Asaph and the
congregation so affectionately lay to heart, is enjoined, with
emphatic iteration, in the Law of Moses, especially in
Deuteronomy. † In its whole substance, it is an ordinance of
perpetual obligation, and well illustrates the dignity and importance of the Family in relation to the salvation of souls.
While it is the bounden duty of the Church to make aggression
on the world, her principal dependence, under God, must ever
be on the godly nurture of her own children. The vast majority
of those who prove pillars in the churches of Christ come forth
from Christian families, and it is in the bosom of such

---

* The "testimony" and "law" commanded by God was, that the fathers should
teach the children the wonderful works of God. The point of the passage is
missed by most of the commentators. It was correctly indicated by Muis and
others of the older critics (see *Poli Synopsis*), who are followed by Delitzsch
and Hupfeld.

† Deut. iv. 9; vi. 7, 21 ; xi. 19.

families that the sweetest graces of the Christian life are
fostered.   The Family is therefore invested with the halo of a
real sanctity, when it is ruled in the fear of God.   It is the
congenial home of the serenest and purest forms of Christian
piety.

II. It will probably surprise those who have not considered
the subject to be told that THE STATE and NATIONAL RELIGION
occupy a place in the Psalter greater even than that which is
assigned to the Family and its duties. A very considerable
number of psalms are strictly political or national in their scope.
There are Psalms for the Kings and Judges of the earth, to
admonish them what manner of men they ought to be, and
what God expects of them in their official stations ; there are
Psalms for the People, directing them how to offer prayer for
their rulers, and admonishing them to do homage and service
to God and His Christ ; there are Psalms for the whole Body
Politic, rulers and people together, directing them how to ask of
God those temporal blessings which civil society was instituted
to procure, and warning them of the peril incurred by casting
off Christ's yoke. *

There is something instructive in the circumstance that the
harp of Zion so often descants on political themes.   It may be
taken as an intimation from God that national affairs—the
moral and material interests of the commonwealth where God
has appointed us our lot—deserve a large place in our thoughts
and prayers.   The Christian is not at liberty to close his ears to
the questions that are being discussed around him and with which
the minds of the community are greatly occupied.   Political life,
especially in free countries, has an honourable part to play in the
providential government of God ; and His people ought to contemplate it with prayerful interest, considering the operation of
His almighty hand.   Nor does devout contemplation exhaust
their duty.   The large place given to National affairs in the
Psalter intimates that political life, in the highest and best sense
of the phrase, as embracing all kinds of ministration in the State,
is an occupation well befitting a Christian man.   "There is not
a perfecter life in this world, both to the honour of God and
profit of his neighbour, nor yet a greater cross, than to rule

* Psalms ii., lxxxii., xciv., ci., cxliv., xx., xxi., etc.

Christianly," * that is to say, to discharge the office of a Christian magistrate. In these words, Tyndale, the martyr and venerable Translator of the Bible, expressed the mind of all the Reformers ; and their judgment respecting the dignity of political life is simply a reflection of that which God Himself has delivered in His Word. The Psalter implies something more than that political life is compatible with a high style of godliness. It implies that, as, in times past, bad laws and unprincipled magistrates have been a principal rod in God's hand to scourge the nations for their sins, even so good laws and God-fearing magistrates will play a great part in the happy time with which the earth is to be blessed. The millennial period will be a Reign of Justice.

Of the political psalms, the Eighty-second is, on several accounts, worthy of special notice. It is from the pen of Asaph, and partakes of the admonitory character which runs through all the psalms that bear his name.

1. God standeth in the congregation of God ;
   He judgeth among the gods.

2. How long will ye judge unjustly,
   And respect the persons of the wicked ?
3. Judge the poor and fatherless ;
   Do justice to the afflicted and destitute.
4. Rescue the poor and needy :
   Deliver them out of the hand of the wicked.

5. They know not, neither do they understand ;
   They walk to and fro in darkness :
   All the foundations of the earth are moved.
6. I said, Ye are gods,
   And all of you sons of the Most High.
7. Nevertheless, ye shall die like men,
   And fall like one of the princes.

8. Arise, O God, judge the earth :
   For Thou shalt inherit all the nations.

It is, of course, to civil governors, especially those entrusted with the administration of justice, that the prophet addresses this stern admonition. He calls them " the gods," and " the sons of the Most High." To the people of Israel this kind of appellation would not seem overbold ; for it was applied to

---

* Tyndale : *Prologue to Exodus* (A.D. 1530), *Doctrinal Treatises*, p. 412.

judges in well-known texts of the Law. Thus, in the code of civil statutes delivered at Sinai,* it is said, "Thou shalt not revile God, nor curse a ruler of thy people," which proceeds on the principle that to curse the ruler is to revile God. Nor is that the only instance of the kind. In two other passages † of the same code, the word rendered in the Authorised Version "the judges" is in the Hebrew "the gods," or "God." Since the ordinary Hebrew word for God (Elohim) is almost always used in the plural form, it is hard to say whether it ought to be rendered in these passages in the singular or plural. In all the three passages, while the Authorised Version reads *the judges*, the Revised Version reads *God*, retaining the other rendering in the margin. The meaning is the same, either way. It is a matter of indifference, for example, whether the law in Exod. xxi. 6 be rendered thus, "His (the bondman's) master shall bring him to *the gods*," or, with the Septuagint, "His master shall bring him to the judgment-seat of God." ‡ In either case, the terms used are plainly meant to imply that the Majesty of God is present in the place of judgment. As it is said of Solomon that he "sat on the throne of the LORD as king," § so it may be said of every magistrate that he sits in God's seat. God has put upon him a portion of His own dominion and authority; and has ordained that he is to be obeyed, not for wrath's sake only, but for conscience' sake. The civil magistrate, in discharging his high function, may justly claim to govern with a divine right.

No one needs to be told that this old doctrine of the divine right of rulers has been woefully abused. Sycophantic divines have often made of it a flattering unction for the ears of princes; teaching them that they owed no obedience to the laws; that they were responsible to none but God for their administration; that any attempt on the part of the people to curb their tyranny, or to depose them from their seats when milder measures failed, was rebellion against God, whose vice-gerents they were. Even now, the same doctrine occasionally makes itself heard from the pulpit and the press; and thus men attempt to subject the consciences of the people to the caprice of rulers. Let it be carefully observed that the harp

* Exod. xxii. 28.
† Exod. xxi. 6, and xxii. 8, 9.
‡ πρὸς τὸ κριτήριον τοῦ Θεοῦ.
§ 1 Chron. xxix. 23.

of Asaph lends no sanction to this "right divine of kings to govern wrong." If the prophet testifies that princes are gods, he includes in the honour the humblest magistrate. The elders administering justice in the gate of Bethlehem, a town "little among the thousands of Judah," sit in God's seat as truly as King Solomon, on his ivory throne, in the porch of judgment at Jerusalem. The common saying that "the divine right of kings is the divine right of constables" is a rough way of expressing a Bible truth. Let this be borne in mind, and no one will allege Scripture in defence of royal claims to indefeasible and irresponsible authority, or claim for such authority the sanction of a divine right.*

But while care ought to be taken to guard the divine right of civil government from abuse, the right itself is not to be forgotten. The State is an ordinance of God, having, like the Family, its foundation in the very constitution of human nature. The officers of the State, whether supreme or subordinate, have a divine right to administer justice in the community over which Providence has placed them. They who resort to the civil magistrate for judgment resort to the judgment-seat of God, just as they who resort to the Ministry of the Word resort to the great Prophet of the Church. Unless the magistrate had received a commission from God, he could not lawfully bear the sword. To take the life of an unarmed fellow-man, without a commission from the Most High warranting the act, would be to commit murder.

It is plainly one design of the Spirit of God in the Eighty-second Psalm to keep the body of the people from forgetting the "divinity that doth hedge" the officers of justice. At the same time, there is significance in the circumstance that this proclamation of the divine right of the civil magistrate, so far from being made subservient to the pride of princes, is made the vehicle of a stern rebuke against those who profane the judicial function by wrongful or partial judgments. They are reminded that, by their crime, the fabric of human society is shaken to its foundation. It is not the least remarkable feature of this psalm, that, although addressed in the first instance to Jewish rulers, it bears no trace of limitation to the Hebrew

---

* Compare Rutherford's *Lex Rex*, chapter xx. ; Paley's *Moral and Political Philosophy*, Book vi. c. 4.

commonwealth—no trace of narrow provincialism. On the contrary, we see that, in the last verse, Asaph's eye sweeps the whole horizon of the world. Commiserating the condition of the nations,—bereft of the benefits which equal laws, administered by God-fearing rulers, would have secured, and made the prey of craft and avarice and violence,—he calls to remembrance the promise respecting the Son of David, " the Ruler over men, the Just One, ruling in the fear of God," whose dominion is yet to rise on the world like a morning without clouds ; * and he prays that His Kingdom may come speedily. As if he had said, " Awake, O Mighty One; hast Thou not received of the Father the nations for Thine inheritance ? Arise, then, and be their Judge. Expel from men's hearts the selfish passions that have bred injustice ; cast down all unrighteous institutions ; and bless the nations with rulers according to Thine own heart."

This fervent prayer of the Church for a Reign of Justice in the earth receives illustration from some parallel passages, which indicate, more distinctly and fully, the manner in which the happy consummation is to be reached. In places without number throughout the Scriptures, and particularly in the Psalter, it is held forth in connection with the mediation of Christ. Christ's proper work is the salvation of souls; but while His right hand distributes the blessings of everlasting salvation, His left hand showers on men innumerable blessings pertaining to the present life. Christian piety is a leaven that is to pervade all human institutions, and especially the mighty institution of civil government. In proportion as it spreads, throned iniquities will be cast down, unjust laws will be repealed, and right will prevail. Christ is the true Prince of Peace, just because He is the Prince of Truth and Righteousness ; and it is instructive to remark how the psalmists anticipate from His dominion the establishment of peace, not only in the invisible and spiritual domain of men's consciences, but likewise in the wide and public domain of civil society and international relations. This is well illustrated in the Seventy-second Psalm :—

> 4. He shall judge the poor of the people,
>   He shall save the children of the needy,
>   And shall break in pieces the oppressor.

---

* 2 Sam. xxiii. 3, 4.

11. Yea, all kings shall fall down before Him :
    All nations shall serve Him.
12. For He shall deliver the needy when He crieth ;
    And the poor, that hath no helper.
13. He shall have pity on the poor and needy,
    And the souls of the needy He shall save.
14. He shall redeem their soul from oppression and violence ;
    And precious shall their blood be in His sight.

It was a true instinct that made ruthless Herod tremble when he heard that Christ was born at Bethlehem. Christ never yet entered into a kingdom but the Herods in it were troubled. Unjust rulers and slave-masters know well that Christ's truth, if it be suffered to enter, will sooner or later overthrow their tyranny.

It would be doing less than justice to the teaching of the Psalter on the subject of National Religion if we limited the duty of civil rulers merely to the executing of justice between man and man, and the extending to the Church of Christ of that protection which is the ordinary right of all peaceable societies. The doctrine that the civil magistrate ought to be neutral in the great conflict between truth and error is not the doctrine of the Psalms. There is, doubtless, much room for the exercise of a wise discretion with respect to the precise ways in which national authorities are to express their allegiance to Christ and give support to His cause. But the general principle that they ought to acknowledge Christ,—that they ought to be in subjection to Him and to further His cause,—is not to be called in question. When the apostle * teaches that Christ, the Church's Head, is also " the Head of all principality and power," he simply repeats a doctrine which the harp of David often descants upon. There is an obvious analogy, in this respect, between the Family and the State. The Family is an institution founded in nature, not in grace. Yet, in this sin-stained world, it can never reach its proper dignity or bring forth its best and ripest fruits unless it be in willing subjection to the Lord Jesus Christ. Christians are to marry only " in the Lord ; " they are to dedicate their households to Christ ; to write His law on the posts of the door ; to sanctify His Day ; to worship Him, and call Him Lord. The case of Nations is substantially the same. Civil

* Col. ii. 10.

society is founded in nature and is competent to heathens. Nevertheless, Christ has received of the Father a moral dominion over nations and their rulers. They are bound, accordingly, to acknowledge and serve Him; and there are many ways in which they may do so without intruding on the ecclesiastical domain, or infringing liberty of conscience in the case of any member of the community. This duty is urged in many places, and is held forth as the article of a standing or a falling nation. Thus, in the Second Psalm, the prophet having, in the first stanza, remonstrated with the peoples and their rulers on account of their rejection of Christ's yoke, devotes the concluding stanza to an earnest inculcation of the duty of doing Him homage and service.

1. Why do the nations rage,
    And the peoples imagine a vain thing?
2. The kings of the earth set themselves,
    And the rulers take counsel together,
    Against the LORD and against His anointed, saying,
3. Let us break their bands asunder,
    And cast away their cords from us.

10. Now therefore be wise, O ye kings:
    Be instructed, ye judges of the earth.
11. Serve the LORD with fear,
    And rejoice with trembling.
12. KISS THE SON, lest He be angry, and ye perish in the way,
    For His wrath will soon be kindled.
    Blessed are all they that put their trust in Him.

The more personal aspects of the magistrate's duty are not forgotten. The Hundred-and-first Psalm, formerly quoted,* may be profitably sung by any householder, but is principally meant to be a "Mirror for Magistrates,"—a prayer and oath of fidelity to the King of kings, to be used by them on entering on their high and onerous function. The Hundred-and-forty-fourth is another Psalm of the same class. It is the prayer of King David for the nation committed to his care, and must be quoted entire.

1. Blessed be the LORD, my rock,
    Which teacheth my hands to war,
    And my fingers to fight:

---

* See p. 47, above.

2. My loving-kindness, and my fortress,
   My high tower, and my deliverer;
   My shield, and He in whom I trust;
   Who subdueth my people under me.

3. LORD, what is man, that Thou takest knowledge of him?
   Or the son of man, that Thou makest account of him?
4. Man is like to vanity;
   His days are as a shadow that passeth away.

5. Bow Thy heavens, O LORD, and come down:
   Touch the mountains, and they shall smoke.
6. Cast forth lightning, and scatter them;
   Send out Thine arrows, and discomfit them.

7. Send forth Thine hand from above;
   Rescue me, and deliver me out of great waters,
   Out of the hand of strangers;
8. *Whose mouth speaketh vanity,*
   And their right hand is a right hand of falsehood.

9. I will sing a new song unto Thee, O God:
   Upon a psaltery of ten strings will I sing praises unto Thee.
10. It is He that giveth salvation unto kings:
    Who rescueth David His servant from the hurtful sword.

11. *Rescue me, and deliver me out of the hand of strangers,*
    Whose mouth speaketh vanity,
    And their right hand is a right hand of falsehood.

12. When our sons shall be as plants grown up in their youth;
    And our daughters as corner-stones, hewn after the fashion of
    a palace.
13. When our garners are full, affording all manner of store;
    And our sheep bring forth thousands and ten thousands in
    our fields;
14. When our oxen are well laden;
    When there is no breaking in, and no going forth,
    And no outcry in our streets;
15. Happy is the people, that is in such a case:
    YEA, HAPPY IS THE PEOPLE, WHOSE GOD IS THE LORD.

What God has taught us to ask, He is minded to give. The peaceful, happy scene King David paints has seldom been witnessed among the nations; but when the nations submit themselves to Christ it will be no longer rare. "Of the increase of peace there shall be no end," under the sceptre of the Prince of Peace.* The Lord hasten it in His time!

---

* Isa. ix. 7.

CHAPTER XI.

THE LAW OF THE LORD.

CONTEMPLATING the piety which utters itself in the Psalms, we soon become aware that it stands in a relation of singular intimacy to a body of sacred writings which are undoubtingly accepted as the Word of God. The thoughts and feelings expressed are not suggested simply by the contemplation of nature in its infinitely various moods; nor by the observation of men and their ways; nor by reflection on the eventful history of which the psalmists were conscious as unfolding itself in the little world of their own hearts. None of these sources of religious sentiment is, indeed, overlooked or despised. There are psalms which, had they stood alone, might have even led us to suppose that the Bible saints found in Nature an all-sufficient revelation of God and the true Tent of Meeting wherein the soul may hold converse with its Maker. This is well exemplified in the Hundred-and-fourth Psalm :

1. *Bless the Lord, O my soul.*
   O LORD my God, Thou art very great ;
   Thou art clothed with honour and majesty.
2. Who coverest Thyself with light as with a garment ;
   Who stretchest out the heavens like a curtain :
3. Who layeth the beams of His chambers in the waters ;
   Who maketh the clouds His chariot ;
   Who walketh upon the wings of the wind :
4. Who maketh winds His messengers ;
   His ministers a flaming fire :

The whole psalm—and it is a long one—moves in the same plain as these opening verses. Everywhere the object of contemplation and worship is the Divine Majesty, as it is to be seen in nature—in the sun and moon, in the winds and clouds and teeming sea, in the rivers and woods, in the birds of the air and the beasts of the field. Once, indeed, near the close, the Psalmist rises for a moment into a higher domain, in his indignant complaint because of the defiling presence of wicked men on this fair earth. With that exception, the poem is occupied throughout with God's revelation of Himself in nature, insomuch that one might be tempted to suppose that its author was of the same mind as the modern poet who wrote,

> "Go thou and seek the house of prayer;
> I to the woodlands wend, and there
> In lovely nature see the God of love."*

If the Psalmists delight in nature, they exercise themselves still more in the contemplation of Society—the ways of men and their various fortunes. Here also they discover food for devout thought, and manifold instruction in the character and counsels of God. The Thirty-seventh Psalm will illustrate this.

> 35. I have seen the wicked in great power,
>   And spreading himself like a green tree in its native soil.
> 36. But one passed by, and, lo, he was not:
>   Yea, I sought him, but he could not be found.
> 37. Mark the perfect man, and behold the upright:
>   For the latter end of that man is peace.

Even more instructive is the way in which the author of the Ninety-second Psalm, looking narrowly into the providential government of the world, not only discovers that the power by which men's lives and fortunes are controlled is a power working for righteousness, but sees on every hand the tokens of a Personal Ruler, whose mind and heart are in His work. In every providential movement he beholds the hand of a personal Deity. Every act of God is in his view the embodiment of a thought of the divine mind. In the long series of divine acts which make up the history of the world, he discovers, not indeed a revelation of redemption, but, at least, a rich and full revelation of the moral government of the Most High, which fools may despise, but wise men will study.

> 5. How great are Thy works, O LORD!
>   Thy thoughts are very deep.
> 6. A brutish man knoweth not;
>   Neither doth a fool understand this:

---

* Southey: *Lines Written on Sunday Morning.*

7. When the wicked spring as the grass,
    And when all the workers of iniquity do flourish ;
    It is that they shall be destroyed for ever :
8. But Thou, O LORD, art on high for evermore.

There is a kind of piety—the piety of the Scribes, as one may style it,—which refuses to lift up its eyes from the letter of Bible texts and the corresponding experiences of the faithful, and declines to look abroad into the wide domains of nature and every-day life, in search of spiritual aliment. It is sufficiently evident that the piety of the Psalmists is of a healthier and more robust type.

I do not make any quotations by way of illustrating the *last* of the three natural sources of religious sentiment which I have named—the eventful history which unfolds itself perpetually in every man's secret conscience. For, although never long out of sight in the Psalms, this seldom comes into view except in conjunction with the higher and supernatural source to be noticed presently. The psalmists, when they turn their thoughts inwards and contemplate the ever-shifting scenes which meet the eye in the private chamber of the soul, do this habitually with the lamp of the written Word in their hands. The Law is the Master to whose teaching they owe their knowledge of themselves. The consequence is that, although the psalmists are found, in many places, contemplating Nature and Society as these are seen apart from the Word, one can hardly come upon any psalmist in the act of contemplating the motions of his Heart, except in the light of the Word. This is well illustrated in the Fifty-first Psalm. The Poet is here, alone, with his own heart. He describes the things which meet his eye in that dark and defiled temple. Yet in listening to him, you never find yourself in the domain of natural religion. What he sees, he sees in the light of the Word. By the law is his knowledge of sin.

This brings us back to the remark with which we set out, that the piety which is expressed in the Psalms stands in a relation of singular intimacy to the sacred Scriptures. It is emphatically scriptural piety. It is rooted in the Word of God, and finds there its most copious and congenial aliment. The First Psalm is believed to owe its place to the circumstance that it forms an appropriate introduction to the whole

Collection. In its description of the godly man and his felicity, the reader is presented with the outline of the picture which it is the business of all the other Psalms to complete. It is not a little significant, therefore, to find that the godly man is here described as one whose "delight is in the law of the Lord," who "meditates in the law day and night;" and that to this habit of meditating continually in God's Word is ascribed that happy exuberance of his religious life, in respect of which he is like a tree planted by the streams of water, which bringeth forth its fruit in its season.

The "Law of the LORD," the "Word of the LORD," the "Statutes and Judgments"—we shall have so much to say about these in the sequel, that it will be expedient to come to an under standing at the outset regarding the meaning of the well-worn phrases, as they occur in the Psalms. What is it precisely that the psalmists have in view when they speak of the Law, and Word, and Statutes of the LORD? The reader who has some acquaintance with the critical questions regarding the authorship and date of the Pentateuch which have been in agitation since the beginning of the present century, and who remembers the extremely divergent conclusions to which the several critical schools have been led, may probably apprehend that, till the battle shall have been fought out, it will be impossible to arrive at any common understanding as to the form and compass of that "Torah" in which the Hebrew saints meditated day and night. It will be a relief to him to be informed that his apprehension is groundless. The critics, whatever else they may differ about, are in substantial agreement regarding the contents of the Bible in which the psalmists meditated; and, in particular, they are of one accord in teaching that the psalmists had in their hands, and were well acquainted with, the Five Books of Moses. No doubt, the more "advanced" of the critics reject the old and current belief that *King David* possessed those books. Some of them think that the Pentateuch was composed under the later kings; others are of opinion (and this is the theory most in vogue at present) that it was composed during the Captivity or shortly after. But if they deny that David knew the Law of Moses, they equally deny that he was the principal writer of the psalms. They are all agreed in striking the harp out of his hands and stripping him of his ancient title of "the sweet

Psalmist of Israel." However low may be the date to which they bring down the origin of the Law, they assign a still lower date to the Psalms. There is therefore no call to arrest progress at this point. It is admitted on all hands that when the writers of the psalms speak of *the Torah, the Word of the* LORD, *the statutes and judgments, the commandments, the testimony of the* LORD, what they have in view is a body of sacred Scriptures of which the Five Books of Moses formed part. Looking to the titles by which the psalmists habitually designate these sacred writings, we may with all confidence add that the place which the Book of the Law of Moses occupied amongst them was one of such paramount honour and importance that the whole collection was popularly named after it.

The fact now stated deserves the reader's careful attention. Not only was the Mosaic Law known to the psalmists, but it was to them, by way of eminence, the Word and Testimony of God. Fully to appreciate the significance of this, it is necessary to remember that some of the psalmists, including (it would seem) the author of the Hundred-and-nineteenth Psalm, lived after the Captivity. The sacred Scriptures known to these later psalmists, and venerated by them as divine oracles, were certainly much more extensive than the Five Books of Moses. The Hebrew Church was already in possession of the great series of historical books from Joshua to 2 Kings. It possessed Job and the Proverbs. Above all, it possessed the three greater Prophets, together with most of the minor Prophets. Yet in speaking of the written Word the psalmists constantly employ terms which, in strict propriety, apply only to the Law of Moses.*

I should not have thought of calling attention to this way of

---

* The reference is especially to Psalm cxix. It is an old and familiar remark that, of the 176 verses of which this psalm is composed, there is only one (the 122nd) in which the Word of God is not mentioned by one title or another. The titles employed are ten in number, some of them being words that were in constant use, others of them words almost peculiar to this psalm. Whether I am right in affirming that the greater part apply most properly to the Mosaic writings, let the reader judge for himself.

    1. *Torah*, the "Law" or Instruction. Occurs 25 times in this psalm.

    2. *Hhuqqim*, the "Statutes." Occurs 21 times.

    3. *Mitsvoth*, the "Commandments:" 22 times.

    4. *Piqqudim*, the "Precepts" or Behests: 21 times. The word is not found except in the psalms and only three times outside of the 119th.

speaking if it had been found only in Davidic psalms, like the Nineteenth; for I believe that the Law of Moses really did constitute much the greatest part of the sacred Scriptures in David's possession. But it is even more characteristic of the Hundred-and-nineteenth, although that was, in all likelihood, written by one whose Bible must have been three times as extensive as the Law. The question is therefore very urgent, How is this remarkable way of speaking to be accounted for?

So far as I am able to see, it cannot be explained at all, except on the principle that the Law of Moses was the fundamental revelation to Israel, the basis on which the whole fabric of the faith and worship of the Hebrew Church was built. The "Book of the Law of Moses" was the great fountain of divine truth, the great institute of salvation, to that Church. The teaching of the Prophets, although exhibiting a great advance at many points on the teaching of the Law, had for its principal intention, not to communicate new revelations, but to open up and inculcate on the minds of the people the instructions which had been, once for all, delivered to their fathers by the mediation of Moses. The prophets never speak as men called to promulgate a new religious system. They speak as men who are simply witnesses for the God of Abraham and whose business it is to recall the people to the religion of their fathers. They assume that the people whom they address already know very well who the LORD is, how He is to be worshipped, and what is the manner of life which is well-pleasing to Him.* This being so, it is quite natural that the

---

5. *'Edoth* and *'Edvoth* (two forms of the same word), the "Testimonies" or Precepts: 23 times. Comp. Deut. iv. 45, vi. 17, 20, also Ps. xcix. 7.

6. *Mishpatim,* the "Judgments:" 23 times. This word occurs perpetually in conjunction with No. 2 throughout Leviticus and Deuteronomy. Comp. also Ps. xviii. 22 and cxlvii. 19.

7. *Imrah,* the "Word" or Promise: 19 times. This term also is rarely found elsewhere.

8. *Dabhar,* the "Word:" 22 times. One of the words of most frequent use in the Bible.

9. *Derek,* the "Way:" 13 times. Comp. Exod. xxxiii. 13; Deut. xxx. 16.

10. *Tsedeq,* "Righteousness:" 12 times.

* This is excellently brought out by Schulz in the Preface to the second edition of his *Alt. Testamentliche Theologie,* as follows:—"I do not agree with these scholars [Kuenen and Thiele] when they assume that Prophets such as Hosea or Amos were really the originators of the religious ideas which occur for the first time in writing in their books. Every time that I examine afresh the most ancient pro-

psalmists, in celebrating the greatness of the heritage belonging to Israel as the depositaries of the divine oracles, should over-leap in thought the goodly fellowship of the Prophets and should expatiate rather on the Law. This they certainly do. They look back to Moses, as the legislator who first indoctrinated Israel in the knowledge of the Lord and His ways. To his writings, rather than to those of the Prophets, they ever turn, as the documents of paramount authority—the highest fountains of divine truth. This comes out in such passages as the following :—

> ciii. 6. The Lord executeth righteous acts,
> And judgments for all that are oppressed.
> 7. He made known His ways unto Moses,
> His doings unto the children of Israel.

> cxlvii. 19. He showeth His word unto Jacob,
> His statutes and His judgments unto Israel.
> 20. He hath not dealt so with any nation:
> And as for His judgments, they have not known them.
> *Hallelujah.*

What has been said may serve for a general answer to the question about the meaning of the psalmists when they speak of *the Word of the* Lord, His *Law*, His *statutes and judgments*. The reference is, without doubt, to a body of Sacred Writings current in Israel, and especially to the Five Books of Moses. The psalmists are fully persuaded that Israel is in possession of an articulate revelation of God and His will. The silence of nature respecting redemption has been broken. " In Judah is God known : His Name is great in Israel." * They are fully persuaded, moreover, that the divine oracles entrusted to them have been put into writing, and have thus been made sure to their successive generations. The Law was not merely a doctrine handed down in Israel by oral tradition, whether in the priestly caste or in some prophetic guild. It was a *written Word.*

phetical literature, I rise with a deepened persuasion that the prophets assume the prevalence among their people of a type of piety agreeing with their own in every essential particular, although doubtless much contested ; and that their chief en-deavour is the practical one of bringing the life of their people into conformity with the will of God, which has been made plain to themselves." An important admission, drawn by the force of truth from an unlikely quarter, and creditable alike to the author's perspicacity and candour.

* Ps. lxxvi. 1.

It was a Book, of which princes might write copies for their private use, and of which the authentic codex was deposited in the sanctuary in the custody of the priests.* Such is the testimony of the Law respecting itself; and the psalmists accept the testimony as true. No one can read the terms in which the Law is described and extolled in the Nineteenth Psalm without perceiving that the writer has in view a body of sacred Scriptures such as are found in the Mosaic books, and that these are to him, what the Bible is to the Christian Church, the Word of God.

Passing now from these preliminary matters, I propose to devote the remainder of this chapter to two questions, the discussion of which will, it is hoped, bring into view, in sufficient detail, the teaching of the Psalms regarding the Word of God. I propose to inquire, first, What were the aspects or contents of the sacred writings which specially attracted the notice and nourished the faith of the psalmists; in other words, What are the things which these holy men have discovered in the sacred Writings, in respect of which they are constrained to receive them as the Word of God? and, secondly, What are the practical uses to which they turn these Scriptures?

1. For an answer to the former of these questions, we naturally turn, in the first instance, to the names and titles by which the Scriptures are habitually designated. These occur most abundantly in the Hundred-and-nineteenth Psalm, and a full enumeration of the titles on which the changes are rung throughout that long poem has been given already. They are such as these: the *law*, the *statutes and judgments*, the *commandments*, the *precepts*, the *testimonies*, the *Word*. It is impossible to mistake the ruling thought which runs through these titles. It is that of legal prescription. The sacred writings are conceived of as, in the first instance, a book of divine Law, a Rule which the Lord has delivered to Israel to walk by.

Every nation has its laws. Every civilised nation has a body of written laws. It was the distinguishing glory of Israel that it had a divinely given code—a body of statutes, moral, ritual, and judicial—drawn up by Moses as the Lord directed him,

---

* Deut. xvii. 18, xxxi. 24-26; Josh. i. 8.

and all built upon the Ten Commandments. The important point here is not the belief that the fundamental laws of the nation are divinely inspired and of divine authority. A similar belief attached to nearly all the codes of antiquity, and we need not hesitate to admit that it had a certain foundation in reason. For indeed that nation is in evil case whose laws are not fortified in the minds of the people with any sanction of divine authority. If, in any nation, the laws prohibiting murder, theft, adultery, and such-like are regarded as mere conventional rules, the dictates of the legislator's arbitrary will, the obedience rendered is not likely to be strict. The important point in the case of Israel was not merely that they were in possession of a Law which claimed to be of divine origin and authority, both in its fundamental principles and in its multifarious details, but that the manner of its delivery had been such as to have made the validity of the claim palpable to the whole nation. Anyhow, the psalmists rejoice in the thought that the statutes which regulate their entire life—their ritual, their personal and domestic conduct, their national affairs—are divinely given, that their statute-book is a body of Divine Oracles. The Lord had dealt with them, in this respect, as He had dealt with no other nation. In their Scriptures, they possessed a Law which had its foundation in the nature of God, and which had been delivered to them by His infallible wisdom.

The subject has another side. It is not an unmixed advantage to be living under Law. However great a comfort it may be to be exempted from doubt as to the right thing to do in our homes, in society, in the sanctuary, and to be living continually, as it were, within earshot of divine oracles, with their articulate *Thou shalt* and *Thou shalt not*, the comfort is sadly clouded, to all serious men, by the reflection that they have often disobeyed the divine precepts delivered to them. Law, although in itself divinely excellent, and able to conduct in the way of life men not already biassed to evil, is impotent to restore fallen men to their integrity and reinstate them in the favour of God. To fallen men a dispensation of pure Law is death. It can only bring home to them the sorrowful conviction that they are indeed fallen. The reasonings by which this view of the matter is demonstrated, in the epistle to the

Romans, merely set forth anew, in a clearer and more articulate form, the doctrine which had been, long before, taught in the Pentateuch, and which had been pathetically confessed in the Psalms. The law delivered to Israel, since it is God's law, is not satisfied with an external and formal obedience. It demands the heart. It is summed up in the precept, " Thou shalt love the LORD thy God with all thine heart, and with all thy soul, and with all thy might."* The Pharisees, no doubt, failed to perceive this, and were able to please themselves with the thought that they had kept the law and could afford to despise the rest of mankind. But the psalmists were of another mind, and the leaven of the Pharisees finds no place in the hymns of the Hebrew Church. This is well illustrated by a passage in the Nineteenth Psalm from which we gather that, as the Psalmist meditated on the law, he became aware of unsuspected shortcomings in his life ; sins which, except for the law, might have escaped his notice altogether, became painfully apparent; so that his conscience was disquieted, and he became sensible that by the law he could not be justified, even when he was at his best. I refer to the verses in which, after extolling the Law as perfect and sure, as right and pure, as clean and true, as more to be desired than gold and sweeter than honey, he exclaims :—

12. Who can discern his errors ?
    Clear Thou me from hidden faults.
13 Keep back Thy servant also from presumptuous sins ;
    Let them not have dominion over me : then shall I be perfect,
    And I shall be clear from great transgression.

Here is an Israelite in whose soul the Law has awakened painful misgivings not merely by detecting and dragging forth into the light sins previously unsuspected, but also by suggesting to his conscience that there must be ever so many other sins—hidden faults of heart and life, which, although they have hitherto escaped his notice, have been all the while naked to the pure eye of God. This is one example of many which show how, by the Law, there came home to the psalmists the knowledge of sin.

This being so, the question occurs, How could these men of

---

* Deut. vi. 5.

God express such delight in the Law ? How was it possible for the peace of God to possess their hearts in the company of this awful Monitor ? How are we to account for the fact that the tone of their references to the Law is so predominantly grateful and even jubilant ? The answer is that the Torah is never conceived of by them as naked law. They do not, like the Pharisees against whom the apostle Paul directs his memorable argument, confine their attention to the prohibitive and preceptive parts. It is not by keeping these to the last jot and tittle that they hope to purchase the favour of God. They have not so interpreted their beloved Torah. Rather, as they listen to its divine oracles, the demands of authority, *Thou shalt* and *Thou shalt not,* are in their ear everywhere qualified with the word of promise, *I will,* and they learn to look to the mercy of God alone for salvation. In thus interpreting the Torah, they certainly do it no more than justice. Any other interpretation would have been unhistorical. The accompaniments of the Sinaitic legislation were such as to exclude the supposition that it was a body of unmixed and naked law. Even the Decalogue is no exception. God did not deliver that law to the people till He had first redeemed them. That which was promulgated to the congregation at Sinai was not law pure and simple, but law embedded in a gracious covenant and prefaced with a solemn declaration of redemption and adoption. The Adoption came first; the giving of the Law came after.* When the people presented themselves, for the first time, before the mount, the LORD's message to them by Moses ran in these terms, " Ye have seen how I bare you on eagles' wings and brought you unto Myself: now, therefore, if ye will obey My voice indeed and keep My covenant, then ye shall be a peculiar treasure unto Me from among all peoples." † When, at length, the Decalogue was spoken from the mountain-top, the words which reached the ears of the awe-struck congregation were these, " I am the LORD thy God, which brought thee out of the land of Egypt, out of the house of bondage. Thou shalt have none other gods before Me. Thou shalt not make unto thee a graven image ;"—and so forth. The bearing of all this on the subject in hand is direct and obvious. If the Pentateuch was to the

---

* Rom. ix. 4. † Exod. xix. 4, 5.

psalmists, in the first instance, the LAW,—the book of the Statutes and Judgments,—it was to them not less truly the book of the Covenant and the Promises.

One who would understand this side of the psalmists' teaching must remember, moreover, that, in the Torah and side by side with the Ten Commandments, they found one of the fullest and clearest declarations of forgiveness and grace which ever cheered the faith of the saints. I refer to the proclamation of the Name of the LORD which was made to Moses in Horeb.* Singularly enough, this great oracle occurs in the very heart of the Levitical code. It would be too much to affirm that in the Torah the Name of the Lord stands out with the same prominence as the Ten Commandments, or that it forms an equally characteristic feature of Old Testament revelation. I do not doubt that in the Mosaic dispensation the legal element was the more outstanding and characteristic one. " The law was given by Moses ; grace and truth came by Jesus Christ." † Still, the revelation of grace was neither absent nor inconspicuous ; and the Psalms everywhere abound in proofs that it was noted and laid to heart. In this connection there is great significance in the fact (I believe it to be a fact) that the terms of the proclamation in Horeb are echoed in the Psalms more frequently than those of any other Bible text.‡ This takes place for the most part informally and perhaps unconsciously ; but in one signal instance it takes place with literal exactness and as formally as if chapter and verse had been given.

ciii. 7. He made known His ways unto Moses,
　　　His doings unto the children of Israel.
　　8. *The* LORD *is full of compassion and gracious,*
　　　Slow to anger and plenteous in mercy.§

These two things, then, the psalmists certainly found in their Sacred Scriptures. They found in them a divinely given code of laws, and also an authentic revelation of God's grace—an evangelical word which enabled them to say with assured faith,

---

　* Exod. xxxiv. 5-7.
　† John i. 17.
　‡ See, for example, Psalms lxxxvi. 15, ciii. 8, cxi. 4, cxii. 4, cxvi. 5, cxlv. 8 ; and comp. xxxi. 19, lvii. 10, cviii. 4, cxxx. 4.
　§ The reader, by turning to Exod. xxxiv. 6 in the Revised Version, will find that the psalmist quotes *verbatim*.

"There is forgiveness with Thee." Must we stop here? Were these two diverse revelations all that the faith of the Old Testament saints had discovered in the Torah as worthy to be called the Word of the Lord? There is very much in Scripture—very much in the Torah in particular—which cannot fairly be reduced either to the category of law or to that of promise. Is there nothing in the Psalms to show how this large residuum of matter in the divine Word was regarded by the faithful? On the topic brought up in this question, I submit the following remarks.

Thoughtful students of the Bible have observed with much interest the historical form into which it has been cast, from beginning to end, by the wisdom of the Spirit. I say, *by the wisdom of the Spirit*, for it is evident that, in this instance, the guiding mind was not that of any one of the sacred writers, nor of them all put together. They lived many centuries apart from each other, and could never confer together on the subject. God's redemptive purpose is set forth in Scripture, neither in the form of a theological manual, nor in the form of a compendious statement of the whole duty of man. It is set forth in the shape of a History which, beginning with the creation and the fall and the first promise, traces the unfolding of God's purpose, through the successive generations, until the advent of Christ, the mission of the Spirit, and the planting of the Gospel Church. The truth about redemption is delivered to us in a history of redemption. This truly remarkable feature of the written Word was impressed even on its earliest instalments. The incomplete Bible of the psalmists was written on the same plan as the perfect Bible of the Christian Church. We style the Five Books of Moses "the Book of the Law.' They are so styled in the colophon of the Pentateuch itself, and throughout the Old Testament.* Yet the book is not thrown into the form with which the world is familiar in codes of law. The legislation is embedded in a narrative of the circumstances attending its delivery, and is prefaced with a long historical introduction.

Taking into view this remarkable predominance of history in the Sacred Writings, speculative minds have sometimes occupied

---

* Deut. xxxi. 26 ; comp. Josh. i. 8 ; Ps. xix. 7 ; cxix. *passim ;* Ezra vii. 10, etc.

themselves with the question whether it may not be possible to disentangle the laws and promises and other divine oracles, strictly so called, from the narrative in which they are found. Moreover, remembering the distinction, of which so much has long been made by Roman Catholic divines, between "matters of faith and morals" and "matters of fact," and the limitation of papal infallibility to the former, they have speculated as to the possibility of separating the dogmatic and moral teachings of the Bible from the narrative in which they occur, and of limiting to the former the divine inspiration and infallible truth claimed for the Bible. The most eminent theologian of the Roman Catholic community, in this country, not long ago expressed himself to the effect that the solution of the critical difficulties which have been raised about the Scriptures is to be sought in the direction to which these speculations point ; and probably there is an arena here for much discussion in the future. For my part, I do not see how it is possible to make the separation proposed, unless one is prepared to break away from the views respecting Holy Scripture which pervade the Psalter. The "Law of the Lord," whose praises are sung by the psalmists, consisted of history quite as much as of law or promise, and their commendations are so expressed as to apply to the whole book. And there is good reason for this. You cannot cut up the sacred text into sections, and label these respectively "law," "promise," and "narrative." Much which is truly narrative is law or promise as well. God was pleased to reveal His redemptive purpose almost as much by what He did as by what He spoke, by His providential acts almost as much as by His verbal revelations through the prophets. This being so, you cannot cut out from the sacred text the history of God's dealings with the covenant people without mutilating the revelation of His purpose. This is the principle underlying the psalmists' treatment of the Torah. They do not value it simply as the miner values a bed of worthless shale in which are found nodules of precious metal. The sacred narrative is, in the judgment of the psalmists, homogeneous in quality and value with the oracles embedded in it. Accordingly several of the most remarkable of the psalms are wholly occupied with a devout recital of the history ; and, in at least one instance, this is accompanied with a distinct statement of the principle involved. I refer to the prologue to the Seventy-eighth Psalm.

1. Give ear, O my people, to my law:
     Incline your ears to the words of my mouth.
2. I will open my mouth in a parable;
     I will utter dark sayings of old:
3. Which we have heard and known,
     And our fathers have told us.

What the psalmist intends by the "law," the "parable," the "dark sayings of old" which he proposes to utter, is made plain by the tenor of the psalm thus introduced. The burden of it is the old familiar story of the Forty Years' Wanderings and the settlement of the tribes in Canaan—the story of the Lord's acts in the redemption and government of His congregation. The story was an acted parable, a real revelation of the mind and purpose of the Lord in relation to the covenant society. The authentic record of it was regarded by the psalmist as a treasure of divine "judgments and testimonies," replete with matter fitted to guide and nourish faith. The author of the Hundred-and-nineteenth Psalm seems to have this part of the contents of the Scripture, especially, in view when he records of himself,

52. I have remembered Thy judgments of old, O LORD,
     And have comforted myself.

II. We have still to take note of the USE which the psalmists make of the Book of the Law. The Lord having set their duty before them in commandments, and declared to them His purpose of grace in promises and foreshadowings of redemption, and having, moreover, delivered to them an authentic record of His acts towards their fathers from the beginning, the question is to what practical account all this is turned. Here three particulars claim special notice.

1. The psalmists take the Law of the LORD for the Rule of their Faith and Life. We know how much value the Jews of the apostolic age set upon their law as the standard of truth; how they rested in the Law, gloried in God, took pleasure in reflecting that they knew God's will and were able to form a correct judgment on matters of right and wrong about which their Gentile neighbours were very much in the dark. "Having in

the law the form of knowledge and of the truth," they were confident that they were in a condition to act as "a guide of the blind, a light of them that are in darkness." * The apostle to whom we owe this graphic account of the state of mind characteristic of his Jewish kinsmen is far from regarding it with entire complacency. He is ashamed of his brethren because their practice fell so far behind their knowledge; so that, all the while that they were glorying in the Law, they, through their transgression of the Law, dishonoured God in the sight of the Gentiles. One can perceive, moreover, that he is grieved at heart to see that instead of being humbled at the thought of the enhanced responsibility consequent on their superior knowledge, they indulged in arrogant and scornful contempt of their less favoured neighbours. Still, his language implies that the Law was worthy of all the esteem in which it was held, and that such a sure Rule of Faith was indeed an enviable possession for any people. Replying to the question, " What advantage hath the Jew ?" he makes answer, " First of all, that they were entrusted with the oracles of God."† This is exactly the view of the matter presented in the Hundred-and-nineteenth Psalm, from which indeed the apostle seems to be unconsciously borrowing.

> 104. Through Thy precepts I get understanding:
>   Therefore I hate every false way.
> 142. Thy righteousness is an everlasting righteousness,
>   And Thy law is truth.
> 144. Thy testimonies are righteous for ever:
>   Give me understanding, and I shall live.
> 160. The sum of Thy word is truth ;
>   And every one of Thy righteous judgments endureth for ever.

The psalmists, it is plain, have a due appreciation of the value of the written Word as a fountain of truth and a standard by which to try doctrines. They do not think lightly of correct views of truth, or regard the Bible as neutral in relation to the great articles of faith. At the same time, it deserves to be noted and laid to heart that, much as they extol the Law as a rule of faith, they extol it even more as a rule of life, and abound in expressions of fervent desire after conformity to it. A merely speculative and disputatious zeal for correct opinions in religion is utterly foreign to their mind. The writer of the Nineteenth

---

* Rom. ii. 17-20.   † Rom. iii. 1.

Psalm rejoices in the Law for this reason, especially, because he sees in it a guide and help towards a purer, healthier, more perfect style of life than he has reached hitherto :

> 8. The precepts of the LORD are right, rejoicing the heart :
>   The commandment of the LORD is pure, enlightening the eyes.
> 11. Moreover, by them is Thy servant warned :
>   In keeping of them there is great reward.

His delight in the Word is not because he finds in it a repertory of themes for barren and ostentatious speculation, or an armoury from which to fetch weapons of assault or defence in controversy, but because he finds in it a manual of practical religion. Hence his meditations on it are so apt to rise into passionate confessions, and vows, and prayers, and aspirations after holiness. This feature, seen everywhere in the Hundred-and-nineteenth Psalm, imparts to it a peculiar charm, and has led to its being taken up, to a quite remarkable extent, into the prayers of the faithful ever since it was written.

> 4. Thou hast commanded us Thy precepts,
>   That we should observe them diligently.
> 5. Oh that my ways were established
>   To observe Thy statutes !
> 6. Then shall I not be ashamed,
>   When I have respect unto all Thy commandments.
> 7. I will give thanks unto Thee with uprightness of heart,
>   When I learn Thy righteous judgments.
> 8. I will observe Thy statutes :
>   O forsake me not utterly.

2. Even more do the psalmists value the Law as a Revelation of God. It is to them much more than a declaration of truth and duty : it is a glass in which is seen the glory of God. The soul of man being so formed that God alone is its adequate and satisfying portion, the written Word, with its incomparably real and sure knowledge of God, meets his supreme need. This holds true of the law even in its most restricted sense, as is well explained by Jonathan Edwards, when he describes the Decalogue as "that grand expression and emanation of the holiness of God's nature." It holds true, more obviously, of the promise of redemption which runs like a golden thread through the whole fabric of Scripture. Devout readers have

often found it to be true even of those shadows of Christ and His work which faith can discern in the structure and ritual of the Levitical sanctuary. The revelation of Himself which the Lord has thus given to the Church in the written Word far excels that which He has spread out before all men in nature and providence and conscience. This seems to be the meaning of one of the psalmists in a saying which is apt to perplex readers inattentive to the biblical idiom: "Thou hast magnified Thy Word above all Thy name."* The name of the Lord denotes "all that whereby He maketh Himself known," including the revelation of Himself which He is perpetually giving in His works and ways. Of that revelation He makes much use to His own glory and the good of men ; but upon the revelation of Himself in the written Word He puts higher honour, turning it to more abundant and honourable account. By means of it more than of the other, He conveys into men's minds that knowledge of Himself which saves.

The property of the Word now under consideration explains certain utterances of the Hundred-and-nineteenth Psalm which to unbelieving critics have seemed flat and meaningless, while to devout readers they have ever seemed singularly pointed and full-laden with thought. Take, for example, these couplets from the third stanza :

18. Open Thou mine eyes that I may behold
    Wondrous things out of Thy law.
19. I am a sojourner in the earth ;
    Hide not Thy commandments from me.
20. My soul breaketh for the longing
    That it hath unto Thy judgments at all times.

Here is one whose eyes have been opened to discern things rare and excellent in the Law. He has got beneath the surface and has discovered veins of precious ore. But what he has discovered has simply brought home to him the persuasion that other veins of ore equally precious are hidden in the Law, able to enrich him with heavenly wisdom and knowledge, if he could only get at them ; and this he earnestly desires to do. The fervour of his desire he cannot find words to express. Its strength is such that his heart is like to break under it.

* Ps. cxxxviii. 2.

One reflection which inflames it greatly is, that he is a stranger in the earth. "Ah, Lord," he exclaims, "this world is to me merely a place of sojourn. Only a few years have passed since I was born into it; and after a few years more I must certainly quit it. I would not lay out my strength in acquiring such treasures as I cannot take with me when I depart—riches, or titles of honour, or secular accomplishments. I have chosen Thee to be my portion and dwelling-place; and I value the Law because I find Thee in it. Thy testimonies I have taken to be my heritage for ever, and they are the rejoicing of my heart. I pray Thee not to let me be baulked in my endeavour to penetrate more deeply into the riches of this heritage. Hide not Thy commandments from me."

3. Experience has taught the psalmists that the Law, besides being a repertory of truth about God, is a medium of fellowship with Him, a divine ordinance in the use of which the soul is conducted into God's presence and converses with Him. This is stated very often, and with a great variety of expression, in the Hundred-and-nineteenth Psalm, and suggests the true explanation of certain features of that long poem which have puzzled the rationalist Commentators. They complain that, of the 176 couplets of which it is composed, there are many in which no coherence whatever can be discovered between the two members, as if the psalmist, having contrived to put in writing a brief meditation on the Law, beginning with the required letter of the alphabet, had completed the distich by adding any pious sentence of suitable length which occurred to him, without taking the trouble to see that it was apposite to the former half. * Misapprehensions of this sort are probably inevitable in the case of divines who are blind to the glory of the Holy Scriptures as the Word of God— the presence-chamber in which He shows Himself to devout readers and admits them to hold converse with Him. Let this function of Scripture be kept in view, and the incoherence complained of will be no longer felt. The truth is, that the Psalmist does not separate God from the Word, nor the Word from God. He does not even distinguish between them with anxious precision. Retiring to meditate in the Word, he becomes aware that he is not alone. The Lord

* See Hupfeld's remarks on vers. 19 and 20.

is with him, shining out of the Word, as He shone out of the cloud on the marshalled host of Israel in the wilderness, speaking to him, enlightening and comforting his soul. The following are examples of the kind of verses referred to— couplets in which the two members, seemingly incoherent, are really nothing else but variations (instructive variations) of one and the same thought.

151. Thou art nigh, O LORD ;
     And all Thy commandments are truth.
135. Make Thy face to shine upon Thy servant ;
     And teach me Thy statutes.
 10. With my whole heart have I sought Thee ;
     Oh, let me not wander from Thy commandments.
 82. Mine eyes fail for Thy word,
     While I say, When wilt Thou comfort me ?
114. Thou art my hiding place and my shield :
     I hope in Thy word.
 55. I have remembered Thy name, O LORD, in the night,
     And have observed Thy law.

The experience unfolded in these and similar utterances is generalised in the First Psalm in its description of the righteous man as "like a tree planted by the streams of water, that bringeth forth its fruit in its season." There is a parallel passage in Jeremiah,[*] where the same beatitude occurs with a significant difference : "Blessed is the man that trusteth in the Lord and whose hope the Lord is. For he shall be as a tree planted by the waters, . . . and shall not be careful in the year of drought, neither shall cease from yielding fruit." This passage again finds its parallel in the saying of our Lord, "Abide in Me, and I in you. As the branch cannot bear fruit of itself, except it abide in the vine ; so neither can ye, except ye abide in Me."[†] Trust in the Lord, communion with Christ by faith, it is this only that makes a man like a tree planted by the waters. The same virtue which Christ attributes to abiding in Himself, and which the Prophet attributes to trusting in the Lord, is accordingly attributed by the Psalmist to the habit of meditating in the Law night and day. The principle on which this is done has been already explained. It is stated by Christ in the sequel of the parable just quoted

---

* Chap. xvii. 7, 8.   † John xv. 4.

from : " If ye abide in Me, and My words abide in you, ask whatsoever ye will, and it shall be done unto you." * Christ will not separate Himself from His Word. It is vain to think of trusting in the Lord and abiding in Christ without habitual meditation in the written Word. Those who would meet Christ and abide in Him must " have their delight in the law of the Lord, and meditate in His law day and night."

Throughout this chapter, in speaking of the thoughts and feelings of the psalmists in relation to the Holy Scriptures, and especially the Law of Moses, I have not found it necessary to institute any laboured argument for the purpose of persuading Christian readers to do justice to the teachings of the Psalter on this head. For indeed there is nothing in the Old Testament which stands less in need of apologetic interpretation, in order to clear away difficulties and put modern readers into a position to read with intelligence and entire sympathy, than the utterances of the Hebrew psalmists regarding God's written Word. Nowhere do Christian readers find themselves more at home than in such psalms as the First, the Nineteenth, the Hundred-and-nineteenth. They recognise in these the just expression of thoughts and feelings which arise in their own hearts continually as they prayerfully read the Bible. This is a fact well worthy of consideration. To hear some men talk, one might imagine that the divine excellence attributed by evangelical writers to the Bible is only a pious imagination ; that orthodox divines, having accepted from tradition a particular doctrine about the Old and New Testament, try to justify it to themselves and others by a variety of more or less ingenious arguments, although it has no root in experience ; and that they and their disciples perform their stated daily task of Bible-reading just as they would take their daily draught of some disagreeable medicine. Doubtless there may be found Bible-readers who answer to this unflattering description. Certainly there are thousands of men and women who would find it a sufficiently irksome task, with their present tastes, to search the Scriptures daily. But they greatly mistake if they imagine that it is so with their devouter neighbours. There are thousands of simple hearts in the world whose delight really is in the law of the Lord and

---

* Ver. 7.

who meditate in it day and night. It is not that they deem this their duty, under the pressure of arguments or of fears. The contents of the Bible are to them full of surpassing interest, more precious than gold and sweeter than the honeycomb. Above all, they find that, while they read, the visitations of God's Spirit make sunshine in their hearts. This, I say, is true of innumerable simple hearts. It is equally true, moreover, of many who belong to the nobles of the earth in respect to genius, learning, and intolerance of everything savouring of cant and unreality. A favourite motto of Luther's was the verse, "Unless Thy law had been my delight, I should have perished in mine affliction." This was the heartfelt experience of the great Reformer, not a mere theory which had somehow got possession of his mind; and his troubled life afforded opportunities in plenty for such experiences. Dr. Chalmers was a man almost singularly intolerant of unsubstantial fancies, especially in religion. Yet in the closing years of his life, during which he spent much time in daily converse with the Bible, he expressed a growing persuasion that the Word of God is everywhere rich in divine treasures, and he made use of a verse of the great Alphabetical Psalm so often quoted in this chapter as expressing, better than any words he could frame for himself, the inmost feeling of his heart in relation to it: "My soul breaketh for the longing that it hath unto Thy judgments at all times." There is in the divine Word a self-evidencing quality which will render futile in the future, as it has done in the past, all the attempts of unbelieving criticism to undermine faith in the divine origin and authority of the Holy Scriptures. Let the Bible be only suffered to speak, it will not fail to make its due impression on serious readers.

BOOK III.

NOTICES REGARDING THE USE OF THE PSALMS IN THE CHURCH.

CHAPTER I.

THE USE OF THE PSALMS UNDER THE OLD TESTAMENT.

THE characteristic ordinances of the Hebrew Church were those included in the Temple Service; and amongst them an honourable place was, from the first, assigned to the singing of the Psalms. Some facts relating to this use of the sacred lyrics have been already noticed in our survey of the history of inspired psalmody. Thus we have seen that the Twenty-fourth was sung at the bringing up of the ark into the city of David; and that, from that time forward, Levitical choirs ministered before the Lord in a perpetual service of song. The frequent mention of the "Precentor" or "Chief Musician," in the titles of the earlier psalms, reminds us that a large proportion of them were originally composed with an eye to the service of the Temple, and were delivered to the leader of the psalmody for public use.

Not many years after the second Temple rose on the brow of Zion, the Psalter was completed, and the Service of Song settled into the form which it thenceforward retained. It would seem that the anthem which is engrossed at full length in the sixteenth chapter of 1 Chronicles constituted the unvarying basis of this service, day by day. It is a kind of lyrical mosaic, * composed of a series of passages culled from the Psalter, and including the whole of the Ninety-sixth Psalm.

Besides this stated song (which finds its parallel in the constant use of the Ninety-fifth and Ninety-eighth Psalms in the Daily Service of the Church of England) there were psalms appropriated to particular days and seasons. † In particular,

---

* Comp. pp. 64, 65, above.

† According to Ewald, Delitzsch, and others, the superscription of Ps. c., which they render literally, *A Psalm for the Thankoffering*, was sung while

every day of the week had its Proper Psalm. One trace of this is seen in the superscription of the Ninety-second, " A song for the Sabbath-day." Other traces of the same usage are found in the superscriptions to the Twenty-fourth, the Forty-eighth, and the Ninety-fourth, in the Septuagint ; for they are entitled respectively " a Psalm of David for the *first* day," " the *second* day," and " the *third* day of the week." In like manner, the superscription of the Eighty-first Psalm in the ancient Latin version entitles it " a Psalm of Asaph for the fifth day of the week." * Jewish tradition enables us to complete the list. It is given by Dr. Lightfoot as follows :—

" The constant and ordinary psalms that they sang were these :
" On the *first* day of the week, the Four-and-twentieth Psalm, *The earth is the Lord's, and the fulness thereof*, etc.
" On the *second* day of the week, the Forty-eighth Psalm, *Great is the Lord, and greatly to be praised in the city of God*, etc.
" On the *third* day, the Eighty-second Psalm, *God standeth in the congregation of the mighty, and judgeth among the gods*, etc.
" On the *fourth* day, the Ninety-fourth Psalm, *O Lord God, to whom vengeance belongeth*, etc.
" On the *fifth* day, the Eighty-first Psalm, *Sing aloud unto God our strength, make a joyful noise unto the God of Jacob*, etc.
" On the *sixth* day of the week, the Ninety-third Psalm, *The Lord reigneth, He is clothed with majesty*, etc.
" On the Sabbath-day they sang the Ninety-second Psalm, which bears the title of *A Psalm or song for the Sabbath-day*.

" These were the known and constant and fixed psalms that the singers sang, and the music played to, on the several days of the week." †

At the great solemnities certain other psalms were sung. More particularly, it was the custom to sing the *Hallel*, or *Egyptian Hallel*, as it was called,—that is to say, the cycle of

the " sacrifice of thanksgiving " was being offered. A similar liturgical reference is attributed to the superscription of Psalms xxxviii. and lxx. : " to bring to remembrance." Referring to Isa. lxvi. 3, "he that burneth (*literally*, maketh a memorial of) incense," Ewald thinks these two psalms were sung at the burning of incense ; Delitzsch prefers the interpretation which connects them with the " memorial" mentioned Lev. ii. 9. It cannot be said that any of these interpretations has been conclusively established.
* For the LXX. see Field's *Hexapla* ; for the old Latin, Sabatier's *Bibl. Sac. Latinæ Versiones Antiquæ.*
† *Temple Service*, chap. vii. 2 (Works, vol. I. p. 922). Comp. Delitzsch I. 25 (3rd Ed.).

Psalms, from the 113th to the 118th inclusive,—on occasion of the great annual Festivals. "This saying over of the *Hallel* is acknowledged by the Jews to be an institution of the scribes; and the reason of the picking out of these psalms for that purpose was because of their beginning or ending with *Hallelujah*, and partly because they contain, not only so high and eminent memorials of God's goodness and deliverance unto Israel, . . . but also several other things of high and important matter and consideration; for the *Hallel*, say they, recordeth five things: the coming out of Egypt, the dividing of the sea, the giving of the law, the resurrection of the dead, and the lot of Messias." *

These Temple Songs were sung or chanted by a Levitical choir. There was an instrumental accompaniment, the performance of which was not so carefully restricted to the sacred tribe; for the vocal music alone was looked upon as "the proper song and the proper service." † The singers were never fewer in number than twelve, commonly a much larger company. The instruments consisted of Psalteries and Harps; the former serving for the *soprano* accompaniment, called in the Hebrew the *alamoth;* the latter for the *bass,* called in the Hebrew the *sheminith,* that is to say, *the eighth* or *octave.* The "loud-sounding cymbals" were struck by the leaders of the choir for the purpose of regulating the time.‡ The Psalms were divided into sections of moderate length; and, at the end of each, there was a pause in the song and instrumental music. At these points the *priests* (not fewer than two, nor more than one hundred and twenty, at once) struck in with the sound of trumpets, making the courts ring again with a loud and joyous *Taratantara.* This sounding of trumpets was a sacerdotal function, being restricted to the sons of Aaron, and is not to be confounded with the Levitical Service of Song, properly so called. At certain points, the general body of *the congregation,* in the courts below, responded to the psalmody, either by chanting again some sentence that had just been sung by the Levites, or by singing *Hallelujah* or *Amen.*§ No one can fail to perceive that

---

* Lightfoot, as above, chap. xii. 5 (vol. I. p. 958).
† Lightfoot, as above, chap. vii. 2 (vol. I. p. 920).
‡ 1 Chron. xv. 19-21. Comp. Delitzsch, vol. II. p. 400, and Lightfoot, as above.
§ 1 Chron. xvi. 36. This usage illustrates the vision in Rev. xix. 1, 3, 4, 6.

this service must have constituted as imposing and magnificent a ritual as ever was witnessed in any sanctuary since time began.

The employment of the psalms in the Temple Service was neither the only nor the principal use to which they were turned in the Hebrew Church. It is to be remembered that, side by side with the ceremonial observances annexed to the "worldly sanctuary" at Jerusalem, there went on in Israel a continual worship of the Lord in the *families and social gatherings* of the people. Nowhere, it is true, do we find in the ancient Scriptures any express and formal institution of this kind of worship; and the notices relating to it are much more scanty than those which relate to the more splendid and imposing ritual of the temple. The paucity of information, considering the importance of the subject, is quite remarkable. We cannot so much as tell at what time Synagogues began to be organised in the several towns, the earliest mention of them by name carrying us no farther back than the eve of the Captivity. As for Family Worship, the notices of it are more scanty still; and there is scarcely a word said regarding the dedication of the Sabbath-day to sacred rest, and the assembling of the people for social worship in their respective towns and villages. From the silence of Scripture on these interesting topics, it has sometimes been inferred that, till the Babylonish captivity, no solemn worship was statedly offered except in the Tabernacle and Temple. But the explanation of the fact is probably to be sought in another direction. The ceremonial worship was prescribed formally and in detail, for this very sufficient reason, that it rested entirely on positive institution. Only the express appointment of God made it obligatory; and when the period of the appointment expired the obligation ceased. Without an express divine appointment it would have been mere will-worship, rejected by God and unprofitable to men. It was otherwise with the more simple and spiritual manner of worshipping God by exercises such as prayer and praise. These being moral in their nature,—moral, not positive,—their obligation was independent of any formal appointment. Adam did not require a formal commandment to pray to God. The moment that he learned "that God is, and that He is a Rewarder of them that diligently seek Him," he was bound to pray. Abraham did not require a formal commandment to train up his children and household for God, and to "proclaim the name of the Lord" in the way of a solemn domestic profession of religion. Nature itself taught him to do so whenever he came to know that the Lord is the God of His people and of their seed. In like manner, so soon as the people received an instalment of the written Word and a book of spiritual Songs, it became their duty to make use of these in domestic worship as they had opportunity. Moreover, being now grown into a nation, and dispersed in villages and towns, it became their duty to devote the leisure of the Sabbath-days to the holding of assemblies for publicly worshipping God, by reading His Word, praying, and singing Psalms. No command respecting any of these modes of worship is set down in Scripture, just because no command was necessary. Before the cessation of prophecy in Malachi's time, Synagogues devoted to the spiritual worship of God had been set up wherever Jews were settled at home or abroad; and at a still earlier period, some centuries before the Synagogue system received such a mighty impulse from the captivity of the nation and the cessation of the Temple Service, we have evidence that the prophets were accustomed to hold religious assemblies in their houses, where the people resorted to them on the New Moons and Sabbath days to hear the word of the Lord.*

As for the Psalms, the use of them in the Family and Synagogue must, from the first, have entered largely into the divine purpose. The greater number are of a kind little suited to the splendid mode of performance characteristic of the temple. I will not affirm that the Hundred-and-nineteenth Psalm, for example, was never sung by the Levitical Choirs; but the likelihood is, that it never was. Certainly it was much better suited to the simpler worship that was offered in the synagogues and families of Israel. But, however this may be, we know that the singing of the Psalms was not confined to the members of the sacred tribe who ministered by course in the Temple. It prevailed also amongst the general body of the people. The *Hallel* which was sung by the Levites on the Passover night, when the heads of families brought in their lambs to be slain at the altar of burnt-offering, was afterwards sung by all the families apart, in the several guest-chambers

---

* 2 Kings iv. 23 ; comp. Ezek. xx. 1, xxxiii. 31.

where they ate the Passover.   The Evangelists mention that
our Lord and the Eleven " had sung an hymn "* before they
went out to the mount of Olives.   The particular " hymn "
they sang is not specified ; but there seems no reason to reject
the general opinion of the learned, that it consisted of the six
psalms of the *Hallel.*†   These are still sung by the Jews, in
their families, at the solemnity of the Passover.   At all events,
it is plain that, without any professional precentor to lead them,
the fishermen of Galilee could sing the Psalms ; and no doubt
they had them by heart.

Evidence is extant to show that this familiarity of the Jews
with the words and melodies of the Bible songs was not confined to the few which were appropriated to the festal seasons.
The kind of evidence that determines a point of this sort is
known to all.   When a colliery accident, some years ago, had
the effect of shutting up a company of miners in an English
coal-pit, and the men thus suddenly encompassed with darkness
and danger comforted their hearts by singing some of the
Wesleyan hymns, no one needed to be informed, that men who
showed such a familiarity with the hymns had been used to
sing them in their cottages and in public worship.   There is
great significance, therefore, in the circumstance related in the
Acts of the Apostles, that, when Paul and Silas were thrown
into the inner prison at Philippi and their feet made fast in the
stocks, they sang praises to God at midnight, till the prisoners
heard them.‡   They were not members of a Levitical choir ;
and they had not been long enough together to have become
habituated to the conjoint singing of new songs ; yet when they
were suddenly imprisoned in the murky dungeon of Philippi,
without candle or book, they were at no loss for either words
or melody.   The explanation doubtless is, that they had been
taught to say and sing the Psalms in their childhood ; and that
their habitual attendance in the Synagogue and participation
in its services had prevented the early familiarity with " the
praises of Israel " from being lost or impaired.

---

* Matt. xxvi. 30.   More literally,   " Having hymned (or sung praise,
ὑμνήσαντες), they went out unto the mount of Olives."   The rendering in the
Geneva Bible is, " When they had sung a song of thanksgiving."

† Namely, Psalms cxiii to cxviii., inclusive.

‡ Acts xvi. 25.

NOTE TO CHAPTER I.

THE MUSIC OF THE SYNAGOGUE AND OF THE EARLY CHURCH.

Regarding the Music of the Hebrews little is known, at least with certainty. The circumstance that Hebrew poetry is destitute of *metre* is sufficient to show that the way of singing the Psalms which is most usual amongst us cannot have had any place in the Old Testament Church. The Hebrew music must have been such as might have been sung to any compositions in the style of our common prose version of the Psalter, —a circumstance which points to a kind of music resembling either the *Anthem* or the *Chant*. It is every way likely that the *Anthem* may have been employed in the Temple Service ; for the Levitical choirs, consisting of some hundreds of families, the members of which were wholly separated to the Service of Song, would be competent to minister before the Lord in the highest style of music to which the nation may have attained. It was otherwise with the Synagogue service. Here the music must have been of the plainest kind. In ordinary circumstances, there could be neither an instrumental accompaniment nor a band of professional singers. Moreover, the singing was congregational, so that the style of music employed must have been such as any ordinary congregation of plain people would be competent to use. This undoubtedly points to some simple style of *Chanting* as the music of the Synagogue. Since, as we shall afterwards show, the worship of the apostolic Church was modelled after the worship of the Synagogue, we are warranted to conclude (apart from all other evidence) that it was the custom of the *early Christians* also to chant the psalms to some simple melody.

The conclusion thus reached, by way of inference, from the circumstance that the Psalter of the Hebrews, and (we may add) the Psalter of the early Christian Churches, were utterly destitute of metre, is corroborated by the more direct evidence which the learned have been able to collect.

The style of chanting still in use in the English Church can be traced back without difficulty to the early centuries of the Christian era. It is known to have been brought over by the monk Augustine of Canterbury, whose master, Pope Gregory, had bestowed much pains on the reformation of the musical part of the Roman service. Some of the changes introduced by Gregory into the public psalmody were ill-advised and mischievous ; but, so far as the music was concerned, his aim was simply to conserve what was, even then, the ancient style. His most distinguished predecessor in the reformation of sacred music was Ambrose of Milan, who was the first to introduce into the West the responsive style of chanting the psalms, " after the manner of the eastern parts." To aid him in the endeavour to improve the psalmody of Italy, this prelate had been at the pains to bring over from Alexandria a person skilled in the Oriental style of music. Ambrose must have made other innovations; for he introduced some *metrical* hymns of his own into the Church, which would, no doubt, be sung to melodies resembling our " Psalm Tunes ; " but the principal feature in his reformation of the Psalmody was the transplanting to the Latin Church of the style of chanting which had been long employed in the East.

The outstanding feature, then, in the psalmody of the early Church was the recitation of the Psalms to appropriate melodies. This recitation took place in several ways. Sometimes the people sang *all together*. This, according to Armknecht,[*] " as it was the most natural, was also the most ancient way, and is doubtless intended in Eph. v. and Col. iii. Even at a later time it continued to prevail in domestic and public worship." Sometimes the congregation sang in two bands, " responsive each to other's note," the one band singing one verse or stanza, the other *responding* by singing the verse or stanza following. It was this method that Ambrose introduced into the West. The *antiphonal* was a third method, according to which the precentor led off by singing one stanza, whereupon the congregation struck in, and sang the psalm to the end. There was yet another method occasionally used, in which the leader of the psalmody sang the psalm alone, the congregation merely singing the *Gloria Patri* at the close. The chants must, in every case, have been rapid as well as simple; for it was the custom to sing an entire Psalm.

The style of psalmody now described is still in use in the Greek, and especially the Armenian Churches.[†] The American missionaries have found it so deeply rooted among the Nestorians, that they have been constrained to fall back upon it, in preference to the more modern style prevalent in the United States. This is reported by Dr. Perkins of Oroomiah in the following interesting communication:[‡]—" The 23rd Psalm was chanted by the graduating class and their Nestorian teacher in a manner exceedingly beautiful, and which could not fail to carry back our thoughts to the style of ' the sweet singer of Israel,' doubtless very similar to the chanting of the Nestorians of this day. In some of our congregations, the chanting of a psalm in the Modern Syriac, in this Oriental style, is taking the place of the first hymn in the Sabbath services, and adds greatly to the interest of our worship. For thirty years and more, I have been straining my lungs to train the organs of these Oriental Christians to sing our occidental tunes in a highly guttural language, and, it must be confessed, with not the greatest success; in the meantime little prizing the fact, that music, rich and melodious, was ready to gush forth upon us in torrents, from living fountains, in airs and chants incomparably better adapted to their organs, language, and tastes, and certainly more promotive of devotional feeling, than the novel, foreign style which we, with so much painstaking, essayed to inaugurate. The best of all books of chants,

---

* *Die heilige Psalmodie,* pp. 69, 70.
† Otto Strauss, *Der Psalter als Gesang-und Gebetbuch,* p. 20.
‡ See " *Christian Work,*" for July 1867.

too, they have had in their hands,—the Psalms of David,—chanted for long centuries by their ancestors, though too long in an unknown tongue."

There can be no doubt, then, that in the early churches the Psalms were chanted to simple melodies in the style of the so-called *Gregorian Tones.* How far (it remains to ask) are we warranted to attribute this style of psalmody to the Synagogue? That the Hebrew music underwent no change after it had passed over into the Christian Church, no one will venture to affirm. The Greek titles of the Gregorian tones ("dorian" and "hypodorian," "phrygian," etc.) would seem to imply that the music of the Greeks exercised an influence more or less. But it is the general opinion of those who have most carefully studied the matter, and is in itself very likely, that the change thus wrought was quite superficial. And this is confirmed by the fact that the music in use among the "Spanish Jews" of the East, who have most faithfully cherished the traditions of their fathers, is essentially the same as that of the Gregorian Tones.*

---

* Strauss, p. 20.

CHAPTER II

THE USE OF THE PSALMS IN THE CHRISTIAN CHURCH.

THE worship of the Christian Church was, for the most part, borrowed from the Synagogue. In addition, therefore, to the reading and preaching of the word, and the offering of united prayer, the singing of the Psalms was in use from the beginning. The earliest picture the Spirit of God has preserved of the infant Church at Jerusalem shows us the disciples "continuing steadfastly in the teaching of the apostles" and "praising God."* It is obvious that the psalmody continued to be, just as it had been in the Synagogue, strictly congregational, without professional choirs or instrumental accompaniment. It was of the simple sort which alone is possible where the whole congregation takes part in the singing, and which is best fitted to minister to the general edification.

The singing of the *Hallel* by Christ and the Eleven in the guest-chamber, on the night of His betrayal, may be said to mark the point at which the Psalter passed over from the old dispensation into the new; for it accompanied the celebration of the new ordinance of the Lord's Supper as well as the celebration of the expiring ordinance of the Passover. Thenceforward, it is assumed† that when the members of a Christian Church come together for mutual edification, some one will "have a psalm" to give out to be sung. Accordingly, Christ's people are commanded to "teach and admonish one another with psalms and hymns and spiritual songs, singing with grace in their hearts unto God."‡ This ordinance of psalmody is urged with a frequency and earnestness which show that it must have been prominent among the religious services of the apostolic age. As winebibbers are accustomed to vent their

---

* Acts ii. 42, 47.   † 1 Cor. xiv. 26.   ‡ Col. iii. 16.

hilarity in songs, so they who are "not drunken with wine, but filled with the Spirit," are enjoined " to sing psalms when they are merry,"* " speaking one to another in psalms and hymns and spiritual songs, singing and making melody with their heart to the Lord."† Among the many advantages which the first preachers of 'the gospel had over our modern missionaries to the heathen, this was not the least, that as they did not require to undertake the preparation of a new version of the Scriptures, so they did not require to spend time in the composition of new hymns or the arrangement of appropriate melodies. The Psalter, in the Greek of the Septuagint, was ready to their hand. They knew the Greek psalms by heart themselves ; and in almost every city where they planted a Church, the first converts consisted of Jews and proselytes who had been used to chant them in the Synagogue and at home.

It is still a moot point amongst the learned whether the first Christians employed in public worship any other hymns than those of the Psalter which they inherited from the Hebrew Church. The New Testament Scriptures do not contain any reference to such a use of uninspired hymns. It is hardly necessary to say that the occurrence of the word "hymn" in the two texts in the epistles to the Ephesians and the Colossians affords no light on the point ; for the word, in itself and as employed in the Septuagint, denotes simply a song of praise. The Gospels apply it (in a slightly different form) to the *Hallel,* which consisted altogether of Bible psalms. The three terms *psalm, hymn, song,* are all used by the Seventy in their translation of the Psalter, as descriptive of various classes of psalms. Some eminent critics think that, in a few texts in the Epistles, they can discern metrical fragments which may be presumed to have 'been quoted from Christian hymns. But the grounds of their surmise are precarious.; ‡ and the circumstance that the employment of *metre* in sacred song was unknown to the Jewish Church admonishes us to examine well the proof, before accepting the conclusion that the first Christians made so great an innovation, as the employment of

* James v. 13.
† Eph. v. 18, 19.
‡ 'Compare, however, Bengel's note on Eph. v. 14, in the *Gnomon.*

metrical compositions would have involved. When we pass from the canonical Scriptures to the memorials of primitive Christianity that are found in profane writers and the early Fathers, we discover the same absence of distinct reference to uninspired hymns. The earliest notice of the psalmody of the primitive Church, after the close of the New Testament Canon, occurs in the well-known letter sent to the Emperor Trajan by Pliny, when he was Proprætor of Bithynia, about A.D. 102. Among other interesting particulars regarding the Christians, whom he found in the province in great numbers, he states that " they had been wont, on a certain day, to assemble before sun-rise, and to sing a psalm to Christ as to a god."* This has been sometimes taken to mean that those Bithynian congregations sang what would now be styled " Christian hymns." But it is plain from Justin Martyr, and the early Fathers generally, that the Christians of those days understood the Forty-fifth and other Messianic Psalms to refer to the Lord Jesus so directly and exclusively, that Pliny's words exactly agree with the account they would themselves have given of the matter to any stranger, who, finding them singing these psalms, had asked for an explanation. They would have answered, that they were singing praise to Christ as to a god. The responsive style of singing which Pliny describes was precisely the way of singing the psalms which the oriental Churches inherited from the Synagogue, and which, some generations afterwards, found its way into Italy and the West.

But, whatever may have been the case during the first age of the Church, there is no doubt that, ere many generations passed away, new hymns began to be employed in public worship along with the more ancient and Biblical songs. This is plain, not only from Eusebius,† but from the relics of early hymnology that are still extant ; and the fact is recognised by the most eminent Church historians. However, the Psalms continued to furnish in all the Churches the far greater part, and in many the whole, of the materials for the service of song. Many facts

---

* " Affirmabant, quod essent soliti stato die ante lucem convenire ; carmenque Christo, quasi Deo, dicere secum invicem."—Plin., lib. x. Ep. 97. The translation given above is Isaac Taylor's (*Process of Hist. Proof*, p. 25). Compare Bingham's *Antiquities of Christian Church*, Book XIII. c. ii. 3.

† *Hist. Eccles.*, Lib. V. c. xxviii.

conspire to prove that the uninspired hymns in use during the first three or four centuries must have been few in number and very brief. For example, the accounts which are extant of the search made for the books of the Christians in times of persecution make no mention either of Prayer Books or Hymn Books; whereas the canonical Scriptures, and especially copies of the Psalter, are constantly named.* It was a rule in the Syrian Churches that no person could be ordained sub-deacon until he had learnt the Psalter by heart.† Jerome mentions that he had learnt the Psalms when he was a child, and sang them constantly in his old age.‡ The small number of the early hymns now extant is another fact that points in the same direction. Dr. Schaff, after remarking that "the Book of Psalms is the oldest Christian Hymn Book, inherited by the Church from the ancient covenant," mentions that "we have no complete religious song remaining from the period of persecution (*i.e.*, the three first centuries) except the song of Clement of Alexandria to the divine Logos—which, however, cannot be called a hymn, and was probably never intended for public use—the Morning Song and the Evening Song in the Apostolic Constitutions, especially the former, the so-called *Gloria in Excelsis*, which, as an expansion of the hymn of the heavenly hosts, still rings in all parts of the Christian world. Next in order comes the *Te Deum*, in its original Eastern form. The *Ter Sanctus* and several ancient liturgical prayers may also be regarded as poems. Excepting these hymns in rhythmic prose, the Greek Church of the first six centuries produced nothing in this field which has had permanent value or general use. It long adhered almost exclusively to the Psalms of David, who, as Chrysostom says, was first, middle, and last in the assemblies of the Christians; and it had, in opposition to heretical predilections, even a decided aversion to the public use of uninspired songs. The Council of Laodicea, about A.D. 360, prohibited even the ecclesiastical use of all uninspired or 'private hymns,' and the Council of Chalcedon in 451

---

* Bingham, Book XIII. v. 3 and 7.

† Diestel, *Geschichte des Alten Test. in der Christlichen Kirche.* Jena, 1869, p. 782.

‡ "Psalmos jugi meditatione decanto."—*Apol. adversus libros Rufini*, Lib. II. § 24. *Opera*, Tom. II. p. 518 (Migne).

confirmed this decree. . . . Hilary, Bishop of Poictiers (368), the Athanasius of the West in the Arian controversies, is, according to the testimony of Jerome, the first Hymn-writer in the Latin Church."* Upon the whole, therefore, it may be accepted as a well-ascertained fact that, down to so late a period as the middle of the fourth century, the Psalms reigned supreme and almost alone in the Service of Song throughout the whole Church, especially in the West.

The remarkable prominence still given to the Psalter in the Latin Church at the beginning of the fifth century comes out perpetually in the life and writings of AUGUSTINE. Born in the north of Africa in the year 354, this distinguished man was finally won by the grace of Christ in his thirty-third year. He was resident at the time in Milan, where he had settled as a Professor of Rhetoric, and used to attend the ministry of Ambrose. When the Spirit of Christ first began to move his heart, it was often by means of the Psalms. Referring to this period, he exclaims in his *Confessions*, "Oh! in what accents spake I unto Thee, my God, when I read the Psalms of David, those faithful songs and sounds of devotion, which allow of no swelling spirit! Oh! what accents did I utter unto Thee in those psalms! and how was I by them kindled toward Thee, and on fire to rehearse them, if possible, through the whole world, against the pride of mankind! And yet (he goes on to say) they are sung through the whole world, nor can any hide himself from Thy heat."† He makes mention of the Fourth Psalm, in particular, as one that greatly stirred his heart at this time. The influence thus exerted in him was much confirmed by the fervour with which the Church at Milan gave itself to the singing of the Psalms. Ambrose was a man who greatly delighted in sacred music; and, with a view to setting on foot in Italy a revival of this excellent handmaid of devotion, he had been at pains to bring to Milan an accomplished musician from Alexandria. This was a short time prior to the

---

* Article on the *Greek and Latin Hymnology*, reprinted in *British and Foreign Evangelical Review*, 1866, pp. 680, 681, 689. Compare Bingham, Book XIV. chap. ii., who gives a full account of the hymns and other devotional writings mentioned by Dr. Schaff. Also Neander, *Church History*, vol. iii. 450, 451 (Bohn).

† Lib. IX. 8, Oxford Translation.

conversion of Augustine ; for, after telling how the divine Hymns and Canticles made him weep, " touched to the quick by the voices of Thy sweet-attuned Church," Augustine adds this piece of information :*—" Not long had the Church of Milan begun to use this kind of consolation and exhortation, the brethren zealously joining with harmony of voice and heart. For it was a year, or not much more, that Justina, mother to the Emperor Valentinian, a child, persecuted Thy servant Ambrose, in favour of her heresy, to which she was seduced by the Arians. The devout people kept watch in the Church, ready to die with their bishop Thy servant. There my mother Thy handmaid, bearing a chief part in those anxieties and watchings, lived for prayer. We, yet unwarmed by the heat of Thy Spirit, still were stirred up by the sight of the amazed and disquieted city. Then it was first ordained that Hymns and Psalms should be sung after the manner of the Eastern parts,† lest the people should wax faint through the tediousness of sorrow ; and from that day to this the custom is retained, divers (yea, almost all) Thy congregations, throughout other parts of the world, following herein."

Augustine himself had a passionate delight in music ; and the Service of Song was, all his life, such a source of pleasure that his heart sometimes misgave him, and he would be haunted with the fear that he might be mistaking the pleasure of the sense for the devout rapture of the soul. " The delights of the ear had more firmly entangled and subdued me ; but Thou didst loosen and free me. Now, in those melodies which Thy words breathe soul into, when sung with a sweet and attuned voice, I do a little repose, yet not so as to be held thereby but that I can disengage myself when I will. But

---

* *Confess.*, Lib. IX. 15.

† " Tunc hymni et psalmi ut canerentur secundum morem orientalium partium . . . institutum est." The Oxford Translation, inverting the order of the words, thus, "Then it was first instituted that, after the manner of the Eastern Churches, hymns and psalms should be sung," would imply that there was no psalmody in the West before this time, which is certainly a mistake. It was only a particular way of singing that Ambrose introduced ; namely, the responsive way which had long prevailed in the East. See Armknecht, *Die heilige Psalmodie*, p. 70, and compare Dr. Palmer, in Herzog's *Encyclopædie*, Article *Gesang*, vol. v. 108. Calvin seems to have fallen into the same mistake as the Oxford Translator : *Institutio*, Lib. III. chap. xx. 32.

with the words which are their life and whereby they find admission into me, themselves seek in my affections a place of some estimation, and I can scarcely assign them one suitable. For at one time I seem to myself to give them more honour than is seemly, feeling our minds to be more holily and fervently raised unto a flame of devotion, by the holy words themselves when thus sung, than when not ; and that the several affections of our spirit, by a sweet variety, have their own proper measures in the voice and singing, by some hidden correspondence wherewith they are stirred up.   But this contentment of the flesh, to which the soul must not be given over to be enervated, doth oft beguile me, the sense not so waiting upon reason, as patiently to follow her ; but having been admitted merely for her sake, it strives even to run before her, and lead her.   Thus in these things I unawares sin, but afterwards am aware of it.   At other times, shunning over-anxiously this very deception, I err in too great strictness, and sometimes to that degree, as to wish the whole melody of sweet music which is used to David's Psalter banished from my ears, and the Church's too ; and that mode seems to me safer which I remember to have been often told me of Athanasius, bishop of Alexandria, who made the reader of the psalm utter it with so slight inflection of voice, that it was nearer speaking than singing.   Yet again, when I remember the tears I shed at the Psalmody of Thy Church in the beginning of my recovered faith, and how at this time I am moved, not with the singing, but with the things sung, when they are sung with a clear voice and modulation most suitable, I acknowledge the great use of this institution.   Thus I fluctuate between peril of pleasure and approved wholesomeness, inclined the rather (though not as pronouncing an irrevocable opinion) to approve of the usage of singing in the Church, that so, by the delight of the ears, the weaker minds may rise to the feeling of devotion." *

When Augustine was ordained to the ministry in North Africa, he appears to have found the Psalter exclusively used in the public service of the Catholic congregations.   This appears from a passage in one of his epistles to Januarius, in which,

---

* Lib. X. 33, 34.

after laying down the rule that, whatever concessions may be due to the customs prevalent in particular Churches, one must boldly carry out everything that is found to promote edification, and especially everything authorised by the Scriptures, he goes on to mention, as an instance of the latter, " the singing of hymns and psalms, forasmuch as we have from the Lord Himself, and the apostles, examples and precepts relating to it ; " and he adds that, " in regard to this matter, so useful for piously moving the soul and kindling the flame of divine love, the custom varies in different places ; and the greater part of the members of the Church in Africa are so slow, that the Donatists make it a matter of reproach against us, that, in the Church, we sing with sobriety the divine songs of the prophets, whereas they inflame the intoxication of their minds by singing psalms of human composition." He goes on to observe that, in his judgment, the singing of God's praises is never unseasonable in public worship, unless when the attention of the congregation is otherwise occupied, either with the reading of the Scripture, or the discussion of the truth, or the offering up of the common prayers.*

No one can look with any attention into the writings of Augustine without perceiving that the Psalms were constantly and very abundantly employed in public worship. The singing or cantillation of them was not an occasional embellishment merely, but was looked upon as an essential part of the service at every diet of worship. That nothing else was ever sung in the congregations which were wont to hang upon the lips of the great African divine, I will not take it upon me to assert ; but nowhere in his writings have I found a single distinct reference to the use of any hymns but those of the Psalter, whereas the references to the Psalms are innumerable.

The order of public worship in the Churches of North Africa was very similar to that which used to prevail in the Synagogue. The reading of the Scriptures—either the Old Testament or the New, or both together—found place, in one form or another, at every diet of worship. The most usual way was to have two sections of the Scriptures read, for example, a lesson from the Gospels, and then a second lesson from the Epistles ;

---

* *Ad Inquisitiones Januarii*, Lib. II. c. 34 (Epist. 55).

and between the two an entire Psalm was sung. In ordinary
cases, the Psalms were sung (as the Scriptures were read)
in regular course, till the whole Psalter was gone through.
It was customary, moreover, to sing particular psalms on
certain days. Thus, at the Easter celebration of the Lord's
Supper, the Twenty-second Psalm was uniformly sung ; and,
indeed, so prevalent was this custom that Augustine, in a
discourse upon the Psalm, delivered at Easter, reminds his
auditors that, on that day, every congregation in Africa would
be occupied like themselves in celebrating the grace of the
Crucified One in the words of that prophetic song ; even the
Donatists would form no exception.   All this, it is to be
remarked, was the result merely of spontaneous concert and
ancient custom ; it was not an enforced uniformity.   There was
no rigid rule prescribed, either with respect to the portions of
Scripture to be read, or the Psalms to be sung.   When a
preacher desired to expound a particular chapter, he would give
it a place in the readings for the day ; and in like manner,
when he wished to expound a particular psalm, he would direct
the Precentor to give it out to be sung.   On one occasion, the
Precentor having, by some mistake, sung a different psalm
from the one prescribed, Augustine, instead of correcting him,
suffered the singing to proceed ; and then (laying aside the
discourse he had premeditated) delivered an extemporaneous
exposition of the psalm which had been thus,—as he thought,
providentially,—laid to his hand.   The singing of the psalms
was, I repeat, an unvarying feature in the public worship.   The
Psalter was the one book the people had in their hands ; and
Augustine observes, that no stranger could enter a church,
even once, without hearing the harp of David, and the voices of
the prophets or apostles.*

In order that the people might sing with the understanding,
Augustine bestowed much pains on the exposition of this part
of Scripture.   In his collected writings, a much larger space is devoted to the Psalter than to any other book of Scripture.   He
published in his own lifetime *Enarrations*, as they were styled
(a kind of running commentaries), on all the psalms ; and of
these, the greater part were discourses actually delivered to

---

* *Opera,* Tom. XII. 360.

Christian congregations. Besides the *Enarrations*, there are some two-and-twenty *Sermons*, founded on texts in the psalm s that happened to be sung on the days in which the respective sermons were preached. In introducing his *Enarration*, the preacher would sometimes say, " I have united with you, beloved, in singing this Psalm ; I beg that you will now, in your turn, unite with me in applying your minds to a devout meditation upon it."* His custom was to embrace an entire psalm in one discourse ; and he would select a short one if he knew he was to be hampered for time. Occasionally, he finds the time ex- hausted before the psalm has been all gone over, in which case he promises to resume the exposition of it at the next diet of public worship—in the afternoon, or on the morrow, or on the next Lord's-day, as the case may be.

There is evidence that Augustine's expositions were listened to with breathless attention by great congregations. At the close of what would now be deemed a very long discourse, he bears witness that it was simply his own exhaustion, not any token of weariness in the people, which admonished him that he must have spoken long. The wide acceptance which these *Enarrations* found bears witness to an uncommon relish for the Psalms on the part of the Christian people. This is the more remarkable because the preacher laboured under peculiar disadvantages in dealing with this part of the divine word. Like all the Latin fathers, except Jerome, he was ignorant of Hebrew ; and, as Jerome's labours upon the new Latin version of the Bible were regarded by him with suspicion and alarm,† he had to content himself with one or other of the rude and inaccurate Translations which were current throughout the West ;—Translations which had been made by persons who themselves knew the Old Testament only in the Greek of the Septuagint. As that ancient version is more than ordinarily imperfect in its rendering of the Psalter, and the old Latin versions had been made from it without any reference to the Hebrew, a preacher who was obliged to trust to them often found himself utterly helpless. The consequence is, that in the greater number of the Psalms, Augustine, being unable to

---

* See *Enarrat.* in Ps. xlv.

† See the letters which passed between them on the subject in the Collective Editions of their Works.

discover any satisfactory literal sense, betakes himself to the usual expedient of helpless expositors, launching out into a boundless sea of allegorising fancies. It speaks much for the people's delight in the Bible songs, and also for the preacher's spiritual insight, that, despite the serious disadvantages under which they were prepared, his *Enarrations* were much read and greatly prized for a thousand years, and, indeed, were only superseded by the expositions of the Reformers, who were able at length to read David in his own tongue, and thus to draw water for the people out of the undefiled fountain of the sacred original.

If Augustine was the chief luminary of the Latin Church at the beginning of the fifth century, the same honourable pre-eminence belonged in the Greek Church to his contemporary JOHN CHRYSOSTOM ; and he too bestowed more labour on the Psalms than on any other part of Scripture. He published expositions of them all, and these were so copious that if they had been preserved, they would have filled two folio volumes. Of only fifty-eight have the expositions come down to our time, and they are pronounced by the Benedictine editors to be the author's most elaborate productions. They seem to have been all delivered originally from the pulpit, and are believed to have been published before the author's removal from Antioch to Constantinople. Chrysostom, as a Greek of Antioch, had singular advantages for the exposition of the New Testament, and especially the Pauline epistles, and it is not surprising that his Homilies on these have been in chief estimation among modern readers. It is a striking testimony to the predilection which he himself had for the Psalms, that he devoted to them so large a proportion of his public discourses and elaborated them with such special care.

All through the Mediæval period, the Psalter was able to retain its hold on the affections of the faithful. Of all the sacred books, "it is the only one of which the Christian peoples were not utterly bereft during the darkest periods of the Middle Age."[*] In the religious houses of the Celtic Church, far away on the utmost limit of the North-west, the multiplication of copies was a favourite employment of the brethren. A task

---

[*] Reuss : *Le Psautier*, p. 27.

of this sort occupied the leisure hours of St. Columba during the last months of his long life ; and his biographer relates that on the June day, A.D. 597, on which he fell asleep in Iona, he was at work on the Thirty-fourth Psalm, and had got as far as the tenth verse, "The young lions do lack, and suffer hunger : but they that seek the LORD shall not want any good thing." The Psalms were early translated into the rude vernacular dialects of Europe. Long before Wyclif's English Bible saw the light, several English psalters had been produced. These must have been sufficiently rude and inaccurate ; nevertheless they put it in the power of the faithful to quench their thirst at this fountain, during the dreary ages when the rest of the Divine Word was closed against them. These and all other vernacular Psalters were, of course, meant for private use exclusively. In the Church Service, the Latin Vulgate alone was employed. In this form, the Psalms continued, for the most part, to retain their ancient pre-eminence in public worship ; but it must be acknowledged that the use of them tended everywhere to become a dead form. This was mainly owing to two changes. First, Pope Gregory (who died A.D. 604), in rearranging the Church Service, put an end to the ancient custom of *congregational* singing, and restricted this heavenliest act of worship to a choir of professional singers. This was a great change ; for by the early Christians "it was considered very important that the whole Church should take part in the psalmody ; "* and the same sentiment had prevailed before, in the Hebrew Church, with respect to the Synagogue service. The change, once made, has never been reversed in the Romish communion. For twelve long centuries, the congregations living under the papal supremacy have been bereft of their right to take part in singing the praises of God in public worship. With a few exceptions—chiefly, I believe, in Germany and Bohemia—there is no congregational psalmody in the stated Divine Service of the Church of Rome. The other change took place more gradually. The early Christians of the West chanted the Psalms, as we have seen, in their own vernacular Latin. As time went on, the Latin language ceased to be spoken or understood by the people, and care

---

* Neander, *Church Hist.*, iii. 450.

was not taken to make a corresponding alteration on the Church Service. The consequence was that, after a few centuries, the whole service, including the chanting of the Psalms, was performed in a language unintelligible to the people, and became to them a sealed fountain.*

At the Reformation, the Psalter was unsealed, and Christ's people might once more drink freely out of this fountain of salvation. LUTHER, like Augustine and Chrysostom, bestowed more labour on it than on any other part of Scripture. Besides executing an admirable German version, he expounded the Psalms with uncommon diligence. He had completed a Commentary on the whole book, after the manner of Augustine, before the commencement of his Reformatory career. The summons to appear before the Diet at Worms, in 1521, found him in the midst of a valuable course of expository lectures to his students at Wittenberg, in which he had got as far as the Twenty-first Psalm. These lectures, together with an exposition of the Twenty-second Psalm written during the Reformer's detention in the Wartburg, were published immediately in Latin.† All through the latter part of his life, one of his favourite ways of ministering counsel and encouragement to the Churches was to throw off expositions of particular Psalms which seemed specially appropriate to the times; and these are uncommonly spirited and valuable. He published, besides, valuable commentaries on particular classes or cycles of psalms, such as the Seven Penitential Psalms and the Songs of Degrees: and two Prefaces which he published,—the *first* in 1531, along with the German Psalter, as it was finally revised by him with the assistance of many learned friends, the *second* in 1545, the

---

* At the adjourned meeting of the Council of Trent, in 1562, the subject of congregational psalmody was brought up by the representatives of the Emperor and the King of France. Having witnessed in their respective countries the advantage derived by the Protestants from the popular Service of Song, these princes demanded the permissive introduction of a similar service alongside of the Latin one. Among other reforms urged by the Cardinal of Lorraine and the French prelates, in the name of their royal master, this, we are informed, was one, " That the psalms might be allowed to be sung, in the French language, in full congregation." The request was refused.—Ranke, *Hist. of the Popes*, vol. i. p. 252 (Bohn).

† *Operationes in duas Psalmorum decades.* Comp. Dr. Walch's *Preface* to the 4th vol. of Luther's Works, p. 7.

year before his death,—rank amongst the most beautiful eulogies that have ever been pronounced on the Songs of Zion.*

At one important point, Luther fell into a serious error. He failed to secure to the Psalter (as indeed to the Old Testament generally) its due place in the public worship of the Church. At first, it is true, the intention was, that Lessons from the Old Testament should alternate with Lessons from the New; and the reading of these was to be accompanied with the chanting of two or three Psalms.† Certainly Luther had no desire to disparage or set aside the Old Testament. Volume after volume of his collected works are filled with expositions of Old Testament Books which were originally spoken from the pulpit; and it was his intention that the Old Testament as well as the New should be constantly read to the congregations. Short services were to be held in every church on the week-days, in addition to the more solemn services of the Lord's-day; and for these week-day services, the readings from the Old Testament were prescribed. It proved to be an unfortunate arrangement; for week-day services were soon found impracticable, and so the Old Testament readings ceased. As for the Psalms, Luther undoubtedly meant that they should retain their ancient place in public worship. With a view to this, he early set about the preparation of metrical Versions of favourite psalms. So early as the year 1524, he had himself composed and published metrical Versions of Psalms xii., lxvii., cxxx.; and he had several able coadjutors in the work. In addition to this, he intended to retain the regular chanting of the whole Psalter, according to the ancient custom. If he did not make provision for this in the *German* service, the reason was that he had a passionate delight in the old Latin Psalter and the accompanying chants. He had the same sort of attachment to these as prevails in the English Church in relation to the Prayer-book Version of the Psalms; and he fondly anticipated that the Latin Psalms would continue to be sung in the Churches always. In this also he was mistaken. Unless in a few quite exceptional places, the Latin Psalter has long since fallen into disuse. Thus it has come about that not only has

---

* A new translation of these famous Prefaces will be given in the following chapter.

† Diestel, *Geschichte des Alten Test. in der Christl. Kirche*, p. 317.

the Old Testament ceased to be read in the Lutheran Churches, but the Psalter has ceased to be sung. The effect has been mischievous in many ways. Besides leading to a dangerous disparagement of the more ancient Scriptures, it has, in the opinion of intelligent Lutherans, exercised an enervating influence on the piety of the Lutheran communities. Voices are being raised, at the present time, for a reform in this whole matter, and especially for the restoration of the Psalter to the place of chief honour in the Church Service.*

In all the branches of the Reformed Church—the Reformed, I mean, as distinguished from the Lutheran—care was, from the first, taken to secure to the Old Testament its due place, alongside of the New Testament, in the public service, that, as Knox beautifully said, the people might "hear that harmony and well-tuned song of the Holy Spirit speaking in our fathers from the beginning."† The Psalter was everywhere employed as the book of Church Song. Like Augustine and Luther, CALVIN took especial delight in the Psalms, and laboured much in the exposition of them. This he did with such distinguished success that the publication of his Commentary on the Psalter marks an epoch in the interpretation of the book. In addition to the profound spiritual insight common to him with the two illustrious predecessors just named, he brought to his task an aptitude for historical criticism far in advance of his age, and an exegetical faculty which has never been excelled. His Commentary, accordingly, remains, upon the whole, the ripest and best we have on the Psalms; and must have powerfully fostered the delight in psalmody that everywhere characterised the Reformed Churches.

The manner in which the Psalms were sung differed in different places. The English Reformers had a certain advantage in this matter, owing to the circumstance that the Gregorian psalmody had been handed down in their cathedral churches with singular purity. Accordingly, they had little to do beyond the translating of the Psalter into the vulgar tongue, and the

---

* The resumption of Psalmody is advocated with learning and ability, among others, by Otto Strauss, *Der Psalter als Gesang-und Gebetbuch*, Berlin, 1859, and Fr. Armknecht, *Die heilige Psalmodie oder Der psalmodirende König David und die singende Urkirche*, Gottingen, 1855.

† Works, vol. iv. p. 139.

restoring to the people of their right to take part in the service of praise. The Book of Common Prayer provides that the Psalter, in prose, shall be said or sung from beginning to end every month.* In the seventeenth century, metrical versions came into use; and, a century later, Hymns also began to be sung; but the use of these rests on custom rather than authority.

In the other branches of the Reformed Church, the use of Metrical Versions prevailed from the first. The Churches of France and French Switzerland led the way with their complete Metrical Psalter by Marot and Beza, the melodies of which were furnished, in part at least, by Goudimel, the famous composer.† It was a new thing for the people to be invited to sing God's praise; and the new psalmody made such an impression on the public mind, that it is reckoned by historians amongst the principal causes of the marvellous spread of the Reformed opinions in France during the latter half of the sixteenth century. One can hardly open any piece of history or biography relating to the French Reformed Church of the seventeenth or eighteenth century, without meeting with incidents illustrating the hold which the Psalms had of the affections of the Huguenot populations. During the war of the Camisards (1702-1704), when the perverse tyranny of the government forced the Protestants of the South to take arms in self-defence, they used to sing the Sixty-eighth Psalm as they discharged their first volley against the royal troops. When the Huguenot pastors were brought to the scaffold, the Psalms furnished them with the words of faith and hope, in which they uttered their last testimony to the truth and commended their souls to God. Alexandre Roussel, who suffered at Montpellier in 1728, sang the Fifty-first Psalm on the scaffold. So also did the youthful martyr Bénezat, who suffered some years after. Louis Rang, a young pastor (he was only twenty-

---

* It is a pity that the rude version made by the first Reformers is still retained in the Prayer Book. The authors of it knew little or nothing of Hebrew, and could only make their translation, at second hand, from the Latin Vulgate and Luther's German Version. It is every way inferior to the Authorised Version.

† Goudimel was the preceptor of Palestrina, the most renowned of the Italian masters of sacred music. The revival of sacred music which Palestrina brought about in the Church of Rome was greatly indebted, therefore, to the influence of the Psalmody of the Reformation.

six when he died) who was condemned by the parliament of Grenoble in 1745, and suffered on the gallows at Die, sang with a loud voice, over and over again, the triumphant words of Ps. cxviii., beginning, " La voici, l'heureuse journée." * It may be added that the Psalms retain something of their ancient prominence in the Genevan and French Churches to this day.

What has been said regarding these communities and their psalmody applies, with little modification, to the Churches of the Reformed Confession in Germany, in Hungary, in Holland, in Scotland. In Holland, a numerous party in the Reformed Church scruple, like the primitive African Church, to employ in public worship any hymns but those of the Psalter; and it is well known that the same scruple is somewhat extensively prevalent in Scotland and the United States of America. In the course of last century, the use of Watts' Adaptations of the Psalms led the way to a general introduction of modern hymns amongst the English Nonconformists, to the exclusion of Bible psalmody; and a similar change took place, contemporaneously, in the greater part of the American Churches. The change has not given universal satisfaction. The English Nonconformists are, in many places, returning to the ancient practice of chanting the Psalms; and earnest voices have been raised beyond the Atlantic † in condemnation of the disuse of the divinely provided materials for the Service of Song. As no one collection of Hymns or of Imitations of Psalms has succeeded in finding acceptance amongst the Churches generally, or been able to hold its ground for many years in any one denomination, it may be anticipated that the Reformed Churches, on both sides of the Atlantic, will, after a while, find their way back to a larger use of the Psalmody of the universal Church. There are few things more important, in the interest of a pure and scriptural and Catholic piety, than that the views of truth and godliness impressed on successive generations, by the combined influences of poetry and song in the worship of the Lord, should be those set forth by the Holy Spirit Himself in the Bible psalms. Apart from any difference of opinion that may

* De Félice, *Histoire des Protestants de France*, Ed. 7, pp. 466, 493, 532, 516.
† M'Master, *An Apology for the Book of Psalms*, 1818, 4th Ed., Philadelphia, 1852. *The True Psalmody; or, The Bible Psalms the Chu ch's only Manual of Praise*, 2nd Ed., Philadelphia, 1859.

exist in regard to the partial employment of uninspired hymns in the public service of the Church, there can be no doubt that it is both wrong and dangerous to eject the Psalter from the place of honourable pre-eminence it has occupied for well-nigh three thousand years, and thus to deprive the Christian people of the inestimable advantage of having their souls brought under the predominant influence of those inspired lyrics that have moulded the sentiments of so many generations, even as they were designed by God to mould the sentiments of all generations to the end of time.

CHAPTER III.

TESTIMONIES TO THE ESTIMATION IN WHICH THE PSALMS HAVE BEEN HELD.

IN ordinary cases it is a vain thing to cite the suffrages of men in commendation of the Oracles of God. "What is the straw to the wheat? saith the LORD. Is not my word like as fire? saith the LORD; and like a hammer that breaketh the rock in pieces?"* Nevertheless, since the notion occasionally finds utterance that the Psalms have, somehow, become antiquated, and savour too strongly of the legal dispensation to be perfectly adapted to guide the worship of God in Christian assemblies; and since many people, who have been brought up in Churches where the Psalter has been disused in public worship for some generations, have got into a way of speaking about Psalm-singing as if it were a provincial or sectarian peculiarity; it seems expedient to occupy a short concluding chapter with some noteworthy examples of the testimonies that have been given to the incomparable excellence of the Psalms by men of recognised eminence in their respective Churches.

Enough has already been said to show the esteem in which the Psalter was held by the most distinguished of the early Fathers. Nor do I think it necessary to quote the fervent admiration of it expressed by Calvin in the Preface to his Commentary. His interest was not merely that of a devout Theologian. It was of an intensely practical kind. In David's songs he saw reflected, with a perfect accuracy that nothing could rival, the manifold conflicts—"fightings without and fears within"—through which he had himself passed in his time, and the comforts by which he had been sustained. The Psalter had therefore much of a personal interest for him, which comes out, very strikingly, in the circumstance that he made the Preface

---

* Jer. xxiii. 28, 29.

to his Commentary upon this portion of Scripture the medium for putting on record and publishing to the world the only autobiographical memoirs extant in relation to his eventful career. After all, the best possible proof of the value he set upon this Manual of Praise is found in the fact, that, when the Order of Public Worship was settled by him at Geneva, the Psalms, with a few Bible canticles, were alone prescribed to be sung.

The judgment expressed by Luther in two famous Prefaces has been already mentioned. I do not know whether there is any English translation of these in print. At all events, the Prefaces are inaccessible to ordinary readers ; and for that reason, as well as on account of their intrinsic excellence, they may be inserted here without abridgment. Some of the considerations urged by the great Reformer can hardly fail, if duly weighed, to produce a deep sense of the benefits which are secured to any Church, when its successive generations are taught the Psalms from their childhood.

Preface to the Revised Edition of the German Psalter, A.D. 1531.*

"The Psalter has been lauded and loved by many holy fathers above the other books of the Scripture ; and, indeed, the work itself doth sufficiently praise its Author. Nevertheless, we also must utter our praise and thanks for it.

"In past years there was handed about almost nothing but a multitude of legends of saints, passionals, lives of saints ; and the world was so filled with them, that the Psalter lay under the seat, and in such great darkness, that not one psalm was rightly understood ; nevertheless, it shed abroad such an excellent precious fragrance that all pious hearts drew devotion and power even from the unknown words, and the book was therefore dear to them.

"For my part, I think that a finer book of lives and legends of the saints has never appeared in the earth, nor ever can appear, than the Psalter. For if one were to desire that out of all the lives, legends, and histories, the best were picked out and brought together and set forth to the best advantage, why,

---

* *D. Martin Luther's sämtliche Schriften herausgegeben von J. G. Walch,* 1744, vol. xiv. pp. 23-28.

the book thus produced would be just the Psalter we now have. For here we find, not what one or two saints only have done, but what the Head of all the saints has done, and what all the saints still do: how they are affected towards God, towards friends, and towards foes; how they bear themselves and act in every sort of peril and tribulation :—and all this, besides the divine wholesome doctrines and precepts of all sorts to be found in it.

"Yea, the Psalter ought to be precious and dear, were it for nothing else but the clear promise it holds forth respecting Christ's death and resurrection, and its prefiguration of His kingdom and of the whole estate and system of Christianity, insomuch that it might well be entitled a Little Bible, wherein everything contained in the entire Bible is beautifully and briefly comprehended, and compacted into an *enchiridion* or Manual. It seems to me as if the Holy Ghost had been pleased to take on Himself the trouble of putting together a short Bible, or book of exemplars, touching the whole of Christianity or all the saints, in order that they who are unable to read the whole Bible may nevertheless find almost the whole sum comprehended in one little book.

"But above all, there is this excellent quality and virtue in the Psalter, that whereas other books prate much about the deeds of the saints, but say very little about their words, the Psalter is the very paragon of books, yielding a most sweet fragrance to the reader, since it relates not only the deeds of the saints, but also their words—how they spake and prayed to God, and do yet speak and pray, insomuch that the other legends and lives, in comparison of it, hold forth to us mere dumb saints, whereas the Psalter sets before us right brave living saints.

"And verily a dumb man, when you compare him with one who speaks, is no better than a man half dead. Of all that a man does, there is nothing more potent or more excellent than speech, since it is by the faculty of speech that man is chiefly differenced from other animals, rather than by his form or his other works. For indeed a block can, by the graver's art, receive the form of a man; and a beast can see, hear, smell, sing, walk, stand, eat, drink, fast, thirst, and suffer hunger and frost, every whit as well as a man.

" Moreover, it is not the poor every-day words of the saints that the Psalter expresses, but their very best words, spoken by them, in deepest earnestness, to God Himself, in matters of utmost moment. Thus it lays open to us not only what they say about their works, but their very heart and the inmost treasure of their souls ; so that we can spy the bottom and spring of their words and works,—that is to say, their heart, —what manner of thoughts they had, how their heart did bear itself, in every sort of business, peril, and extremity. This is what neither is done nor can be done by the legends and lives of the saints, which relate nothing but their works and miracles. For I cannot know how a man's heart is affected, although I should see or hear tell of ever so many excellent works he has done.

" And as I had much rather hear a saint speak than behold his works, even so would I yet much rather spy his heart and the treasure in his soul, than hear his words. And this the Psalter enables us to do most plentifully with respect to all the saints ; so that we can certainly know how their hearts were affected, and what was the tenor of their words, both towards God and man.

" For a human heart is like a ship on a wild sea tossed by the four winds of heaven. Here it is smitten with anxiety and the dread of future mischance ; there it is driven with dismay and sadness by reason of present evils. Now, there is a soft breath of hope and presumption of future welfare ; again, there is a breeze of security and gladness in present possessions.

" Now winds like these make a man earnest in his words, make him open his heart and utter its secrets. For one who is shut up in fear and necessity will discourse of calamity much otherwise than one who swims in gladness ; and one who swims in gladness will discourse and sing of gladness much otherwise than one who is shut up in fear. It does not come from the heart (so the saying is) when a mourner laughs and a frolicker weeps ; that is, the bottom of his heart is not uncovered nor utters itself at all.

" What is the Psalter, for the most part, but such earnest discourse in all manner of such winds ? Where are finer words of gladness than in the Psalms of Praise and Thanksgiving ? There thou lookest into the hearts of all the saints as into fair and pleasant gardens, yea, as into the heavens, and seest what fine, hearty, pleasant flowers spring up therein, in all manner of fair gladsome thoughts of God and His benefits. And again, where wilt thou find deeper, more plaintive, more sorrowful words of grief than in the Psalms of Complaint? There thou lookest again into the hearts of all the saints, as into death, yea, as into hell. How they are filled with darkness and gloom by reason of the wrath of God! So also, when they discourse of fear and hope, they use such words, that no painter could so pourtray, nor any Cicero or orator could so express, the fear or hope.

"And (as I said) the best of all is, that these words of theirs are spoken before God and unto God, which puts double earnestness and life into the words. For words that are spoken only before men in such matters do not come so mightily from the heart, are not such burning, living, piercing words. Hence also it comes to pass that the Psalter is the Book of all the Saints; and every one, whatsoever his case may be, finds therein psalms and words which suit his case so perfectly, that they might seem to have been set down solely for his sake, in such sort that anything better he can neither make for himself, nor discover, nor desire. One good effect of which, moreover, is that if a man take pleasure in the words here set forth and find them suit his case, he is assured he is in the communion of the saints, and that all the saints fared just as he fares, for they and he sing all one song together, particularly if he can utter them before God even as they did, which must be done in faith, for an ungodly man relishes them not.

"Finally, in the Psalter we find such safety and such well-assured guidance, that in it we can without danger follow all the saints. For other exemplars and legends of dumb saints bring forward works which it is impossible to imitate; and many more works do they bring forward which it would be dangerous to imitate, and which commonly engender sects and parties, seducing and withdrawing men from the communion of the saints. But the Psalter holdeth thee back from parties and keepeth thee in the communion of the saints; for it teacheth thee how thou mayest, in gladness, and fear, and hope, and sorrow, cherish the same temper and speak the same words, as all the saints have cherished and spoken.

" To sum up ; wouldest thou see the Holy Catholic Church pourtrayed to the life in form and colour, as it were in miniature ? Open the Psalter. Thus thou shalt have before thee a fine, bright, spotless mirror, that will show thee what kind of thing Christianity is. Yea, thou shalt therein find thine own self, and the right γνῶθι σεαυτὸν, God Himself also and all the creatures.

" Let us, therefore, take heed also to thank God for such unspeakable benefits, and to accept and make use of them to the praise and honour of God, that we bring not upon ourselves wrath by our unthankfulness. For, formerly, in the time of darkness, what a treasure it had been esteemed if men had been able rightly to understand one psalm, and to read or hear it in plain German ! and yet they were not able. Blessed now are the eyes which see the things that we see, and the ears which hear the things that we hear ! And yet take heed,—alas, we already see, that we are like the Jews in the wilderness, who said of the manna, ' Our soul loatheth this light bread.' It behoves us to mark what is written in the same place, how they were plagued and died, that it may not befall us also after the same sort.

" To this end, may the Father of all grace and mercy help us, through Jesus Christ our Lord, to whom be blessing and thanks, honour and praise, for this German Psalter, and for all His innumerable, inexpressible gifts, for evermore ; Amen and Amen ! "

Preface to the Edition of the Psalter published in 1545.

" Every Christian who would abound in prayer and piety ought, in all reason, to make the Psalter his manual ; and, moreover, it were well if every Christian so used it and were so expert in it as to have it word for word by heart, and could have it even in his heart as often as he chanced to be called to speak or act, that he might be able to draw forth or employ some sentence out of it, by way of a proverb. For indeed the truth is, that everything that a pious heart can desire to ask in prayer, it here finds psalms and words to match, so aptly and sweetly, that no man—no, nor all the men in the world—shall be able to devise forms of words so good and devout. Moreover, the Psalter doth minister such instruction and comfort in the act of supplication ; and the Lord's Prayer doth so run through it, and it through the Lord's Prayer, that the one helpeth us finely to understand the other, and the two together make a pleasant harmony.

"Not only, therefore, ought the Prayer Books * formerly in use to be forbidden and done away with (being little else but unchristian lies and abuses, and that even in their best parts, wherein our Lord's Passion is indeed introduced, not, however, for the edification of faith, but only to be shamefully abused for temporal gain), but care ought to be taken that no new prayers break in again. For already it looks as if everybody were beginning to compose Prayers, and Paraphrases of the Psalter, according to his own devotional feeling, and were seeking thus to have his work famous and in general use in the Church and amongst the Christian people ; just as if the Psalter and the Lord's Prayer had been some wretched trifle of a thing. If care be not taken to keep within measure, the Psalter and Lord's Prayer will come to be despised as before. I admit that some of these new compositions are good ; but it is to be presumed that the Psalter and Lord's Prayer are better, yea, the best. One who hath learnt to pray them aright hath learnt to pray well, far above all prayers, especially since the Psalter has now, by God's grace, been rendered into intelligible German.

"I have heard the story of a godly person to whom the Lord's Prayer was so dear that he would ever pray it with tears in his eyes, for deep devotion. A well-meaning Bishop, thinking to improve the man's devotion, took from him the Lord's Prayer, and gave him a multitude of other good pious prayers ; but thereupon he lost all devotion, and was fain to let those pious prayers go their ways, and resume the Lord's Prayer. In my opinion, any man who will but make a trial in earnest of the Psalter and the Lord's Prayer will very soon bid the other pious prayers adieu, and say, Ah, they have not the sap, the strength, the heart, the fire, that I find in the Psalter ; they are too cold, too hard, for my taste !

"Our Blessed Lord, who hath given us the Psalter and Lord's Prayer and taught us to use them in prayer, grant us also the Spirit of prayer and of grace, that with gladness and earnest faith we may pray mightily and without ceasing ; for

* By " Prayer Books " here are plainly meant *Collections of devotional pieces in prose and verse.*

we have much need.   So hath He commanded, and so will He have it at our hands.   To Him be praise, honour, and thanks, for ever.   Amen."

Passing to our own country, HOOKER may be taken to have expressed the judgment of the English Church, in the Elizabethan age :—

"The choice and flower of all things profitable in other books, the Psalms do both more briefly contain, and more movingly also express, by reason of that poetical form wherewith they are written. . . . What is there necessary for man to know which the Psalms are not able to teach ?   They are to beginners an easy and familiar introduction, a mighty augmentation of all virtue and knowledge in such as are entered before, a strong confirmation to the most perfect among others.   Heroical magnanimity, exquisite justice, grave moderation, exact wisdom, repentance unfeigned, unwearied patience, the mysteries of God, the sufferings of Christ, the terrors of wrath, the comforts of grace, the works of Providence over this world, and the promised joys of that world which is to come, all good neces- sarily to be either known, or done, or had, this one celestial fountain yieldeth.   Let there be any grief or disease incident into the soul of man, any wound or sickness named, for which there is not in this treasure-house a present comfortable remedy at all times ready to be found.   Hereof it is that we covet to make the Psalms especially familiar unto all.   This is the very cause why we iterate the Psalms oftener than any other part of the Scripture besides ; the cause wherefore we inure the people together with their minister, and not the minister alone to read them as other parts of Scripture he doth."*

That this high estimate has not failed to perpetuate itself in the mind and heart of the English Church, even to our own time, is sufficiently attested by the glowing eulogy pronounced on the Psalms by one of the most gifted of her sons, the fore- most British statesman of our age :—

"But most of all does the Book of Psalms refuse the challenge of philosophical or poetical composition.   In that book, for well-nigh three thousand years, the piety of saints

---

* *Eccles. Polity*, Book V. c. xxxvii. 2.

has found its most refined and choicest food, to such a degree, indeed, that the rank and quality of the religious frame may, in general, be tested, at least negatively, by the height of its relish for them.   There is the whole music of the human heart, when touched by the hand of the Maker, in all its tones that whisper or that swell, for every hope and fear, for every joy and pang, for every form of strength and languor, of disquietude and rest. There are developed all the innermost relations of the human soul to God, built upon the platform of a covenant of love and sonship that had its foundations in the Messiah, while in this particular and privileged Book it was permitted to anticipate His coming."*

The late Mr. Isaac Taylor may be said to have occupied a position midway between the English Establishment and the Nonconformist communions.   His judgment regarding the un-approachable excellence of the Psalter, given to the world in one of his latest works, is expressed with great decision :—

"It is but feebly, and as afar off, that the ancient liturgies (except so far as they merely copied their originals) come up to the majesty and the wide compass of the Hebrew Worship, such as it is indicated in the Hundred-and-forty-eighth Psalm. Neither Ambrose, nor Gregory, nor the Greeks, have reached or approached this level; and in tempering the boldness of their originals by admixtures of what is more Christian-like and spiritual, the added elements sustain an injury which is not compensated by what they bring forward of a purer, or a less earthly kind : feeble indeed is the tone of those anthems of the ancient Church—sophisticated or artificial is their style.   Nor would it be possible—it has never yet seemed so—to Christian-ise the Hebrew anthems—retaining their power, their earth-like riches, and their manifold splendours—which are the very splendours, and the true riches, and the grandeur of God's world, and withal attempered with expressions that touch to the quick the warmest human sympathies. . . . And as to the powers of Sacred Poetry, those powers were expanded to the full, and were quite expended too, by the Hebrew bards.   What are modern hymns but so many laborious attempts to put in a new form that which, as it was done in the very best manner

---

* Right Hon. W. E. Gladstone, *Studies on Homer and the Homeric Age.* 1858. Vol. II. p. 526.

so many years ago, can never be well done again, otherwise than in the way of a verbal repetition ? "*

To these powerful testimonies I will add another, from the pen of Edward Irving; for although at some points he swerved, in his later years, from the opinions and sentiments his infancy had imbibed in the Scottish Reformed Church, his warm eulogy of the Psalms is but the eloquent expression of a feeling deeply rooted in her heart; so that, in this instance, he may still be regarded as her spokesman :—

"The reason why the Psalms have found such constant favour in the sight of the Christian Church, and come to constitute a chief portion of every missal and liturgy, and form of worship, public or private, while forms of doctrine and discourse have undergone such manifold changes, in order to represent the changing spirit of the age and the diverse conditions of the human mind, is to be found in this,—that they address themselves to the simple instinctive feelings of the renewed soul, which are its most constant and permanent part; whereas the forms of doctrine and discourse address themselves to the spiritual understanding, which differs in ages and countries according to the degree of spiritual illumination and the energy of spiritual life. . . . The souls of believers recur to these psalms as the home of their childhood, where they came to know the loving-kindness of their heavenly Father,—the fatness of His house and the full river of His goodness, His pastoral carefulness, His sure defence, and His eye that slumbereth not nor sleepeth,—with every other simple representation of divine things to the simple affections of the renewed soul. Therefore are these Psalms to the Christian what the love of parents, and the sweet affections of home, and the clinging memories of infant scenes, and the generous love of country, are to men of every rank, and order, and employment, of every kindred, and tongue, and nation.

"There hath grown up in these lean years a miserable notion, that the Psalms are not so appropriate for expressing the communion of the Christian Church, for the reason that they contain allusions to places and events which are of Jewish and not of Christian association. And some have gone so far as to weed out all those venerable associations, by introducing

---

* *The Spirit of the Hebrew Poetry.* 1861. Pp. 157, 158. Comp. the other passage from the same work (pp. 179, 180), quoted above, at p. 278.

modern names of places in their stead. Why do they not, upon
the same principle, weed out the Jewish allusions of the Four
Gospels and the Epistles? But it is as poor in taste and
wrong in feeling, as it is daring in the thought and bold in the
execution. . . . If we take not our forms for expressing
spiritual patriotism from those inspired songs through which,
in the old time, the Church breathed the spirit of her high
privilege and separate community, where shall we obtain them
of like unction and equal authority in the experience of times
during which no prophet hath arisen in the holy city? For,
though the Church hath been as sorely tried under the Gentile
as under the Jewish dispensation, it hath not pleased the Lord
to bestow upon any of her priests or people the garment of
inspiration, with which to clothe in spiritual songs the depths
of her sorrow or the exaltation of her joy. And we are shut up
to the necessity, either of responding to the voice of the Spirit
in the ancient psalmist, or to re-echo the poetical effusions of
uninspired men,—either to address the living God in the
language of His own Word, or in the language of some vernacular poet, whose taste and forms of thinking, whose forms of
feeling, yea, and forms of opinion, we must make mediators
between our soul and the ear of God, which is a great evil to be
avoided, whenever it can be avoided. For Christians must be
forms of the everlasting and common Spirit, not mannerists of
mortal and individual men."[*]

It would be easy to cite other testimonies not less strong. I
have confined myself to those which, besides proceeding from
different branches of the Church, are intrinsically valuable for
the matter contained in them. The observations of Luther are
deserving of special attention at the present time. The tide of
Christian hymnology which has been running with ever-increas-
ing volume and strength in the Reformed Churches during the
past century threatens, in many quarters, to displace the Psalms
(although it can only be for a season) from their place of
unrivalled prominence and authority in public worship. This I
cannot help regarding as a great evil. It threatens very
seriously to compromise that catholicity of feeling and that

---

[*] *Essay on the Book of Psalms* in Irving's Collected Writings, vol. I. pp.
389-396.

harmony of devotional language which the general use of the Psalms has so admirably fostered, as well as to remove the barrier it has placed in the way of those local and temporary and abnormal forms of religious feeling which are so apt, especially in times of excitement, to mar the symmetry of the Christian character. In Churches where the prayers are offered by means of fixed liturgical forms, one can well understand both that the call for modern hymns will be more clamant, and that the danger will be less felt. But where the prayers are free, it is of incalculable importance that the other half of the devotional service should be moulded in forms of ancient authority ; and surely the best possible mould is that which the Holy Spirit Himself gave by the Psalmists, and which has left its divinely traced lines on the general Church for these three thousand years.

INDEX OF AUTHORS AND TOPICS.

INDEX OF TEXTS.

Printed by Hazell, Watson, & Viney, Ld., London and Aylesbury.

John Eadie Titles

Solid Ground is delighted to announce that we have republished several volumes by John Eadie, gifted Scottish minister. The following are in print:

Commentary on the Greek Text of Paul's Letter to the Galatians
Part of the classic five-volume set that brought world-wide renown to this humble man, Eadie expounds this letter with passion and precision. In the words of Spurgeon, "This is a most careful attempt to ascertain the meaning of the Apostle by painstaking analysis of his words."

Commentary on the Greek Text of Paul's Letter to the Ephesians
Spurgeon said, "This book is one of prodigious learning and research. The author seems to have read all, in every language, that has been written on the Epistle. It is also a work of independent criticism, and casts much new light upon many passages."

Commentary on the Greek Text of Paul's Letter to the Philippians
Robert Paul Martin wrote, "Everything that John Eadie wrote is pure gold. He was simply the best exegete of his generation. His commentaries on Paul's epistles are valued highly by careful expositors. Solid Ground Christian Books has done a great service by bringing Eadie's works back into print."

Commentary on the Greek Text of Paul's Letter to the Colossians
According to the New Schaff-Herzog Encyclopedia of Religious Knowledge, "These commentaries of John Eadie are marked by candor and clearness as well as by an evangelical unction not common in works of the kind." Spurgeon said, "Very full and reliable. A work of utmost value."

Commentary on the Greek Text of Paul's Letters to the Thessalonians
Published posthumously, this volume completes the series that has been highly acclaimed for more than a century. Invaluable.

Paul the Preacher: A Popular and Practical Exposition of His Discourses and Speeches as Recorded in the Acts of the Apostles
Very rare volume intended for a more popular audience, this volume begins with Saul's conversion and ends with Paul preaching the Gospel of the Kingdom in Rome. It perfectly fills in the gaps in the commentaries. Outstanding work!

DIVINE LOVE: A Series of Doctrinal, Practical and Experimental Discourses
Buried over a hundred years, this volume consists of a dozen complete sermons from Eadie's the pastoral ministry. "John Eadie, the respected nineteenth-century Scottish Secession minister-theologian, takes the reader on an edifying journey through this vital biblical theme." - Ligon Duncan

Lectures on the Bible to the Young for Their Instruction and Excitement
"Though written for the rising generation, these plain addresses are not meant for mere children. Simplicity has, indeed, been aimed at in their style and arrangement, in order to adapt them to a class of young readers whose minds have already enjoyed some previous training and discipline." – Author's Preface

Call us Toll Free at 1-877-666-9469
Send us an e-mail at sgcb@charter.net
Visit us on line at solid-ground-books.com

Printed in the United Kingdom
by Lightning Source UK Ltd.
119456UK00002B/4-33